Contemporary Applied Management

Behavioral Science Techniques for
Managers and Professionals

Contemporary Applied Management

Behavioral Science Techniques for Managers and Professionals

Andrew J. DuBrin
Rochester Institute of Technology

Third Edition 1989

Homewood, Illinois 60430

To Douglas

© RICHARD D. IRWIN, INC., 1982, 1985, and 1989

Executive editor: Gary L. Nelson
Project editor: Rita McMullen
Production manager: Bette Ittersagen
Cover Design: Studio M
Compositor: TCSystems, Inc.
Typeface: 10/12 Times Roman
Printer: Malloy Lithographing, Inc.

Library of Congress Cataloging-in-Publication Data

DuBrin, Andrew J.
    Contemporary applied management : behavioral science techniques for managers and professionals / Andrew J. DuBrin. — 3rd ed.
        p.   cm.
    Bibliography: p.
    Includes index.
    ISBN 0-256-05822-9 (pbk.)
    1. Management.   2. Organizational behavior.   I. Title.
HD31.D79 1989
658.3—dc19   88–22626
                                                                        CIP

Printed in the United States of America
1 2 3 4 5 6 7 8 9 0 ML 5 4 3 2 1 0 9 8

Preface

Management thought and action has been influenced by the work of behavioral scientists. Many students of organizational behavior, management, and human resource management (or personnel and human resource management) have been exposed to general information about behaviorally based techniques and concepts. Examples of these concepts include team building, negotiating techniques, career development, and employee involvement programs. Students could also benefit from information about the specific application of these approaches.

The purpose of this book is to provide managers, aspiring managers, and staff professionals with a look at the application of a current selection of both behavioral science and management techniques, methods, and strategies. (*Management* in this context refers to the classical or functional school.) Toward this pupose, each chapter begins with a brief statement of why a technique was chosen and a hands-on description—in a job setting—of the technique, method, or strategy under consideration.

The underlying theme of this book is that applied management techniques serve such useful ends as increased productivity and job satisfaction, despite some of their disadvantages and shortcomings. In support of this theme, each chapter considers both the advantages and disadvantages, or strengths and weaknesses, of the technique or method. In addition, guidelines are presented for the appropriate application of each technique, method, or concept.

This book is written for two audiences. One is students of organizational behavior, human relations, organizational psychology, management, personnel, or human resource management. The other is managers and staff specialists (or individual contributors) seeking professional development on their own, or within the context of internal management development programs. The book is designed to be used as a supplement to a formal text, alone in application courses, or in management development programs.

Generally the user of this book will have some understanding of or will have completed some reading in organizational behavior, management, supervision, or human resource management. *Contemporary Applied Management* intentionally does not duplicate the vital theoretical and conceptual background contained in various readings on behavioral science and classical management applications to management practice. Current texts in organizational behavior, management and the human resource management (or personnel) fields provide the student with an adequate theoretical background and research orientation for benefitting from an applications text of this type.

In addition to providing a concise look at the application of current applied management techniques and methods, this book has several other objectives. A major objective is to provide an explanation of techniques that can be applied by managers acting alone with some assistance from a specialist in organizational behavior or human resource management. Two examples would be a career-development specialist or an organization development specialist. Some of the techniques described, such as negotiating with others or managing in a crisis, can be implemented by the individual without the assistance of a formal program sponsored by the organization.

Another objective is to offer a balanced presentation of the methods described, looking at both strengths and potential pitfalls. However, if a particular technique is considered of neutral or negative value, it is not included here.

Still another objective is to provide readers an opportunity to enhance their managerial skills. One approach to this objective is to include discussions of managerial skill development at various places in the manuscript. Another approach is to provide the reader with concrete guidelines for the effective use of the techniques described. We therefore include a Guidelines for Action and Skill Development section at the end of each chapter. The guidelines can also be regarded as generalizations for applying the technique or method under disscussion. A final objective is to increase the self-awareness of the reader in relation to such key aspects of job behavior as assertiveness, negotiating skill, creativity, teamwork, and burnout. To accomplish this purpose, self-examination question-naires are included as appendixes to appropriate chapters. Although these instruments are not scientifically validated, they can serve as potent launching points for personalized discussions about the technique under examination.

CHANGES IN THE THIRD EDITION

The third edition has substantial changes in content, and it updates research evidence and opinion about the methods and techniques de-scribed in the book. Eight new chapters have been added and seven old ones deleted. About half the case illustrations from the 12 remaining chapters are new. The eight new chapters deal with crisis management, production work teams, building quality awareness, intrapreneuring, creating flat organization structures, employee involvement programs, telecommuting (working at home), and outplacement. The one structural change in the text is to shift assertion skills from the individual to the interpersonal section.

Part I, Improving Individual Effectiveness, describes four techniques individuals can use to improve personal productivity and enhance their careers. Part II, Improving Interpersonal Relationships, deals with four techniques, methods, and programs designed to overcome or prevent problems among people in organizations. Part III, Improving the Functioning of Work Groups, describes four methods designed to enhance both productivity and morale.

Part IV, Improving Productivity and Quality at the Organizational Level, describes four methods for boosting productivity, enhancing innovation, and sometimes elevating morale. Part V, Human Resource Management Programs, describes four programs typically administered through the personnel department.

The five-part structure of this text helps the student organize and conceptualize the information. However, several of the chapters in this book could be logically placed in more than one of the parts. For example, employee involvement programs could be conveniently placed into Part IV or Part V.

ACKNOWLEDGMENTS

Producing a book of this nature is a team effort. Among the key contributors to this project were my editors Rhonda K. Harris and John R. Weimeister. Professor John M. Ivancevich receives my appreciation for presenting me with the basic concept for the first edition of this book. The outside reviewers for this edition and previous ones provided major suggestions for improving the structure and content of the book. In alphabetical order they are: M. K. Badawy, Virginia Polytechnic Institute; John D. Blair, Texas Tech University; Lawrence G. Brandon, The American Institute for Property & Liability Underwriters, Inc.; Angelo S. DeNisi, University of South Carolina; Bill Fannin, University of Houston; William G. Hahn, Savannah State College; Richard M. Hodgetts, Florida International University; Pamela A. Posey, The University of Vermont; and Mary Van Sell, Michigan State University.

The many professors, trainers, and students who had kind words about the two previous editions of this book also receive my appreciation.

Andrew J. DuBrin

Contents

Part III

Improving the Functions of Work Groups   *141*

Part IV

Improving Productivity and Quality at the Organizational Level   *213*

Quality Awareness.   Questions and Activities.   Notes.   Some Additional References.

Part I

Improving Individual Effectiveness

The four chapters in this section concentrate on developing skills, techniques, and attitudes that can help the individual perform more effectively on the job, thus simultaneously improving organizational performance. Frequently these same skills, techniques, and attitudes can be applied to improving effectiveness in personal life. These four chapters provide insight into overcoming problems that face many managers and staff specialists. The four major problems covered here are low personal productivity, insufficient job creativity, poor crisis management, and burnout.

Chapter 1, Work Habits and Time Management, covers the always current topic of improving personal productivity. The goal of improving organizational productivity can often be partially met by improving efficiency and effectiveness among organizational members. Improvement of work habits and time management results in control of time and work and often prevents stress caused by feeling overwhelmed on the job.

Chapter 2, Improving Your Creativity, presents several do-it-yourself techniques for making better use of creative potential. A case description of how brainstorming works in practice is included. The chapter concludes with a scientifically validated instrument for measuring creative potential.

Chapter 3, Crisis Management, presents information about one of the most demanding tasks facing a manager—gaining control in a crisis situation. To date, very little information on this topic has worked its way into the scientific literature. However, some valid information about this topic has appeared in trade books and is the topic of long-range research by this author.

Chapter 4, Preventing and Overcoming Job Burnout, deals with a problem of ever-present concern—burnout in managerial work. During the last decade behavioral scientists have come to recognize that many managerial workers become depleted and exhausted as a consequence of long-term stress. Large numbers of workers at every level may suffer from burnout when two organizational conditions are present: The firm is in decline while, at the same time, workers are given limited recognition from management for their efforts. Some of the remedial suggestions are based on direct experience in helping individuals and organizations cope with burnout.

Chapter One

Work Habits and Time Management

In order to achieve his high-level goals, the executive described below by the editor in chief of *Success!* magazine developed finely tuned work habits and time-management practices.

Mark H. McCormack walked into the room, and I sized him up. I knew right away I had never met anyone so organized. A picture of the well-organized executive began taking shape in my mind. Over the past 25 years McCormack has built an empire, and he runs it with a personal touch. It's called the International Management Group, and it specializes in sports and entertainment around the world.

"Mark is so organized it is frightening," says Lodwrick M. Cook, chairman and chief executive officer (CEO) of Tichfield. "He sets standards all of us should emulate. He prepares as if he were an athlete and doesn't leave anything to chance."

The rudiments of McCormack's success system are the three-by-five index cards he carries in his jacket and on which he writes meticulous notes in script. He copies these notes onto legal pads, which he divides down the middle, with "People to Call" on the left and "To Do" on the right. He dates the pages several months into the future, he says, "so when someone asks you to call next Wednesday at 10:30, go the sheet for that day and put the name and number about one third of the way down on the left side of the sheet."

Another empire builder, Alexander the Great, said the secret of his accomplishing so much was never putting off anything until tomorrow. Similarly, McCormack says that if you get behind on your agenda, "don't eliminate anything—you'll just have to do it tomorrow. Pick up the pace a bit, and you'll catch up.'' McCormack stresses that you should write down everything you intend to do; then forget it until it turns up on your pad on the appropriate day and time.

Emperors in ages past lacked telephones and jet planes, which McCormack uses to an extraordinary degree. He logs 250,000 miles a year in the air. He keeps his 15 offices around the world hopping with his practice of "management by phoning around," and believes "the well-timed phone call can be a great management tool, forcing people to act, to get answers they've been avoiding, or simply to learn they are not forgotten.''

I've heard that genius lies in combining unlike elements in new ways. McCormack, a lawyer, combined the sports hero with the marketing needs of the modern corporation and created a new era of product endorsements. His list of 500 clients includes top athletes in every field from golf to windsurfing who endorse everything from perfume to tires. Other clients include the Olympics, Wimbledon, the Nobel Prize committee, and the pope, to name a few.[1]

STRATEGIES FOR PERSONAL PRODUCTIVITY

Why improve your work habits and time management? The major justification is to increase your personal productivity by making you both more efficient and more effective. *Efficiency* means that you accomplish tasks with a minimum of wasted time, material, and fanfare. This ratio of output to input represents the traditional concept of productivity. *Effectiveness* refers to the importance and quality of what you actually accomplish. As the popular management cliché states, "Efficiency is doing things right, while effectiveness is doing the right things." Nevertheless, efficiency and effectiveness are not unrelated. Being efficient often clears the way for being effective. If you are on top of your job, it gives you time to work on the major tasks facing you. To be productive in the contemporary meaning of the term, you must be both efficient and effective.

There are other significant reasons for improving your work habits and time management. People with good work habits and time management practices tend to be more successful in their careers than poorly organized individuals. In addition, good work habits and time management allow you to have more time to spend on your personal life. You will also enjoy your personal life more if you are not preoccupied with unfinished tasks.

Our discussion of suggestions for improved personal productivity is divided into two major categories: productive attitudes and values, and productive skills and techniques. If these suggestions are practiced, they should lead to improved productivity as a manager or individual contributor.[2] Readers with work experience will be familiar with many of these attitudes, skills, and techniques. In that case, the discussion can serve as a reminder to put into practice familiar ideas.

Productive Attitudes and Values

Developing good work habits and time-management practices is often a matter of developing the right attitude toward your work and toward time. If for example, you think that your job is important and that time is precious, you will be on your way toward developing good work habits. Summarized in this section are a group of attitudes, values, and beliefs that can help a person make good use of time and develop productive work habits.

Be Aware of the Dangers of Procrastination. Beyond question, procrastination is the major way in which employees at all levels waste time. People procrastinate for many different reasons. One reason is that they perceive the task to be done as unpleasant—such as conducting a performance appraisal with a problem employee. We procrastinate also when we perceive the job to be overwhelming, such as preparing a strategic plan for the department. Procrastination also takes place when we fear the consequences of our actions. One possible negative consequence is a poor evaluation of your work. Bad news is another uncomfortable consequence of action that procrastination can sometimes delay. For example, if an executive thinks that a budget analysis will reveal a deficit, he or she may delay preparing the report.

A deep-rooted reason for procrastination is self-destructive behavior.[3] For instance, a person might have the chance to make a presentation to top management that could represent a major career boost. Yet the person delays preparing the report until top management loses interest or assigns the project to somebody else. Self-destructive behavior is related to another remote reason why some people procrastinate—fear of success. (The person who fears success will sometimes procrastinate to avoid taking on the added responsibilities brought forth by success.) Self-destructive behavior may be a symptom of fear of success.

Procrastination is a major hindrance to personal productivity. The following suggestions can help in dealing with the problem. First, calculate the cost of procrastination.[4] For example, by not having a résumé prepared on time, a person may miss out on a high-paying job opportunity. The cost of procrastination includes the difference in salary between the job the person finds and the one really wanted. Another cost is the loss of potential job satisfaction. Another way to overcome procrastination is to create momentum to get moving. A useful tactic is to find a leading task (an easy, warm-up activity) to perform.[5] If you have to prepare a strategic plan, it is helpful to get momentum going by performing such tasks as getting a new file folder, sharpening a few pencils, and reaching for a text dealing with the subject.

Breaking the task down into manageable units is a method of conquering procrastination caused by facing an overwhelming task. The problem is more acute when more than one of these "elephants" is facing you. A well-accepted principle in this situation is to "Eat the elephant one bite at a time." Break the project down into logical parts and begin with a few simple parts of the project. For example, a manager in charge of an office relocation might begin by scheduling an interview with a commercial real estate broker.

Settling for less than perfection in performing an assignment can also reduce procrastination because striving for perfection blocks the completion of a project.[6] You can also fight procrastination by rewarding yourself for progress you make toward not delaying activity. If you do go ahead and schedule the performance appraisal with the problem employee, treat yourself to a new sweater or pair of athletic shoes. Finally, making a commitment to other people that you will accomplish something by a certain date *may* help you curb procrastination. If you fail to meet the deadline, you are likely to experience embarrassment or guilt.[7]

Try to Discover Your Mental Blocks.   Some forms of low productivity are caused by personal problems or mental blocks. If you can figure out the nature of the block(s), you may be able to increase your productivity. Ronald Ashkenas and Robert Schaffer have discovered, for example, that many managers engage in busy work to help them deal with the anxiety caused by the major tasks facing them. By observing managers in a large assortment of industries, these two consultants have identified three job characteristics common to almost all management levels that create anxiety. All of them lead to busy work:

1. Modifying one's daily work patterns and routines.
2. Responding to heavy pressure from above to improve performance.
3. Obtaining improved results from subordinates.[8]

An example of a retreat to a relatively unproductive task is a quality control director who scans the detailed results of every quality trial but cannot find the time to organize a much-needed quality improvement project. By asking himself or herself, "What is blocking me?" the director may recognize the problem and begin to tackle the major project. The anxiety-related block is only one of hundreds. Another block to getting an important project completed is dislike of being controlled by others. Some people feel overcontrolled when they have to conform to somebody else's deadline.

Avoid Perfectionism.   Thoroughness is a virtue on most jobs until it reaches the point of diminishing returns. Two time-management specialists, Peter A. Turla and Kathleen L. Hawkins, note that it is worthwhile to be interested in quality, but you must also be fair with yourself. "Compulsive striving for unrealistic goals can impair your creativity, cause tension between you and others, and waste valuable time. Is it worth the price? Or is this the time to break these self-defeating patterns?"[9]

Appreciate the Value of Rest and Relaxation.   In your zeal to multiply your productivity, watch out for work becoming an addiction. True workaholism sets in when nonwork activities no longer yield pleasure, making rest and relaxation difficult to achieve. The workaholic sets up a work schedule devoid of family and personal responsibilities. The link to productivity is that the person who takes very little time off from work may be less productive than employees who do not work on weekends and during vacations. Time away from work can refresh the spirit and increase personal efficiency on return from work.[10] Thomas R. Horton, CEO of the American Management Association and former IBM executive, presents this personal analysis of the pitfalls of avoiding rest and relaxation:[11]

> At one time in my career at IBM, I became so committed to succeeding that 14-hour days and 7-day weeks became my regular schedule. I was not really a workaholic (so I kept telling myself); it was just that the job demands required this dedication. As I dug myself deeper and deeper into the rut I had created, I finally realized how stale I had become. Lacking perspective, I simply plowed ahead, my efforts on the job becoming less and less effective.
>
> When I faced the fact that I was mismanaging my time and my life, I forced myself to break away and devote some time to my family and myself. Not surprisingly, this made me more productive on and off the job.

Although work addiction can lower productivity, some workaholics find so much pleasure in their jobs that work becomes a form of relaxation. One observer notes that people can only work themselves to death when they are working laboriously and without excitement.[12]

Value Cleanliness and Orderliness.   An orderly desk, file cabinet, or attaché case does not inevitably indicate an orderly mind, but it does help most people become more productive. Less time is wasted, and less energy is expended if you do not have to hunt for information that you thought you had on hand. Knowing where information is and what information you have available is a way of being in control of your job. When your job gets out of control, you are probably working at less than peak efficiency.

Cleaning up one's work area is a good starting point for a work-habit–improvement program. Even the most orderly career people should clean out their work areas every six months. Two hours devoted to office housekeeping may give you some hints as to whether or not you are taking care of all the things that you should do on your job. You might be surprised as to what has filtered down to the bottom of your in-basket.

Learn to Say No.   "Of all the time-saving techniques ever developed, perhaps the most effective is the frequent use of the word *no*," points out Edwin C. Bliss. You cannot take care of your own priorities unless you learn tactfully to decline requests from other people that interfere with your work. If your boss interrupts your work with an added assignment, point out how the new task will conflict with higher-priority ones and suggest alternatives. When your boss recognizes that you are motivated to get your major tasks accomplished and not to avoid work, you'll have a good chance of avoiding unproductive tasks.[13]

A word of caution. Do not turn down your boss too frequently. Much discretion and tact is needed in using this approach to improving personal productivity. In other words, knowing *when* to say no is also very important.

Appreciate the Importance of Paperwork.   Although it is fashionable to decry the necessity of having to do paperwork in responsible jobs, the effective career person does not neglect paperwork. (Paperwork refers here to taking care of administrative details such as correspondence, expense reports, and inventory forms.) Unless paperwork is efficiently attended to, a person's job may get out of control. Once a job is out of control, it may lead to a stress reaction for the jobholder. Ideally, a small amount of time should be invested in paperwork every day. Nonprime time (when you are at less than your peak of efficiency, but not overfatigued) is the best time to take care of routine paperwork.

Many people who do a slipshod job of handling their paperwork offer rationalizations for their actions. A sales representative may say, "I can't be bothered with paperwork. I'm paid to sell." Not taking care of paperwork usually creates problems for others in the organization. In the sales example just cited, the accounting and market research departments may have a critical need for the information generated by sales representatives.

Productive Skills and Techniques

In addition to developing the right attitudes, values, and beliefs, you also need the right skills and techniques to become productive. Below we summarize the most important skills and techniques for personal productivity.

Clarify Your Own Objectives. Knowing what you want to accomplish can improve your work habits and time management in additional ways. A basic starting point in improving your work habits and time management is to know what it is you are supposed to accomplish. A careful review of your job description and objectives with your boss is of fundamental importance. Some people are accused of being ineffective simply because they do not know what is really expected of them. A manager in a computer software firm was chastised by the owner for being ineffective. Asked why he was considered ineffective, the owner replied "You have failed to keep the systems analysts off my back." The manager rightfully replied, "This must have been some hidden purpose of my job. You never told me that before." From that point on, the manager increased his effectiveness by dealing with the complaints and concerns of the systems analysts.

Prepare a "To Do" List. Few people are so innately well organized that they can make good use of time without preparing a list of activities that need doing. You will recall that Mark McCormack, similar to many other busy people, uses three-by-five index cards to establish his To Do list. Because so many people lose these lists, it is advisable to place these lists on a combined desk calendar and planner.[14] These planners are orderly systems of allocating your time among various activities. Some of these planners suggest apportioning your time into 30-minute or one-hour chunks. In addition to time allocation, such planners serve as record-keeping devices for luncheon engagements, expense account items, and important dates. Figure 1–1 presents two pages from a representative planner, *The American Management Association Executive Appointment Book.*

Time-management specialists advocate assigning an A, B, or C rating to each item on the list. A items have the highest value; B items have medium value; and C items have the lowest value. Taking care of a few C items first can be a morale booster because it feels as if progress is being made. Many people describe a therapeutic feeling when they knock off a few C items from a formidable To Do list.

Challenge Your Use of Time. A major tool for improving your efficiency and effectiveness is to ask Lakein's question: "What is the best use of my time right now?"[15] This question helps you to justify your every action. Lakein notes that a particularly good time to ask this question is when you have been interrupted by a visitor or phone call. When it's over, he advises to check whether you should go back to what you were doing or on to something new.

Your answer to Lakein's question may be different when asked about what seems to be a comparable situation. One day you are waiting for an elevator in your office building. You ask, "What is the best possible use

Figure 1-1 Pages from an Executive Appointment Book and Planner

THIS WEEK	MONDAY JUL. 11	TUESDAY JUL. 12	WEDNESDAY JUL. 13	THURSDAY JUL. 14	FRIDAY JUL. 15
THINGS TO DO:	A.M.	A.M.	A.M.	A.M.	A.M.
	LUNCH	LUNCH	LUNCH	LUNCH	LUNCH
	EVENING	EVENING	EVENING	EVENING	EVENING

	SATURDAY JUL. 16
	SUNDAY JUL. 17

PEOPLE TO CALL:	THIS WEEK I'LL GIVE FEEDBACK TO:

JUNE

S	M	T	W	T	F	S
			1	2	3	4
5	6	7	8	9	10	11
12	13	14	15	16	17	18
19	20	21	22	23	24	25
26	27	28	29	30		

JULY

S	M	T	W	T	F	S
					1	2
3	4	5	6	7	8	9
10	11	12	13	14	15	16
17	18	19	20	21	22	23
24	25	26	27	28	29	30
31						

AUGUST

S	M	T	W	T	F	S
	1	2	3	4	5	6
7	8	9	10	11	12	13
14	15	16	17	18	19	20
21	22	23	24	25	26	27
28	29	30	31			

Turning Commuting Into Productive Time

You can make idle commuting hours productive by asking yourself these questions:

1. What are the priority items in the current work load?
2. What problems can be expected today?
3. Which jobs from the previous day need to be cleaned up?
4. What special opportunities exist that are particularly challenging or call for special skills?
5. What personal contributions to company goals are likely or possible today?

SOURCE: Reprinted, by permission of the publisher, from *The American Management Association Executive Appointment Book*, 1988. © 1988 American Management Association, New York. All rights reserved.

of my time right now?" Your answer is "Certainly not waiting for an elevator. I'll jog up the stairs and get some needed exercise."

One week later you are again waiting for the elevator. You ask the same question. This time your answer is, "Waiting for the elevator is a good use of my time right now. It's about time I touched base with a few employees from different departments in the company."

Be Decisive and Finish Things. A good deal of time is wasted by managers who vacillate too long before choosing among the alternative solutions to a problem facing them. If you value decisiveness, you should learn the skill of being decisive, assuming you have a reasonable degree of self-confidence. If a person has too little self-confidence, he or she may never become a rapid decision maker. Business school graduates are often criticized for being so analytical that they are indecisive. The productive individual will invest a reasonable amount of time in weighing alternatives, but then will make a decision.

Dru Scott has developed a technique for helping people become more decisive. In general, it follows the logic of the steps involved in problem solving and decision making. Its unique thrust is that it asks you to define what you most want to accomplish before you begin comparing alternatives.[16] To illustrate, if you were trying to decide which office automation system to purchase, you should define precisely what you want the system to accomplish. One such answer could be, "We want a system that will take care of the computing demands of our managerial, professional, and clerical employees without having to purchase a variety of equipment." You would then narrow down your choice to office automation systems with software and hardware capable of satisfying these three sets of demands simultaneously.

Another productivity drain stemming from not finishing things is the *Ziegarnik effect*—the phenomenon of incompleted tasks creating a disturbing level of tension. Not finishing a task can thus serve as a distraction that interferes with productivity on future tasks.

Carefully Schedule Activities. The use of a To Do list and a desk planner enable a person to schedule activities in a productive manner. Four other important scheduling suggestions are described next:

1. *Allow time for emergencies.* Because many managerial and professional jobs require the handling of emergencies, enough slack has to be built into one's schedule for handling these unpredictable problems.[17] In essence, the careful scheduler creates room for unscheduled events. Similarly, a household budget must allow enough room for the inevitable *miscellaneous* category.

2. *Minimize unscheduled interruptions.* Although legitimate emergencies must be handled quickly, most other types of un-

scheduled interruptions should be minimized in order to maintain productivity. One solution to the problem of interruptions is for you to schedule a period of time during the day in which you have uninterrupted work time. You give co-workers a definite time during which you want to be disturbed with emergencies only. It is also helpful to inform co-workers of the nature of the important work you ordinarily conduct during your quiet period.[18]

3. *Schedule similar tasks together.* An efficient method of accomplishing small tasks is to group them together and perform them in one block of time. To illustrate, you might make most of your telephone calls in relation to your job from 11 to 11:30 each workday morning. Or you might reserve the first hour of every workday for correspondence; this will allow for secretarial processing if needed. When you go downtown, think of all the errands that you have that can best be done downtown. Over a period of time you save a number of wasted trips.

By using this method, you develop the necessary pace and mental set to knock off chores in short order. In contrast, when you flit from one type of task to another, your efficiency may suffer.

4. *Schedule yourself by computer.* Software is available that allows one to use a personal computer as an electronic calendar to help keep track of appointments and list of chores.[19] The first step in implementing these programs would be to enter into the computer's memory your appointments, tasks, and errands. For instance, a person might use these items as input:

April 2	Meet with Brady to discuss budget.
April 17	Get strategic plan for department started.
May 3	Lunch with Rachel to discuss affirmative action plan.
May 18	Make request for new office furniture.

From this point forward, the computer's information-processing capabilities could be tapped. Suppose you couldn't remember the date of your lunch with Rachel. You would command the computer to "Find lunch date with Rachel." Or, if you were an extremely busy person, you might have reason to ask the computer to tell you when you had the next opening for lunch. Another use of this type of software is to command the computer to flag key appointments and tasks. An indicator such as **URGENT** might be used. Some managers who use electronic calendars (and word processing) believe that their personal computers take over many secretarial chores.

Concentrate on High-Output Tasks.   To become more effective in your job, you have to concentrate on tasks where superior performance could have a big payoff for the organization.[20] This is the familiar distinction between breakthrough versus routine or trivial tasks, or the 80–20 principle. The 80–20 principle (also referred to as the Pareto principle) states that 80 percent of the results of most transactions derive from 20 percent of the activity. Thus, if you work on the right 20 percent of your job, you will be achieving bigger results.

In following the A-B-C system, you should devote ample time to the A items. You should not pay more attention than absolutely necessary to the C items. However, if you find that working on C items is tension-reducing, proceed, but recognize that you must return to A items as soon as you feel relaxed. When the suggestion of working on high-output items is offered, many managers respond, "I don't think that concentrating on important tasks applies to me. My job is so filled with routine, I have no chance to work on breakthrough ideas." True, most jobs are filled with routine requirements. What a person can do is spend some time—even one hour per week—concentrating on tasks that may prove to have high output.

Eliminate or Minimize Low-Output Tasks.   It is critical to your job success to avoid doing work that has no real payoff to the organization. Consultant John Humble says, "The major opportunities for elimination lie in stopping meetings that no longer serve a useful purpose and in cutting out time-consuming, needless paperwork. For some international managers the elimination of regular trips is usually possible."[21]

Eliminating or minimizing low-output items is tied in with most of the suggestions presented in this chapter. Michael LeBoeuf notes that once you know what is important to you, you can use the entire gamut of time-management techniques to take care of external time wasters such as interruptions, unnecessary meetings, and excessive telephone calls and paperwork.[22]

Work at a Steady Pace.   In most jobs, working at a steady pace pays dividends in efficiency. The spurt worker creates many problems for superiors, co-workers, and subordinates. An important advantage of the steady-pace approach is that you accomplish much more than someone who puts out extra effort just once in a while. Trying to catch up for lost time may result in a high error rate even in managerial work.

In the steady-pace approach, you strive for a constant expenditure of energy every working day. (As one person describes this strategy, "Every day is Monday.") The payoff is that you develop a precious supply of bonus time that you can use for planning and thinking creatively about your job. If you find yourself with an afternoon of discretionary time, you can figure out ways of doing your job more effectively. Such improvements should ultimately enhance your reputation wherever you work. Despite the advantages of maintaining a steady pace, some peaks and valleys in your work may be inevitable. The seasonal demands placed on employees in public accounting firms are a prime example.

Keep an Accurate Time Log. Another good starting point in improving your work habits and time management is to analyze how you are currently spending your time. If you are privileged to have a secretary or assistant, that person might help compile the log. A time analysis of this nature often reveals some surprises because we tend to exaggerate the importance of the tasks to which we devote our time. One bank required that its branch managers record time spent under three headings: (*a*) time with customers, (*b*) time on administration, and (*c*) time with their own staff. The analysis demonstrated that too much time was expended on internal administration to the detriment of marketing and staff development.[23]

Time should be logged only for a defined period—perhaps one or two weeks to identify how time is spent and/or wasted. Too much time spent in logging time can be counterproductive.

Identify and Plug Time Leaks. Wasted time is costly enough to justify your identifying and plugging time leaks. By putting more of normal working hours to good use, you can increase your output without increasing your number of hours worked. A common time leak is the practice of conducting informal discussions unrelated to the job that are held during working hours, including social phone calls. Other common leaks include 90-minute lunch breaks, excessive time spent in warming up to get started working, too much time spent winding down to stop working, and visiting other people in the office instead of phoning them to discuss a work problem.

GF Business Equipment has developed a guide to protecting your privacy from small-talkers in the office. They suggest that a direct statement is the most effective. Simply say, "I'm sorry, but I'm busy and can't be disturbed. I will get back to you later." They also suggest that if you are concerned that others will take this personally, or consider you to be antisocial, compensate by going out of your way to be friendly with these people at other times.[24]

Concentrate on One Task at a Time. Effective executives have a well-developed capacity to concentrate on the problem or person facing them, however surrounded they are with other obligations. Intense concentration leads to crisper judgment and analysis and also minimizes major errors. The thousands of fingers lost each year by the owners of home power tools attest to this observation! Another useful byproduct of concentration is that it helps reduce absent-mindedness. If you concentrate intensely on what you are doing, you decrease the chance of forgetting what you intended to do. Walter Olesky provides a dramatic statement of the link between concentration and personal productivity.

> Most of the really successful people, in whatever field, subordinate everything to the main purposes of their lives. When they are working, they display extraordinary powers of concentration. These men and women often bewilder their fellow workers, because they never seem to work hard, or for any period of time. Their secret lies in their power to concentrate, and thus obtain maximum results with a minimum of apparent effort.[25]

Deal with Distracting Problems.   When you are preoccupied with a personal or work problem, it is difficult to concentrate in the manner just described. The solution is to address the problem so that its impact on the job is kept at a minimum. Suppose a person is so far in debt that his or her monthly debt payments and fixed living expenses allow no room for unanticipated expenses that seem to arise every month. As dire as the solution seems, it might be to that person's advantage to obtain a debt-consolidation loan. The monthly payment might be low enough to allow breathing room. Once the consolidation loan is paid off, that person might choose to never reenter debt, thus contributing to his or her peace of mind for the long term.

Sometimes a relatively minor problem such as being long overdue for a dental checkup can impair your work concentration. At other times, a major problem such as a child custody dispute between divorcing parents interferes with work. In either situation, your concentration will suffer until you take appropriate action.

Delegate When Feasible.   A boss who tries to do too many tasks alone eventually becomes overwhelmed and somewhat unproductive. A sounder approach is to delegate that portion of those assignments that can be properly handled by a subordinate. In order to delegate effectively, it is necessary to have competent and willing subordinates. Even under such conditions, it is important to exercise some control (follow up) on work that is delegated. If the subordinates do not produce results, *you* are still responsible for the lack of results.

Delegation provides another important boost to productivity. Charles D. Pringle observes that managers who delegate wisely have higher performing subordinates, and hence more effective departments, than do managers who are poor delegators. In turn this leads to a personal benefit for the manager because managers of successful departments are more likely to be promoted.[26]

Harness Your Natural Energy Cycles.   People vary somewhat as to their hours of peak efficiency. Most are aware of the hours at which their mental and physical energy is apt to be highest or lowest. First, determine your strong and weak energy periods (such as morning versus afternoon). You should then be able to arrange your work schedule accordingly. Tackle your intellectually most demanding assignments during your energy peaks. If possible, avoid creative work or making major decisions when fatigue has set it. Many errors in judgment take place when people are working outside their time of efficiency, such as one or two in the morning.

Make Use of Bits of Time.   A truly productive person makes good use of miscellaneous bits of time, both on and off the job. Time spent waiting in lines can be profitably invested in professional reading, reading work memos and reports, or composing a fresh list of chores. While waiting for an elevator you might be able to read a 100-word report. And if you have finished your day's work 10 minutes before quitting time, you can use that 10 minutes to clean out a drawer in your desk. By the end of the year, your productivity will have increased much more than if you had squandered these bits of time.

Set Time Limit for Certain Tasks.   As managers and professionals become more experienced with certain projects, they become able to make more accurate estimates of how long a project will take to complete. A department head might say, for example, "Getting this preliminary budget ready for my boss's approval should take seven hours." A good time-management practice to develop is to estimate how long a job should take and then proceed with a strong determination to get that job completed within the estimated period of time.

A productive variation of this technique is to decide that some low- and medium-priority items are only worth so much of your time. Invest that much time in a project, but no more. Preparing a file on advertisements that cross your desk is one example.

Remember Where You Put Things.   How much time have you wasted lately in looking for such items as an important file, your keys, or your appointment book? If you can remember where you put things of this nature, you can save a lot of wasted time and motion. Turla and Hawkins offer two practical suggestions for remembering where you put things.[27] First, have a parking place for everything. This would include putting your keys and appointment book back in the same place after each use. Second, make visual associations. In order to have something register in your mind at the moment you are doing it, make up a visual association about that act. Thus you might say, "Here I am putting my budgeting proposal in the back section of my attaché case."

Use the Telephone Efficiently.   Much business today is conducted over the telephone, including both internal and external calls. Using the telephone efficiently can thus save a substantial amount of time. Many callers are slow to get to the point, thus consuming time. A good way of handling this problem is to take the initiative to ask, "How can I help you?" or "What can I do for you?" Such an approach decreases the chances that the caller will engage in small talk. Long distance callers, for example, particularly enjoy comparing their weather to the receiver's weather.[28]

Another point to consider about the use of telephones is that sometimes phone calls can be a productive use during a brief lapse between meetings and appointments. It is best to make fairly routine calls during these intervals to avoid the tension that results when a lengthy phone call makes you late for the next appointment.

Be Aware of Diminishing Returns.   A time-management principle closely related to setting time limits for tasks is to know when to get off a project to avoid low productivity. Stephanie Winston points out that "knowing when to stop a project is as important as knowing when to start one."[29] If you can only concentrate on doing a spreadsheet analysis on a computer for three hours, stop as soon as your time in front of the computer approaches three hours. If your neck muscles ache, and you are making too many errors, it is time to quit. If it is not the end of your normal workday, move on to some other less tedious task such as making telephone calls.

As you acquire more skill on a difficult task, you are likely to find that you are able to work productively on the same task for longer periods of time. Thus, the point of diminishing returns takes longer to reach. One reason is that as people become more skilled in performing a task, they become less tense and more relaxed. Working under moderate tension, in turn, leads to fewer errors than working under high tension. For example, air traffic controllers are prone to more errors when they are stressed from congestion in the airport and sky.

The Case for Good Work Habits and Time Management

Common sense and experience suggest that there is much to be gained by improving your approach to work along the lines suggested in this chapter. Good work habits, including time management, may be as important as high intelligence and appropriate personality characteristics in bringing about career success. To use an extreme example, if you are in charge of issuing payroll checks, your employees will be more concerned about your timeliness than your personal warmth and enthusiasm.

Another important reason for improving your work habits is that they make a multifaceted contribution to your life. Good work habits can improve job performance, personal life, and mental health. A person who performs efficiently and effectively on the job has more time (and often money) for personal life. Simultaneously, he or she escapes the stress stemming from a constant feeling of being behind in work.

Good work habits are also important because, to a large extent, they underlie the basic management functions of planning and controlling. To illustrate, planning involves setting priorities, and controlling includes following up on progress toward achieving goals.

The Case Against Using These Methods to Improve Productivity

Almost no experienced manager or individual contributor would say that poor work habits and time management are the keys to success, yet the converse is not always true. Many successful, creative people do not appear particularly well organized. Successful executives often behave in an impulsive manner, responding to the demands of the moment. Their work is characterized by frequent interruptions.

Another fundamental argument against placing too much emphasis on good work habits is that they are a reflection of underlying personality characteristics. As such, they are difficult to change. For instance, if you are a compulsive personality (tidy, highly concerned about details), your natural inclination will be to have good work habits and time management. If you are not compulsive, trying to behave compulsively may not be worth the effort. Also people who are basically patient have an easier time developing good work habits than do impatient people.

Another important issue to consider is whether the attitudes, methods, and techniques described here actually contribute to personal productivity. Some critics of this approach believe that people who take time-management techniques too seriously become rigid and obsessed with making optimum use of time. In their quest for personal efficiency they drive themselves to a stress disorder. (Note that rest and relaxation is an important time-management technique.)

Critics of popular approaches to the improvement of work habits and time management also note that these techniques do not work for everybody. Each individual has to discover what works best for him or her. For example, John Kotter reports that the best executives do not necessarily map out their daily schedules in advance. Instead, they react to events as they occur.[30]

Despite these arguments that could conceivably be advanced against improving your work habits and time management, almost any manager or professional person would become more productive by practicing some of the suggestions made in this chapter.

OVERVIEW OF WORK HABITS AND
TIME MANAGEMENT

So many methods and techniques have been covered in this chapter that a quick overview is in order. The general point is that by improving your work habits and time management you can improve your job productivity and enhance your personal life. Developing good work habits and time-management practices is often a matter of developing the right attitudes toward work and toward time. An important starting point is to be aware of the dangers of procrastination. Other key attitudes and values include discovering your mental blocks, appreciating the value of rest and relaxation, and appreciating the importance of paperwork.

In addition to developing the right attitudes, values, and beliefs, you also need the right skills and techniques to become productive. Among the most important skills and techniques for this purpose are preparing a To Do list, carefully scheduling activities, concentrating on high-output tasks, concentrating on one task at a time, and delegating when feasible.

Guidelines for Action and Skill Development

As you embark on a program of improved personal productivity, guard against becoming an annoyance to everybody else. Try not to convert everybody to your ways. If you become too concerned about time squandering and inefficiency, it is possible that you will irritate more than motivate others. The true goal of the suggestions in this chapter is to improve your productivity but still retain some flexibility in your work and compassion for people.

To get started improving your work habits, select an aspect of work where you are hurting the most; then choose an appropriate remedial strategy. A good starting point for most people is to clean up their work area or develop a priority list.

Practice faithfully and patiently whichever work habits and time-management approaches you select. Poor work habits and time management usually develop over the years and therefore require at least several months to turn around. Once you have mastered one new habit or habits, proceed to another strategy appropriate to your situation.

DISCUSSION QUESTIONS AND ACTIVITIES

1. Much has been said about the evils of procrastination. Nevertheless, provide an example of how procrastination can sometimes work in a person's favor.

2. Does it appear to you that Mark McCormack (see the opening case) has learned to use the telephone efficiently?

3. Some highly productive scientists work in chaotic-appearing offices. How does this fact reconcile with statements made in this chapter about orderliness and time management?

4. When you meet a stranger, how can you tell if he or she is well organized?

5. In what types of work will good work habits and time management most likely lead directly to increases in earnings for the individual?

6. How applicable are the suggestions made in this chapter to (a) school work and (b) running a household?

7. Some tidy and perfectionist people never become highly successful from a career standpoint. Which time-management strategy are they probably neglecting?

8. What is your reaction to the statement, "A clear and orderly desk reflects a clear and orderly mind"?

9. Interview a person you know to be highly productive. Determine which of the time-management and work habits presented in this chapter that person practices regularly.

NOTES

1. Scott De Garmo, "The Organized Executive," *Success!,* December 1986, p. 4. Excerpted and adapted with permission.
2. Strategies for improving work habits and time management tend to be similar from source to source. Where credit to one particular source is deserved, it will be indicated by footnotes.
3. Andrew J. DuBrin, *Human Relations: A Job Oriented Approach,* 4th ed. (Englewood Cliffs, N.J.: Prentice Hall, 1988) p. 477.
4. Alan Lakein, *How to Gain Control of Your Time and Your Life* (New York: Peter H. Wyden, 1973), pp. 141–51.
5. Michael LeBoeuf as cited in Priscilla Petty, "Saying No to Unproductive Jobs Frees Time for High-Priority Goals," Rochester *Democrat and Chronicle,* June 21, 1983, p. 10D.
6. "Procrastinators Need to Be Dealt with Now," *Research Institute Personal Report for the Executive,* January 1, 1987, p. 8.
7. DuBrin, *Human Relations: A Job Oriented Approach,* p. 479.
8. Ronald N. Ashkenas and Robert H. Schaffer, "Managers Can Avoid Wasting Time," *Harvard Business Review,* May–June 1982, p. 99.
9. Peter A. Turla and Kathleen L. Hawkins, "The Flaws of Perfectionism," *Success!,* December 1982, p. 23.
10. "All Work and No Play Makes for an Unproductive Employee," *Research Institute Personal Report for the Executive,* August 6, 1985, p. 5.

11. Thomas R. Horton, "How Dedicated Must You Be?" *Success!*, March 1987, p. 16.

12. "Confessions of a Happy Workaholic," *Success!*, June 1983, p. 8.

13. Edwin C. Bliss, "Give Yourself the Luxury of Time," *Mainliner*, December 1976, p. 55.

14. R. Alec Mackenzie, "The 'To Do' List Is Obsolete," *Supervisory Management*, September 1985, pp. 41–43.

15. Lakein, *How to Gain Control of Your Time and Your Life*, p. 99.

16. Dru Scott, *How to Put More Time in Your Life* (New York: New American Library, 1980), pp. 92–100.

17. "Total Time Management," American Management Association Audio-Cassette Workbook Program, 1988.

18. Peter A. Turla and Kathleen L. Hawkins, "A Personal Achievement Guide to Time Management," *Success!*, November 1982, p. A6.

19. William Brohaugh, "Computerizing Your Calendar," *Success!*, November 1983, pp. 14–16.

20. Among the many places in which this concept is espoused is Andrew Grove, *High Output Management* (New York: Random House, 1983).

21. John Humble, "Time Management: Separating the Myths and the Realities," *Management Review*, October 1980, pp. 29, 40.

22. LeBoeuf, cited in Petty, "Saying No to Unproductive Jobs Frees Time for High-Priority Goals," p. 10D.

23. Humble, "Time Management," p. 27.

24. "Protecting Your Privacy," *Success!*, April 1982, p. 10.

25. Walter Olesky, "Concentration," *Success!*, October 1983, pp. 28, 30.

26. Charles D. Pringle, "Seven Reasons Why Managers Don't Delegate," *Management Solutions*, November 1986, p. 30.

27. Peter A. Turla and Kathleen L. Hawkins, "Remembering to Remember," *Success!*, May 1983, p. 60.

28. Bernardo, "Time Is Money," p. 52.

29. Stephanie Winston, *Getting Organized* (New York: Warner Books, 1979), p. 40.

30. Cited in "Time Management Techniques—A Rundown," *Personal Report for the Executive*, August 1, 1987, p. 4.

SOME ADDITIONAL REFERENCES

Davis, Sandra L. "How to Overcome Procrastination." *Business Week Careers*, February 1987, pp. 46–49.

Feinberg, Andrew. "Artists of Organization." *Success!*, October 1987, pp. 60–64.

Hanson, M. R. "To-Do Lists for Managers." *Supervisory Management*, May 1986, pp. 37–39.

Januz, Lauren R., and Susan K. Jones. *Time Management for Executives*. New York: Scribner's, 1981.

Kotter, John. *The General Managers*. New York: Macmillan, 1986.

Winston, Stephanie. *The Organized Executive*. W. W. Norton, 1986.

Appendix to Chapter One

IMPROVING YOUR WORK HABITS AND TIME MANAGEMENT

Casually reading this chapter will probably not lead to improvements in your personal productivity. You need to back up these ideas with a specific action plan for improvement. A useful mechanical aid toward achieving this end is to scan the checklist presented below. It covers the attitudes, strategies, techniques, and tactics described in this chapter. Select the six areas on this checklist in which you need the most help. For each item you select, write a one- or two-sentence action plan. Suppose you checked "Concentrate on high-output tasks." Your action plan might take this form:

> I tend to put too much effort into performing tasks well that do not have a big payoff. I'm going to carefully review my job and figure out which tasks could really have a big payoff. I will consult my boss to get his or her opinion also. Then I will put more effort into tasks with a potential for a big breakthrough.

The Work Habits and Time-Management Checklist

Attitude, Skill, or Technique
  1. Be aware of the dangers of procrastination.   _____
  2. Try to discover your mental blocks.   _____
  3. Avoid perfectionism.   _____
  4. Appreciate the value of rest and relaxation.   _____
  5. Value cleanliness and orderliness.   _____
  6. Learn to say no.   _____
  7. Appreciate the importance of paperwork.   _____
  8. Challenge your use of time.   _____
  9. Be decisive and finish things.   _____
 10. Clarify your own objectives.   _____
 11. Prepare a To Do list.   _____
 12. Carefully schedule activities.   _____
     a. Allow time for emergencies.   _____
     b. Minimize unscheduled interruptions.   _____
     c. Schedule similar tasks together.   _____
     d. Schedule yourself by computer.   _____
 13. Concentrate on high-output tasks.   _____
 14. Eliminate or minimize low-output tasks.   _____
 15. Work at a steady pace.   _____

16. Keep an accurate time log.   ———————
17. Identify and plug time leaks.   ———————
18. Concentrate on one task at a time.   ———————
19. Deal with distracting problems.   ———————
20. Delegate when feasible.   ———————
21. Harness your natural energy cycles.   ———————
22. Make use of bits of time.   ———————
23. Set time limits for certain tasks.   ———————
24. Remember where you put things.   ———————
25. Use the telephone efficiently.   ———————
26. Be aware of diminishing returns.   ———————

Chapter Two

Improving Your Creativity

A small business owner faced a problem at home—his five-year-old son was experiencing difficulty learning to write. The man's creative solution to the problem launched a new business and a new career for himself and his wife.

Several years ago, Chris E. Rusk noticed that his five-year-old son was learning how to write but did not know how to hold a pencil. "He was holding it like a steak knife," Rusk recalled. Rusk took some cookie dough, placed it over the end of the pencil, and molded it to fit Troy's thumb and two of his fingers. Troy took to the device immediately.

Rusk said, "Here was a five-year-old, proud as punch, writing correctly. The next morning I got up and he was using it again, and I thought, 'Everyone ought to have one.' It's named Stetro after my daughter and son, Stephanie and Troy. That was my wife's idea."

Rusk began coverting his idea into a business shortly after this incident. Some lean times have followed, but the gadget has now attracted some attention in school systems. "It's ready to explode," Rusk says. "A lot has happened in the last five months. I couldn't believe it." In those five months, Rusk has gone from filling orders for 250 or 300 of the grips to signing contracts for 2 million units. The addition of two production molds is boosting output fivefold to 1 million per week.

Teachers who have tried the Stetro have described it as "absolutely wonderful" and "magic." One teacher wrote Rusk that "no amount of words can tell you how helpful these are." Available in every color of the rainbow and retailing for 39 cents, the Stetro has worked its way into other markets. People suffering from arthritis and other physical handicaps say the device makes it easier for them to grip a pen or pencil.

"So many people are interested in the product now. It's a new wheel or something. I was just trying to make things easier for my son."

Shortly after inventing Stetro, Chris and his wife Susan spent time on weekends in libraries poring through patent files. When they and a lawyer did not find anything similar, Rusk obtained a patent. Soon Rusk dropped his small construction business, sold his share in a local tavern, and flew the family to California for a school supply trade show. He did not have a booth, but he had 10 urethane prototypes that caught the eye of suppliers.

Pretending to take orders, he soon found people interested in buying as many as 15,000 Stetros. He returned home and ordered an $11,000 mold capable of making eight at a time. "Before I ever saw a penny come back, over the last four years I had put $20,000 in it. We were putting everything we had into it. I was about to run out of money."

At the start of their first full year of operation, Rusk and his wife stuffed Stetros in 20,000 envelopes for a bulk mailing to schools chosen randomly across the country. The Rusks received 3,500 responses, and Susan saw their home transformed from the day-care center she had started to help pay bills. "We had our whole house with mailbags up to the ceiling," she said. "The phone never stopped ringing."

Stetro is now being sold through about 500 sales representatives for various supply houses. It can be found in pharmacies, convenience stores, and school bookstores. It is nontoxic, being made from a pliable plastic approved by the Food and Drug Administration. Rusk said he ate the first one off the line to make sure.

"It still looks like a glob of bubble gum, but it's cute," he said.[1]

SELF-HELP APPROACHES TO CREATIVITY IMPROVEMENT

Chris Rusk hit upon a creative idea in response to a troublesome problem. The chances of a person being able to find creative solutions to problems are likely to increase when that person engages in exercises and techniques designed to increase creativity. As used here, creativity is the ability to develop novel ideas that can be put into action.[2] Creativity leads to creative problem solving—the ability to overcome obstacles by approaching them in novel ways. After first describing a well-accepted view of the creative process, in this chapter we also describe a group of techniques useful in developing creativity.

The Stages of Creative Thought

Because the importance of creativity has long been recognized, much effort has been devoted to understanding the process by which creative ideas surface. Here we are concerned with the five stages in a person's thinking and behavior that produce a creative result.[3]

1. Problem Finding. The individual discovers that something is worth working on or becomes aware that a problem or disturbance exists.

2. Immersion. The individual concentrates on the problem and becomes immersed in it. He or she will recall and collect information that seems relevant, dreaming up alternatives without refining or evaluating them.

3. Incubation. After assembling the information, the individual keeps it in the back of his or her mind for a while. It has been hypothesized that the subconscious mind begins to take over. Although the individual is not actively working on the problem, it is simmering in the mind. It is therefore justifiable to go for a walk during working hours to engage in creative problem solving. While the problem is simmering, the subconscious may be trying to arrange the facts into a meaningful pattern.

4. Insight. If you have ever experienced a sudden insight about a vexing problem, you will understand this step in the creative process. The problem-conquering solution flashes into the mind at an unexpected time, such as while about to go to sleep, showering, or jogging.

5. Verification and Application. The individual sets out to prove that the creative solution has merit. Verification procedures include gathering supporting evidence, logical persuasion, and experimenting with the new idea. Tenacity is usually required at the application state of creative thought because most novel ideas are rejected as being impractical.

Techniques Useful in Developing Creativity

Overcome Traditional Mental Sets. The most important part of learning to behave creatively is to overcome familiar approaches to problems that lock us into one way of doing things. These familiar approaches have been referred to as perceptual blocks, mental locks, or traditional mental sets. According to Roger von Oech, founder of a creativity consulting firm, people have become prisoners of familiarity. The more often a person manages a project, runs a meeting, or designs a marketing strategy the same way, the more difficult it becomes to think about doing it any other way. Originally, he concentrated on developing creativity-training programs to help high-technology companies arrive at more creative solutions to scientific and marketing problems. The application of his methods has spread to many different organizations and individuals. Von Oech suggests a few ways he believes will help most people overcome mental locks and thus get in a creative frame of mind.[4]

Allow the Foolish Side of You to Come Out. Humor has long been observed to be a helpful way of getting into a creative mental set. "For example, one of my clients manufactures satellites. They had a design meeting not too long ago, and everyone started making fun of the satellites. They made weird jokes about them, bad puns, and were just really silly with it. In the course of this, they came up with two major innovative design breakthroughs.''

Be a Hunter.   Says von Oech, ''I've worked with creative people in many industries, disciplines, and professions, and the really good ones are hunters. These people look outside their areas for ideas, and when they find an idea, they bring it back to their own area and apply it.''

Use Stepping Stones.   Crazy-sounding, impractical, infrequent ideas, even though you are unable to execute them, can sometimes serve as a stepping stone to a practical, creative new idea. A paint company representative said a few years ago, ''Let's put gunpowder in our housepaint. Then when the paint cracks and it's a real pain to get off, we could just blow it right off the side of the house.''

Von Oech notes the silliness of the idea. However, that idea was used as a stepping stone to ask another question: ''What other ways could we put additives in our paint at the front end so they would remain inert, but combined with another solution a few years later, would react and make the paint easy to get off?'' This paint is now available commercially.

Be a Revolutionary.   Most new ideas and advances in technology, science, and business come about when someone either breaks or bends the rules. Microprocessors and recombinant DNA break the rules. Ask yourself, ''What if we tried it another way?'' ''What if we didn't do this?'' One company president says his most difficult task is getting his subordinates to challenge the rules.

Don't Be Afraid to Try and Fail.   The late Sydney Harris contended that it is fear of failure more than anything else that separates the imitators from the innovators.[5] If you try a large number of projects, ideas, or things, a large number of them are likely to fail. Yet your number of ''hits'' will be much higher than if you tried only a few projects, ideas, or things. It is the absolute number of successes that counts the most—not the percentage of successes.

Conduct Brainwriting Sessions.   Brainstorming is widely recognized as a group method of finding creative alternatives to problems. A variation of the same method, which can be used to advantage by individuals, is referred to as *brainwriting*. In brainwriting, the individual works alone and writes down a number of alternatives to the problem at hand. It is often helpful to give oneself a quota of ideas along with a time deadline.

A good deal of self-discipline is required to conduct private brainstorming sessions because you do not have the support of the group. The idea is to discipline yourself to develop a number of alternatives to the job problem you are trying to solve—or the opportunity you are trying to create. Faced with a situation calling for a creative response, you might sit quietly with a pencil and pad and begin to generate possible solutions. For example, "How can I shorten the time it takes our customers to pay their bills without creating ill will?" Most people accept the first one or two alternatives to such a problem. Through private brainstorming, you can learn to search for many alternatives.

An example of the potential yield from brainwriting took place at a fast-food restaurant in New England where low-paying service jobs are particularly difficult to fill. The franchisee was convinced that the uniforms the restaurant employees were required to wear were a big irritant to employees. He noticed that the teenage employees immediately changed into street clothes even for their 20-minute in-store breaks. One alternative solution chosen by the franchisee was to take four employees and one mother down to a local uniform shop. He asked his people what uniforms they wanted, and then he purchased those selected. Four months later his applicant pool had soared, including college students whom he wanted to recruit. At last report the parent company had not complained about his deviation from the company dress code.[6]

Develop a Synergy Between Both Sides of the Brain.   Until recently it was generally believed that the left side of the brain is the source of most analytical, logical, and rational thought. It performs the tasks necessary for well-reasoned arguments and for working with standard applications of a computer. The right side of the brain, it was believed, grasps the work in a more intuitive, overall manner. It is the source of impressionistic, creative thought. People with dominant right brains thrive on disorder and ambiguity—both characteristics of creative people.

Current scientific thought indicates that any mental activity is carried out by both sides of the brain simultaneously. Joined by the corpus callosum, the two hemispheres work together in harmony. Creativity is the result of both sides of the brain working in harmony. Creative thought arises from the symbiotic cooperation of various parts of the brain in both the left and right hemispheres.[7] Therefore the highly creative individual achieves *synergy* (the combination is more than the sum of the parts) between the two sides of the brain. Both brain hemispheres are used as needed. Robert Gundlack, a physical scientist who had been awarded 128 patents in his first 30 years of work, explains this approach to creativity improvement in these terms:

> Being creative means developing a synergy between the left half of the brain—the analytical half—and the right half of the brain—the creative half. I learned that at home during my childhood. My mother was an artist, a painter of landscapes. My father was a chemist and inventor of Wildroot hair oil. Both my parents influenced me equally well.[8]

Identify Your Creative Time Period.   As you begin to make creativity a habit, it is helpful to identify those times of the day or week when your capacity for creative thought is the highest and lowest. For most people, creative capacity is best following ample rest. It is, therefore, helpful to tackle creative problems at the start of a workday. Some executives and researchers tackle their biggest thought problems while on vacation or while jogging. The solution to the problem is conceptualized in broadest outline, and the details are worked out back on the job. Among such "vacation problems" might be "What new service might our agency offer?" or "What hypothesis is worthy of researching?"

Other individuals report that their best time for creative thought is immediately before falling asleep. We have all heard of the energetic people who keep a pen and notebook adjacent to their bed in order to jot down such nocturnal flashes of inspiration. One manager reports that he gets his best ideas during meetings conducted for other purposes. The point is to chart your individual creative time period.

Be Curious. Curiosity frequently underlies creative ideas. The person who routinely questions why things work or don't work is on the way toward developing a creative suggestion to improve on what already exists. Many new ideas for products and services stem from the curious attitude of their developer. An office supervisor in a plumbing supply company encouraged his firm to develop a new mechanism that would help stop leaking water closets. His suggestion stemmed from his curiosity as to why so many places he visited had troubles with continuously running toilets. The resultant product is built on a new principle. It uses water pressure to replace the troublesome floating bulb arrangement found in most water closets.

Get a Balanced Cultural Media Diet. To gather creative ideas, Stephen J. Bennett recommends that you obtain a "balanced cultural media diet." His reasoning is that few people can keep up with reading in their own fields, let alone a general sense of what is happening in other fields. The information glut should not act as a deterrent for expanding knowledge. Scan publications in other fields, as well as newspapers, news magazines, and books. Frequently a creative idea will jump out of an article.[9] People should therefore force themselves to read material outside their field or industry.

Using the ideas obtained in reading, or in talking to others, is referred to as duplication. Knowing when and which ideas to borrow from other people can help you behave as if you were an imaginative person yourself. Many useful ideas brought into an organization are lifted directly from others or a simple combination of them. We are, of course, referring to borrowing ideas that are public information, not trade secrets. It is also important to properly credit the source of these creative ideas.

An example of a creative idea borrowed from others concerns the challenge faced by suburban department stores and fast-food restaurants in obtaining an ample supply of teenage help. Abraham and Strauss, an upscale department store chain in the metropolitan New York City area, apparently originated the idea. Faced with a critical shortage of teenage help in their Westchester store (located near New York City), they bused in teenagers from New York City. The cadre of workers proved to be of high quality. Today many other stores have duplicated this creative idea.

Use Individual Synectics. Similar to brainstorming, *synectics* is primarily a group method of generating creative ideas, but it can also be used by individuals working alone. The technique uses analogies to provide mental images to the brain. By using analogies, the unfamiliar becomes familiar. Follow these guidelines to use synectics acting alone:[10]

1. Begin with a personal analogy by projecting yourself into the essence of the problem. As an example, a product development specialist might think of herself or himself as a print wheel in a printer. Einstein viewed himself as a light beam on his way to discovering the theory of relativity.

2. Think of a direct analogy. A direct analogy looks for something that solves the same problem but in a different setting. For example, a high-speed electronic typewriter prints by moving the printing head across the page—rather than moving the carriage back and forth. Why not use this same principle in a computer printer (as is now done)?

3. Develop a symbolic analogy. A symbolic analogy is looser and more visual. The development of Pringles involved symbolic analogy. The synectics group was asked to solve the problem of compressing the potato chips into a small place without squashing them. Part of the creative task was to find an instance in which nature had solved the problem. In the end, the group members found an analogy in leaves. Although fragile, leaves were found compressed and undamaged. The feat is accomplished because the leaves are compressed while moist. It was decided to make Pringles by compressing moist potato chips.[11]

4. Use a fantasy analogy. Wild and imaginative thinking is called for in this step. An example of this step was an engineer who was attempting to develop a device to link two electrical wires. Operating in the fantasy stage, the engineer visualized the wires being held in the teeth of two people facing each other. Out of this fantasy came the idea for the alligator clip.

Maintain an Enthusiastic Attitude. A major hurdle faced by the manager or professional in being creative is resolving the conflict between being judicial and imaginative. In many work situations, being judicial (or judgmental) is necessary. Situations calling for judicial thinking include reviewing proposed expenditures and inspecting products for quality or safety defects. Imaginative thinking is involved when searching for creative alternatives. The late Alex F. Osburn, a well-known advertising executive and the originator of brainstorming, notes how judgment and imagination are often in conflict:[12]

> The fact that moods won't mix largely explains why the judicial and the creative tend to clash. The right mood for judicial thinking is largely negative. "What's wrong with this? . . . . No, this won't work." Such reflexes are right and proper when trying to judge.
>
> In contrast, our creative thinking calls for a positive attitude. We have to be hopeful. We need enthusiasm. We have to encourage ourselves to the point of self-confidence. We have to beware of perfectionism lest it be abortive.

The action step to be taken is therefore to project yourself into a positive frame of mind when attempting to be creative. The same principle applies when attempting to be creative about a judicial task. For instance, a manager might be faced with the task of looking for creative ways to cut costs. The manager would then have to think positively about thinking negatively!

Use SCAMS. *SCAMS* is a creativity-enhancing exercise developed by Eugene Raudsepp. Its purpose is to help people build their fluency of thought and expression.[13] Although difficult to perform successfully at first, it gets easier with persistency. These are the instructions. Write five-word sentences. Each of the five words must begin with the following letters in the order given: S–C–A–M–S. Here are a few examples:

Soldiers care about many subjects.

Sarcastic comments are meant seriously.

Scientists can arrange meetings successfully.

Give SCAMS a try. See how many sentences you can produce in five minutes.

Maintain and Use an Idea Notebook. It is difficult to capitalize on creative ideas unless you keep a careful record of them. A creative idea trusted to memory may become forgotten in the press of everyday business. An important suggestion kept on your daily log of errands to run or duties to perform may become obscured. Because it is creative ideas that carry considerable weight in propelling your career forward, they deserve the dignity of a separate notebook. The cautious or forgetful person is advised to keep two copies of the idea book: one at home and one in the office.

The Demand for Creativity in Managerial Work

Managerial work requires more creativity than most people realize. Above all, the manager or professional is frequently faced with a complex problem to solve for which programmed alternatives are not available. By searching for a new alternative, the manager engages in creative behavior. Robert E. Kaplan, a behavioral scientist and project manager at the Center for Creative Leadership, contends that good managers are creative all the time: "They have to be to meet the confusing, fast-changing procession of demands on their intelligence, adaptability, and people-handling skill."[14]

Some of the need for creativity in management stems from the hectic nature of a manager's job. A manager's day includes such diverse activities as scheduled meetings, reading, writing, making presentations, greeting visitors, and going on tours. Managers jump from one task to another. According to Kaplan, to fashion order out of this potential chaos is a creative act.[15]

Entrepreneurial managers are continuously faced with the need to be creative. The entrepreneur needs to be creative in such matters as identifying a new product or service that customers will accept, getting by with a small staff, and arranging for financing—particularly when business is bad or the firm is facing bankruptcy.

Another way of developing one's managerial skills is thus to improve one's creativity. The suggestions described in this chapter and the Guidelines section are directly relevant. In addition, the essential skill to develop in becoming more creative is to search for several good alternatives to the problem at hand before reaching a decision. The less creative manager or professional will tend to grab at the first alternative rather than stretching his or her mind one step further.

The Strengths of Creativity Improvement

Few people would argue that improving your creativity is not of some benefit to the individual and the organization. As stated by the Director of the Innovation Consulting Group (Netherlands):

Considering the rapid changes in markets, fierce competition, and fast-paced technological developments, a large "innovation capacity" has become an important condition for survival and growth in many industries. . . . In a survey among nearly a thousand senior executives from the United States, Europe, and Japan, 90 percent indicated a growing need for innovation in their companies.[16]

Assuming the suggestions for creativity improvement described here (or in additional references) worked for you, it could propel you forward in your career. Many high-ranking executives gained early momentum in their careers because they spearheaded a breakthrough idea. Steven Jobs and Steven Wozniak with the Apple Computer, and Lee Iacocca with the Mustang are three legendary examples. On a lesser scale, Spencer Silver the 28-year-old chemist who invented Post-it Note Pads was treated better by his company (3M) after the product's success. It became easier to get equipment and assistance, and "they give me a lot more support with some of the stranger ideas I come up with."[17]

A key strength of these methods of creativity improvement is that they are highly cost effective. For a modest investment of time, and virtually no money, they can yield a major return. Brainstorming, both in groups and individually, has helped bring forth thousands of creative suggestions.

The Weaknesses of Creativity Improvement

Improving your creativity is not without some disadvantages. For one, many organizations are not looking for more creative ideas. They already have too many good ideas floating around that they are unable to implement, or even process, because of limited resources. Being imaginative is usually far removed from creating change. As articulated by a past president of a manufacturing association in reference to the developer of a new type of water bed, "He is one of the few persons who ever invented anything who has business sense. There is no end of ideas that are going to revolutionize the world. But there are few people with the ability and patience to put them into practice."[18]

Another problem with heavy emphasis on creativity from the organization's viewpoint is that it may lead to a de emphasis on mundane products and services. Yet many of these ordinary products and services are highly profitable and useful. One example is the products made by Pretty Neat Industries, Inc. These products are simply inexpensive organizers—boxes and trays of all sizes and shapes designed for use in the home and office. Over a 10-year period the company's compounded growth rate exceeded 60 percent.[19]

If the individual carries creativity improvement too far, he or she may be perceived as more of a dreamer than a realist. Most organizations are looking for an occasional good idea, not a spate of them.

A related argument against creativity improvement is that some organizations do not want creativity because the key people are unclear as to the true meaning of creative behavior. They may perceive creativity as being synonymous with far-fetched thinking, rather than as primarily looking for new alternatives to solving problems. Thus, the creative individual may be shunned as a person with unworkable ideas.

An argument against the creativity-improvement exercises described in this chapter is that they are not validated with substantial empirical evidence. Therefore, a person could be investing time in exercises that will not really achieve their purpose.

Guidelines for Action and Skill Development

Select several or a combination of creativity-improvement techniques that seem best suited to your personal preferences. To illustrate, you might find it comfortable to conduct brainwriting sessions but to try to develop synergy between both sides of your brain too much of a long-term commitment. Unless you have an extraordinary gift for remembering things, using an idea notebook will be beneficial to you.

Improving your creativity requires a great deal of self-discipline and concentrated effort. The techniques and strategies described here and in the references are intended to supplement, not substitute for diligent application of your mental efforts toward finding creative alternatives to problems.

Avoid overemphasizing creativity to the point that you develop a distaste for the repetitive aspects of your job. Every position from the data-entry specialist to the chief executive officer includes some noncreative tasks.

An idea cannot be considered truly creative until other people pass judgment on its utility. The reason is that your idea must be converted to action before it is classified as creative. It is, therefore, helpful to give your ideas a "pilot run" by asking others for their reaction to your innovative suggestions. To keep the process alive, it is important that you establish a reciprocal relationship with those people by providing them feedback about their ideas.

If you develop a creative concept that you think will sell, the authors of a book about creativity suggest: (1) Bounce your idea off bright co-workers with different specialities, such as manufacturing and marketing. (2) Find a senior management sponsor to protect and later promote your idea. (3) Don't ask for too big a budget commitment too soon because a large budget request is often rejected. (4) Be persistent and don't be discouraged by naysayers and skeptics.[20]

DISCUSSION QUESTIONS AND ACTIVITIES

1. Business organizations are currently emphasizing creativity among employees by such means as creativity training and hiring creativity consultants. What factors do you think are behind this renewed emphasis on creativity?

2. Which method of creativity improvement discussed in this chapter do you think is best suited to you? Why?

3. To what extent is the type of creativity displayed by inventors and artists the same type as that displayed by businesspeople?

4. It has been said that the best creative ideas in business are magnificently simple. Furnish an example of a successful yet magnificently-simple business idea.

5. Name a few periodicals you think would help people achieve a balanced cultural diet.

6. Some creativity experts contend that doing crossword puzzles and writing poems help build creativity. Why might this be true?

7. Try one or two of the creativity-improvement suggestions in this chapter for 10 days. See if you actually become more proficient at searching for creative solutions to problems. Be ready to report your observations to the class.

NOTES

1. Ken Kusmer, "Hot New Teaching Tool Started As a Glob of Dough," Associated Press story, March 23, 1986. Adapted with permission.

2. Edward H. Meyer, "Creativity in Business," *Business Week's Careers*, September 1985, p. 27.

3. Robert R. Godfrey, "Tapping Employee's Creativity," *Supervisory Management*, February 1986, pp. 16–17.

4. Roger von Oech, *A Whack on the Side of the Head* (New York: Warner Books, 1984). Some of the information in this section is based on two interviews with von Oech; Priscilla Petty, "Break Out! Routine Thinking Can Be Hazardous to On-the-Job Creativity," *Rochester Democrat and Chronicle*, November 22, 1983, p. 1D; Robert S. Wieder, "How to Get Great Ideas," *Success!*, November 1983, pp. 29–31, 59, 60. All the quotes in this section are from the Petty article.

5. Sydney J. Harris, "Fear of Failure Separates Imitators from the Innovators," syndicated column, October 3, 1986.

6. Tom Peters, "Management Action Ideas Get Results," syndicated column, November 23, 1986.

7. Terrence Hines, "Left Brain/Right Brain Mythology and Implications for Management and Training," *Academy of Management Review*, October 1987, pp. 600–606.

8. John J. Byczkowski, "Invention's a Necessity at Xerox," *Rochester Democrat and Chronicle*, January 9, 1983, p. 1F.

9. Steven J. Bennett, "Entrepreneurial Thinking: 5 Ways to Make It Work for You," *Business Week's Careers*, Spring–Summer 1987, p. 30.

10. Marilyn Goldstein, David Scholthauer, and Brian H. Kleiner, "Management on the Right Side of the Brain," *Personnel Journal*, November 1985, p. 44. Synectics was first described in William J. J. Gordon, *Synectics* (New York: Harper & Row, 1961).

11. Niles Howard, "Business Probes the Creative Spark," *Dun's Review*, January 1980, pp. 35–36.

12. Quoted in "Breakthrough Ideas," *Success!*, October 1987, p. 50.

13. Eugene Raudsepp, "Test Your Creativity Quotient," *Success!,* March 1985, p. 59.
14. Robert E. Kaplan, "Creativity in the Everyday Business of Managing," *Issues & Observations,* May 1983, p. 1.
15. David R. Wheeler, "Creative Decision Making and the Organization," *Personnel Journal,* June 1979, p. 374.
16. Hans Smeekes, "The Innovation Program," *Issues & Observations,* Fall 1986, p. 9.
17. Ruth Hamel, "Wish You'd Thought of That? They Did," *USA Weekend,* October 10–12, 1986, p. 14.
18. Phil Ebersole, "Air-Water Mix Makes Bed," *Rochester Democrat and Chronicle,* November 3, 1987, p. 7D.
19. Nancy K. Austin, "Marketing the Mundane," *Success!,* May 1986, p. 16.
20. John M. Ketteringham and P. Ranganath Nayak, *Breakthroughs!* (New York: Rawson Associates, 1987).

SOME ADDITIONAL REFERENCES

Bennett, Steven, and Michael Snell. *Executive Stress.* New York: New American Library, 1987.

Glassman, Edward. "Leadership Style's Effect on the Creativity of Employees." *Management Solutions,* November 1986, pp. 18–25.

Godfrey, Robert R. "Tapping Employees' Creativity." *Supervisory Management,* February 1986, pp. 16–20.

Gryskiewicz, Stanley S. *Stein on Creativity* (videotape). Greensboro, N.C.: Center for Creative Leadership, 1986.

Kuhn, Lawrence Robert, ed. *Frontiers in Creative and Innovative Management.* New York: Ballinger Publishing Company, 1986.

Meehan, Robert H. "Programs That Foster Creativity and Innovation." *Personnel,* February 1986, pp. 31–35.

Appendix to Chapter Two

HOW CREATIVE ARE YOU?*

By Eugene Raudsepp

President Princeton Creative Research, Inc., Princeton, New Jersey

In recent years, several task-oriented tests have been developed to measure creative abilities and behavior. While certainly useful, they do not adequately tap the complex network of behaviors, the particular personality traits, attitudes,

---

motivations, values, interests, and other variables that predispose a person to think creatively.

To arrive at assessment measures that would cover a broader range of creative attributes, our organization developed an inventory type of test. A partial version of this instrument is featured below.

After each statement, indicate with a letter the degree or extent with which you agree or disagree with it: **A** = strongly agree, **B** = agree, **C** = in between or don't know, **D** = disagree, **E** = strongly disagree. Mark your answers as accurately and frankly as possible. Try not to second guess how a creative person might respond to each statement.

1. I always work with a great deal of certainty that I'm following the correct procedures for solving a particular problem.   _____

2. It would be a waste of time for me to ask questions if I had no hope of obtaining answers.   _____

3. I feel that a logical step-by-step method is best for solving problems.   _____

4. I occasionally voice opinions in groups that seem to turn some people off.   _____

5. I spend a great deal of time thinking about what others think of me.   _____

6. I feel that I may have a special contribution to give to the world.   _____

7. It is more important for me to do what I believe to be right than to try to win the approval of others.   _____

8. People who seem unsure and uncertain about things lose my respect.   _____

9. I am able to stick with difficult problems over extended periods of time.   _____

10. On occasion I get overly enthusiastic about things.   _____

11. I often get my best ideas when doing nothing in particular.   _____

12. I rely on intuitive hunches and the feeling of "rightness" or "wrongness" when moving toward the solution of a problem.   _____

13. When problem solving, I work faster analyzing the problem and slower when synthesizing the information I've gathered.   _____

14. I like hobbies that involve collecting things.   _____

15. Daydreaming has provided the impetus for many of my more important projects.   _____

16. If I had to choose from two occupations other than the one I now have, I would rather be a physician than an explorer.   _____

17. I can get along more easily with people if they belong to about the same social and business class as myself.   _____

18. I have a high degree of aesthetic sensitivity.   _____

19. Intuitive hunches are unreliable guides in problem solving.   _____

20. I am much more interested in coming up with new ideas than I am in trying to sell them to others.   _____

21. I tend to avoid situations in which I might feel inferior.   _____
22. In evaluating information, the source of it is more important to me than the content.   _____
23. I like people who follow the rule "business before pleasure."   _____
24. One's own self-respect is much more important than the respect of others.   _____
25. I feel that people who strive for perfection are unwise.   _____
26. I like work in which I must influence others.   _____
27. It is important for me to have a place for everything and everything in its place.   _____
28. People who are willing to entertain "crackpot" ideas are impractical.   _____
29. I rather enjoy fooling around with new ideas, even if there is no practical payoff.   _____
30. When a certain approach to a problem doesn't work, I can quickly reorient my thinking.   _____
31. I don't like to ask questions that show ignorance.   _____
32. I am able to more easily change my interests to pursue a job or career than I can change a job to pursue my interests.   _____
33. Inability to solve a problem is frequently due to asking the wrong questions.   _____
34. I can frequently anticipate the solution to my problems.   _____
35. It is a waste of time to analyze one's failures.   _____
36. Only fuzzy thinkers resort to metaphors and analogies.   _____
37. At times I have so enjoyed the ingenuity of a crook that I hoped he or she would go scot-free.   _____
38. I frequently begin work on a problem that I can only dimly sense and not yet express.   _____
39. I frequently tend to forget things such as names of people, streets, highways, small towns, etc.   _____
40. I feel that hard work is the basic factor in success.   _____
41. To be regarded as a good team member is important to me.   _____
42. I know how to keep my inner impulses in check.   _____
43. I am a thoroughly dependable and responsible person.   _____
44. I resent things being uncertain and unpredictable.   _____
45. I prefer to work with others in a team effort rather than solo.   _____
46. The trouble with many people is that they take things too seriously.   _____
47. I am frequently haunted by my problems and cannot let go of them.   _____
48. I can easily give up immediate gain or comfort to reach the goals I have set.   _____
49. If I were a college professor, I would rather teach factual courses than those involving theory.   _____
50. I'm attracted to the mystery of life.   _____

Scoring Instructions. To compute your percentage score, circle and add up the values assigned to each item.

	Strongly Agree	Agree	In-Between or Don't Know	Disagree	Strongly Disagree
	A	B	C	D	E
1.	−2	−1	0	+1	+2
2.	−2	−1	0	+1	+2
3.	−2	−1	0	+1	+2
4.	+2	+1	0	−1	−2
5.	−2	−1	0	+1	+2
6.	+2	+1	0	−1	−2
7.	+2	+1	0	−1	−2
8.	−2	−1	0	+1	+2
9.	+2	+1	0	−1	−2
10.	+2	+1	0	−1	−2
11.	+2	+1	0	−1	−2
12.	+2	+1	0	−1	2
13.	−2	−1	0	+1	+2
14.	−2	−1	0	+1	+2
15.	+2	+1	0	−1	−1
16.	−2	−1	0	+1	+2
17.	−2	−1	0	+1	+2
18.	+2	+1	0	−1	−2
19.	−2	−1	0	+1	+2
20.	+2	+1	0	−1	−2
21.	−2	−1	0	+1	+2
22.	−2	−1	0	+1	+2
23.	−2	−1	0	+1	+2
24.	+2	+1	0	−1	−2
25.	−2	−1	0	+1	+1
26.	−2	−1	0	+1	+2
27.	−2	−1	0	+1	+2
28.	−2	−1	0	+1	+2
29.	+2	+1	0	−1	−2
30.	+2	+1	0	−1	−2
31.	−2	−1	0	+1	+2
32.	−2	−1	0	+1	+2
33.	+2	+1	0	−1	−2
34.	+2	+1	0	−1	−2
35.	−2	−1	0	+1	+2
36.	−2	−1	0	+1	+2
37.	+2	+1	0	−1	−2
38.	+2	+1	0	−1	−2
39.	+2	+1	0	−1	−2
40.	+2	+1	0	−1	−2
41.	−2	−1	0	+1	+2

	Strongly Agree	Agree	In-Between or Don't Know	Disagree	Strongly Disagree
	A	B	C	D	E
42.	−2	−1	0	+1	+2
43.	−2	−1	0	+1	+2
44.	−2	−1	0	+1	+2
45.	−2	−1	0	+1	+2
46.	+2	+1	0	−1	−2
47.	+2	+1	0	−1	−2
48.	+2	+1	0	−1	−2
49.	−2	−1	0	+1	+2
50.	+2	+1	0	−1	−2

80 to 100 Very creative   20 to 39 Below average
60 to 79 Above average   −100 to 19 Noncreative
40 to 59 Average

Further information about the test, "How Creative Are You?" is available from Princeton Creative Research, Inc., 10 Nassau St., P.O. Box 122, Princeton, NJ 08540.

Chapter Three

Crisis Management

Donald D. Lennox, currently chairman of the board of the Schlegel Corporation, faced an organizational crisis when he was the president of International Harvester (now called Navistar). Lennox turned to crisis-management techniques to help the firm regain equilibrium.

"The biggest crisis I faced in my career was an organizational problem," said Don Lennox. "The problem occurred around the time I joined International Harvester. Top management, with the assistance of outside consultants, decided that the company's poor performance was due to their five business units being run as a centralized organization. The five businesses were trucks and engines, gas turbines, agricultural equipment, components manufacturing operations, and financial services.

"International Harvester was a paternalistic, autocratic, and unimaginative organization that was dead on its feet. They paid the highest salaries, had lucrative employment contracts with executives, and were not demanding of their employees. There was layer upon layer of staff, everybody had a secretary, and executives rode around in limos. A common saying around IH was 'You never go up very fast, but you never go out.' Lack of performance was never a reason for dismissal.

"The alternatives I saw to solving the problem were decentralizing the five businesses, selling off one or more of the businesses, or leaving the organization centralized. The consultants advised us to make the five businesses separate and autonomous operations.

"To implement the solution we eliminated the corporate staff with the exception of a financial unit for tax purposes and statement consolidation, a legal unit, and a human resources unit to deal with pension administration and union bargaining. We reorganized the five new businesses. However, the end result was five bureaucratic businesses instead

41

of one. The management staff therefore attempted to identify those who had the potential to be innovative. It was found that many of the employees couldn't or wouldn't change. We eliminated these employees.''

Lennox also launched a far-reaching move to reduce IH's operating expenses. ''There were things that had to be done that had been obvious for a long time, but management—unwilling to endure the stigma of big write-offs—was reluctant to move,'' said Lennox. ''There was a psychological block about doing things that would cause us to approach a negative equity position. To me it just didn't matter whether you're $200 million positive or $200 million negative in a multibillion company like IH. The important thing was to get rid of nonperforming assets.''

The biggest sale (prior to selling the agricultural equipment business to Case two years later) was of the construction equipment unit to Dresser Industries, Inc. for about $70 million. Lennox also took IH out of the manufacture of truck axles and transmissions, airliner tow trucks, and off-highway haulers. Divestments were also made of the life insurance business and numerous joint ventures such as mining.

During this period of divestments, Lennox closed the Fort Wayne truck plant that had been a company fixture since 1923. Two thousand workers were laid off, all that remained of the 10,000 who had worked there in 1979. To some old-timers, Lennox recalls, ''Fort Wayne *was* International Harvester, but in the end I concluded that we had to get rid of the plant. I doubted the plant could be turned to profitability because it had not turned a profit in 20 years.''

Another facility closed was the corporate science and technology group, which was headed by an old friend. Lennox asked himself, ''In the long run do we need that activity. Yes. Can we afford it? No.'' So he shut it down.

In describing his attempt to turn around the company, Lennox said, ''The bottom line was that the culture of the organization had to be changed. Executive search firms were used to help recruit replacements for key people who could not adapt to the changes. The total reorganization of the company took over one year. Our efforts were successful because we did escape bankruptcy.

''I was able to convince the organization that our drastic efforts were in the employees' best interests because bankruptcy was impending. Most employees came to believe that action was necessary.

''To decide what actions were necessary to bail out of the crisis, I relied more on intuition than logical analysis. The urgency of the situation prohibited too much complicated analysis. We were running out of cash so fast that drastic action was necessary. For example, forecasts made on May 1, 1982, showed that there wasn't enough cash to make it until the end of June.

"I certainly had self-doubts about what I was doing and a deep concern for the havoc that was created. Making those brutal cutbacks was the most unpleasant task in my life. It was such a depressing way to operate. Employees were getting laid off, and orders to vendors were eliminated when a product was discontinued.

"There wasn't any elation because the agricultural business was losing money daily. I finally experienced elation when the agricultural business was sold off in 1984. At that point, I felt we were home free."

Asked if the crisis could have been predicted earlier, Lennox responded, "The previous chairman of the board knew there was a problem and hired the consultants. He also brought in new top management, which included me. They tried to correct the problem by spending money rather than getting to its root. But 20–20 hindsight helps to see that.

"An important lesson I learned from my experiences at International Harvester is that you have to take action rather than procrastinating. If you have an 80 percent confidence level for an alternative, take it."[1]

Crisis-Management Strategies and Techniques

Don Lennox was engaged in crisis management. Although executives and managers have dealt with crises in the past, the formal label of *crisis management* emerged with the publication of Steven Fink's book, *Crisis Management*, published in 1986. A *crisis* is a turning point for better or for worse, or a situation that has reached a critical phase.[2] Crisis management can be regarded as taking control of a crisis that has already surfaced, or preparing in advance for one. The phrase *turnaround management* also refers to managing in a crisis (or a situation that requires drastic improvement in a hurry). Enough knowledge has been accumulated about crisis management to offer some tentative principles for those people faced with handling crises.

Identify, Isolate, and Manage the Crisis.   The core of crisis management, according to Fink's framework, is to identify, isolate, and manage the crisis.[3] Although this statement contains three principles, they can rightfully be considered a flow of interrelated activities. *Identifying the real crisis* refers to diagnosing the true nature of the critical problem, similar to any type of decision making. The real crisis facing International Harvester was that the company was on the brink of bankruptcy and would therefore be unable to continue as a corporation. The fact that demand had slacked for many of their products was a problem, but not the real crisis.

Another example is the Tylenol poisonings that took place in 1982. (A deranged individual bought bottles of Tylenol, placed cyanide-laced capsules back in the bottles of Extra-Strength Tylenol, and replaced them on shelves in Chicago.) According to Fink, the real crisis facing Johnson & Johnson was the demise of the Tylenol brand and of the subsidiary company, MacNeil Consumer Labs.

Isolating the crisis refers to containing it so it will not contaminate anything else, much like quarantining a patient with an infectious disease. Isolation in this sense meant that the CEO and any other members of the crisis team focused on the crisis to the exclusion of other responsibilities. Nothing can or should take precedence over a crisis.

Once the decision maker has identified and isolated the crisis, it becomes easier to manage the crisis because any misleading and diversionary paths have been blocked off. The manager also has a clearer idea of what actions must be taken to rectify the problem. According to Fink, managing a crisis involves primarily managing decisions. The right alternative has to be chosen among the available options. In weighing alternatives, it is important not to engage in "analysis paralysis." Instead decisive action must be taken.

Part of making the right decision in a crisis is to investigate the causes of the crisis. When the fifth floor of a high-rise office tower under construction in Los Angeles collapsed in December 1985, the general contractor was besieged by outsiders. The firm hired a crisis-management consulting firm, which in turn assembled a team of safety engineers to determine the most likely causes of the collapse.[4]

Adapt a Crisis-Decision-Making Style. Because managing a crisis concerns making the right decisions, it may prove helpful to fine tune one's decision-making style toward the crisis mode. John Ramée offers these decision-making rules:[5]

> **Rule 1:** *Avoid the quick fix.* It is important to correct the underlying problem rather than grab an almost immediate solution— such as borrowing money at exorbitant interest rates rather than cutting costs when faced with a cash crisis.

> **Rule 2:** *Seek new information.* A crisis fosters rapid change, thus making information obsolete quickly. Gathering ample new information will inform decision makers facing a crisis if their current strategies are valid or if new strategies must be formulated.

> **Rule 3:** *Revise strategies.* A vigilant crisis manager, or crisis-management team, will stay prepared to modify new strategies whenever new information indicates the need. A typical strategy when a company is faced with a profit crisis is to sell off assets to raise cash. In one company facing this problem, the CEO decided to purchase a small company that made laser printers because of its growth potential. The gamble paid off because the sale of laser printers infused new cash into the firm.

Rule 4: *Have one center of authority.* Lacking a central crisis-management authority, strategies can become fragmented and lower-ranking power centers can emerge. This principle is an aspect of isolating the crisis because the strategy involves only a few key people concentrating on the crisis.

Rule 5: *Act as the need arises.* An unfortunate aspect of crisis management is that the cure often seems worse than the problem, particularly when massive numbers of employees are laid off and valuable assets are sold. Procrastination, however, only deepens the crisis. It is important to select the best strategies and act quickly and decisively (as Don Lennox observed).

Place the Crisis in a Problem-Solving Mode.   A general method of dealing with crises at the individual level is to regard the crisis as yet another important work problem that requires resolution. One way or another, when you successfully cope with a crisis, you use some aspect of (or the entire) problem-solving method. In essence, it involves these familiar steps:

1. *Clarify the problem.* What is the real problem created by this crisis? Perhaps the crisis has created a credibility problem or a financial problem.
2. *Search for creative alternatives.* What options are open? Many managers facing a crisis choose stonewalling the problem over dealing with it openly, thus digging a deeper hole for themselves.
3. *Make a choice.* If the crisis is to be resolved, you must make a tough decision at some point.
4. *Develop an action plan and implement.* What steps must be taken to get out of this mess? You will recall that Don Lennox at International Harvester (now Navistar) took a series of urgent steps to deal with the crisis facing him and his company.
5. *Evaluate outcomes.* Did the crisis-management plan work or will you have to try another alternative?

Explain the Problem to the Public and Employees.   Adopting a "bunker mentality" is another common trap poor decision makers in a crisis often fall into. The *bunker mentality* means that the decision maker collects facts, hides behind them, and does not deal with the facts publicly. It also means that the manager facing a crisis avoids communicating with the public by erecting barriers. Moving aggressively to explain the problem was one of the successful strategies employed by Johnson & Johnson to deal with the Tylenol crisis. An equally important strategy was taking decisive action to remove the product from the stores.[6]

Retrenchment, both in private and public organizations, is another common crisis that should be dealt with openly. It is important, however, to inform employees before informing the public that resources are declining and that major cuts are necessary. One or two announcements concerning necessary cuts are insufficient. Top management must explain with many reports, speeches, and fact sheets that the retrenchment is real and necessary.[7] Public statements about retrenchment that specify how many employees will be laid off result in less further probing than vague estimates of the number of people to be laid off.

Deal Effectively with the Media.   An inescapable aspect of making public information about a crisis is dealing with the media. The communicator in a crisis must have immediate access to top-level authority or have authority himself or herself. Without such authority, the media-contact person may be forced to hedge or act evasively. A key general principle of communicating with the media is to be honest. Honesty, however, can include presenting the truth in the most advantageous way. Fink provides a specific example: "If you are a chemical plant's spokesperson and a potential crisis may be pollution or toxic waste, you should be prepared to report immediately on your plant's health and ecological record with the government with such statements as:

• While this plant has been cited by the Environmental Protection Agency (EPA) for leaks, it has been cited only three times in the past six years, and the last time was two years ago.

• We have spent more than $X million in the past 12 months alone in improving our waste-removal system."[8]

Another important principle for dealing with the media is that nobody should be appointed as spokesperson, not even the CEO, if that person is not fully qualified to withstand the media inquiry and present the organization in the most positive way that circumstances permit. Also, the presentation to the media must be carefully prepared. Lack of preparation may result in false information, misstatements, and publicly embarrassing gaffs.[9] One of the many embarrassments that Morton Thiokol (the aerospace company) endured in relation to the Challenger explosion was the inconsistent statements about the reliability of the O-ring seals.

Obtain Information from the Original Source.   When a crisis hits, an important question to find answers to is "How bad is it?" Experienced crisis managers suggest that asking customers, clients, and suppliers provides valuable information about the gravity of a crisis. Michael D. Dingham, the CEO of a company that specializes in turning around troubled companies, points out that a key principle of turnaround management is to get close to the customer.[10]

Another turnaround specialist, John Whitney, notes that armed with accurate information about the company's cash position, turnaround managers seek out additional sources of information. Included here are customers, employees, competitors, vendors, bankers, the investment community, government agencies or regulators, and the media. The most useful information comes from the source such as sitting in a customer's office and listening to complaints about product quality or late shipments. Building communications bridges to the source is valuable as revealed by this incident:[11]

> The CEO of a troubled $50 million consumer products company made all his senior officers, himself included, take part in a 30-day sales blitz. In so doing, he learned that a $2 million original equipment manufacturer (OEM), thought to be safe, was so unhappy with the company's work, it was considering withdrawing its business. Worse, the CEO had been counting on that customer's continued support to keep a plant open. Fortunately, his timely call helped him save the customer and sparked a critical assessment of his consumer goods operation.

Turnaround managers also maintain open communication channels with some of the firm's major vendors. Because these vendors conduct business with competitors and other customers, they may be aware of trends or important shifts in the marketplace. They may also provide marketing information about pricing and discount schedules. Vendors can also provide new insights about the strengths and weaknesses of the company and its employees.[12]

Take Advantage of the Hidden Opportunity.   An important principle of managing adversity in general is to look for hidden opportunities within the negative circumstances. Following this principle, a manager whose new-product group is dismantled by the company may decide to quit the firm and start a new company to make the new product. Crisis managers also follow this principle in managing organizational assets. Following the stock market crash of 1987, many chief financial officers (CFOs) directed their firms to capitalize on the sudden downturn in stock prices.[13]

When stock prices fell, bonds rebounded creating opportunity in the midst of adversity for many firms. Eastman Kodak Co. raised $300 million in four-year notes at an interest rate of 8.84 percent. The Kodak treasurer took the opportunity to replace some short-term adjustable-rate debt with fixed-rate debt (at 8.84 percent). Around the same time, Consolidated Natural Gas Co. sold $100 million in five-year debentures at 9 1/8 percent—a rate they considered quite favorable.

A more widespread tactic for capitalizing on hidden opportunity was for corporate treasurers to buy back stock at bargain prices. IBM spent about $1 billion repurchasing its shares. Olin Corporation bought close to 300,000 shares of its own stock. Advantages of a company purchasing its own stocks include stabilizing prices for the stock and taking advantages of good values. For instance, when the stock market rebounds, the company can sell the repurchased stocks at a sizeable profit.

Cut Costs and Management Layers.   Turnaround managers are usually called in from the outside by boards of directors, often under pressure from bankers who are worried about the company's deteriorating financial position. The core strategy of turnaround managers is to slash costs, including excising layers of management, in order to improve the firm's financial position. Once the firm is in improved financial health, it is often sold at a favorable price. Part of this cost-cutting strategy is to decide what part of a company is healthy, then act decisively to sell anything that isn't.[14]

A representative example of the cost-cutting program enforced by turnaround managers is the approach used by James Sullivan. He zealously goes after what he describes as corporate fat. When assigned to turn around a company, he immediately enforces a temporary pay cut of 10 percent and reduces corporate overhead by 25 percent. Sullivan usually eliminates company cars and will frequently sell the company headquarters building and lease it back. In one instance, the owner of the troubled company was also the owner of the headquarters building. Sullivan ordered him to reduce the rent.[15]

Decreasing the number of management layers reduces costs because payroll costs are lowered. At times revenue is increased because the displaced managers are assigned to sales positions. Although the cost-reduction from flattening the structure may be substantial, other benefits may be greater according to John O. Whitney. A flat organization presents fewer barriers to the flow of information and reduces the filtering effect of the hierarchy. It also opens opportunities for a dialogue between top management and those close to operations and market information. The shortened chain of command also improves mobilizing people for action, especially when task forces are used to implement new programs.[16]

Link Bonuses to Profits.   An axiom of the effective use of money as a motivator is to link pay to performance. High performers thus receive more money than average or low performers. During a financial crisis, linking bonuses to profits is particularly important because profits become so necessary. Also, a contributing factor to a company's problems may be that executives receive healthy bonuses independent of the company's profits. The executives therefore lack financial motivation to improve company performance. (Pride and other intrinsic motivational factors, however, may still compel them toward high performance.)

The tactic of linking bonuses to profits was an important part of the strategy for turning around York, the manufacturer of air conditioners.

York had become a seriously ailing division of Borg-Warner Corporation. The company called in Stanley Hiller, Jr., a turnaround specialist. Although not ruthless, he was demanding, requiring that managers shorten the time between order-taking and delivery. Only 2 of the company's top 100 executives were fired, while 20 of them were reassigned. Hiller also linked once automatic bonuses to profits. Within two years, York posted a fivefold increase in profits in one six-month period (to $14.7 million on sales of $456 million). Bonuses also increased dramatically. Comments Hiller: "If you score big, you score big for everyone."[17]

Practice Transformational Leadership. An organization in crisis requires decisive and bold leadership to move it from a morass to higher ground. This type of leadership is now referred to as *transformational*. The transformational leader is called on to create something new out of something old. The transformational process aims at moving individuals beyond normal expected performance to higher achievement and maturity levels. Charisma, individualized consideration, and intellectual stimulation are considered by Bernard M. Bass to be the major traits and behaviors distinguishing transformational from transactional leaders.[18] Conventional leadership, in contrast, involves a series of transactions between the leader and group members. Transactional leaders give followers something they want in exchange for something the leaders want.[19]

Transformational leaders are likely to help the troubled organization perform better in the long range. Some turnaround managers, however, are concerned more with the short range. The "slash and burn" manager turns around the company in a hurry and then departs to fix another broken organization.

Having headed Wickes since 1982, Sanford Sigiloff (dubbed Ming the Merciless) is an example of a charismatic crisis manager who is now concerned with the long range. When Sigiloff took over the reins of Wickes, he faced a disaster and his largest rescue mission ever. Wickes had limited merchandise, not enough sales associates, hardly any credit, and no cash. Sigiloff's first move was to file for bankruptcy in order to protect the firm's dwindling assets. In the 15 months previous to Sigiloff's appointment, the firm had lost $400 million.

Sigiloff fired about 10,000 of Wickes 40,000 employees, sold off 15 money-losing operations, and closed Aldens (the catalogue-showroom retailer) because a buyer could not be found. Many of the 2,600 Aldens employees had been employed there all their working lives. Wickes now concentrates on the home-improvement markets and has annual sales of $6 billion.

Sigiloff has become a charismatic leader to many Wickes employees despite the slashing he spearheaded when he first joined the company. His leadership image was helped along by his frequent appearance on television commercials. His script in one ad read, "Sure they call me the toughest retailer in America. But you have got to be tough."[20]

The Case for Crisis-Management Strategies and Techniques

The case for crisis-management techniques involves two major issues. First is whether or not crises are worth worrying about. Based on the experience of John Ramée and his associates, corporate crises exert substantial potential damage to a company's operation. A crisis, such as the Three Mile Island meltdown or the Union Carbide poison gas leak in Bhopal, can have the following effects: (1) a severe negative impact on company profits, (2) unwanted public and government scrutiny, (3) damage to corporate integrity and name, (4) unproductive diversion of effort to quell the crisis, (5) employee morale problems,[21] and (6) physical and emotional damage to the public.

Second is the issue of whether or not crisis-management strategies and tactics are effective. Case-history evidence suggests that these approaches to crisis management are useful because companies that follow them are able to cope with crises. For example, Tylenol's market share actually increased several months after the poisonings. Johnson & Johnson acted aggressively and positively, as described above. Companies that do not follow these principles do not fare as well. A case in point is the Star-Kist subsidiary of H. J. Heinz that was accused of shipping one million cans of rancid tuna in Canada. Even after the Canadian prime minister impounded the fish, Heinz executives refused to communicate with the public or the press. The episode became a major embarrassment to the firm.[22]

Another case for crisis management strategies and tactics is that the cumulative impact of turnaround managers has been substantial. A *Business Week* survey of 30 turnaround consultants found that in a 10-year period they have worked with hundreds of companies totaling $60 billion in sales. According to some estimates, these consultants have turned around 75 percent of their clients. A top bank executive contends that turnaround managers' efforts have saved billions of dollars in bank loans.[23]

The Case against Crisis-Management Strategies and Techniques

Crisis-management strategies and techniques can be criticized on philosophical, humanitarian, and empirical grounds. Philosophically, crisis management is really a special case of managerial decision making. Decision making follows the same process in good times and bad times. According to this argument, crisis management has no separate existence in the same way that international management and small-business management are not really separate fields of study.

The humanistic argument is that turnaround management is unsavory because it results in so many lost jobs and personal hardships. Rather than shrink a troubled firm so drastically, other steps could be taken, including pay cuts for all employees, shorter work weeks, decreased stock dividends, and substantially reduced pay for top managers. Plant closings, for example, aside from economic hardship dramatically escalate the suicide rate of laid-off employees.[24]

An empirical argument against crisis-management methods is that they often do not work—they may result in a company so trimmed down that it cannot survive in the long run. In an attempt to trim fat, muscle tissue is also sacrificed.

Sanford Sigiloff notes that too many turnaround managers liquidate to generate cash without regard for the future. A specific example is L. B. Foster Co., the Pittsburgh manufacturer of rail products and oil field tubing. When oil prices declined substantially, Foster could no longer service the debt it had assumed to diversify into new lines of equipment. To avoid bankruptcy, a turnaround manager slashed jobs and sold off the new units. The emergency measures eliminated the debt and tripled the stock price, but Foster's renewed dependence on oil equipment may have hurt its future profits.[25]

Guidelines for Action and Skill Development

Many suggestions for dealing with both general crises and financial crises have been presented so far. In this section we therefore describe mostly guidelines for action and skill development that relate to advance preparation for a crisis.

The first step is to engage in crisis forecasting and planning. Based on past experiences, estimate the type of crises that could occur. For instance, an automotive company might be able to predict future recalls based on the percentage of previous recalls. Appropriate action can sometimes be taken in advance. Many consumer products now have relatively tamper-proof packing to prevent poisoning of the contents of packages already on store shelves.

Early-warning signals of crises can come from such information sources as exceptional performance deviations, employee observations, and customer input.[26] For example, an internal Union Carbide report warned that the plant in Institute, West Virginia, "faces a possible runaway reaction of methyl isocyanate." The initial report was dated September 11, 1984—three months before the crisis at the sister plant in Bhopal, India.[27]

Another preparedness tactic is to set up corporate crisis-management teams composed of employees who are trained to take charge in the event of a sudden disaster. Among the companies that have crisis-management teams ready to swing into action if needed are United Airlines, Dow

Chemical, Heinz, and Waste Management. Some companies now conduct simulated crises with the crisis-management team and/or members of top management.

Another way of managing a crisis in advance is to build up substantial cash reserves. In Whitney's opinion, nothing is more important to a successful turnaround than cash. Financial managers therefore have to devise a system for gathering accurate information about the company's true cash picture.[28]

Do not cry wolf too often. Forecasts of impending crises will ultimately be ignored if too many predictions were made in the past of crises that did not materialize.

A final word about crisis management is that it should be reserved for legitimate crises and the early stages of a turnaround. Yet, used unnecessarily, too often, or too long, crisis management creates fear and confusion and can lower morale. For that reason the head of a healthy company will use it judiciously and will replace it with conventional-management practices and organization structures as soon as feasible.[29]

DISCUSSION QUESTIONS AND ACTIVITIES

1. Give an example of how several of the techniques described in this chapter might be used to handle a personal crisis.

2. How might the stock market crash of 1987 have called for crisis management on the part of brokerage firms?

3. What seems to be the difference in emphasis between crisis management and turnaround management?

4. Some turnaround managers hire body guards. Why might such action be advisable?

5. How might customers be helpful in warning a firm about a future crisis it could be facing?

6. Give any example from personal observation or the media of a transformational leader. Explain why you consider that person to be a transformational leader.

7. Attempt to find somebody who was working at a company during a period of crisis management, including turnaround management. Get that individual's perception of what it was like to live through those conditions.

NOTES

1. Case researched by Julie Hardis, Rochester Institute of Technology, 1987. Some of the facts in the case are as reported in "Can Don Lennox Save Harvester?" *Business Week*, August 15, 1983, pp. 80–84.

2. Steven Fink, *Crisis Management: Planning for the Inevitable* (New York: AMACOM, 1986), p. 15.
3. Ibid., pp. 71–85.
4. "Coping with Catastrophe," *Time,* February 24, 1986, p. 53.
5. John Ramée, "Managing in a Crisis," *Management Solutions,* February 1987, pp. 28–29.
6. "How Companies Are Learning to Prepare for the Worst," *Business Week,* December 23, 1985, p. 74.
7. Perry Moore, "The Problems and Prospects of Cutback Management," *Personnel Administrator,* January 1985, p. 92.
8. Fink, *Crisis Management,* p. 97.
9. Ramée, "Managing in a Crisis," p. 28.
10. "Mike Dingman Tunes 'Em Up, Turns 'Em Around, Spins 'Em Off," *Business Week,* October 5, 1987, p. 90.
11. Adapted from John O. Whitney, "Turnaround Management Every Day," *Harvard Business Review,* September–October 1987, p. 52.
12. Ibid., p. 52.
13. Christopher Farrell, "Companies Are Staying Cool—But Moving Fast," *Business Week,* November 9, 1987, p. 37.
14. "The Green Berets of Corporate Management," *Business Week,* September 21, 1987, p. 111.
15. Ibid., p. 112.
16. Whitney, "Turnaround Management Every Day," p. 54.
17. "The Green Berets of Corporate Management," p. 112.
18. Bernard M. Bass, *Leadership and Performance beyond Expectations* (New York: The Free Press, 1985).
19. Karl W. Kuhnert and Philip Lewis, "Transactional and Transformational Leadership: A Constructive Developmental Analysis," *Academy of Management Review,* October 1987, p. 649.
20. "On the Comeback Trail," *Time,* March 12, 1984, p. 54.
21. John Ramée, "Crisis Management: Looking for the Warning Signs," *Management Solutions,* January 1987, p. 5.
22. "Coping with Catastrophe," p. 53.
23. "The Green Berets of Corporate Management," p. 111.
24. Angelo Kinicki, "Socially Responsible Plant Closings," *Personnel Administrator,* June 1987, p. 116.
25. "The Green Berets of Corporate Management," p. 114.
26. Ramée, "Crisis Management: Looking for the Warning Signs," p. 6.
27. Fink, *Crisis Management,* p. 12.
28. Whitney, "Turnaround Management Everyday," p. 51.
29. Ibid., p. 55.

SOME ADDITIONAL REFERENCES

Bunker, Barbara Benedict, and Howard O. Williams, Jr. "Managing Organizational Decline." *Personnel,* June 1986, pp. 31–40.

Cameron, Kim S.; David A. Whetten; and Myung U. Kim. "Organizational

Dysfunctions of Decline." *Academy of Management Journal,* March 1987, pp. 126–38.

Conger, Jay A., and Rabindra M. Kanungo. "Toward a Behavioral Theory of Charismatic Leadership in Organizational Settings." *Academy of Management Review,* October 1987, pp. 637–47.

Greenberg, Eric Rolfe. "Downsizing: Results of a Survey by the American Management Association." *Personnel,* October 1987, pp. 35–37.

Meyers, Gerald C. *When It Hits the Fan: Managing the Nine Crises of Business.* Boston: Houghton Mifflin, 1986.

Mitroff, Ian I.; Paul Shrivastava; and Firdaus Udwadia. "Effective Crisis Management." *The Academy of Management Executive,* November 1987, pp. 283–92.

Ramée, John. "Corporate Crisis: The Aftermath." *Management Solutions,* March 1987, pp. 18–22.

Shrivastava, Paul. *Bhopal: Anatomy of a Crisis.* Boston, Mass.: Ballinger, 1987.

Sloma, Richard S. *The Turnaround Manager's Handbook.* New York: The Free Press, 1985.

Chapter Four

Preventing and Overcoming Job Burnout

Troy Bannister, sales manager at a large branch of a financial services firm, by his own admission was becoming emotionally exhausted and cynical. He and his manager agreed that Troy should attend a burnout workshop—to learn techniques designed both to remedy and prevent burnout. This chapter describes portions of the workshop Bannister attended.

Drew Jordan, the workshop leader, began the session by making a few introductory comments about the nature of burnout to the 21 participants: "At one time we believed that burnout was a special type of stress disorder that affected workers in the human services field almost exclusively. It was thought to be a form of battle fatigue from trying to be a conscientious people helper. When the rewards weren't there, conscien tious human services workers would eventually lose their spark. Individuals would suffer a host of mild stress symptoms such as backaches, muscle aches, and headaches.

"Later burnout was observed among people not directly involved in the mental health or human services field. Police workers, fire fighters, and high school teachers were found to be frequent victims of burnout. Then, specialists in the field began to notice that conscientious workers in any type of work, and at any job level, could suffer from job burnout. So long as you are subject to long-term stress or you work under oppressive organizational conditions, you could become emotionally exhausted, depleted, cynical, irritable, and impatient. The victim of severe burnout is also known to suffer from low personal accomplishment and to begin treating other people like objects. Treating people like objects is referred to as *depersonalization*.

"You people may be interested in knowing that managers are known to be frequent victims of burnout. It's partly because managers are often conscientious, well-motivated people, and so much is expected of them. Often managers are supposed to reward other people, but they may not be receiving much stroking themselves." (More than half the attendees nod their head in approval at the last statement.)

"Later on this morning we'll get into some of the techniques and strategies for treating and preventing job burnout," said Dr. Jordan. "But for now, I think we should start learning from each other. I would like each person here to explain to the rest of the group, why you are here. Tell us about the specific concerns you have that brought you to this workshop. Between now and the coffee break, let's hear from you five people seated to my right."

Person A:

I came here, quite frankly, because I'm frightened. I'm not nearly the hard-driving, hard-charging sales rep I used to be. After 20 years in the territory, I really don't care too much whether or not customers buy from us. Our line of office furniture is pretty good, but our competition also has good equipment. I'm also tired of jumping up and down telling people that what we sell is service, when our service really isn't that hot.

Dr. Jordan, if you can recharge my battery, I'll consider this day time and money well spent. (A spontaneous burst of laughter takes place within the group.)

Person B:

My reason for being here is to try to help some of my supervisors. As plant superintendent, I see burnout every day. You didn't mention it in your little speech, but burnout has driven some of my best supervisors into overdoing it with drugs and alcohol. My team is suffering from trying to motivate employees who are suffering from a weak work ethic. Also, the heavy turnover among our production workers leads to burnout for the supervisor. Training new employees all the time gets very discouraging.

Person C:

I'm a manager of a technical publications group in a large company. I've been in the same spot for about 10 years. There's not much hope of a promotion, and I'm not seeing many problems that I haven't seen before. But that's not the real reason I feel burned out. It's the lack of appreciation and recognition that's getting to me and my whole group. Management treats us like a necessary evil. There's not much glamor in "tech pubs."

Person D:

I'm Troy Bannister, sales manager of a large suburban branch of one of the big financial services firms. I supervise about 20 people all together. If the group doesn't mind, I'd like to take an extra minute or so to describe my situation. I think that most of us here today are experiencing some of the same problems that I am facing.

First of all, both my boss and I agreed that I need help. I'm definitely a classic case of burnout. I'm exhausted; I'm cynical; I've lost my zip; and most of the time, I'm not much fun to be around. It all started a couple of years ago. I began to notice that I was no longer so concerned about our branch making quota. I used to think that making or exceeding quota was one of the biggest items in my life. I would call my wife immediately once I learned that we made or surpassed quota.

I began to question the value of my work when I read a report concluding that most of our customers would have been better off financially if they had not taken our advice. They would have fared just as well by putting their money in no-load mutual funds, money market funds, and bank certificates of deposit. Soon thereafter I began to experience tension and anxiety when I tried to get our representatives excited about getting our clients to invest more money with us.

I also began to see that the whole financial services industry was involved in some very nonproductive work, particularly mergers and acquisitions. I'm especially referring to hostile takeovers. The only people who benefit in these games are lawyers, financial analysts, and some stockholders who are wealthy enough to own large numbers of shares. But no new jobs are created.

My level of discouragement with our business also increased when our clientele became increasingly unsophisticated. In years past, most of our customers were knowledgeable about investments. For many it was a hobby. Today our sophisticated investors are more sophisticated than they ever were because there is so much valid information available for them to read. However, we are also serving customers today who know absolutely nothing about investments. These are the people who literally used to stuff their money under their mattresses in the past. One man came to our office last month with $10,000 in $100 and $50 bills. He said, "Will you please put this in a safe place for me? I've heard that you guys are doing the same kinds of things banks used to do."

After awhile my disenchantment with my work began to spill over into my home life. Sometimes I would feel so down that I couldn't get involved with my wife and two children. Soon they started to do things without me. I heard my six-year-old say one day, "Why has Dad turned into such a sour-puss?"

I know it's break time, so I'll make just one more statement. It really helps explain the magnitude of my burnout problem. My boredom with my job sometimes interferes with my sex life. When I'm depressed about having to face another week in the office, I lose my interest in sex. And that's really bad because it hurts the feelings of somebody I love very much—my wife.

Person E:

My reasons for being here are not very complicated. A problem I face, however, is that by being here I'm digging myself a deeper hole. I'm a partner in a national public-opinion polling firm. To compete against the giants in the field, we really have to extend ourselves. I've been caught up in the race of working 70 hours per week for two years in order to manage my workload. Many Sundays I work eight hours, which gives me very little time for my family. I feel like I'm grinding myself into oblivion, but I don't want to lose my business. My nerves are frazzled, and work is no longer any fun.

I need help with my problem, but I'm not sure what kind of help. I'm looking for some answers today.

After the break, the remaining 15 workshop participants presented a brief description of their problem. The workshop leader then described a number of techniques and strategies all people might use to combat burnout. Jordan then asked each participant to spend 30 minutes writing down some tentative approaches to dealing with his or her problem. Participants would then be asked to share their plans with the other members of the group. In addition, Jordan would react to their plans. Other participants were also encouraged to comment.

When it was Troy Bannister's turn to present his action plan, he offered these comments to the other workshop participants:

"First of all, as Dr. Jordan has suggested, I should take care of the stress aspects of my burnout. Combined with my occasional down-in-the dumps feelings, I am very tense and wound up. I have kind of slipped away from regular, robust physical exercise. I think I'll get back into chopping wood and jumping rope. That should make me feel better. A bigger issue is that I take my job too seriously. I like the strategy of not putting all my emotional eggs in one basket. If I could convince myself that kicks from personal life are as legitimate as kicks from work life, I think my burnout problem would benefit.

"I also like your suggestion of getting a new toy or gadget to play with on the job. Most of the customer representatives use the computer, but I rarely do. If I learned to use it well, it could conceivably give me a new kick on the job that would serve me well.

"I think I'll stick with these three suggestions as a starting point. Implementing them will keep me pretty busy for awhile."

Dr. Jordan had these reactions to Bannister's action plans:

"I think your approach is sound. Yet I have the feeling that you are overlooking one of the most important factors that is behind your particular burnout situation. Earlier today you mentioned your growing concern about whether or not your firm was really helping people. I think you should give careful thought to the number of people you really are helping. Your branch is probably making a positive impact on more lives than you realize. I suspect that without the services of your firm—or a comparable one—many of your customers would not have been able to send their children to college or purchase a home.

"One of the core reasons many conscientious people like Troy suffer burnout is that they want to help everybody. Learn to relish in the victories of the lives that you have touched."

STRATEGIES FOR MANAGING BURNOUT

Burnout is an evolving concept centering on the idea of a job-related condition of emotional, mental, and physical exhaustion, along with cynicism, stemming from the presence of long-term stressors.[1] It is also regarded as stress out of control. As implied from the statements made by the seven workshop participants, each case of burnout is based on a slightly different set of factors. An appropriate method for managing burnout must therefore be based on individual circumstances.

This section of the chapter describes a variety of measures that can be taken both to treat and prevent burnout. Described first are actions the individual can take, followed by actions that the organization might take to help manage burnout. Each burnout victim should select several techniques and strategies that make the most sense in his or her unique circumstances—as illustrated by the comments of Troy Bannister and the response from Drew Jordan.

Individual Strategies

Take the Problem Seriously.   Unfortunately many career people are reluctant to admit that they are experiencing burnout. They deceive themselves into believing that the situation will mysteriously pass away, similar to many bodily aches and ailments. It is strategically sounder to admit that the problem exists and formulate remedial action quickly. Toward this end, hundreds of workshops have been conducted for teachers who are victims of burnout. Only recently has it been recognized that managerial workers might also need such help.

Reading the vignette about the burnout workshop may have helped sensitize you to the phenomenon of burnout. The appendix to this chapter might prove useful in providing preliminary insight into whether or not you are experiencing a similar problem.

Deal with the Stress Aspects of Burnout.   Job burnout and stress are inextricably related. The usual conception is that burnout stems from being exposed to uncomfortable stressors. The threat of physical violence and violence itself, for example, are documented stressors contributing to teacher burnout. Another conception is that burnout itself becomes a stressor—it is stressful to feel discouraged, apathetic, and cynical. Whether burnout is a reaction to job stress or a stressor itself, the burnout victim is therefore well advised to practice relaxation techniques. Among the more successful everyday methods of relaxation are physical exercise, rest, maintaining a nutritious diet, and learning to relax your muscles. Information about stress management techniques is widely available today.[2]

Develop Realistic Expectations.   Management development specialist Ivan was the quickest victim of burnout known to this author. After two months in his position, he began to exhibit the classic symptoms of burnout—apathy, irritability, and disappointment. The sudden onset of his condition seemed closely tied in with his unrealistic expectations of what he could accomplish. As Ivan describes it:

> Was I deceived. My first assignment as management development specialist was to conduct a leadership training program for middle managers. I thought I would hit them with some of the latest developments in leadership theory and practice. My boss and higher management liked the basic idea of my program and gave me the green light. Once the programs actually began, I knew something was wrong. Some of the managers yawned during the sessions. They laughed; they joked; they bragged about having stayed up half the night. A few of them patronized me. One woman in her 50s told me that after I had some practical knowledge under my belt, I would become a first-rate trainer.
>
> I don't think that more than 1 in 10 was really interested in the program. I thought since everybody assigned to the training program was a manager they would automatically be interested in leadership theory. I thought they would be eager to sop up any information I could give them. I was crushed by their lack of response.

Realign Goals.   Closely related to developing realistic expectations is the process of realigning your goals once it appears that they might be too difficult to achieve. For instance, in the future Ivan might strive to capture the interest of one third of his trainees, not all of them. Hundreds of case workers have burned out because they expected poor people to take their admonitions about food habits and financial management seriously. You can only save a small proportion of people in any occupation. (Troy Bannister received similar advice.)

Here is an illustration of how developing realistic goals might help prevent burnout for an occupational safety and health specialist. Jim, one such worker in a large firm, has decided that despite its importance, "Not everybody is sold on safety and health." He claims that he intends to fight one battle at a time and will be happy if he has a positive impact on safety and health in his area. He puts it this way, "I can bang my head against the wall until the year 2000, but my company will never make safety and health its number 1 priority. However, at least they are beginning to listen to me."

Try New Activities.   "Remember, the more well rounded your life is, the more protected you are against burnout," contends a psychoanalyst who specializes in treating the problem.[3] New activities could include hobbies, sports, community activities, attending different restaurants, eating different foods, or enriching your social life. This advice is similar to the old idea of taking a vacation when things are not going well for you. Trying out new activities is helpful but is only supplemental to strategies designed to change your work activity or modify your perception of them.

Find a Second Career or New Job.   For many burnout victims the only real solution is a drastic one—placing yourself into a new occupational role. Finding a second career requires long-range planning. The economy can absorb only so many small retail store owners or free-lance operators. Sometimes a long-term avocation can be converted into an occupation, provided a high level of skill has been developed. One manager had been hand-crafting furniture since age 20. By age 43 he was tired of spending so much time working directly with people. He converted his savings plus a bank loan into an initial investment in his own custom furniture business. He worked longer hours in his new occupation at slightly lower net income, but his psychic income increased dramatically. He enjoyed shifting the balance of his activities from so much concern with people to more concern with things (furniture).

Finding a new job can also be an antidote to burnout providing the new job does not contain the same contributors to the problem as did the old one. A guidance counselor may experience temporary relief from the condition if he or she becomes a human resources specialist. But after awhile, the ex-guidance counselor may feel unappreciated and unrewarded as a personnel worker. One manager dealt with his burnout problem by joining a firm that placed more emphasis on the development of subordinates. He felt that in his previous firm the efforts he invested in developing subordinates were largely unappreciated by management. The new firm rewarded such activity. Consequently he felt rejuvenated in his new position.

Build a Network of Social Support.   Burnout victims often feel isolated from one another. Research evidence and opinion suggests that if the burned-out person develops a group of friends who give him or her social support and reassurance, the feelings of isolation will be softened.[4] For most people, a spouse and family are the primary and most important support. Support from superiors can also help soften the impact of burnout. In one study with public school teachers it was found that teachers who reported that they had supportive supervisors were less vulnerable to burnout.[5] Social support is also helpful because, as with any problem, just talking it over with a friend helps.

Establish a Decompression Period.   Sharon Levin of the Stanford University Health Centers says that the best and simplest remedy for job burnout is to create a time interval between work and nonwork time. She refers to this as a *decompression period*. It can be anything that takes your mind off your work such as listening to the radio, window-shopping, or working out at a health spa. Rather than being frustrated by commuting, use the time to relax. Levin believes that inserting the decompression period into your schedule allows you to take control over what's happening to you. Regaining control is important because some cases of burnout can be attributed to a feeling of having lost control.[6]

Reward Yourself.   Burnout is a form of mental depression. As with mild depression, a sometimes workable antidote is to pamper yourself with small rewards, or in modern terms *stroke yourself*. Give yourself rewards for a job well done, such as a luxurious meal. Suppose you perform well on a people-related task such as conducting a performance evaluation. The world may not pay you a compliment, but you can tell yourself that you did a good job and deserve to be complimented. Or when you do something well, buy yourself a new piece of athletic equipment, suit, jacket, or dress. In short, take care of yourself rather than waiting for others to reward you.

Rewarding yourself becomes particularly important when placed in a work environment in which few contingent rewards are given to employees. Although this strategy sounds simplistic, experience suggests that it is effective in combating burnout. Rewarding yourself, as with realigning your goals, has a built-in problem: It often suffers from a lack of authenticity. Realigning your goals is sometimes perceived by the individual as lowering personal standards or copping out. Self-rewards, to many people, don't seem nearly as potent as those conferred by other individuals.

Get a New Gadget.   A broad generalization about managing burnout is that something must be done to initiate a process of constructive change. Sometimes the change may appear to be small, like a manager using a personal computer in his or her daily work. We mention personal computers because there is something both partially addictive and tension reducing (sometimes) about working with a computer. For some managers and staff specialists, the high point of their day arrives when they can "play" with their computers. Another gadget that might help combat burnout is video equipment. It could be used for such purposes as practicing sales presentations and presentations to top management.

Try Humor and Laughter.   A minor tactic for coping with burnout is to find ways to inject humor and laughter into the stressful aspects of one's job. A good example of gallows humor took place at International Harvester (now called Navistar) when the company was experiencing financial losses. The chief executive, Don Lennox, took a vacation to play in an American Airlines, Inc., golf tournament in Hawaii. Some old friends noticed that Bethlehem Steel Corporation had just amassed a loss larger than Harvester. They sent Lennox this telegram: "Forget American tourney. Harvester needs you. Bethlehem now in first place."[7]

Humor and laughter can actually produce physiological changes in the body, and these can help combat some forms of disease. Similarly, laughter can be effective in displacing stress that can push a person toward burnout.[8]

Get Professional Help.   Some cases of burnout are a form of mental depression and may therefore require assistance beyond the self-help techniques or organizational interventions described in this chapter. In these instances it may be necessary to receive assistance from a mental health professional. Discussions with a professional may help properly identify the causes of burnout. Counseling can also be useful in helping the person cope with the stress aspects of burnout. In some instances the burnout victim may be advised to take antidepressant medication to help deal with distracting stress symptoms. Despite the potential contribution of counseling and psychotherapy, the burnout victim may also need to modify his or her work environment by such means as switching assignments.

Maintain a Growing Edge.   An almost philosophical strategy for preventing burnout is to maintain a lifelong positive attitude toward self-development and self-improvement. By so doing, the individual continues to receive a new trickle—and sometimes a flood—of rewards. The logic behind this strategy is that if you avoid going stale, you decrease the probability of burning out. Here is how the situation might work for a manager whose work primarily involves supervising word processing technicians:

Over a period of time, the manager begins to hear the same complaints from her subordinates; she watches person after person leaving the word processing center for transfer, promotion, or personal reasons; she hears the same old rush requests week after week. Under these circumstances many managers would experience burnout. Using the growing-edge strategy, the word processing manager would continue to develop as a manager and as an individual. One month she might learn a new technique of disciplining subordinates. She tries it, and the method works. The manager thus receives the reward of self-satisfaction for having used a personnel technique that proved effective. Each new increment of personal development yields a new reward. Fed by a long series of rewards, the word processing manager avoids burnout.

Maintaining a growing edge could prove to be the most important technique for improving your professional effectiveness and personal vitality.

Organizational Strategies

Several valid reasons exist why organizations should take constructive action in the treatment and prevention of burnout. Many instances of burnout are triggered by adverse organizational conditions, thus creating an obligation on the part of management to solve problems it creates. Burnout also adversely affects performance. Remedying the problem would thus elevate performance and productivity. Further, managing burnout is part of a humanitarian obligation to provide employees a good quality of work life. Described next are some potentially effective organizational strategies for managing burnout.

Confront the Burnout Victim.   A starting point in effectively managing burnout is to confront burnout victims with the consequences of their problem. The confrontation should be done in a helpful and sympathetic manner, focusing on the work behavior that is suffering. Although a given individual may talk about being burned out, he or she may not realize the full implications of the problem. In addition, burnout is often said to be contagious.

Establish a Contract with the Burnout Victim.   After the burned-out person is confronted and shows some awareness of the problem, a verbal contract between the organization and the individual should be established. It should specify what is expected of the individual in terms of performance improvement and what types of help the employer is willing to offer.[9] A clause in one such contract specified, ''We are willing to find you a special assignment for a month or two. In return we expect you to stop telling your subordinates how oppressive it is to work here.'' One form of help is a stress-management program.

Allow for Job Rotation and Varied Assignments.   A natural antidote to burnout is for management to create the opportunity for constructive change in work assignments. An example of this approach is the antiburnout policy at Casto Travel in San Francisco. The owner, Maryles Casto, sends her employees on a work-related trip at least once every three months. She also tries to cross-utilize them by transferring them to different locations to work at the same job level. In addition to preventing staleness (one contributor to burnout), these rotating assignments give employees a broader view of the business.[10]

Alter Working Conditions.   Sometimes a constructive way of alleviating burnout is to modify job conditions so that the primary contributor to the problem is softened in impact. Often this modification can be made for a group of workers. One hospice for dying patients was faced with an unacceptably high turnover among nurses. Management intervened by giving the nurses places to eat lunch and take breaks by themselves. Previously, they had to share lunches and cafeterias with the patients. In that hopeless environment, the nurses had limited opportunity to offer each other peer support or advice and encouragement. After this modified work condition, the turnover rate fell to a more acceptable level.[11]

Conduct a Stress-Management Program.   Previously we described the necessity of individuals managing their own stress levels. The process is facilitated when organizations offer a company-sponsored stress-management program. Oliver L. Niehouse has worked with the United States federal government in helping several of its agencies develop such programs. Aside from helping individuals deal with stress disorders in general, these programs are useful in combating the stress associated with burnout. A popular program of this nature is the READ program of relaxation, exercise, attitude and awareness, and diet. Niehouse argues that the READ program is cost effective. Its cost of several hundred dollars per participant can be contrasted to the much larger (yet unknown) cost of a decline in a burned-out staff member's productivity.[12]

Employee assistance programs can also be used to help individuals cope with burnout. At a minimum, employees can receive help in dealing with stress. Today, most assistance programs have a counselor on the staff who is familiar with the problem of job burnout.

Alter Stressful Working Conditions.   A macro solution to the burnout problem is for the organization to make the total environment less stressful, both physically and mentally. The less chronic stress experienced by employees, the less the likelihood of burnout. Physical working conditions can be improved by such relatively small factors as improved ventilation, heating, and lighting. Recent research evidence suggests that managers play a more important role than family members in helping subordinates cope with stress. It has been found that managers can reduce stress levels by offering encouragement and other forms of emotional support. Stress researcher, Kenneth Pelletier, reports these findings about another aspect of the boss's role in controlling stress: "The boss is crucial in how much stress his or her workers feel, and whether their health will suffer. One key is whether the boss lets subordinates feel in control of their jobs."[13]

Give Ample Rewards, Including Recognition.   Many burnout sufferers believe that their apathy and indifference stems from not receiving the recognition (and other rewards) they think they deserve. The self-stroking strategy described earlier is designed to help with this problem. Of greater potential impact, the organization should implement a carefully designed system of rewards that includes recognition from superiors for a job well done. Susan E. Jackson and Randall S. Schuler recommend that supervisors be trained to offer more rewards based on performance to employees, thus reducing the frequency of the comment, "If you don't hear anything, you must be doing okay."[14]

Give Increased Feedback on Performance.   A general case of the point just mentioned is to provide substantial feedback on performance to employees at all levels. It has been noted that in human service organizations, for example, there is a dominant tendency for employees not to receive feedback for a job well done.[15] Presumably, this is one factor contributing to a high burnout rate among human service professionals.

Increase the Use of Participative Decision Making.   A major contributor to job stress is the feeling that the job controls you rather than your controlling the job. Previously it was mentioned that the manager can reduce stress by helping subordinates gain more control. When opportunities for control are missing, and employees feel trapped in an uncontrollable and unpredictable environment, both their physical and mental health are likely to suffer.[16] A standard technique for turning over more control to subordinates is participative decision making (PDM). Besides increasing employees' feelings of control, participation may help prevent burnout by clarifying what is expected of employees and giving employees a chance to reduce some of the role conflict they experience. In the process of PDM, for instance, the employee might contribute the input that he or she cannot satisfy the competing demands of two bosses.

Strengths and Weaknesses of Burnout Strategies

Although we do not yet have much research-based information about the prevention and treatment of burnout, many of the strategies described earlier have proven clinically effective. In other words, counselors and therapists have recommended them to people experiencing burnout and they seem to work. Also of significance, the strategies suggested for managing burnout are based on well-established principles of human behavior (such as the value of establishing realistic goals).

Except for suggesting that you switch your job or career, these strategies are relatively conservative. They are unlikely to do any harm even if they fail to help you cope with burnout. Should you misdiagnose your situation (you are not really experiencing burnout), these strategies would still prove valuable for your personal development. The radical strategies of job or career switching are things a person might do for any type of chronic job dissatisfaction.

Also on the positive side, the organizational strategies for managing burnout suggested above are likely to help the organization in other ways even if they do not cure or prevent burnout. A case in point is the establishment of an effective reward system. Almost any organization would benefit from such a strategy.

On the negative side, many instances of burnout could be explained away as situations of extreme job dissatisfaction. And we know that a small percentage of the work force is going to be dissatisfied no matter what action management takes. It could therefore be a waste of resources to try and eliminate some cases of burnout. Another weakness is that most of the strategies suggested here are superficial if your basic problem is that you hate your work. To illustrate, no matter how many new gadgets you try you are unlikely to become happy about supervising a group of ungrateful and resentful subordinates.

Guidelines for Action and Skill Development

Burnout is a serious problem that concerns your basic means of earning a living. Problems of burnout are, therefore, worth discussing with a mental health professional, career counselor, or professional human resource specialist. Reading about the problem should be an important supplement, not a substitute for, seeking outside assistance.

Move cautiously in choosing a radical solution to burnout such as changing jobs or careers. First try to modify that portion of your work that seems to produce the most frustration. Observe the results and see if burnout sensations still abound.

Recognize that every form of job dissatisfaction is not burnout. After reading this chapter and the additional references, do not talk yourself into a case of burnout.

If you are a manager, a potentially valuable human skill to develop is to be able to detect burnout among your subordinates. This skill begins with an awareness of burnout symptoms (such as apathy, indifference, cynicism, and emotional exhaustion). When these symptoms are manifested repeatedly by a person in your group, it would be time for you to intervene. You could ask the subordinate if he or she wanted to talk about the dissatisfaction and loss of enthusiasm you have observed. You might also discuss the possibilities of sponsoring the person at a burnout workshop or make a referral to an employee assistance program.

DISCUSSION QUESTIONS AND ACTIVITIES

1. To what extent do you think a burned-out manager creates burnout among subordinates? Explain your reasoning.

2. In what way might a burned-out manager contribute to the demotivation of subordinates?

3. Many managers and professionals talk openly about being burned out, almost to the point of bragging. What reasons do you think underlie this behavior?

4. Is early retirement an effective cure for burnout? Explain your reasoning.

5. Identify several techniques described in other chapters of this book that you think might be helpful in dealing with burnout.

6. Why do you think it is true that perfectionistic people are more likely to suffer from burnout than their less perfectionistic counterparts?

7. Should burnout victims receive workers compensation benefits?

8. What do most students probably mean when they say they are burned out?

9. What managerial and organizational practices might contribute to employee burnout?

NOTES

1. Susan E. Jackson and Richard L. Schwab, "Toward an Understanding of the Burnout Phenomenon," *Journal of Applied Psychology,* November 1986, p. 630.

2. A representative current book is Walt Shafer, *Stress Management for Wellness* (New York: Holt, Rinehart & Winston, 1987). See also SOME ADDITIONAL REFERENCES.

3. Quoted in "Are You Burning Out?" *Personal Report for the Executive,* March 15, 1986, p. 4.

4. Robert A. Baron, *Understanding Human Relations: A Practical Guide to People at Work* (Newton, Mass.: Allyn & Bacon, 1985), p. 294; Daniel C. Ganster, Marcelline R. Fusilier, and Bronston T. Mayes, "Role of Social Support in the Experience of Stress at Work," *Journal of Applied Psychology,* February 1986, pp. 102–10.

5. Daniel W. Russell, Elizabeth Altmaier, and Dawn Van Velzen, "Job-Related Stress, Social Support, and Burnout among Classroom Teachers," *Journal of Applied Psychology,* May 1987, pp. 269–74.

6. "Beating Burnout," *Success!,* January 1985, p. 11.

7. "Can Don Lennox Save Harvester?" *Business Week,* August 15, 1983, p. 83.

8. Oliver L. Niehouse, *The Road Away from Burnout: A Traveler's Guide for Public Management,* AMA Management Briefing (New York: AMA Pub-

lications Division, 1982), p. 55; Dan Oldenburg, "Corporate Man 1986?" *Washington Post* story, March 17, 1986.

9. Ibid., p. 64.
10. Katy Koontz, "Beating Burnout," *Success!,* May 1986, p. 32.
11. Jerry E. Bishop, "The Personal and Business Costs of 'Job Burnout'," *The Wall Street Journal,* November 11, 1980, p. 39.
12. Oliver L. Niehouse, "Controlling Burnout: A Leadership Guide for Managers," *Business Horizons,* July–August 1984, p. 85.
13. Quoted in Daniel Goleman, "Controlling Stress Starts with the Boss," *New York Times* story, January 31, 1984.
14. Susan E. Jackson and Randall S. Schuler, "Preventing Employee Burnout," *Personnel,* March–April 1983, p. 63.
15. Jackson and Schuler, "Preventing Employee Burnout," p. 67.
16. Ibid., p. 65.

SOME ADDITIONAL REFERENCES

Batten, Julie. "Ten Jobs That Cause Burnout." *Business Week's Careers,* December 1985, pp. 41–43.

Dworkin, Anthony Gary. *Teacher Burnout in the Public Schools: Structural Causes and Consequences for Children.* Albany, N.Y.: State University of New York Press, 1987.

Freudenberger, Herbert J., and Gail North. *Women's Burnout: How to Spot It, How to Reverse It, and How to Prevent It.* New York: Doubleday, 1985.

Latack, Janina C. "Coping with Job Stress: Measures and Future Directions for Scale Development." *Journal of Applied Psychology,* August 1986, pp. 377–85.

Matteson, Michael T., and John M. Ivancevich. *Controlling Work Stress: Effective Human Resource and Management Strategies.* San Francisco: Jossey-Bass Inc., 1987.

Pines, Ayala, and Elliot Aronson. *Career Burnout: Causes and Cures.* New York: The Free Press, 1988.

Zauderer, Donald, and Joseph Fox. "Resiliency in the Face of Stress." *Management Solutions,* November 1987, pp. 30–35.

Appendix to Chapter Four

THE BURNOUT CHECKLIST

Directions.   Answer the following statements as mostly true or mostly false as they apply to you.

	Mostly true	*Mostly false*
1. I feel tired more frequently than I used to.	____	____
2. I've been experiencing heavy job stress for far too long.	____	____
3. I think that I quite often treat other people on the job like objects.	____	____
4. I seem to be working harder but accomplishing less.	____	____
5. I get down on myself too often.	____	____
6. My job is beginning to depress me.	____	____
7. I often feel I'm headed nowhere.	____	____
8. I've reached (or am fast approaching) a dead end in my job.	____	____
9. I've lost a lot of my zip lately.	____	____
10. It's hard for me to laugh at a joke about myself.	____	____
11. I'm not really physically ill, but I have a lot of aches and pains.	____	____
12. Lately I've kind of withdrawn from friends and family.	____	____
13. My enthusiasm for life is on the wane.	____	____
14. I'm running out of things to say to people.	____	____
15. My temper is much shorter than it used to be.	____	____
16. My job makes me feel sad.	____	____
17. Most days I feel emotionally exhausted.	____	____
18. I look forward to vacations much more than I do to work.	____	____
19. I know I have a problem, but I just don't have enough energy to do anything about it.	____	____
20. I don't get nearly enough appreciation from my employer.	____	____

Interpretation.   The more of these questions you can honestly answer mostly true, the more likely it is that you are experiencing burnout. If you answered 15 or more of these statements mostly true, it is likely you are experiencing burnout or another form of mental depression. Discuss these feelings with a physical or mental health professional.

Part II

Improving Interpersonal Relationships

The next four chapters concentrate on methods and techniques of strengthening one-to-one relationships in organizations. However, these interpersonal relationships also take place within the context of a group.

Chapter 5, Effective Negotiating, describes strategies and tactics for improving your ability to negotiate for what you want in a wide variety of situations. Information about negotiating receives attention in the organizational behavior and management literature and is also the subject of many trade books, magazine articles, and management development programs. The negotiating methods presented are rooted in behavioral approaches to conflict resolution and the social psychology of bargaining. Several of the strategies stem from research conducted in the Harvard Negotiation Project.

Chapter 6, Nonverbal Messages in Organizations, deals with the most speculative topic in this book. Although nonverbal communication has been widely researched, its readiness for direct application is subject to debate. Despite this, the practicing manager should know something about the transmission of nonverbal messages in the workplace because a substantial portion of communication is nonverbal. Improving nonverbal communication skills can therefore enhance job effectiveness.

Chapter 7, Developing Assertion Skills, provides some specific tips for helping people attain their goals by expressing their thoughts and feelings and by taking action. Assertiveness training (AT) is an offshoot of principles of behavior therapy, which itself is based on principles of behavior modification. AT is often used to help managers deal more effectively with group members and to help customer-service personnel deal more effectively with customers.

Chapter 8, The Prevention and Control of Sexual Harassment, presents information about a sensitive topic that has received widespread attention both in the formal literature and popular press in recent years. The purpose of this chapter is not to present another exposition indicating that sexual harassment is prevalent in the workplace, but to describe experience-based suggestions for its control. Both human resource managers and managers throughout the organization are responsible for controlling sexual harassment on the job.

Chapter Five

Effective Negotiating

The chief administrator at a health maintenance organization (HMO) was one of the key figures involved in negotiating the terms for her HMO's acquisition of a smaller HMO. To prevent the takeover from falling through, she relied heavily on the general negotiating strategy of looking for win-win solutions to the points at issue.

Maxwell Health Center is a health maintenance organization that functions much like a large self-contained health clinic, or a "medical supermarket." It currently has a membership of 45,000 subscribers. To belong, members pay a fee of $200 per family, per month. All medical and nursing care received at the center is covered by this monthly fee in addition of a $4 per visit charge. Medicine and medical supplies (such as crutches and back braces) are paid for directly by the patient.

The Maxwell Health Center is divided into eight medical departments including ophthalmology, obstetrics and gynecology, pediatrics, and radiology. Each department is administered by a medical director and an office supervisor. The patient intake and billing departments are managed by nonmedical personnel. Each medical department is staffed by physicians, nurses, nurse practitioners, licensed practical nurses, medical assistants, and other appropriate health service professionals. Top management of Maxwell consists of the chief medical director, Frank Whitcomb, M.D.; Lisa Tonnelli, M.S.H.A. (M.S. Health Administration); a chief financial officer, Al Canton, C.P.A.; and several administrative assistants.

About six months ago, Canton submitted a report on the health center's financial status to Whitcomb, Tonnelli, and the board of directors. The report pointed out that although the membership of the Center was growing steadily and the membership fee structure was appropriate for local circumstances, operating expenses were cutting heavily into profits. Canton's recommended action plan to increase profitability was to acquire Northside Group Health, a competitive HMO. Both top management and the board thought highly enough of Canton's plan to empower him to speak to Northside top management about the proposed acquisition.

Northside Group Health is located about 12 miles north of Maxwell in another section of the city. Northside has an organization structure quite similar to Maxwell's; however the total operation is about two thirds the size, both in membership and employees. The top management team is headed by medical director Barry Phillips, M.D.; chief administrator Clint Griffin, M.B.A.; and chief financial officer Karen Lacey, M.B.A.

At the time of Canton's original inquiries, Northside was operating at a loss and therefore was willing to discuss terms of a possible acquisition by Maxwell. Karen Lacey thought the acquisition would bring consolidated advertising costs, centralized billing, less need to have expensive specialized medical equipment at both HMOs, and reduction in payroll costs, among other benefits. One day a month for as long as needed was set aside for the negotiating terms to work out the details of an acquisition agreement. Both boards agreed the acquisition would be approved providing the negotiating teams could arrive at some mutually satisfactory agreements.

The negotiating teams for each side consisted of the three members of top management, each headed by the chief administrative officer of the HMO: Lisa Tonnelli for Maxwell and Clint Griffin for Northside. Portions of the final negotiating session are presented below.

Tonnelli:

Welcome back, gang, to what we all hope could be the final session needed to reach agreement on big issues causing us some concern. For openers, we haven't yet agreed on a suitable name for the surviving HMO. Since we are the acquiring organization, I thought it would be appropriate for both places to carry the name Maxwell Health Center. What problems does this create for you people?

Phillips:

I'm much older than anybody else in this room, so perhaps that's why I'm more sentimental. I just can't see us dumping entirely the good Northside Group Health name. It means too much to too many people. [*Griffin and Lacey nod in agreement.*]

Tonnelli:

Now I understand. You feel there is goodwill attached to the Northside Group Health name. You have a good point. We think the Maxwell name is valuable for similar reasons. Also, we are the acquiring organization. Let me suggest a name for the new HMO that might serve both our purposes: Maxwell Group Health. In that way the Maxwell fans could refer to it as "Maxwell," and the Northside fans could refer to it as "Group Health."

Griffin:

I've just conferred with my two colleagues. We buy your idea. The new name should work just fine.

Canton:

We still have some key items to resolve in terms of reducing overhead in the new organization. We have already reached agreement about the clerical and data processing staffs. After normal attrition, one early retirement, and the laying off of two problem employees, those support groups will be down to the right size. At the top of the major issues is the problem of two medical directors. Dr. Phillips, what are your current feelings about your position?

Phillips:

I'm 63 and I intend to remain professionally active until retirement.

Tonnelli:

We think a person of your stature should remain active. Here's what we have in mind. We would like you to become a member of the board of directors and also to serve as a consultant to Maxwell Group Health, effective the first day of acquisition.

Phillips:

That's not exactly what I meant by remaining professionally active, but I'll give your offer warm consideration.

Griffin:

I'm happy to know that Dr. Phillips is taken care of. We now have to deal with my situation. You tell us, Lisa, that Al Canton will have to stay as chief financial officer, and I could stay on as office manager of the combined office operations, providing we find other jobs for our two present office managers. Well, that's not satisfactory to me. If that's my only alternative, I won't be in favor of the acquisition. One of the major tentative agreements we reached is that all personnel would be handled equitably.

Tonnelli:

What do you see as the biggest problem with your proposed new job as officer manager?

Griffin:

It's the pits. I don't want a decrease in status at this point in my career.

Tonnelli:

What career alternative do you see that would give you the status you need, aside from your present job?

Griffin:

To be candid, I want to establish my own consulting firm to provide data processing and financial services to small medical and dental offices.

Tonnelli:

Our negotiating team has the authority to give a key executive up to six-month's salary and benefits as severance pay if that person's job is collapsed as a result of the acquisition.

Griffin:

Although I would prefer one year's salary as severance pay, I think I could live just fine with that deal. It could fund me while I'm getting my new business started.

Tonnelli:

Another major issue we face is the salary differentials for physicians at our two HMOs. Al Canton has shown me the figures. Apparently physicians at Northside Group Health receive salaries that are about 20 percent higher than paid by other HMOs in this area. For example, your two ophthalmologists are paid $175,000 per year. That's out of line; $150,000 per year is much more in line with our salaries.

Phillips:

But if you tell a doctor today that he or she is going to receive a pay cut, you can say goodbye to that doctor.

Tonnelli:

You think, then, that the underlying problem is that physicians on your staff would want to maintain their same total income?

Phillips:

I don't think so, I *know* so.

Tonnelli:

In that case, hear my proposal. I think it will satisfy everybody. We'll explain to the overpaid doctors that their salaries are out of line with our pay scales, but that we do not want to cut their incomes. As a compromise, we'll ask them to forgo cost-of-living increases for the next three years. However, we will do what we can to help them maintain their current income levels. We will authorize them to spend an additional five hours per week on private patients if they so desire. This should enable them to maintain their same high incomes during the time the Maxwell pay scales are catching up with those of Northside.

Phillips:

Your idea just won't work. If you think you can cut the pay of our physicians, you're wrong. They'll quit for sure, under the terms you propose.

Tonnelli:

But, as I explained, their total income won't be reduced. We will be giving them time for private practice.

Lacey:

You're being too naive, Lisa. Our doctors are already seeing some private practice patients. No matter how you try to work the deal, you're asking our doctors to take a pay cut. And they won't buy it. I'm beginning to think you're not bargaining in good faith.

Tonnelli:

You're the one who is intractable, not me. It looks like we're getting nowhere today. Think through carefully our offer about the pay for our doctors before we meet again.

By the end of this negotiating session, one major issue remained to be resolved. However, the issue of the disparity between physicians' pay at the two HMOs was such a major one, that it threw negotiations into a serious deadlock. Unless the parties can effectively negotiate a solution to this problem, the merger acquisition will not be consummated.

NEGOTIATING STRATEGIES AND TACTICS

Negotiating strategies and tactics warrant attention because negotiating is required in such diverse activities as finding a job, agreeing on goals, agreeing on provisions of a contract, buying and selling, settling customer complaints, determining the size of a departmental budget, and allocating resources to a project. And, as illustrated in the HMO case, negotiation is a vital part of working out the provisions of a merger or acquisition.

A helpful starting point in sorting out the many negotiating strategies is to classify them as either *collaborative* or *competitive*.[1] Collaborative strategies and tactics are based on a win-win (or everybody wins) philosophy. The user of these approaches is genuinely concerned about arriving at a settlement that meets the needs of both parties, or at least does not badly damage the welfare of the other side. Competitive approaches are based more on a win-lose philosophy. Each side is trying to maximize gain with little regard for the needs and welfare of the other side. We also classify as competitive those techniques that are more devious or "tricky," than open, honest, or sincere.

The strategies and tactics described below are classified as collaborative or competitive. Two limitations to this dichotomy should be kept in mind. First, a good deal of subjective judgment is used in classifying the strategies and tactics. Second, the intent of the person using a given strategy or tactic counts heavily as to whether it is collaborative or competitive. For example, one person may use the strategy of making small concessions gradually as a way of outsmarting the other side. Another person may rely on this tactic in a genuine attempt to arrive at a fair negotiated settlement.

Collaborative Approaches to Negotiation

The approaches placed into this category are generally aimed at gaining one's fair share in a negotiation without sacrificing the rights of the other side.

Use the Harvard Negotiation Project Strategy.   The best field-tested and researched overall program for effective negotiation has been developed by the Harvard Negotiation Project, as described in the book *Getting to Yes.*[2] Their program for resolving conflict through negotiation encompasses many of the other strategies described in this chapter. As you read through the four-step Harvard program, you will observe that the HMO negotiating teams negotiated in the same spirit. The underlying philosophy is that one bargains over underlying issues, not positions. The strategy is referred to as *principled negotiation,* meaning about the same thing as collaborative negotiation.

The basic point is to decide issues on their merits rather than through a haggling process focused on the position held by each side. It implies that you look for mutual gains wherever possible. In situations where your interests conflict, the parties insist that the result be based on some fair standards independent of the will of the other side. (For instance, it was determined that the physicians' salaries should be brought in line with wage rates at other HMOs in the area.) Principled negotiation is based on the merits of the situation, and uses no tricks or posturing.

Principled negotiation, or negotiation by merit, centers on four basic points (described next). These points define an open and honest form of negotiation that its developers believe can be used in almost any negotiating situation.

I. People. Separate the People from the Problem.   According to this point, human beings, unlike computers, are not entirely rational problem solvers. People have strong emotions, and often have radically different perceptions of the same event. When negotiating, their emotions become entangled with the objective merits of the problem. It is therefore important to disentangle the people problem before working on the substantive problem. Fisher and Ury recommend, "The participants should come to see themselves as working side by side, attacking the problem, not each other."[3]

Lisa Tonnelli showed good sensitivity to human behavior when she suggested a solution to the problem of having one surplus medical director. She appealed to Dr. Phillip's need for status by offering him a position as a board member and a consultant. (Whether or not displaced executives in a merger ever do much consulting, their egos are usually satisfied by having the title, consultant.) Fisher and Ury point to another of the infinite possible applications of this general principle. If you should be negotiating with a company to repair your broken machinery, focus on the problem, but do not attack the company representative. Here is an example:

> Our rotary generator that you serviced has broken down again. That is three times in the last month. The first time it was out of order for an entire week. This factory needs a functioning generator. I want your advice on how we can minimize our risk of generator breakdown. Should we change service companies, sue the manufacturer, or what?[4]

II. Interest. Focus on Interests, Not Positions.   The intent here is to overcome the drawback of focusing on peoples' stated positions when the true object of a negotiation is to satisfy the underlying interests on both sides. A negotiating position often obscures the nature of what a person is really trying to achieve. The standard remedy of compromising positions infrequently produces an agreement that effectively takes care of the human needs that led people to adopt these positions.

A detail not provided in the HMO acquisition case is that both sides initially took the position that they wanted to retain the original organizational name. During the session, the underlying interest was revealed: Both sides were looking for a way of preserving the identity of their HMO. The proposed solution of combining the key elements of both names—Maxwell Group Health—was therefore a workable compromise that satisfied both sides. An unworkable compromise might have been for the acquiring firm to give the acquired firm a cash bonus for scrapping its name.

III. Options. Invent Options for Mutual Gain.   An effective negotiating strategy is to generate several workable options before you enter into the heat of the actual negotiating session. Trying to select a good option in the presence of your adversary may create emotional interference with your thinking. When the stakes are high, the stress created by the negotiating session may be at such a high level that creativity is dampened. Thus, you may not arrive at creative alternatives to the points at issue.

Under ideal circumstances, the two parties can join together in a brainstorming session to arrive at options that will satisfy the needs of both. Or, both parties may engage in brainstorming separately and then bring these new options to the negotiating session or bargaining table. However, a major hurdle must be overcome before a systematic search for options is possible. Both sides must realize that the outcome of negotiation is not inevitably one position winning out over the other.

Here is an example of how the manager of the data processing department of a bank invented options when she was faced with a surge in workload. The peak demand was attributed to a large number of bank customers shifting their funds from stocks and mutual funds to financial instruments offered by the bank. Recognizing that her department could not handle the load, the manager pleaded for more staff support and more equipment. Higher management refused her request because hiring new employees and purchasing new equipment would result in a budget overrun for the fiscal year. The manager returned three days later with a proposal for hiring temporary employees and leasing equipment for the peak load period. Her proposal was accepted, and her department caught up with the backlog.

IV. Criteria. Insist on Using Objective Criteria.   To overcome stubbornness and rigidity on one or both sides, it is helpful to insist that the agreement reached must reflect some fair (objective) standard such as market value, expert opinion, customary settlements, or law. For instance, if you are negotiating with a new car dealer about repairing your "lemon," you can insist that the amount paid for by the dealer is in line with customary handling of this problem. Similarly, the dealer should not be forced to make a settlement with you exceeding this standard.

Base Your Demands on a Solid Rationale.   Related to the above point, it is useful to base your demand on a solid rationale. A typical setting for applying this strategy is when asking for a raise. A weak rationale is to demand an above average raise because you need more money. It is more tactically sound to provide a valid reason why you deserve a big raise. Gerard I. Nierenberg, founder of the Negotiation Institute, offers this example of how to get results: "I want a raise so I can work harder for both of us. I want a raise because if you can't give me one, I'll have to take another job that is offered to me at a higher salary."[5]

Prepare in Advance for the Negotiation Session.   A negotiation session is a meeting. As such it will proceed more smoothly if both sides agree on an agenda and make other necessary preparations (including looking for creative options, as described above). You should plan in advance what major and minor points you plan to negotiate. Your opponent should do the same. Ideally, the two sides should agree beforehand on what items will be dealt with during the formal negotiating session. The agenda places control on what will be said and not said. It has also been suggested that one should plan for the negotiating session by role-playing the opponent's most likely responses to your suggestions.[6]

James F. Rand, a labor relations officer, says that the key questions in the preparation phase of negotiations are as follows:

Have you defined and analyzed the situation in terms of resources, organization, and environment?

What are the issues to be negotiated?

How do time constraints influence the negotiations?

What are the interests, motives, and concerns of each party?

Do the parties have alternatives to the negotiated agreement?

Who should make the first offer?

Has a reasonable pattern of concessions been defined?

Who should negotiate?[7]

A separate part of preparing for negotiations is to set objectives relating to what is to be accomplished through the negotiations. The objectives should be realistic and measurable. As an example, one of the principal players in the opening case established the objective of arriving at a new name for the merged HMO that would be acceptable to both sides.

Philip L. Morgan recommends that negotiators should make a list of all their objectives. Next, the objectives should be divided into two lists: *likes* and *musts*. *Likes* are things that would be nice to have but could be forgone if necessary. *Musts* are objectives one must attain for the negotiation to be successful—such as large enough budget to maintain a desired level of customer service. As negotiations proceed, the manager may give up on many *like* items but will persevere in trying to achieve the *must* items.[8]

Give Yourself Time to Think.   A hasty decision made in a negotiating session is often a poor one. Although it may seem that you are pressed to make a fast decision, there are many legitimate and ethical stalling tactics that will enable you to reflect on the proposition coming from the other side. You might call for a lunch break, request time to obtain some backup information from your files, demand that you first consult an expert advisor before committing yourself, or suggest that both sides resume negotiations in the morning.

Create a Positive Negotiating Climate.   Negotiation proceeds much more swiftly if a positive tone surrounds the session. It is therefore helpful to take the initiative to take a positive outlook about the negotiation meeting. Nonverbal behavior such as smiling and making friendly gestures both help create a positive climate. Nierenberg maintains that by staying positive, you'll stop a negative person cold. "It will be like a child who throws a tantrum until the child sees that it's not working, that nobody's giving in. Then he or she will move on to something else."[9]

Avoid Macho-Chicken.   Many tough-minded negotiators play a standoff game in which they become bullheaded, entrenched, and committed to a win-lose conception of the outcome (defined in this chapter as the essence of competitive bargaining). Howard Raiffa cautions that if the negotiation gets down to macho-chicken, it has escalated out of your control.[10] The antidote is to focus on the many collaborative bargaining tactics described throughout this section of the chapter.

Allow Room for Negotiation.   The most basic negotiating strategy is to begin with a demand that allows you room for compromise and concession. Anybody who has ever negotiated the price of an automobile, house, or used furniture recognizes this vital principle. If you are the buyer, begin with a low bid. If you are the seller, begin with a high demand. If you are negotiating next year's budget for your department, begin by asking for a liberal budget—one higher than the absolute minimum required for your functioning. Labor unions typically allow themselves negotiating room by bringing many more items into negotiating than they believe will be granted (such as complete dental coverage or treating a person's birthday as holiday). As negotiations proceed, the union will drop several of these lesser demands.

Begin with a Plausible Demand or Offer.   Allowing room for negotiation does not preclude the importance of beginning negotiations with a plausible demand or offer. To begin with an unreasonable and potentially destructive demand will often be interpreted by the other side as bargaining in poor faith. Thus serious negotiations will be delayed or even cancelled. In one situation a union negotiator had initially demanded a 25 percent increase in all wage rates. Both sides realized this demand was unjustifiable. When asked to respond with a counterproposal, the company representative made this comment:

> I am not going to insult you and your membership with a ridiculously low initial offer. When your wage demands are more realistic, we will come forward with a specific wage package. And then we can really negotiate and come up with something we can all live with. But you have to be realistic before we will offer anything.[11]

The mini-max strategy (or what should I give and what should I get?) leads the negotiator toward a plausible initial demand or offer. The mini-max strategy thus points toward a range of acceptable solutions. Each side may find it helpful to answer these questions.

1. What is the minimum I can accept?
2. What is the maximum I can ask for without getting laughed out of the room?
3. What is the maximum I can give away?
4. What is the least I can offer without getting laughed out of the room?[12]

Try to Make the Opposing Negotiator Feel Good.   A useful, positive negotiating tactic is to make the adversary feel good, to facilitate that person thinking in a win-win mode. One "feel-good" tactic is to reward the opposing negotiator's concession. A series of laboratory simulations of union-management negotiations over wages showed that granting counter-concessions (or reciprocating) serves as a reward. It results in large concessions by a quick agreement with the opponent.[13] Of considerable value, these large concessions continue after the rewards cease—as would be predicted from reinforcement theory. An example of a reward might be, "Since you were gracious enough to decrease the number of forms we have to process per week, we'll set higher quality standards in the department.''

Another way of making the opponents feel good is to simply let them know you understand their position. One way to accomplish this is to paraphrase their position accurately. This lets them know that you understand their objective even if you do not necessarily agree with it. You may recall that when Barry Phillips said that he could not see dumping the Northside Group Health name, Lisa Tonnelli replied, ''Now, I understand. You feel there is goodwill attached to the Northside Group Health name.''

Be Truthful.   In many instances, laying all the cards out on the table is an effective negotiating tactic. It communicates the fact that you are not game playing and that you respect the intelligence of the opponent. It may also encourage the other side to make more honest demands since their distorted demands will be contrasted to a set of more honest ones. Howard Raiffa has concluded from his experiments that subjects who did the best in negotiating games were the ones who simply announced the truth.[14] One reason is that most people expect negotiation to be filled with duplicity. Consequently they are overwhelmed by the truth.

Another way of being truthful is never to ask for something you don't want or cannot justify. In following this guideline, ethical negotiators do their homework and justify what they want to the other side. For instance, a purchasing agent might provide documentation as to why delivery of custom-made supplies is needed within two weeks: The agent's company is facing pressure for a quick delivery date from one of their customers.

Use Negotiation Jujitsu.   It sometimes becomes necessary to parry the aggressive thrusts from your opponent. A tactic for this purpose, negotiation jujitsu, focuses on the idea that you ''sidestep their attack and deflect it against the problem.''[15] One such approach is to look at the consequences of their proposal or position. Here is an example:

Union representative:

Our last and final offer is a wage rate of $21.75 for machinists in this labor grade.

Company representative:

That certainly is a handsome rate of hourly pay. But what do you think that would do to the cost of our gear-cutting equipment?

Union representative:

The cost would go up, I guess.

Company representative:

You guessed right. It would raise the price so high that foreign competition would take over our market. Then we would probably have to close our Michigan plant.

Union representative:

Let me get back to my people and study this issue some more.

Know Your Best Alternative to a Negotiated Agreement (BATNA). The reason people negotiate is to produce something better than the results obtainable without negotiating. When you are aware of your best alternative to a negotiated agreement, it sets a floor to the agreement you need to accept. Your BATNA thus becomes the standard that can protect you both from accepting terms that are too unfavorable and from walking away from terms that would be beneficial for you to accept.[16]

In the situation above, the company representative may know ahead of time that if machinists are to be paid more than $18.50 per hour, it would be more cost effective for the company to subcontract out a good portion of its manufacturing. Thus, he or she can negotiate calmly and accept only an option that the company can afford. The union representative may not have a BATNA in this situation. One conceivable option is to ask the union members to vote on a strike. However, this could lead quickly to the subcontracting option on the part of the company.

Overcome the Fixed-Pie Assumption. An underlying reason that negotiation and bargaining are necessary is that resources are fixed—the parties involved assume that what each one grants to another side represents a loss to him or her. To move negotiation away from this fixed-pie assumption, it is sometimes possible to choose an integrative trade-off. Here is an example: Two business partners were in dispute over who should get which office in their new headquarters. A third party helped resolve this dispute by asking each partner what features of an office were the most important. It worked out that one partner valued status while the other wanted ample space. The solution chosen was to give one partner the corner office (high status) and to give the other partner the central office, which was 50 square feet larger than the corner office.

Allow Room for Face Saving. People prefer to avoid looking weak, foolish, or incapable during negotiation or when the process is completed. If you do not give your opponent an opportunity to save face, you most probably will have created a long-term enemy. The president of a small company was committed to the idea of relocating the office in a setting overlooking a body of water within the same city. Steve, the office manager, was given the tough assignment of locating a suitable property. One such piece of property was found that overlooked a scenic canal. After weeks of negotiation, Alice, the person negotiating the deal for the seller, would only agree to a price 30 percent above what the president wanted to pay originally. The president then reluctantly agreed to the deal. During the formal closing on the property, Alice made this face-saving statement in the presence of Steve and the president: "Steve must have been psychic in agreeing to the minimum price at which we could afford to let this property go. Only this morning another party made a tentative offer at $38,000 over what you are paying."

Competitive Approaches to Negotiation

The emphasis in the approaches described in this section is win lose or to try to maximize gain for one's side even it involves some trickery, deceit, and manipulation. A collaborative approach is strongly recommended wherever possible, but a discussion of negotiation tactics and strategies would be incomplete without a description of competitive approaches. Besides, some of these competitive approaches are not particularly devious.

Establish an Appeal to Legitimacy. People tend to respect the authority of written guidelines. For example, prices printed in a catalog appear more authoritative than an oral price quote, and a letter from a top executive stating the company's official position carries weight in negotiations. The advice here is "Win the advantage by carrying some kind of written support for your position. Conversely, don't believe everything you read."[18]

Frame the Outcome of Negotiations in Positive Terms. A series of laboratory experiments suggest that your mental set about conflict can influence your success in negotiating a favorable outcome. People who frame the outcomes of negotiation in terms of gains or profits are more willing to grant concessions to obtain the sure outcome available in a negotiated settlement. In contrast, negotiators who frame the outcome in terms of losses or costs are more likely to take the risky action of holding out and possibly losing all in an attempt to force further concession from their adversary.

A closely related finding is that if individuals view potential outcomes in terms of what they have to lose, both parties become risk seekers, an impasse develops, and arbitration (third-party–imposed solution) invoked. Conversely, if the parties evaluate potential outcomes in terms of gains, they become risk averse and are more likely to reach a negotiated settlement.[19]

The implication of the above findings is that all things being equal, you are likely to be more successful in negotiating when you attempt to achieve gains rather than prevent losses. This strategy is akin to raising your level of expectation or having a positive mental attitude when you enter into negotiations.

Raise Your Level of Expectation.   People who set higher targets for themselves in negotiation and stick firmly to them will do better than those people willing to settle for less. In an experiment testing this proposition, a barricade was built between bargainers so that neither could communicate with the other. Demands, offers, and counteroffers were passed under the table. Instructions to both sides were identical except for one fact: One side was told that he or she was to achieve a $7.50 settlement; the other, a $2.50 settlement. From an arithmetical standpoint, both sides had an equal chance to get $5. In test after test, subjects who expected $7.50 received about $7.50, while those told to expect $2.50 got close to $2.50.[20]

Make Small Concessions Gradually.   Experimentation suggests that making steady concessions leads to more mutually satisfactory agreements in most situations. Concession granting is referred to as the soft approach to bargaining. The hard approach to bargaining is to make your total concession early in the negotiation and to grant no further concession. ("Okay, you can have three of my people for your project. That's my final concession to you.") Another extreme approach (which is really neither hard nor soft) is to make no concession until the very last moment and then surrender all your concession amount. ("Okay, I've decided to lend you three of my people for your project.")

Negotiating consultant Karrass recommends that if you are a buyer (leading from strength), start low and give in very slowly over a long period of time. If you are a seller (leading from weakness), just turn it around. Start higher and give in slowly over a long period of time. Buyer or seller, the principle remains the same—grant small concessions over the length of the negotiating session.[21]

Use Deadlines.   Many deadlines imposed on us are fictitious. You can still obtain the same deal after the deadline is passed. One example came in my mail. It stated, "A free $500 camera is waiting for you just for using our film processing service. But you must act within five days." I called 20 days after the deadline and was informed that the free $500 camera was still waiting for me. (The only hooker was that I had to purchase 200 rolls of film and processing in advance!) Despite these fictitious deadlines, many deadlines do force people into action. Among them are file your income tax by April 15 or begin work by 8:30 in the morning. Here are several examples of deadlines that will usually move the negotiation in your favor:

Will I be receiving that promotion to senior engineer by December 31? If not, I will feel impelled to act on this job offer from another firm. It has become a matter of pride.

If we don't have your order in by February 1, you will not receive your supplies for 45 days after ordering.

My boss has to approve this deal, and she'll be leaving for the west coast tomorrow.

Be Patient.   A patient negotiator is often a successful negotiator. If negotiations proceed at a deliberate pace, both sides learn more about the real issues involved. Another value of patience is that it enables the negotiator to probe more carefully before taking a stand. Howard Raiffa reports on a negotiation experiment in which Israeli subjects played against Americans. It was found that the Israelis fared better because they were less impatient to arrive at negotiated settlements. Many Americans become anxious with long pauses in the give-and-take of negotiations. Instead, they prefer to say something or do something to move negotiations forward.[22]

Defer to a Higher Authority.   According to John L. Graham and Roy A. Herberger, Jr., overseas executives use the concept of limited authority quite effectively when negotiating with North Americans. In reality the foreign executive is saying, "To get me to compromise you not only have to convince me; you've got to convince my boss, who is 5,000 miles away." This may force the other side to come up with very persuasive arguments (and very good deals). Graham and Herberger believe that Americans, on the other hand, are generally uncomfortable about checking with the home office in the midst of negotiations.[23]

A consumer-oriented version of deferring to a higher authority is called *the big bad bear in the back room.* Often relied on by automobile sales people, it works in this manner. The sales person claims he or she wants to offer you a certain low price, but "The sales manager will never go for it." You and the salesperson then try to arrive at a price that the "big bad bear" will accept.[24]

Use Impasse Breakers.   When negotiations are at an impasse, something needs to be done to get things moving. Sometimes a minor change in the nature of the deal can break an impasse. Suppose, as a manager, you are given additional responsibility but not enough new help to accomplish the job properly. An impasse breaker might be to request that you be temporarily relieved of some minor responsibility that your department is now performing. Among the many other possible impasse breakers are changing a negotiating team leader, calling in a mediator, making changes in specifications or terms, or setting up a joint study committee.[25]

Make a Last and Final Offer. In many circumstances offering the other side your final offer, or "doorknob price," will break a deadlock. A key part of the tactic is to exit from negotiations shortly after making your offer. A partner in a consulting firm used this technique to advantage in negotiating a completion date for a study asked for by a potential client. The potential client wanted a study done in one month of now to reach new customers for its services. The consultant wanted the business but did not have the resources to do the study immediately. After some thought the consultant said, "We would like very much to conduct this study for you. However, the fastest turnaround we can offer is 60 days. If another firm can do a satisfactory job in less than 60 days, have them do it. You know where to reach me." The potential client called the consultant two days later to sign a contract for the study to be completed within 60 days.

Play Hard to Get. Another common sense negotiating strategy is for you to make it appear that you will not readily grant concessions to the other side or buy their proposition. The job applicant who is overly anxious to land employment may meet with less success than the applicant who remains mildly aloof. "I might be interested under the right circumstances," is a more effective tactic than, "Please let me have the job. I'll begin as soon as you want."

Use Final-Offer Arbitration. Under conventional arbitration, a third party is asked to resolve the issues in dispute so that the final outcome balances the organizational and political needs of each party. Three problems with this conventional approach have been identified. First, the possibility that the arbitrator will split the difference compels the negotiators to make extreme demands (maintain polar positions) to offset the arbitrator's expected compromise. Second, since the arbitrator makes the final decision, negotiators feel less responsibility for resolving the dispute and consequently have less incentive to bargain. (This is referred to as the *narcotic effect*.) Third, negotiators may feel uncommitted to the outcome since the final outcome was not their decision.

Under final-offer arbitration, if negotiators do not reach an agreement among themselves, each must submit a final offer to the arbitrator. Instead of compromising, the arbitrator must choose a final offer from one of the parties. Resolutions tend to occur more frequently under final-offer arbitration, partly because each side fears that the other side's final offer would be the one accepted by the arbitrator.

Final-offer arbitration can also be used outside of labor-management negotiations. So long as the two parties agree to have a third party accept one of their final offers, the process can be used. Suppose two department heads are negotiating over who will get how much office space in an upcoming move to a new location. Under normal human self-interest, both sides will make exaggerated claims about their needs for new space. If final-offer arbitration is agreed to, or imposed, both sides may behave differently. Rather than risk a reasonable demand of the other side being selected as the best final offer by an arbitrator, both sides may bargain in a more collaborative mode.

Avoid Overconfidence in the Reasonableness of Your Position.   Experiments conducted by Margaret A. Neale and Max H. Bazerman demonstrated that realistically confident negotiators grant more concessions and win more often than overconfident negotiators. Overconfidence shows itself in two areas. In simple two-party negotiations, negotiators consistently predicted the other side to be confident more than objective analysis would suggest. In final-offer arbitration, negotiators overestimated the probability that their final offer would be accepted.[26] As described by the researchers:

> While obviously only half of all final offers can be accepted in final-offer arbitration, the people in our experiments estimated, on the average, a 65 to 68 percent probability that their offer would win out. This overconfidence reduces the incentive to compromise, while a less optimistic assessment makes a negotiator more uncertain and thus more likely to compromise further.[27]

Be Sensitive to International Bargaining Styles.   Sensitivity to cultural differences in negotiating styles is important in today's global economy. Oriental negotiators prefer to spend much more time in negotiation than do their American counterparts, as described above. Latin-American businesspeople also prefer to prolong negotiations: They typically insist on lengthy socializing before getting to serious business.

Nierenberg has observed several other differences in bargaining styles. American executives typically expect to grant small concessions and receive concessions in return. French business-people thrive on deadline negotiations and wait until the last minute to commit themselves. And Far Eastern executives prefer to stall graciously until they are offered what they want.[28]

Know When to Quit.   Competitive negotiations can sometimes get out of hand—conflict escalates while both sides feel committed to justify their past positions and obtain their demands. Recognizing this tendency can help the negotiator avoid bargaining beyond the point of diminishing returns. Legal fees alone can eliminate the cost effectiveness of some types of negotiating, such as paying $30,000 in legal fees to win a $25,000 claim against another party. Prolonged negotiations can also be intellectually and emotionally draining, thus diverting attention away from more constructive tasks. A counterargument here is that litigation to protect a principle sometimes justifies economic loss, even in the event of victory. An example is litigation to protect a trademark.

Negotiating Tactics: Pro and Con

Improving negotiating skills has surged in acceptance as a management development activity in recent years. Nevertheless, the approaches described in this chapter arouse some controversy.

Pro.   An impressive argument in favor of effective negotiating skills is that they lead to increased cooperation from colleagues, subordinates, superiors, and businesspeople from outside the organization. In addition, they help one achieve a reputation as a results-oriented, fair-minded problem solver. It has also been argued that effective negotiating skills are a requirement for executive success.[29]

Despite the importance of negotiating in work and personal life, it is often carried out ineffectively. Many negotiating practices today "lead to long and tedious dickering which brings severe hardship to many who should not be involved and many who cannot bear such a hardship."[30] If more people followed the guidelines presented in this chapter, more agreements between people would be settled in an equitable and amiable fashion.

Con.   Many of the tactics described are manipulative in nature. Some of the tactics that appear valid need to be researched more carefully. In many instances, they are based on small support from simulated negotiating sessions with college students. A person may not need to pay heed to these strategies if he or she has good common sense and a well-developed sense of ethics. Finally, if people strived for openness and honesty with each other, there would be very little need for negotiating tactics.

Guidelines for Action and Skill Development

A starting point in developing your negotiating skills is to recognize when a situation calls for negotiation. According to the research of Richard E. Walton, bargaining to reach a decision occurs when the joint pool of resources available to the parties is fixed, yet so far their relative shares have not been determined.[31] The situation described previously of two departments heads each trying to capture a larger share of the new office space fits this category. Whatever one side gains is at the expense of the other—the classic case of the zero-sum game. On the other hand, if the potential gain to both parties is variable, joint problem solving can take place. If the two department heads could help each other decide on how much space each really needed, without having to worry about dividing up a fixed amount of resources, they could engage in joint problem solving.

After learning to identify which situations call for negotiation, the next step in skill development would be to practice negotiating in nonthreatening and relatively inconsequential situations. For instance, one might try out one or two negotiating tactics when buying a piece of furniture or home appliance. Once confidence is developed in these lesser situations, one might try negotiating for bigger stakes—such as buying an automobile or arriving at a starting salary on a new job. Again, it is important to incorporate several of the strategies described into one's negotiating.

Another recommended method for improving one's negotiating skills is to use role playing. Two people can first study the description of one of the many strategies described here. Next, they can develop a scenario approximately a bargaining situation they have faced on the job. The tactic of using negotiation jujitsu, described earlier in this chapter, lends itself well to role playing.

DISCUSSION QUESTIONS AND ACTIVITIES

1. Many experienced negotiators contend that they would prefer to negotiate against another experienced—rather than an inexperienced—negotiator. Why might this be true?

2. How effective a negotiator is the current president of the United States or prime minister of Canada? Explain.

3. Based on your own observations, what are two frequent errors made by people when negotiating for themselves?

4. It is common practice these days for movie stars, big name singers, and professional athletes to hire agents to negotiate contracts for them. What do you see as the advantages and disadvantages of this practice?

5. To what extent can you negotiate the sale price of home appliances at large department stores?

6. To what extent can you negotiate with the Internal Revenue Service about the amount of taxes they think you owe them?

7. Identify a professional negotiator, such as a labor relations specialist or an attorney involved in frequent negotiations, in your community. Interview that person to discover the several negotiating tactics he or she thinks are the most effective. Report your results back to the class.

NOTES

1. Robert W. Johnson, "Negotiation Strategies: Different Strokes for Different Folks," *Personnel,* May 1981, pp. 36–44.
2. Roger Fisher and William Ury, *Getting to Yes* (New York: Penguin Books, 1981).
3. Ibid., p. 11.
4. Ibid., p. 26.
5. "Negotiating: A Master Shows How to Head Off Argument at the Impasse," *Success,* October 1982, p. 53.
6. Gary G. Whitney, "Before You Negotiate: Get Your Act Together," *Personnel,* July–August 1982, p. 14.
7. James F. Rand, "Negotiating: Master the Possibilities," *Personnel Journal,* June 1987, p. 93.
8. Philip I. Morgan, "Resolving Conflict through 'Win-Win' Negotiating," *Management Solutions,* August 1987, p. 9.
9. "Negotiating: A Master Shows How to Head Off Argument at the Impasse," p. 53.
10. Howard Raiffa, *The Art and Science of Negotiation* (Cambridge, Mass.: Harvard University Press, 1983).
11. Joseph F. Byrnes, "Negotiating: Master the Ethics," *Personnel Journal,* June 1987, p. 99.
12. Fred E. Jandt, with Paul Gillette, *Win-Win Negotiations: Turning Conflict into Agreement* (New York: John Wiley, 1985).
13. James A. Wall, Jr., "Operantly Conditioning a Negotiator's Concession-Making," *Journal of Experimental Social Psychology,* 1977, pp. 431–440.
14. Raiffa, *The Art and Science of Negotiation,* p. 306.
15. Fisher and Ury, *Getting to Yes,* p. 114.
16. Ibid., p. 104.
17. Max H. Bazerman, "Why Negotiations Go Wrong," *Psychology Today,* June 1986, p. 54.
18. Minda Zetlin, "The Art of Negotiating," *Success!,* June, 1986, pp. 37–38.
19. Bazerman, "Why Negotiations Go Wrong," p. 58; Margaret A. Neale and Max H. Bazerman, "The Effects of Framing and Negotiator Overconfidence on Bargaining Behaviors and Outcomes," *Academy of Management Journal,* March 1985, p. 45.
20. Chester L. Karrass, *Give & Take: The Complete Guide to Negotiating Strategies and Tactics* (New York: Thomas Y. Crowell, 1974), p. 2.
21. Ibid., p. 45.
22. Raiffa, *The Art and Science of Negotiation,* p. 306.
23. John L. Graham and Roy A. Herberger, Jr., "Negotiators Abroad—Don't Shoot from the Hip," *Harvard Business Review,* July–August 1983, pp. 160–168.
24. Zetlin, "The Art of Negotiating," p. 37.
25. Karrass, *Give & Take,* p. 25.
26. Neale and Bazerman, "The Effects of Framing," p. 34.
27. Bazerman, "Why Negotiations Go Wrong," p. 58.
28. Quoted in Zetlin, "The Art of Negotiating," p. 39.

29. "The Art of Negotiating," Xerox Learning Systems program, undated, page 2.
30. Frank L. Acuff and Maurice Villere, "Games Negotiators Play," *Business Horizons,* February 1976, p. 70.
31. Research reported in Bernard M. Bass, *Organizational Decision Making* (Homewood, Ill.: Richard D. Irwin, 1983), p. 109.

SOME ADDITIONAL REFERENCES

Hoffman, Harold M., and James Blakey. "You *Can* Negotiate with Venture Captitalists." *Harvard Business Review,* March–April 1987, pp. 16–18, 22–24.

McAllister, Hunter A., and Norman J. Bregman. "Plea Bargaining by Prosecutors and Defense Attorneys: A Decision Theory Approach." *Journal of Applied Psychology,* November 1986, pp. 686–90.

McNulty, Maureen. "How to Negotiate Your Salary." *Business Week's Careers,* April 1986, pp. 113–14.

Nunan, James C., and Thomas J. Hutton, "How to Negotiate an Executive Job Offer." *Personnel Journal,* November 1987, pp. 52–56.

Brooks, Earl, and George S. Odiorne. *Managing by Negotiations.* New York: Van Nostrand Reinhold, 1984.

Wall, James A., Jr. *Negotiation: Theory and Practice.* Glenview, Ill.: Scott, Foresman, 1985.

Appendix to Chapter Five

WHAT IS YOUR NEGOTIATION STYLE?

To find out, answer these questions:

1. A friend offers you used equipment for $75. New, it would cost $150. Then he gets a bid for $100. You:
   a. Match the offer—you still save $50.
   b. Tell him that as a friend you expect him to keep his promise.
   c. Find other sources from whom to buy your used equipment.

2. You have recently started your own consulting firm. A Fortune 500 company wants to hire you for a project. They won't pay more than $1,500. You would normally charge $2,000. You say:
   a. "As an introductory offer, I'll give you a 25 percent discount for the project."
   b. "I'm sorry: $2,000 is my firm price."
   c. "Let's get started and talk price later."

3. Your landlord paints the lobby an ugly purple. Then he sends you a $50 bill for improvement fees. You:
   a. Pay it, but make him promise to consult you before painting next time.
   b. Refuse to pay it.
   c. Keep the bill and find out what other tenants are doing.

4. You own a small shoelace company. Most of your sales are made to a shoe company that has resisted price increases. With rising costs, now you barely break even on this business. You:
   a. Tell the shoe company owner his business is no longer profitable and ask how much more he can afford to pay.
   b. Send him a price list with your new increased prices.
   c. Try to find other customers before raising the issue.

5. You have been planning a trip to the Caribbean for a year. A week before your departure, an "emergency" comes up and your boss asks you to change your vacation dates. You will lose money if you cancel, and you're sure he can handle the crisis. The *first* thing you say:
   a. "If I reschedule, will I be compensated for cancellation fees?"
   b. "I expect a refund for losses and a bonus toward my next vacation."
   c. Nothing. First ask around to find out if you're *really* indispensable.

6. You are negotiating the price of a used car. You can spend $3,000 but believe the car is worth $2,000. The seller has already dropped the price from $4,000 to $2,500, but he refuses to go any further. You:
   a. Offer to split the difference at $2,250 if he will throw in a set of new snow tires.
   b. Tell him it's $2,000 or nothing.
   c. Tell him you'll shop around first.

7. Your new company has grown, and you and your partner must hire your first employee. After several interviews, you each select a candidate. You feel yours is far superior. You say:
   a. "I'll agree to your candidate if I can make the choice next time."
   b. "If you'll agree to my candidate, I'll let you choose next time."
   c. "Let's see a few more people; maybe we can find someone we *both* like."

Answers

What the quiz means: *a* answers show you are cooperative, eager to close the deal; *b* answers show you are competitive. You try for the most you can get but risk losing the deal; *c* answers show you are noncommittal. You favor a strategy called *forbearance*—waiting it out, while also seeking alternatives.

Four or more *a* answers: You're settling for less than you could get. Be a little bolder. Sometimes holding your ground brings big dividends. Remember: You can usually back down later.

Four or more *b* answers: You're a good, tough negotiator, but at times you'll do better by toning it down. Sometimes preserving a relationship is worth more than the extra dollar.

Four or more *c* answers: You have a lot of patience, but you may be missing opportunities. Forbearance can be a very useful strategy in some situations and disastrous in others.

A good mix of answers means you're on the right track. You know there are times to give in, times to stand firm, and times when patience turns situations to your advantage. A recent study showed that dealing with conflicts in a *variety* of ways is a strategy top executives favor.

SOURCE: Minda Zetlin, "The Art of Negotiating," *Success!,* June 1986, p. 38.

Chapter Six

Nonverbal Messages
in Organizations

The stockbroker described in the following case history wanted to increase his chances of being accepted by clients and prospective clients. Part of his self-improvement program was to enhance the image he projected—an important aspect of nonverbal communication.

When a client enters James Hansberger's office, the first item the person sees is a well-burnished reproduction of an ornate Queen Anne desk with matching armchairs. No spare modern lines for this stockbroker—Hansberger prefers to define himself against a backdrop of elegant detail from the past.

This may not be the image one customarily associates with a broker. But then Hansberger is no ordinary broker. In his early forties, the senior vice president at Shearson Lehman Hutton in Atlanta is at the pinnacle of the firm. For seven consecutive years he has earned more than $1 million in commission income—plus the right to a style associated with the upper echelon.

Everything about Hansberger suggests certainty about who he is and what he does. His manners are impeccable, his bearing assured, his dress crisp and conservative; confidence, poise, and sophistication are qualities he clearly embodies. The method behind his meticulous image is simple: "Look and act like your clients," says Hansberger. "Create the same image they do."

Indeed, Hansberger seems cut from the same cloth as his clients, and that is no accident. Those whose investments he handles are the executive elite—CEOs and law firm partners with custom-made suits, hand-carved desks, and private jets. Hansberger understands their needs. "These people identify with quality. They don't want to entrust portfolios worth hundreds of thousands, even millions, of dollars to someone who is not of their class."

Although the native Georgian is certainly of that class now, twelve years ago he was just another broker with a group of modest portfolios. He stood out mainly because of his appearance: He was thirty pounds overweight. But what kept him out of the spotlight was a lack of in-depth knowledge necessary to do business with the real titans of the corporate community. Yet this group was Hansberger's target. "I wanted to be their financial advisor." So Hansberger embarked on a self-improvement plan. To tone up, he took up jogging before work and tennis every week, and he even developed a year-round tan. Once he felt confident about his appearance, Hansberger turned his attention to the financial concerns of the executives he wished to advise. He steeped himself in tax law, studied various investment strategies, and pored over any and all legislation that could possibly affect high-powered business people. Within a year, Hansberger had transformed himself from a broker into a full-fledged financial consultant.

Only then did he feel equipped to circulate with those in the top tier. He joined two prominent business clubs in Atlanta, where he could meet prospective clients. "I knew I had built an image around knowledge, so I spoke and acted with confidence."

Soon, Hansberger had acquired a roster of powerful and prestigious investors, and it wasn't long before their friends began calling him. By the early 1980s, Hansberger had hit the $1 million-a-year mark.

Today Hansberger has such stature in the industry that his good name enhances his clients' standing as much as their name enhances his. "Image works two ways," he says. "You can help solidify your image by associating with the right people, and they can solidify theirs by associating with you. It's a symbiotic relationship."[1]

MODES OF TRANSMITTING NONVERBAL MESSAGES

The financial consultant described above emphasized image and appearance as a ways of communicating messages about himself. Nonverbal, or silent, messages can also be sent in many other ways. Summarized here are the major nonverbal modes of communication used in job settings. In addition, we present some of the research evidence that supports their validity. Research evidence is especially important when discussing nonverbal communication because of the many outlandish claims made for the meaning of minor, often random, body movements and gestures. Body language does not always mean what someone says it does. Misreading nonverbal acts can be just as dangerous as miscommunicating verbally.

Head, Face, and Eye Behavior.   According to anthropologist David Givens, a head tilted forward or sideways indicates receptiveness. A face turned sideways even slightly suggests distance or rejection. A head tilted back so the person can "look down his or her nose" at you is a clear indicator of disdain. Rapid blinking or constriction of the pupils are signals of discomfort or disagreement. A stare of longer than two seconds is often used as a challenge or a reprimand.[2]

When used in combination, the head, face, and eyes provide the clearest indication of attitudes toward other people.[3] Lowering your head and peering over your glasses is the nonverbal equivalent of the idiom, *You're putting me on.* As is well known, maintaining eye contact with another person improves communication with that person. In order to maintain eye contact, it is usually necessary to correspondingly move your head and face. Moving your head, face, and eyes away from another person is often interpreted as defensiveness or a lack of self-confidence. Would you buy a used car from somebody who didn't look at you directly?

The face is often used as a primary source of information about how we feel. We look for facial cues when we want to read another person's expression. You can often judge an employee's morale just by looking at his or her face. The popular phrase *sourpuss* attests to this observation. Happiness, apprehension, anger, resentment, sadness, contempt, enthusiasm, and embarrassment are but a few of the emotions that can be expressed through the face. Two communications experts offer this sage advice about facial messages in a work setting:

> The ability to read these emotional cues . . . is extremely important, because it is through these cues that you can get . . . the feedback you are seeking from others. A subordinate, for example, might not be able to put in words exactly what it was that he or she did not understand in your instructions, but perhaps an expression of bewilderment might give you a clue that there was some misunderstanding. Being able to read this nonverbal message would then allow you to adapt your verbal message, that is, to rephrase the instructions so that they are understandable.[4]

Some research evidence has shown that eye contact is an important supplement to verbal messages. Messages accompanied by eye contact are more favorably interpreted by observers than are messages sent without eye contact.[5] An implication drawn from this study is that if a manager maintains eye contact with subordinates, communication with them will often be significantly improved. At a minimum do not deliver an important message if you do not have people's visual attention.

Posture.   "Walk into your prospect's office straight and tall. Show him that you represent the finest line of ball bearings in the world," shouted the sales manager of the past. Observations made today by specialists in nonverbal communication support the sales manager's exhortation. Posture does communicate a message. Leaning toward another individual suggests that you are favorably disposed toward his or her messages; leaning backwards communicates the opposite. Openness of the arms or legs serves as an indicator of liking or caring. In general, people establish closed postures (arms folded and legs crossed) when speaking to people they dislike. Standing up straight (assuming a person is physically capable of such behavior) generally reflects high self-confidence. Stooping and slouching could mean a poor self-image.

A shrug of the shoulders can be a clear indicator of receptiveness or submission to the ideas of another person. Squaring of the shoulders indicates a rigid, authoritarian attitude meaning that the person engaging in such behavior wants to be in control.[6]

Body Position and Interpersonal Distance.   The placement of one's body relative to someone else's body is another meaningful way of sending a message. Leaning toward someone shows attention; leaning back or angling the body or face from a person is a distancing signal.[7] One study showed that people located in relatively close proximity are seen as warmer, friendlier, and more understanding than people located farther away. The implication is that if you want to convey positive attitudes to another person, get physically close to that person. As common sense suggests, putting your arm around somebody else in a job setting is interpreted as a friendly act.

Cultural differences must be kept in mind in interpreting nonverbal cues. For example, a French male is likely to stand closer to you than a British male even if they have equally positive attitudes toward you. Practical guidelines for judging how close to stand to another person (in the North American or similar culture) are shown in Figure 6–1 and described as follows:

Intimate distance is from actual physical contact to about 18 inches. Physical intimacy is usually not called for in business, but there are exceptions. For one, confidential information might be whispered within the intimate distance zone.

Personal distance is the distance from about one and one half to four feet. The interaction that takes place in this zone includes friendly discussions and conversation. An exception is a heated argument between two people, such as a baseball coach getting close to an umpire and shouting in his face.

FIGURE 6–1   Four Circles of Intimacy

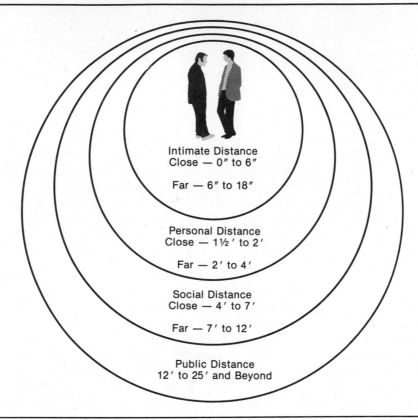

Intimate Distance
Close — 0″ to 6″

Far — 6″ to 18″

Personal Distance
Close — 1½′ to 2′

Far — 2′ to 4′

Social Distance
Close — 4′ to 7′

Far — 7′ to 12′

Public Distance
12′ to 25′ and Beyond

SOURCE: Barry L. Reece and Rhonda Brandt, *Effective Human Relations in Organizations,* Third Edition, p. 36. Copyright © 1987 by Houghton Mifflin Company. Used with permission.

Social-consultative distance is about four to eight feet and is usually reserved for businesslike, impersonal interaction. We usually maintain this amount of distance between ourselves and strangers, such as retail store clerks and cab drivers.

Public distance is from 12 feet to the outer limit of being heard. This zone is typically used in speaking to an audience at a large meeting or in a classroom. An important exception is the insensitive individual who sends ordinary messages by shouting across a room. The unstated message communicated in such an interaction is that the receiver of the message is not worth the effort of walking across the room.[8]

Kenneth Blanchard observes that if an employee feels at ease with your style of management, he or she will face you in a casual, relaxed manner. If the employee turns away, you are receiving the cold shoulder. Arms folded across the chest could mean that the employee is probably feeling defensive.[9]

Gestures.   Gestures refer to movements of the body, head, hand, or face that expresses meaning. Gestures made with the hand are universally recognized as conveying specific information to others. Positive attitudes are shown by frequent gesticulation (hand movements). At the other extreme, dislike or disinterest usually produces few gestures. An important exception here is that some people wave their hands furiously while in an argument. Some of their hand movements reflect anger. The type of gesture displayed also communicates a particular message. To quote one observer of body language:

> Random fidgeting, such as drumming the fingers or twiddling the thumbs, is a set of gestural activities which convey extremely negative attitudes. Similarly, aggressive gestures with clenched fists and menacing postures convey hostile feelings, while frequent use of relaxed, open-palm gestures toward the other person typically conveys positive attitudes.[10]

An attempt has been made to classify the many functions served by hand gestures. Some of these are familiar to anybody who has ever cut off another driver on a highway or watched an irate coach communicate displeasure to an umpire or referee. From time to time, obscene gestures present themselves in the workplace. For instance, a foreman asked his boss one day, "Can I fire an employee who 'gives me the finger'?" Gestures can be used as illustrators, regulators, affect displays, and emblems.[11]

Illustrators are gestures that are used to add emphasis or drama or to clarify a message. Examples of illustrators include pointing toward the floor while saying "Our profits are nosediving," and punching your fist into an open palm while saying "I know we can do better than this." A less dramatic example of an illustrator is to point toward a door or explain the nature of a spiral staircase by twirling your finger.

Regulators are gestures we use to regulate both conversation and human interaction. Raising your hand or finger when you want to talk at a meeting or in class is a regulator. Raising one hand with the fingers pointed upward and the palm outward is used to tell another person to stop talking (usually interpreted as a rude nonverbal message). Parts of the body other than the hand can also be used as regulators. You might raise your eyebrows or nod your head to send the message that it is your turn to speak.

Affect displays are gestures used to communicate emotion that we are experiencing. Such displays are generally used in conjunction with other modes of nonverbal behavior, especially facial expressions. Clenched fists to communicate tension illustrates an affect display. Intensified nail biting and cuticle nibbling are obvious examples of affect displays in response to tension or worry. Belly scratching in a relaxed manner is often a tipoff that an individual is feeling contented (or itchy). Scratching the back of one's head usually suggests that a person is perplexed. Hand-over-mouth gestures usually indicate shock, surprise, or remorse.

Emblems are basically hand signals, not too different from the manual communication that is used by many deaf people. They are nonverbal signals or cues that have a specific verbal equivalent. A popular emblem is the OK signal. The OK emblem, however, communicates more enthusiasm than a simple OK; it seems to mean very OK. An emblem in contemporary use is the hearty approval shown by an upward pointed thumb, combined with a clenching of the four other fingers—both done with the vigor and motion used in hammering a nail. It is similar to the spoken message, "Right on!" Conversely, a thumbs-down signal at a business conference indicates strong disapproval.

Traffic hand signals, manual signals used on the playing field (such as the time-out signal of placing the index fingers at right angles to each other), and certain obscene gestures are other examples of emblems.

Gestures are also useful in revealing dominant and submissive behavior according to the research of anthropologist David Givens and psychiatrist Albert Scheflen. Their findings pointed out that the gestures of the dominant person are usually directed outward, toward the other person. Examples include touching of partner; fingers splayed and pointed toward partner; palm-down gestures; and a steady, unwavering gaze. Submissive gestures are usually protective like shrugging one's shoulder, gazing downward, and touching oneself.[12]

Tone of Voice. We often attach more significance to the way something is said than to what is said. Voice tone is critical, but other aspects of the voice, such as volume, quality, and rate, are also part of the nonverbal message. As with all nonverbal cues, there is an ever-present danger of overinterpreting a single voice quality. A subordinate of yours might speak to you about the status of a project in a high-pitched voice, not out of fear but because of laryngitis. Anger, boredom, joy—three emotions frequently experienced on the job—can often be interpreted from voice quality. Two communication specialists summarize these nonverbal cues in this manner:

Anger is best perceived when the source speaks loudly, at a fast rate, in a high pitch, with irregular inflection and clipped enunciation. Boredom is indicated by moderate volume, pitch and rate, and a monotone inflection; joy by loud volume, high pitch, fast rate, upward inflection, and regular rhythm.[13]

Voice tone is also used to emphasize various elements of the verbal message. Through the use of voice tone, you are able to question, make exclamations, to give extra emphasis to one part of the message at the expense of another part. A clever example is presented in *Communication for Supervisors and Managers* of how emphasizing a particular word in a message through voice tone can lead to different interpretations of the same statement:

The *boss* is giving Sheila a promotion.
The *BOSS* is the one giving a promotion, not the president of the company, not the boss's supervisor, but the boss.
The boss is *giving* Sheila a promotion.
The boss is *GIVING* the promotion, implying that perhaps Sheila is not qualified.
The boss is giving *Sheila* a promotion.
The person getting the promotion is *SHEILA*, not Art, not Betty, not Ken, but Sheila.
The boss is giving Sheila a *promotion*.
Sheila is receiving a *PROMOTION*, not a raise, not a demotion, not "the sack."[14]

The general quality of a person's voice is often used to make inferences about a telephone caller. How a person sounds over the phone provides us with clues about the person's age, education, intelligence, masculinity-femininity, and self-confidence. One employment recruiter insists he can size up a person's physical attractiveness based on his or her telephone voice quality. In reality, the recruiter may be reacting to the degree of self-confidence communicated by the quality of the caller's voice. People who perceive themselves to be attractive often communicate in more decisive terms.

A person's voice tone can also be used to help detect how well you are dealing with him or her. Blanchard notes that when the person speaks in a steady, calm tone of voice, you know that you are properly handling that person. Quick, staccato speech indicates the person is excited. If the person speaks tentatively, it may mean the person finds you intimidating.[15]

Environmental Cues.   The environment in which you send a message can influence the receiving of that message. Important environmental cues include room color, temperature, lighting, and furniture arrangement. The physical aspects of an office communicate a message about a person's official status. Indicators of high status include a large office, one located higher in the building, the presence of several windows, and a corner location.

Office furniture, in combination with its neatness and orderliness, can project information about the office occupant. A person who sits behind an uncluttered large desk appears more powerful than a person who sits behind, a small, cluttered desk. This power illusion may hold even if the two people express the same message such as "What you say has merit."

Another aspect of the environment, the business dining location, is said to communicate clear messages. *Power dining* (breakfast, lunch, and dinner included) is a concern of many businesspeople who want to project a powerful image. Michael Korda suggests that the primary purpose of a business meal is to spend one and a half to two hours in the company of someone more important or powerful than yourself—or at least who could do you some good. Furthermore, the real reason to lunch with important people is that by doing so, it elevates your own importance. In certain businesses, being seen at lunch regularly in the right places and with the right people is enough to make you successful. Korda's suggestions for power lunching include:

1. Always eat at the best restaurant in town.
2. Be careful not to overdrink—lunch is for making deals or a good impression.
3. Tip generously.
4. Pick the restaurant yourself when making a lunch date in order to maintain control.
5. Always meet your lunch date at the restaurant, in order to get there first and make sure the arrangements are satisfactory.
6. Open a house account. It connotes power to simply rise from the table when lunch is over, without ever looking at the bill, and say to the maitre d', "Just add on my usual tip, please."[16]

Although several of Korda's suggestions must be interpreted as tongue-in-cheek, the message is valid: The circumstances under which you dine, and your behavior at lunch, does send a message about your amount of power.

Clothing, Dress, and Appearance. Few people would disagree that your external appearance plays a role in communicating messages to others. Job seekers implicitly recognize this aspect of nonverbal communication when they carefully groom themselves for a job interview.

People pay more respect and grant more privileges to people they perceive as being well dressed and attractive. Should you like to gather empirical evidence for this proposition, conduct this simple experiment. Try paying for merchandise by check at several stores under two different sets of conditions. In one condition, dress as businesslike and affluent as possible. In the other condition, dress in clothing that you use for such chores as yard work, car washing, or helping a friend move. Compare your degree of success under the two experimental conditions.

Dress and appearance are often said to influence how powerful and successful you appear to others. An extreme case in point is Bill Zanker, CEO and founder of The Learning Annex, an adult education company that offers brief courses. He attributes the start of his career climb to having purchased, and worn frequently, a $1,000 custom-made suit.[17] Establishing a power presence includes developing a firm handshake, having an attractive hair style, a healthy physical appearance, and fashionable clothing. The general principles are the same for men and women. One person's opinion of the proper power presence for men and women is shown in Figure 6–2. A cautionary note about this analysis of the "power look" is that it is highly subjective and may be irrelevant in many situations. If it were entirely true, most sales associates in posh retail stores would be powerful people.

Use of Time. A subtle mode of nonverbal communication in organizations is the use of time. Ambitious people attempting to climb the organizational ladder are seldomly late for appointments (in the American culture). If we are late for meetings, it *might* be interpreted that we are careless, uninvolved, or unambitious. However, a high-ranking official might be late for a meeting, and that same amount of lateness might be perceived as a symbol of importance or being busy. Looking at your watch is usually interpreted as a sign of boredom or restlessness.

Mirroring to Establish Rapport. A form of nonverbal communication used to achieve rapport with another is mirroring (or posturing). To mirror someone is to subtly imitate that individual. It is one small aspect of a new discipline called *neurolinguistic programming,* a method of communication that combines features of hypnosis, linguistics, and nonverbal behavior. *Neuro* refers to the way the human nervous system processes communication. *Linguistic* refers to the way that words, tone, timing, gestures, and inflection can be used in communication. *Programming* refers to using a systematic technique of communication with others.[18]

The most successful mirroring technique for establishing rapport is to imitate another's breathing pattern. If you adjust your own breathing rate to match someone else's, you will soon establish rapport with that

FIGURE 6–2   The Power Appearance for Businesspersons

Basic Power Presence Wardrobe for Men

Suit	Conservative; two-button with narrow lapels; slope shoulders; navy or grey; solid pinstripe or shadow plaid.
Tie	Contrasting color (maroon, rust, or brick-red); small patterns, bias stripe, club tie, or dots. Check current fashions for proper tie width.
Shoes	Basic lace-up, tassel loafers, or wingtips; black, brown, or oxblood; well-shined and in good condition.
Shirts	Solid white, 100 percent cotton; narrow pointed, round, or button down collars.
Accessories	Gold pen; solid-color, leather briefcase; gold watch of simple elegance.
Hair	Short haircut with no sideburns or beard.

Basic Power Presence Wardrobe for Women

Suit	Conservative; navy, grey, black, burgundy, or brown; pinstripe or solid.
Dress	Coat style with the look of the suit with white collar and cuffs; one-piece, solid color, accented with necklace or scarf.
Shoes	Plain pumps with medium-high heels in solid color (black, navy, brown, grey, or burgundy); well-shined and in good condition.
Accessories	Gold pen; solid-color, leather briefcase; gold watch of simple elegance.
Hair	Short and away from the face.

SOURCES: Camille Livingston, "How to Establish a Power Presence," *Business Week's Guide to Careers,* Fall/Winter 1983, p. 69; updated with information in John T. Molloy, "Executive Style," *Success!,* September 1986, p. 49.

individual. Mirroring is of relevance here because it is a method of establishing rapport through a nonverbal message. Eric H. Marcus describes one example of how mirroring can be used to solve a management problem:

> A manager is confronted by an angry shop steward concerning disciplinary action taken against a member. In the normal course of events, the breathing rate of both people will fluctuate in keeping with the progress of the discussion. In this case, rapid, shallow breathing, a subconscious signal of anger, will only elicit anger in response. But if the manager instead deliberately paces his own breathing rate to that of his antagonist, and gradually decreases his breathing rate, tension will be dispelled and rapport established.[19]

Marcus notes that it is also possible to engage in cross-over mirroring, or using a different part of your body to mirror another person. For instance, you could mirror a breathing rate by moving your hand at the same rate. Effective communicators, according to Marcus, engage in this kind of nonverbal behavior intuitively, and sometimes unconsciously.

The Case For and Against Making Systematic Use of Nonverbal Messages in Organizations

On the positive side, the fact that we send nonverbal messages along with verbal messages cannot be denied. As much as 60 percent of communication is nonverbal. If you learn to recognize the more reliable nonverbal messages (such as eye contact), you will become adept at sending and receiving messages. Support for this conclusion comes from studies conducted by John T. Molloy.

Based on research with 100 men and 62 women, he demonstrated that one can learn to read the nonverbal messages of people he or she deals with on a daily basis. Ninety percent of the study participants believed that the people around them gave off reliable nonverbal signals indicating mood. In some cases, the signals predicted specific actions. All participants agreed that the information they gained from studying nonverbal signals was useful in solving everyday problems. Molloy reports, for example, that "Two men and six women told us they asked for raises when they knew their boss was in a good mood, and all, except one woman, received them."[20]

A telling point about the validity of nonverbal communication is that if it were not meaningful, anybody could be an effective actor. You could act by simply reciting lines in a monotone; nonverbal behavior would not be required to communicate feelings and moods. Similarly, all managers would be equally effective at communicating enthusiasm to subordinates. They would merely have to recite words of enthusiasm such as "You're doing a fine job." How the message was sent would not be of significance.

On the negative side, a reliable dictionary of nonverbal communication does not yet exist and is not ready for preparation. Much of what we label *nonverbal communication* is basically frivolous and an overinterpretation of minor cues. What is true about nonverbal messages is so obvious that it does not merit formal study. Admittedly a sweaty palm, a yawning mouth, or chain smoking communicate messages, but you do not have to study nonverbal communication to interpret these signals. The nonverbal cues that are not so obvious, such as placing your hands at your side or lowering an eyebrow, are not consistent enough in their meaning to serve as guidelines for action.

Another problem with nonverbal messages is that, as a result of the attention nonverbal behavior has received, too many people are willing to overinterpret trivial nonverbal cues, such as random fidgeting or facial movements. One manager, for example, accused one of his subordinates of being disinterested in his proposal, based on the subordinate's body language. When confronted about the matter, the subordinate replied that he was interested in the topic, but a toothache was causing the pained expression.

Guidelines for Action and Skill Development

Dr. David Givens offers some suggestions for using body language to present a confident yet friendly image to superiors, clients, co-workers and subordinates.[21]

Eyes. Removing your glasses (but not your contact lenses) in the middle of a point increases the intensity of eye contact while "humanizing" your face.

Tie. A loosened tie and slightly exposed throat can portray openness and informality. However, if the dress code does not permit, such behavior would suggest rebelliousness.

Toes. Superiors tend to stand with their toes pointing outward, while subordinates point their toes inward. Position your toes according to the image you want to project.

Shoulders. Shrugged or rounded shoulders make you appear less threatening. Taking off a jacket with padded shoulders can make you appear less authoritative and warmer.

Hands. Placing your forearms on the table, palms up, will make your words seem more sincere. If you disagree with your boss, open your palms to send out the subliminal message that you defer to his or her authority even while disagreeing.

Body. Matching your body movements to those of the person you are communicating with (mirroring), without being too obvious, creates a sense of solidarity that conveys a feeling of agreement with the other person.

In addition, here are several suggestions to consider in order to develop your nonverbal communications skills:

Obtain feedback on your body language by asking others to comment on the gestures and facial expressions that you use in conversations. Have a videotape prepared of you conferring with another individual. After studying your body language, attempt to eliminate those mannerisms and gestures that you think detract from your effectiveness (such as moving your leg from side to side when being interviewed).

Learn to relax when communicating with others. Take a deep breath and consciously allow your body muscles to loosen. A relaxed person makes it easier for other people to relax. Thus, you are likely to elicit more useful information from other people when you are relaxed.

Use facial, hand, and body gestures to supplement your speech, but do not overdo it. A good starting point is to use hand gestures to express enthusiasm. You can increase the potency of enthusiastic comments by shaking the other person's hand, nodding approval, smiling, or patting that person on the shoulder.

Avoid using the same nonverbal gesture indiscriminately. To illustrate, if you want to use nodding to convey approval, do not nod with approval even when you dislike what another employee or subordinate is saying. Also, do not put everybody on the back. Nonverbal gestures used indiscriminately lose their communication effectiveness.[22]

DISCUSSION QUESTIONS AND ACTIVITIES

1. What methods of nonverbal communication are frequently used to communicate enthusiasm to other people in a job setting?
2. Give a couple of specific examples of nonverbal signals that are more appropriate for the executives suite than the shop floor (or similar setting).
3. Give a couple of specific examples of nonverbal signals that are more appropriate for the shop floor (or similar setting) than for the executive suite.
4. What is your opinion of the validity of the power presence suggestions presented in Figure 6–1. Explain your reasoning.
5. In recent years many managers and sales people in their late thirties and forties have undergone plastic surgery as a potential boost to their careers. What nonverbal messages do you think they hope to send with their new look?
6. What nonverbal signals might managers use to appear confident in front of their subordinates?
7. This week engage two different people in conversation and mirror their breathing rate. Observe what happens and report your observations to the class. (An interesting test of this technique would be to try it with someone who is angry with you.)

NOTES

1. Adapted with permission from "Portrait of a Broker at the Top of his Form," *Success!*, September 1986, p. 51.
2. Quoted in "Body Language Says It All," *Personal Report for the Executive,* July 1, 1987, pp. 3–4.
3. John E. Baird, Jr., and Gretchen K. Wieting, "Nonverbal Communication Can Be a Motivational Tool," *Personnel Journal,* September 1979, p. 609. Most of the basic categories of nonverbal behavior described in this chapter stem from the literature review included in this article.
4. Lyle Sussman and Paul D. Krivnos, *Communication for Supervisor and Managers* (Sherman Oaks, Calif.: Alfred Publishing, 1979), p. 75.
5. Kenneth Blanchard, "Translating Body Talk," *Success!,* April 1986, p. 10.
6. "Body Language Says It All (Part 1)," p. 4.
7. *Ibid.*
8. Miles H. Patterson, "Spatial Factors in Social Interaction," *Human Factors* 3, 1968, pp. 351–61.
9. Blanchard, "Translating Body Talk (Part 1)," p. 10.
10. Baird and Wieting, "Nonverbal Communication," p. 609; "Body Language Says It All (Part 1)," p. 4.
11. Sussman and Krivnos, *Communication,* pp. 78–79.
12. Research reported in Salvatore Didato, "Our Body Movements Reveal Whether We're Dominant or Submissive," *Rochester Democrat and Chronicle,* December 20, 1983, p. 1C.
13. Baird and Wieting, "Nonverbal Communication," pp. 610, 625.
14. Sussman and Krivnos, *Communication,* p. 83.
15. Blanchard, "Translating Body Talk," p. 10.
16. Michael Korda, "Power Lunch," *Success!,* May 1986, pp. 42–49.
17. "The Secret of the $1,000 Suit," *Success!,* September 1987, pp. 66–67.
18. Eric H. Marcus, "Neurolinguistic Programming," *Personnel Journal,* December 1983, p. 972.
19. Ibid., p. 975.
20. John T. Molloy, *Molloy's Live for Success* (New York: Bantam Books, 1982), p. 32.
21. "Body Language Says It All (Part 2)," *Personal Report for the Executive,* July 15, 1987, p. 3.
22. Andrew J. DuBrin, *Human Relations: A Job Oriented Approach,* 4th ed. (Englewood Cliffs, N. J.: Prentice Hall, 1988), pp. 262–63.

SOME ADDITIONAL REFERENCES

"The Body Language of Executive Success." *Research Institute Management Reports, Inc.,* undated.

Davis, Flora. *Inside Intuition.* New York: New American Library, 1986.

Ellyson, Steve L., and John F. Dovidio, eds. *Power, Dominance, and Nonverbal Behavior.* New York: Springer-Verlag, 1985.

Gibson, Jane Whitney, and Richard M. Hodgetts. *Organizational Communication: A Managerial Perspective.* Orlando, Florida: Academic Press, 1986, Chapter 5.

Mehrabian, Albert. *Silent Messages: Implicit Communication of Emotions and Attitudes.* 2nd ed. Belmont, Calif.: Wadsworth Publishing, 1981.

Stickler, Nicole A., and Robert Rosenthal. "Sex Differences in Nonverbal and Verbal Communication with Bosses, Peers, and Subordinates." *Journal of Applied Psychology,* February 1985, pp. 157–63.

Chapter Seven

Assertiveness Training

> The company described below was concerned that its managers were not assertive enough; they were either too aggressive or too passive in dealing with subordinates, co-workers, and superiors. The president thought that some managers also needed to become more assertive in dealing with customers in order for the company to receive more favorable contracts. The company therefore looked toward assertiveness training (AT) as a way of improving managerial effectiveness.

Sunny Chang, a management development specialist, welcomed the first group of participants to the management development program:

During our two days together, you'll be participating in an assertiveness training workshop designed to improve your leadership effectiveness. Assertiveness training, or AT as we often call it, has four important goals: We want you to know how you feel, to say what you want, to defend your rights, and to get what you want.

I suspect some of you are wondering why you have been invited to participate in assertiveness training. In other words, what organizational and individual problems are we attempting to solve? To be truthful, we are hoping to improve your leadership effectiveness by giving you the skills to deal more openly, honestly, and candidly with employees and customers. There is some evidence that assertive leaders are more productive. At the same time we want you to be aware of the rights of others and to recognize that you cannot always achieve your demands. I recognize that many of you are already assertive managers. For those of you who fit this category, this workshop will be a review of fundamentals.

AT can help any individual who experiences problems in the area of self-assertion. AT can also help people who are obnoxious when they try to get what they want. The human resources department has received several complaints this year from employees who contend that their managers try to bully and intimidate them. Before we begin with our first exercise, what questions might you have about AT or our workshop?

After 10 minutes of questions and answers, Sunny Chang proceeded with the first role-playing exercise designed to teach assertion skills:

To begin we must make the vital distinction among the three types of behavior—assertive, passive, and aggressive. *Assertive behavior* is when an individual makes a clear statement of what he or she wants, or how he or she feels in a given situation. All this is accomplished without being abusive, abrasive, or obnoxious. *Passive* or *nonassertive* people let things happen to them without letting their feelings be known. They are hesitant to take the initiative to express their point of view. *Aggressive* people are obnoxious and overbearing. They push for what they want with almost no regard for the feelings of others.

Another way of looking at it is that the nonassertive person is stepped on and the aggressive person steps on others. The assertive person deals with a problem in a mature and explicit manner.

In our first role-playing situation, Bob Katz, one of our workshop trainers, will play the role of the boss. A couple of you will play the role of the subordinate. After you have acted out the role for a few minutes, I'll present my critique of the interaction that I have observed. Here is the scenario: You are the manager of product development in your company. The new vice president of marketing has sent down a suggestion for a new product idea for your group to develop. The product is a lightweight, high-speed tricycle designed for senior citizens who want more excitement while bike riding. Your research has shown that those senior citizens who ride adult tricycles favor stability and ease of stopping but dislike speed.

Your boss, to be played by Bob, says to you: "I know your analysis reveals that senior citizens who purchase adult tricycles prefer slowness and safety. But you must realize that our new vice president of marketing believes strongly that a high-speed, adult trike will create a new demand. Couldn't you manipulate your data just a bit, so our department does not appear to be contradicting the vice president's first big suggestion? As you know, market research is not infallible."

Our first volunteer will respond to the statement from Bob. Go ahead Pam Farnsworth.

Pam:

You mean to say, Bob, that you will not accept my findings as they are. That I'm going to have to adjust my conclusions to fit the vice president's opinions?

Bob:

You're not getting the point, Pam. It would be kind of naive to throw cold water on the vice president's first big contribution to marketing. He has built his reputation on having a good feel for the market.

Pam:

I've worked long and hard on this survey. I would hate to junk it. But I do see some data here suggesting that about 15 percent of three-wheel bicycle users do regard speed as an attractive feature. Maybe the idea would catch on, once the fast three-wheelers were promoted and in the hands of dealers.

Sunny:

The two of you can stop now. I like your acting ability, Pam, but I'm somewhat concerned about your assertiveness. You did get your feelings across a little bit. Yet you were completely bulldozed by your boss. It could be an authority problem. Both Bob and the vice president of marketing have much more power than you do. However, it is important to assert oneself with authority figures. Let's get another person to play the role of the manager of product development. Thanks, Pam, for being our first volunteer. Okay, how about Rich Falk?

Rich:

I hear you saying, Bob, that I should reinterpret my data to fit the vice president's brainstorm. I understand how you feel, but I am unwilling to change my conclusions about the market potential for lightweight, fast three-wheelers.

Bob:

How nice to hear from Mr. Perfect, but even market research must sometimes face up to harsh political realities. How can you be so sure you're right?

Rich:

As my boss, you are certainly entitled to your opinion about the accuracy of my work. If you do not think my report is accurate, do not use it. However, I would not be able to change my interpretations of the data.

Sunny:

Good enough for now. Let's stop at this point for a brief analysis. Rich must have done his homework. He is being assertive without being totally inflexible. He has offered an alternative to his boss that could be interpreted as a workable compromise. He continues to assert his right to his professional opinions. Yet, he is suggesting to his boss the option of not using the report. Bob is probably not compelled to present all market research reports to top management. Nevertheless, Rich goes on record as having stood by his professional position. He was appropriately assertive.

To finish up this role play, could we please have a volunteer to act in an aggressive mode? Thank you, Nancy Rice.

Nancy:

Hold on, Bob. I resent your telling me to lie just to please the new marketing vice president. He's making a foolish mistake, and you're willing to sacrifice ethics to avoid confronting him.

Bob:

I think you're taking a harsh position.

Nancy:

> If we manufacture a lightweight, high-speed tricycle for senior citizens, we'll be the laughing stock of the industry. Whatever the company decides to do is okay with me. But I will resign from my job before I fake data.

Bob:

> If you want to resign, that's your decision.

Sunny:

> Thank you, Nancy, for a clever role-play. You have seen how Nancy placed herself in an untenable position by being aggressive and abusive. A disagreement over market-research ethics has escalated almost to the point of resignation from the company. Nancy Rice does not seem headed toward a constructive resolution of the problem.

FOURTEEN STEPS TO ASSERTIVENESS

The sample role-playing interchanges just presented have given you preliminary insight into the mechanics of an AT workshop. Assertiveness training usually also involves a series of steps that, if properly followed, lead you toward becoming an assertive individual. These steps are provided in some detail here to provide further insight into the process involved in changing your behavior from passive to assertive (or from aggressive to assertive).[1]

Step 1: Observe Your Own Behavior. Above all, are you asserting yourself adequately? Or are you being too pushy, obnoxious, or abrasive? Do you believe you get what you want when you want it, without stepping on the rights of others? A frequent work situation, that of being appointed to a committee, can be used to help sensitize you to the differences among passive (nonassertive), aggressive, and assertive behavior.

Opening her morning mail, supervisor Phyllis notices a memo from the human resource director, which says in part, "Congratulations, you have been appointed chairperson to organize the holiday party for needy children. You will find it both an honor and a privilege to serve your community in this manner."

Unfortunately, Phyllis is already heavily committed to community activities, including serving as a special representative to change zoning laws to encourage more industrialization of her town. She also thinks that perhaps her being female contributed to the decision to appoint her to organize the children's party. Phyllis can respond in three different ways:

1. *Passive behavior:* Phyllis does nothing and awaits further instructions. She is simmering with anger but grits her teeth and hopes that the assignment will not be as time-consuming as she now estimates.

2. *Aggressive behavior:* Phyllis grabs the phone, calls the human re-

sources director, and says: "Who do you think you are, assigning me to head up this committee? When I want to run a children's holiday party, I'll volunteer. Try asking a man next time. Maybe a man should be organizing children's activities for a change."

3. *Assertive behavior:* Phyllis calls the human resources director and says, "I appreciate your thinking of me as the head of the committee to organize the holiday party. However, I choose not to serve. It sounds like an interesting assignment, and I doubt that you will have trouble finding another chairperson. If this is an assignment that is rotated between males and females, please keep me on your list of potential committee heads."

The appendix to this chapter will provide you some clues to your present level of assertiveness.

Step 2: Keep a Record of Your Assertiveness.   Devote an entire week to this project, keeping a careful log or diary of situations in which assertive behavior might have been called for. Record each day when you behaved assertively, when you were too passive, or when you were too aggressive. Also, look carefully at situations you avoided altogether in order to avoid confrontation. Such a diary entry might be, "The head of the duplicating department told me I would have to wait two weeks to have my report duplicated. I needed it within 10 days. I guess I should have pursued the matter further rather than just grumbling to myself." It is crucial that you be candid and systematic in keeping this diary.

Step 3: Concentrate on a Specific Situation.   As instructed by two pioneers in AT, "Spend a few moments with your eyes closed, imagining how you handle a specific incident (being shortchanged at the supermarket, having a friend 'talk your ear off' on the telephone when you had too much to do, letting the boss make you 'feel like two cents' over a small mistake). Imagine vividly the actual details, including your specific feelings at the time and afterward."[2]

The manager of product development in the situation described earlier in this chapter might express feelings of this nature:

> Here I was facing my boss in a heavy ethical situation. Bob actually wanted me to fake data in order to agree with some mammoth blunder about to be initiated by the new marketing vice president. It seemed like I was caught between a rock and a hard place. If I agreed with my boss, I couldn't live with myself as a professional person. On the other hand, if I stood up to the boss, it would be like criticizing him and the president. It won't be easy to assert my rights in this situation.

Step 4: Review Your Responses.   Write down your behavior in Step 3 in terms of the key components of assertiveness (eye contact, body posture, gestures, facial expression, voice, and message content). Ask yourself questions such as these: Did my body language communicate how I really felt about the situation? Did I look disappointed about being asked to reinterpret my research data? Did I express my disagreement in a forceful, well-modulated conversational statement? Or did I murmur or fly off the handle? Was I able to look Jed straight in the eye? Did I state clearly that it would be upsetting to me to interpret my data in a manner contrary to what I really believed?

As you review your responses, it is helpful to note the things you did right. Also be aware of those statements that represent passive or aggressive behavior. An example of passive behavior is Pam's statement: "But I do see some data here suggesting that about 15 percent of adult three-wheel bicycle users do regard speed as an attractive feature. Maybe the idea would catch on. . . ."

Step 5: Observe an Effective Model.   People who attend AT workshops are encouraged to observe another person in action who appears to be assertive. It is as important to observe that person's style, as well as what that person says. Observing an assertive person in a staff meeting is one method of finding an appropriate model. Interviews shown on public television are useful in providing a variety of effective models. Some public figures are adept at behaving assertively when interviewed by a television reporter.

Style refers to body language rather than content. The timing of messages is also part of a person's style. A good person to model is one who times his or her assertions well. For instance, it is poor practice to behave assertively with your boss when the both of you are around others in the office. The boss may be forced to behave defensively in such a situation.

Step 6: Consider Alternative Responses.   Think of a situation you recently handled. How else could it have been handled? Larry was using a public photocopying machine at a library. Those waiting in line in back of him could readily see that he had a large stack of papers to be photocopied. Four different people said something to the effect, "Do you mind if I jump in for a second and use the machine? I only have two pages to copy." Larry did mind, but each time his response was "Well, okay, if you only have one or two pages."

An assertive response Larry might have tried would be, "It may not be what you would prefer, but you will have to wait 10 minutes until I've completed my copying. My time is very valuable today."

Step 7: Use Negative Inquiry.   This technique refers to the active encouragement of criticism in order to elicit helpful information or exhaust manipulative criticism. At the same time you prompt your critic to be more assertive and less manipulative. Negative inquiry involves asking a series of questions to get at the true nature of the criticism. Assume that a co-worker of yours expresses displeasure with your performance in a recent department meeting. You find his criticism uncomfortable and undeserved. Here is how negative inquiry might be used in this situation:

Co-worker:

That was a pretty bad show you put on in yesterday's meeting.

You:

What was bad about it?

Co-worker:

You took up too much of the meeting pushing your own ideas.

You:

Whose ideas was I supposed to push?

Co-worker:

I'm not sure. I just know that you pushed too many of your own ideas.

You:

What is it that you disliked about my pushing my own ideas?

Co-worker:

I guess I wanted you to tell the boss about some of the great ideas I had. I wanted some credit too.

You:

Now I see why you're upset with me.

Step 8: Visualize Yourself Handling the Situation. Close your eyes and visualize yourself behaving assertively in the situation reported in Step 6. You might act similarly to the model you have used for Step 5. It is important to be assertive but not to behave in a manner out of character with yourself. This step is much like a rehearsal or role-play, except that it all takes place by yourself. You might also practice saying the assertive statement: "I appreciate your asking me first, but I cannot let other people in to use this machine until I have finished. My time is very valuable today."

Some readers will think to themselves at this point, "AT is much like the old standby 'I should of said' when you have recently argued with somebody." The difference is that in AT, you relive the past and rehearse the future.

Step 9: Try It Out. At this point you have examined your own behavior, explored alternatives, and observed a model of an assertive individual. You are now prepared to begin trying out assertive behavior in a specific problem situation or two. It may be helpful to repeat Steps 6, 7, and 8 until you are ready to proceed. Prior to trying out your new assertive behavior, it may be beneficial to role-play the situation with a friend.

One engineer used role-playing to prepare herself to assertively handle an annoying situation at work. Although she was equal in organizational rank to other engineers in her department, her boss typically introduced her to strangers by her first name only: "This is Pam, one of our mechanical engineers." Males were introduced to visitors in a manner such as "This is Pete Nowacki, one of our mechanical engineers." Pam's assertive response to her boss was:

> Gerry, something has been troubling me. I notice that when I'm introduced to visitors, you only use my first name. When you introduce male engineers to visitors, you use their first and last names. I would like to be given the same courtesy as males.

Pam's boss apologized and never repeated this personal slight.

Step 10: Get Feedback. Here you try to obtain feedback on how well you did in trying out the assertive behavior. Step 4 called for the same type of self-examination. In this step you emphasize what you did right. Pam might provide herself this type of feedback, "You handled things well. You leveled with Gerry in a way that did not make him defensive or retaliatory. You now feel much more comfortable when Gerry introduces you to new people. Although I thought I would appear nervous in making my assertion, I came across pretty cool."

Step 11: Behavior Shaping. Steps 7, 8, 9, and 10 should be repeated as often as necessary to shape your behavior in the desirable direction. Step by step you build up toward the final desired result. You build yourself up to a point where you feel comfortable dealing in a self-enhancing manner with a situation that was bothersome in the past. Suppose you work for a superior who characteristically tells you, "Don't you see that my way is better?" Your final goal might be to say, "I must disagree. Your way has some merit, but my careful analysis of the situation reveals . . . ." Since you are somewhat fearful of disagreeing with somebody in a position of authority, you may have to begin with a very mild assertion such as, "You could be right. But could you explain your position to me more fully?"

Step 12: No Further Delays in Trying Out the Assertive Behavior. The illustrations presented earlier indicate that many people will have put their AT to actual use from Step 9 forward. However, some particularly nonassertive people may have still restricted their assertive behavior to practice sessions. Rehearsals and role-plays are a relatively secure environment. It is now time to do what Pam did—behave assertively in a natural setting. As a final preliminary, some people will try out AT in low-stake situations such as demanding a larger portion of french fries at a restaurant, or asking a dry cleaning store to replace a button broken during the dry cleaning process. People who still cannot behave assertively through Step 11 may need professional assistance in defending their rights and expressing what they think and feel.

Step 13: Further Training. The developers of this program of AT state, "You are encouraged to repeat such procedures as may be appropriate in the development of the behavior pattern you desire.[3] Some people will repeat steps 1 through 11 for one or two other situations in life that call for assertiveness. A person with a work-related problem of assertiveness might want to repeat the same process for a vexing marital problem.

Step 14: Social Reinforcement. No program of self-development will work unless the new behavior receives frequent reinforcement. As you practice assertive behavior, observe the beneficial consequences. (For example, "Yes, it felt great to explain patiently to my boss that I want to be considered for promotion to another division even if I have a husband and three children.") Positive comments from other people about your assertions will prove of more value than self-reinforcement. A shy systems analyst went through a program of assertiveness training. He practiced the new skills back on the job with apparent success. His self-confidence elevated a notch when he overheard the comment, "Whatever happened to Tim? He's a new man these days. He lets people know exactly what he thinks of their work procedures."

The Argument for Assertiveness Training

A compelling argument for the use of assertiveness training in personal development programs is that a substantial number of career-minded people are either too shy or too outspoken. AT is designed to help with both extremes of behavior. AT is also quite useful in reducing and preventing stress. Many people develop psychosomatic disorders because they overcontrol their feelings instead of expressing them directly to people with whom they are in contact. Assertiveness training is also valuable because it can contribute to leadership effectiveness. Competent leaders are usually assertive individuals—they lay out their demands clearly to subordinates, and they express their feelings and attitudes constructively. Finally, AT is at worst harmless and can be conducted for a relatively modest cost.

Another important benefit of AT is that it teaches people the skill of having their demands met without being pushy or overbearing. Research conducted by Stuart M. Schmidt and David Kipnis strongly supports the value of such behavior. Workers who refused to take no for an answer were labeled as *shotguns,* while those who actively try to influence others with reason and logic were referred to as *tacticians.* (Shotguns are aggressive, while tacticians are essentially assertive.) Shotguns received relatively low performance evaluation and salaries and also experienced less job satisfaction and more job stress. The same patterns of consequences were found at different organizational levels and in numerous occupations and firms.[4]

An important caution here is that some people who complete AT misinterpret the program; they confuse assertiveness with being a pest about one's demands and thus behave like shotguns. The unintended negative consequence is that assertiveness training leads them to behavior unwelcomed by the organization.

Another potential benefit of AT is that it teaches people how to handle anger properly, by directing anger in a sensible way toward its source—such as irritating an employee. Gordon L. Lippitt observes that "Instead of channeling anger toward its source, managers bury hostile, aggressive feelings beneath a charming exterior. The feelings, however, dramatically surface through indirect, manipulative tactics. Individuals may have difficulty describing wants, for example. They set unrealistically high standards or start and abort projects on whim. The people around them don't know what to expect from one moment to another. The longer the behavior persists, the more destructive it becomes."[5]

The Argument against Assertiveness Training

A major argument against AT is that only anecdotal evidence exists that it does work. It has been observed that people who undergo assertiveness training often become assertive over minor issues such as not losing their place in a movie theatre line. Changes in more significant aspects of behavior are not forthcoming. Another disadvantage of AT is that despite its claims, it has an adverse impact on people who are already too assertive. Instead of making them more tactful, they become overly abrasive. As one insurance company executive told a personnel manager, "Please stop sending women to assertiveness training indiscriminately. Some of the women you sent were already assertive. They are now much too outspoken in making their demands known to management."

Another potential concern about AT is that if too many people in the work force became assertive, management would spend an inordinate amount of time responding to their demands. Even if they are tactful and many of their demands are legitimate, assertive people require a lot of individual attention. For instance, one man who returned from assertiveness training began to make such demands as wanting new office furniture, more secretarial help, and a larger salary increase. Because of these large number of demands, his manager began to dread meeting with him.

Guidelines for Action and Skill Development

Three things should be remembered when becoming more assertive. First, avoid behaving in ways that will probably make others overly defensive or angry or lead them to shun you. Such behavior will guarantee that you will not get what you want. Second, remember that others have the same rights as you. "You should not try to get what you want by ignoring the legitimate needs and rights of other people." Third, behaving assertively does not mean that you will get what you want everytime. Sometimes a compromise is necessary; at other times you will simply fail to get what you want.[6]

In deciding how frequently to be assertive, consider the guidelines summarized in Figure 7–1. The areas under the bell-shaped curve represent the proportion of time appropriate for each behavior in the workplace. *Understanding/assertive* behavior focuses attention on hearing the other person's ideas and less on asserting your own ideas. *Assertive/understanding* behavior is just the opposite; it focuses more on asserting your own

FIGURE 7–1 Proportion of Time Appropriate for Assertive Behaviors

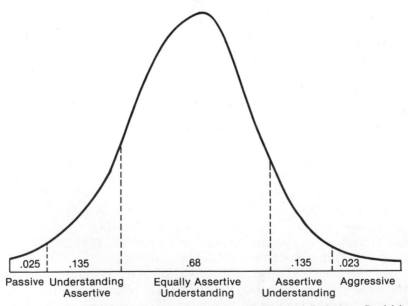

| .025 | .135 | .68 | .135 | .023 |

| Passive | Understanding | Equally Assertive | Assertive | Aggressive |
| | Assertive | Understanding | Understanding | |

SOURCE: Adapted with permission from W. Alan Randolph and Ruth Anne Randolph, "Asserting Your Way to Better Planning," *Supervision Training Update,* Spring 1985, p. 4. (A McGraw-Hill Training Systems Publication.) © W. Alan Randolph, Professor of Management in the Merrick School of Business, University of Baltimore, and Ruth Anne Randolph, Consultant with Blanchard Training and Development, San Diego, CA.

ideas. *Equally/assertive* understanding behavior is a balance between asserting your ideas and hearing the other person's ideas.

About 95 percent of the time, one of the three assertive and understanding behaviors will lead to a more productive interaction with another person. According to Randolph and Randolph, "When people learn to use appropriate behaviors, they become better planners, better team members, better implementers, and better communicators with their boss."[7]

Use flexibility in applying the program of assertiveness training featured in this chapter. One important factor subject to individual differences is the amount of rehearsal you will need before carrying out an assertion. A few people can modify their behavior from passivity to assertiveness or from aggressiveness to assertiveness after just being made aware of the differences. Other people require considerable rehearsal in order to overcome the anxiety associated with behaving assertively.

As with any program of self-development, there is no appropriate substitute for active practice of assertive behavior in real settings. Behave assertively when you choose to, not as an arbitrary exercise. The basic steps in becoming more assertive are deceptively simple. Executing these steps, however, requires knowledge, skill, sensitivity, and substantial practice.

To prompt subordinates to be assertive, it is important for managers to serve as models of assertiveness, to listen to employees, share information with them, and give them regular feedback. To be assertive, employees need to know that their opinions are valued.[8]

DISCUSSION QUESTIONS AND ACTIVITIES

1. How does being assertive contribute to managerial effectiveness?

2. Many obnoxious, overbearing people are quite successful (if success is measured in terms of income and position). Why then be concerned about not being aggressive on the job?

3. If you were the product development manager who discovered that senior citizens did not prefer high-speed, adult tricycles, how would you deal with the situation?

4. Describe how AT might be a useful technique for helping sales representatives become more comfortable in making cold calls.

5. Describe how AT might help an employee receive a generous salary increase.

6. From top management's standpoint, what are some of the potential problems with using AT at lower levels in the organization?

7. Take an informal poll of about six experienced businesspeople and get their opinions on the following question: In what organizational functions is assertiveness the most important and/or appropriate? Be prepared to discuss your findings in class.

NOTES

1. The core of this program is from Robert E. Alberti and Michael L. Emmons, *Your Perfect Right: A Guide to Assertive Behavior* (San Luis Obispo, Calif.: Impact Publishers, 1970), Chapter 2. The program also contains features from "Assertive Management," a seminar conducted by David Gootnick Associates, 1988, and they are also found in other AT programs. The examples and illustrations within the 14 steps, however, are original.
2. Alberti and Emmons, *Your Perfect Right,* p. 35.
3. Ibid., p. 37.
4. Stuart M. Schmidt and David Kipnis, "The Perils of Persistence," *Psychology Today,* November 1987, p. 34.
5. "Defusing Your Anger," *Research Institute Personal Report for the Executive,* October 29, 1985.
6. Anthony F. Grasha, *Practical Applications of Psychology,* 2nd ed. (Boston: Little Brown, 1983).
7. W. Alan Randolph and Ruth Anne Randolph, "Asserting Your Way to Better Planning," *Supervision Planning Update,* Spring 1985, pp. 4–5.
8. Fred Pryor, "Encourage Assertiveness—In Yourself and Your Employees," *The Pryor Report,* September 1987, p. 3.

SOME ADDITIONAL REFERENCES

"Assertiveness for Career and Personal Success." American Management Association tape cassette program, not dated.

People Skills. New York: John Wiley, 1983.

Davis, Sandra L., and Mary Lund. "The Perils of Shyness." *Business Week's Guide to Careers,* April 1986, pp. 125–28.

Drury, Susanne S. *Assertive Supervision: Building Improved Teamwork.* Champaign, Ill.: Research Press, 1984.

Morgan, Philip I., and H. Kent Baker. "Building a Professional Image: Learning Assertiveness." *Supervisory Management,* August 1985, pp. 14–20.

Appendix to Chapter Seven

ARE YOU PASSIVE, ASSERTIVE, OR AGGRESSIVE?

The following questionnaire is designed to give you tentative insight into your current tendencies toward nonassertiveness (passivity), assertiveness, or aggressiveness. As with other questionnaires presented in this book, The Assertiveness Scale is primarily a self-examination and discussion device. Answer each question mostly true or mostly false, as it applies to you.

	Mostly True	Mostly False
1. It is extremely difficult for me to turn down a sales representative when that individual is a nice person.	_____	_____
2. I express criticism freely.	_____	_____
3. If another person were being very unfair, I would bring it to that person's attention.	_____	_____
4. Work is no place to let your feelings show.	_____	_____
5. No use asking for favors, people get what they deserve on the job.	_____	_____
6. Business is not the place for tact; say what you think.	_____	_____
7. If a person looked as though he or she were in a hurry, I would let that person in front of me in a supermarket line.	_____	_____
8. A weakness of mine is that I'm too nice a person.	_____	_____
9. If my restaurant bill is even 25 cents more than it should be, I demand that the mistake be corrected.	_____	_____
10. I have laughed out loud in public more than once.	_____	_____
11. I've been described as too outspoken by several people.	_____	_____
12. I am quite willing to have the store take back a piece of furniture that has a scratch.	_____	_____
13. I dread having to express anger toward a co-worker.	_____	_____
14. People often say that I'm too reserved and emotionally controlled.	_____	_____
15. Nice guys and gals finish last in business.	_____	_____
16. I fight for my rights down to the last detail.	_____	_____
17. I have no misgivings about returning an overcoat to the store if it doesn't fit me properly.	_____	_____
18. If I have had an argument with a person, I try to avoid him or her.	_____	_____
19. I insist on my spouse (roommate, or partner) doing his or her fair share of undesirable chores.	_____	_____
20. It is difficult for me to look directly at another person when the two of us are in disagreement.	_____	_____
21. I have cried among friends more than once.	_____	_____
22. If someone near me at a movie kept up a conversation with another person, I would ask him or her to stop.	_____	_____

23. I am able to turn down social engagements
    with people I do not particularly care for.   _____   _____
24. It is poor taste to express what you really feel   _____   _____
    about another individual.
25. I sometimes show my anger by swearing at or   _____   _____
    belittling another person.
26. I am reluctant to speak up in a meeting.   _____   _____
27. I find it relatively easy to ask friends for small   _____   _____
    favors such as giving me a lift to work when
    my car is being serviced or repaired.
28. If another person was smoking in a restaurant   _____   _____
    and it bothered me, I would inform that
    person.
29. I often finish other people's sentences for   _____   _____
    them.
30. It is relatively easy for me to express love and   _____   _____
    affection toward another person.

Scoring and Interpretation

Score yourself plus 1 for each of your answers that agrees with the scoring key. If your score is 10 or less, it is probable that you are currently a nonassertive individual. A score of 15 through 24 suggests that you are an assertive individual. A score of 25 or higher suggests that you are an aggressive individual. Retake this about 30 days from now to give yourself some indication of the stability of your answers. You might also discuss your answers with a close friend to determine if that person has a similar perception of your assertiveness. Here is the scoring key.

1. Mostly false	16. Mostly true
2. Mostly true	17. Mostly true
3. Mostly true	18. Mostly false
4. Mostly false	19. Mostly true
5. Mostly false	20. Mostly false
6. Mostly true	21. Mostly true
7. Mostly false	22. Mostly true
8. Mostly false	23. Mostly true
9. Mostly true	24. Mostly false
10. Mostly true	25. Mostly true
11. Mostly true	26. Mostly false
12. Mostly true	27. Mostly true
13. Mostly false	28. Mostly true
14. Mostly false	29. Mostly true
15. Mostly true	30. Mostly true

Chapter Eight

The Prevention of Sexual Harassment

The company involved in the case described below had not developed a formal policy about sexual harassment of one employee by another, nor had it communicated a complete definition of sexual harassment to its employees. An incident of "environmental sexual harassment" made the company more aware of the importance of developing formal mechanisms to deal with sexual harassment on the job.

"This is going to be a great job. The guy I'm working with is super nice. He seems to really care about me as a friend," thought Heidi after her first week on the job as a computer programmer. She and Darryl would be working together for the next six months on developing software for a human resources information system. After this project was completed, Heidi would be assigned to another. She was assigned to work with Darryl because he needed assistance to complete the project on time.

The first two months went by rather smoothly. Heidi and Darryl worked together well and talked freely with each other about a variety of topics. She learned very quickly about the system, the programming language incorporated into the system, and the project itself. Darryl often complimented Heidi on her quick learning ability and gave their boss Mike several excellent status reports.

Darryl picked up the tab several times when he and Heidi went out to lunch together. He also invited her to his house for dinner with Mary Lou, a computer analyst with whom she had become friends.

Mary Lou expressed no surprise about Darryl's having bought Heidi's lunches. She told Heidi that a year ago she had to work closely with Darryl. After six months she went to Mike to ask to be transferred away from Darryl's project. Mary Lou said she couldn't handle his coming on to her and his perfectionism about work. Mary Lou then told Heidi that Mike had asked her how the new programmer (Heidi) was getting along with Darryl.

"I told him that things seemed to be going along pretty well," said Mary Lou, "except that I detected Darryl was getting a little too personal. He was beginning to act differently than in the past. Darryl began commenting on how sexy he thought I was. Often he would rub his shoulder against mine when he made such comments. He also said he wished we could spend some time together alone. He was dressing better and was in the office earlier than usual, casually glancing out the window as if watching for someone. Mike than told me he would keep an eye on the situation. I thought he meant that he would either talk to you or Darryl, but I guess that wasn't his intention."

Heidi decided her best course of action was to avoid Darryl as much as feasible. She also decided to behave rudely toward Darryl in order to discourage any further advances. In response to one of her short comments, Darryl asked Heidi if she was having problems with her car or with another person. Heidi soon felt repelled by Darryl's presence and began to hate working with him. Heidi thought to herself, "Why would a married man with two step-daughters my age think that I would be interested in him?"

Heidi decided to write Darryl a long letter explaining how uncomfortable she was in his presence because of his persistent comments about her as a person. She also pleaded with him to talk only about work with her. Darryl responded by urging Heidi not to be so hasty in making a decision about the potential in their relationship. One morning as they were reviewing some details about a program, Darryl said to Heidi, "Let's you and I plan on dinner this Thursday to really talk through our relationship."

That afternoon Heidi went to see Mike and gave him a detailed account of all her concerns about Darryl's words and actions directed toward her. Mike thanked Heidi for her candor and said that he would investigate the problem immediately. The next morning Mike told Darryl to meet with him at 10 o'clock to discuss an urgent matter. "Darryl we have something quite unpleasant to talk about," said Mike. "Heidi has told me about the nonstop harassment you have placed her under during her employment. We cannot allow the type of behavior she described to me."

"I would hardly call my relationship with Heidi to be an act of harassment. She's a cute kid so I acted a little extra friendly toward her. I never fondled her or anything like that. You know me, I'm very friendly."

"You ought to develop a clearer definition of what friendly means," said Mike. "I'm not going to recommend to the president that you be fired this time. But if any woman ever lodges a justified complaint of harassment against you again, I'll see to it that you are fired. What I am going to do though is make a comment on your performance appraisal about your insensitivity to the welfare of one of your programmers. I am also going to recommend that you receive no merit increase for this year's performance.''

"I still think you and Heidi are overreacting," said Darryl. "Nobody ever warned me that I was doing something wrong."

One week later Mike met with the president and the human resources manager to discuss the importance of the company establishing a policy about the prevention and control of sexual harassment. The president was surprised to learn that many other firms in the area already had implemented such policies.[1]

ELEMENTS OF AN EFFECTIVE PROGRAM OF PREVENTION AND CONTROL

The firm described spontaneously handled an incident of sexual harassment involving a senior male employee making unwanted sexual advances toward a junior female employee. Many organizations today rely less on spontaneous judgment and more on formalized procedures in managing sexual harassment. These formalized procedures have arisen in response to the related forces of government involvement in the problem and a growing awareness of sexual harassment in the workplace.

Below we describe the elements of an effective program for the prevention and control of sexual harassment based on experience in a variety of work organizations. The program is designed to deal with the many varieties of sexual harassment (presented in decreasing order of frequency): males against females, males against males, females against males, and females against females.

Be Aware of the Meaning of Sexual Harassment

An effective program of prevention and control begins with an agreed-upon definition of the problem. The definition of sexual harassment provided by the Equal Employment Opportunity Commission (EEOC) is widely accepted because it has legal stature. It defines the problem as

Unwelcome sexual advances, requests for sexual favors, and other verbal or physical conduct of a sexual nature when (1) submission to such conduct is made either explicitly or implicitly a term or condition of an individual's employment, (2) submission to or rejection of such conduct by an individual is used as the basis for employment decisions affecting the individual, or (3) such conduct has the purpose or effect of unreasonably interfering with an individual's work performance or creating an intimidating, hostile, or offensive working environment.[2]

The Supreme Court has upheld the validity of the definition of sexual harassment just presented. In its landmark decision of *Meritor Savings Bank* v. *Vinson* (June 19, 1986) the Court declared that both tangible job benefits and environmental harassment are prohibited forms of sexual discrimination. Tangible job benefits (or quid pro quo) harassment exists when managerial personnel impose on subordinates sex-oriented conditions to employment status, such as trading sexual favors for promotion. Environmental harassment is based on the existence of an intimidating, hostile, or offensive work environment that interferes with the employee's work performance. Various federal court rulings have included the following behaviors as environmental harassment: leers, obscene gestures, being rubbed against, being subjected to several months of questionable language, off-color jokes, and sexual jokes and innuendos.[3]

It is helpful to supplement a legalistic definition of sexual harassment with an informal, comprehensive definition provided by the Working Woman's Institute: "Sexual harassment is any unwanted attention of a sexual nature from someone in the workplace that creates discomfort and/or interferes with the job."[4]

Establish a Policy about Sexual Harassment

A large number of private, public, and nonprofit organizations have developed formal policies about sexual harassment. Such policies make a major contribution to the prevention and control of sexual harassment, particularly if they are widely disseminated throughout the organization. It will be helpful to examine two representative policies dealing with the issue under discussion.

Here is a policy statement following the often-used approach of linking sexual harassment policy to the law:

The Equal Employment Opportunity Commission (EEOC) has issued guidelines setting forth the Commission's interpretation regarding sexual harassment as a violation of Title VII of the Civil Rights Act of 1964. These guidelines are consistent with our long-standing policy that conduct creating an intimidating, hostile, or offensive working environment will not be tolerated and those violating this practice may be subject to disciplinary action up to and including discharge. To make sure employees are aware of management's position toward sexual harassment, the following should be considered:

1. Review policies to determine if sexual harassment is adequately identified as unacceptable conduct.

2. Examine the need for additional communication.

3. Encourage employees to discuss their sexual harassment concerns with supervision.

4. Include in supervisory training programs a discussion of sexual harassment and the need for supervision to take timely corrective action when the problem exists.[5]

An organizational policy on sexual harassment, backed up with procedures for implementation, has been recommended by William A. Nowlin and George M. Sullivan.[6] This policy is outlined below.

Corporate Policy Concerning Sexual Harassment

This organization does not support or condone sexual harassment. Any employee who believes that she or he is being sexually harassed by any co-worker, supervisor, or customer should do the following:

1. Notify the person harassing you that you are offended by his or her actions, you consider that person's behavior to be sexual harassment, and you expect it to cease.

2. If the offending person does not react to your complaint with sensitivity, then immediately contact the sexual harassment compliance offer by telephone, written correspondence, or in person.

3. If you believe that your work area is characterized by lewd comments, obscene gestures, sexual remarks, or any other offensive conditions, contact the sexual harassment compliance officer.

4. If within a reasonable period of time you feel that your complaint is not being processed adequately, communicate directly with the director of human resources or other top management official.

A logical corollary of a formal policy against sexual harassment is to treat employees equitably, thus reducing chances of a sexual harassment complaint. An example would be for a male supervisor not to give preference to a female subordinate when making assignments that involve long periods of working alone together. *Equitably,* however, does not mean that males should avoid choosing females to accompany them on business trips, or vice versa.

Adopt Sanctions

Policies against sexual harassment will be strengthened to the extent that policy violators are punished. Donald J. Petersen and Douglass Massengill recommend that the penalties for sexual harassment be made a part of regular company rules. They note that a major-minor system of rule violations is used in many organizations. Major rule violations lead to discharge for one offense, but lesser offenses lead to lesser sanctions such as verbal warnings, written warnings, and suspensions. For blatant sexual harassment such as rape or attempted rape (a major rule violation), discharge may be the appropriate response. For lesser acts of harassment, the harasser may receive a smaller penalty based on the nature of the offense, and the schedule of the organization's penalties.[7]

In support of this reasoning, the EEOC guidelines suggest considering each case on its own merits. Thus, the penalty imposed on Darryl—no merit increase and a negative performance appraisal—would seem stiff because the charges are based exclusively on the testimony of Mary Lou. No corroborating evidence was presented.

Develop Mechanisms for Investigating Complaints

For a program of sexual harassment and control to be effective, it is important for the organization to encourage the complaining employees to protest through formal channels developed for that purpose. Petersen and Massengill found that 40 of the 68 *Fortune* 500 firms responding to their survey had a formal complaint procedure. Those firms with a formal complaint procedure (for harassment) were more likely to have dealt with such a problem than those without a formal procedure (74 percent versus 29 percent).[8]

A related study showed that if clear organizational policies against sexual harassment are developed, information about sanctions disseminated, and standard procedures for dealing with incidents of harassment are developed, a predictable trend occurs. At first there is an increase in the number of complaints of sexual harassment by employees. However, if the anti-harassment policies are maintained, complaints will begin to decline.[9]

The four more frequently used formal complaint channels are these:

1. Arrange appointment with top-level director of human resources.
2. Open door policy—bring in complaint anytime to top level manager without having to go through the chain of command.
3. Follow chain of command in making complaint.
4. Contact equal employment opportunity (EEO) manager.[10]

Develop Mechanisms for Handling the Accused

The individual accused of sexual harassment should receive sanctions that are commensurate with the particular offense. Nevertheless, the person accused of harassment must be assured of a fair and thorough investigation that protects his or her individual rights. Employment law specialist David S. Bradshaw points out that terminating a harasser without strong evidence can lead to another set of problems. An employer should ensure that it is not trading a potential sex harassment claim for a wrongful termination lawsuit by insisting on accurate documentation that the charges of harassment actually took place.[11]

One of the difficulties in documenting charges of harassment is that some instances are based on a subjective interpretation of what constitutes harassment. In one company a new recruit complained that her boss had sexually harassed her. The substance of the complaint was that when the woman inquired about advancement opportunities, the boss replied, "Maybe we can talk about that topic over lunch sometime." (Poor judgment yes; sexual harassment no!)

Another reason for carefully investigating complaints of harassment is that these complaints are sometimes used as a form of blackmail. A male maintenance worker in an office building told his boss (a male), "If you don't get me a raise, I'm going to tell the company that you refused to get me one because I wouldn't have sex with you." The worker did bring forth the complaint, but it was later dismissed as frivolous.

According to Jeanne Bosson Driscoll, employees who are accused of sexual harassment may require assistance to understand the point of view of the accuser. They may also need personal counseling to obtain further insight into how to control their behavior. If termination is required, outplacement may be advisable.[12] (See Chapter 20 for a description of outplacement.) In short, the sexual harasser should be granted the same due process granted employees charged with other offenses.

Develop Mechanisms for Handling Victims of Harassment

Employees who feel sexually harassed may require counseling support and assurance that the organization will protect their rights as well as investigate all allegations. Some employees are reluctant to make formal charges of harassment out of fear of reprisal. The harassment victim should also be assured that appropriate disciplinary action will be taken. It may also be necessary to help the harassed persons realize that they are not responsible for the actions of the initiator. Victims of harassment often feel guilty for somehow having encouraged such behavior on the part of their harasser.[13] For instance, the harassed individual is sometimes accused of having acted in a sexually provocative manner toward co-workers and superiors.

In some cases, the feelings of the harassment victim are similar to those experienced by rape victims. Driscoll observes that "The combination of rage and guilt can be long-lasting and can affect one's ability to be productive. Counseling should be provided to help the victim sort out those feelings and gain understanding of the situation and the feelings it generated."[14]

Provide an Appropriate Training Program

A comprehensive strategy for preventing sexual harassment is to provide appropriate training at all levels in the organization. As mentioned in one of the policy statements above, the topic should be introduced in supervisory training programs. These programs should communicate the type of information presented in this chapter, such as definitions of sexual harassment, company policy statements on the issue, EEOC rulings about harassment, and the rights of both the accused and victims. An underlying purpose of the training program is to increase the level of awareness about the problem throughout the organization.

Another major purpose of a sexual harassment training program is to overcome the credibility problem surrounding the subject. George K. Kronenberger and David L. Bourke report that many male employees cannot believe that their language, attitudes, and jokes can be construed as sexual harassment. The training program, therefore, has to be quite specific and well planned. Kronenberger and Bourke suggest that the following should be incorporated into an EEOC training program about sexual harassment.[15]

Moderately Technical Level.   The program should present a brief description of relevant law and court rulings. Yet, if the discussion enters into great detail, the audience may become confused and alienated. Human resource specialists and company lawyers can be consulted for more legal detail when it is needed. It is illuminating to discuss the prevalence of sexual harassment in the workplace. A current estimate is that 50 percent of working women and 15 percent of working men have experienced sexual harassment in the workplace.[16]

Organizational Policies.   The training program on sexual harassment may present a timely opportunity to reaffirm existing organizational policies on equal employment opportunity and training. The message can be communicated that concern about sexual harassment fits into existing concern about decreasing discrimination in the workplace.

Judicial Examples.   Actual judicial actions should be presented to emphasize the legal implications of the issue and to show how the courts are likely to view acts of sexual harassment. A representative case used in these training programs is *Miller* vs. *Bank of America*. Its essential points are as follows:

Margaret Miller alleged that she was discharged from the Bank of America because she refused her supervisor's demands for sexual favors. The bank argued that it had established (1) a policy prohibiting sexual harassment, and (2) an inhouse grievance mechanism. Therefore, Bank of America contended that it was not liable for its supervisors' actions. The Ninth Circuit Court of Appeals ruled that despite the administrative policies and mechanisms, Bank of America was still liable because supervisors were acting as its agents.

Miller is considered a value training case because it shows that human resource specialists and managers from other functions must take affirmative action to stop acts of sexual harassment and that concerted action is necessary to limit company liability.[17]

Corporate Examples.   If it can be done with sensitivity and confidentiality, it is helpful to review company cases of sexual harassment. Such cases are more readily used in large organizations where the participants may not be aware of the case under discussion.

Extent of Employee Involvement.   Ideally, all employees should participate in the program. At a minimum, all first-level managers should attend the training program. Those employees who do not attend the program should be made aware of its major aspects. Supervisors can conduct staff meetings to disseminate some of the information, particularly the EEOC guidelines and company policy.

Competent Trainers.   To enhance credibility, the training program should be administered by employees with sufficient company experience and adequate background in EEO matters so that all questions can be answered authoritatively. Training of this type can sometimes be conducted externally. Among the sources are management consultants and education associations (such as the American Management Association) who sometimes offer programs on the prevention and control of sexual harassment.

Specific Techniques for Dealing with Harassment

Although the program just presented is of merit, it may need to be supplemented with specific techniques for controlling the sexual harassment of one individual by another. At times the discussion of specific strategies will suffice, but at other times role-plays may be more effective. Following are specific suggestions for dealing with harassers that have been incorporated into training programs:

The easiest way to deal with sexual harassment is to nip it in the bud. The first time it happens respond with a statement of this type: "I won't tolerate this kind of talk." "I dislike sexually-oriented jokes." "Keep your hands off me."

A woman's best defense against harassment is a polite, nonthreatening, "No." That is particularly true for verbal harassment unconnected to receiving preferred treatment on the job. Sometimes ordinarily sensitive men will engage in this kind of talk or action, unaware that they are being offensive. If the man persists despite receiving a repeated "No," the woman should consider a surprise act of physical retaliation. Suppose the man continues to pat the woman's rump from time to time. The woman might try punching *him* in the rump. The shock effect may very well work.[18]

When it is difficult to confront the harasser personally, or attempts to do that have not stopped the unwanted behavior, writing a letter to that person may stop the harassment. Three parts should be included in the letter: First, list any instances of harassing behavior, with all pertinent details such as time, place, date, nature of the behavior, and witnesses, if any. Second, describe the consequences of harassment whether emotional, behavioral, or financial. For example, "I was so upset by your actions that I missed three days of work resulting in the loss of $550 in commissions." Third, state the outcome that you want such as, "From now on, I want all our interactions to be strictly business."

Keep a written record of what the harasser has been doing to you, perhaps in a diary entry. For instance, "January 9: Today, Matt brushed against me while I was reaching down to obtain a record from the file cabinet."

Find witnesses to the harassing acts. Although harassment is usually a private affair, some harassers enjoy the additional humiliation derived from making demeaning remarks in public, or in kissing or touching another person in front of co-workers. Because many harassers are repeaters, it is usually possible to find witnesses for past acts of harassment.[19]

The Case For and Against Formal Programs Relating to Sexual Harassment and Control

There are several pressing reasons why organizations should embark on a formal program of preventing and controlling sexual harassment. One primary consideration is humanitarian. Sexual harassment is one of the major employment problems of the decade. (Sexual harassment has probably always been a problem, but it is now being addressed due to more women in the labor force and a greater sensitivity to human rights.) Surveys indicate that up to 88 percent of women believe they have been victims of sexual harassment on the job.[20] Another justification for such programs is that they have a large potential for being cost-effective. A survey of more than 17,000 federal employees concluded that sexual harassment cost taxpayers $205 million during a two-year period in sick leave, lost productivity, and turnover.[21]

Potential employer liability for acts of sexual harassment committed by employees is another reason top management should favor programs of sexual harassment prevention and control. The Supreme Court issued a split ruling on the question of employer liability for acts of sexual harassment committed by its employees. It ruled that the Court of Appeals erred in concluding that employers are always automatically liable for sexual harassment by their supervisors. However, the court also maintained that the employer is not insulated from liability just because the harassed employee did not use an established grievance procedure.[22]

The issue of employer liability in a given case is likely to be settled in lower courts. Several major court cases in the past have supported the EEOC position that the employer is responsible for sexual harassment by its employees—even if they were forbidden by the employer and regardless of whether the employer knew or should have known of their occurrence.[23] The governing legal principle states: "The fact of delegation of authority to the supervisor by the employer makes the employer responsible for any exercise of that authority in violation of Title VII."[24]

The case against formal programs of this nature does not dismiss the significance of sexual harassment in the workplace. One argument is that sexual harassment is simply another form of misconduct and as such does not require a separate policy.[25] This is true because the employer is responsible for providing a safe environment. Another argument is that mature adults should take responsibility for their own behavior without external control exerted by both the employer and the government. If an employee is harassed by another, the former should handle it in the way that he or she would handle another employee who violated his or her rights in any other way. The harassment victim could retaliate directly by filing a complaint with the employer or police.

It can also be argued that an astute individual should be able to prevent a potentially harassing situation from progressing too far. The suggestions about warding off harassment mentioned in the training program above could be implemented by any person with good insight and interpersonal skills.

Guidelines for Action and Skill Development

Although the elements of an effective program for the prevention and control of sexual harassment presented above should be interpreted as action steps, a few summary tips are in order.

Based on his review of legal cases, Robert H. Faley advises that the most significant thing an employer can do is to take the problem of sexual harassment seriously. Top management should demonstrate by its actions a genuine concern for the sensitivity to the issues.[26]

The best preventive measure the supervisor can take is to avoid harassing behavior. The *appearance* of innocence can sometimes be as important as actual innocence. A survey showed that male supervisors should avoid placing themselves in compromising situations such as driving female employees home after work, engaging in sexually suggestive conversations, and having unnecessary "business dinners."[27]

Because sexual harassment is a sensitive and ambiguous subject, the person conducting a training program about it should try to know the audience and not be viewed as condescending or dogmatic. An improper attitude may alienate the group and render the program ineffective.[28] Humor should be used sparingly and with sensitivity. A tasteful joke can relieve tension, while a tasteless joke will be interpreted as a sexist slur and alienate members of the audience.

Top management must make it absolutely clear that sexual harassment will not be tolerated. Senior management should act as role models to others throughout the organization.

All parties concerned with sexual harassment should recognize that it is not simply another human resources management problem such as tardiness, absenteeism, or turnover. The emotional nature of sexual harassment sets it apart from other problems, thus requiring more sensitive handling.

DISCUSSION QUESTIONS AND ACTIVITIES

1. How fair do you think Mike was in his handling of Darryl?
2. Can you offer Heidi any constructive criticism for the way she handled the situation with Darryl?
3. How is the prevention of sexual harassment related to conflict resolution?
4. Is asking another employee (whether subordinate, co-worker, or superior) to join you for dinner a form of sexual harassment? Explain.
5. Identify two suggestions made in this chapter that deal more directly with the prevention (rather than the control) of sexual harassment.
6. According to any of the definitions of sexual harassment presented in this chapter, is telling sexually oriented jokes to another employee a form of sexual harassment? Explain.
7. Interview a couple of managers or human resource specialists to obtain their answers to the following: Identify two sexually oriented statements or actions that are (*a*) clearly a form of sexual harassment and (*b*) clearly not.

NOTES

1. Case researched by Karen Gunkel, January 1988.
2. Equal Employment Opportunity Commission Guidelines on Sexual Harassment, April 10, 1980. (29 C.F.R. No. 1604.11 [a])
3. William Nowlin and George M. Sullivan, "Sexual Harassment Issue Intensifies for the Business Community," *Nevada Review of Business & Economics,* Summer 1986, pp. 6–10; David S. Bradshaw, "Sexual Harassment: Confronting the Troublesome Issue," *Personnel Administrator,* January 1987, pp. 51–53.
4. Kay Bartlett, "Is Sexual Harassment in the Work Place the 1980's Glamour Cause?" Associated Press story, February 28, 1982.
5. Donald J. Petersen and Douglass Massengill, "Sexual Harassment—A Growing Problem in the Workplace," *Personnel Administrator,* October 1982, p. 83.
6. Adapted from Nowlin and Sullivan, "Sexual Harassment Issue Intensifies," p. 9.
7. Petersen and Massengill, "Sexual Harassment—A Growing Problem," p. 87.
8. Ibid., p. 84.
9. Ibid.
10. Jeanne Bosson Driscoll, "Sexual Attraction and Harassment: Management's New Problems," *Personnel Journal,* January 1981, p. 36.
11. Bradshaw, "Sexual Harassment: Confronting the Troublesome Issues," p. 52.
12. Driscoll, "Sexual Attraction and Harassment," p. 36.
13. Ibid., p. 36.
14. Ibid., p. 36.
15. George K. Kronenberger and David L. Bourke, "Effective Training and the Elimination of Sexual Harassment," *Personnel Journal,* November 1981, pp. 880–81.
16. Bradshaw, "Sexual Harassment: Confronting the Troublesome Issues," p. 51.
17. Adapted from Kronenberger and Bourke, "Effective Training," p. 881.
18. "Abusing Sex at the Office," *Newsweek,* March 10, 1980, p. 82.
19. Susan Kaufmann, "Sexual Harassment," *Business Week's Guide to Careers,* February/March 1985, p. 76.
20. Data summarized in Robert H. Faley, "Sexual Harassment: Critical Review of Legal Cases with General Principles and Preventive Measures," *Personnel Psychology,* Autumn 1982, p. 584.
21. Bartlett, "Is Sexual Harassment in the Work Place the 1980's Glamour Cause?" p. 1C.
22. Frederick L. Sullivan, "Sexual Harassment: The Supreme Court's Ruling," *Personnel,* December 1986, p. 41; Nowlin and Sullivan, "Sexual Harassment Issue Intensifies," p. 10.
23. Elizabeth C. Wesman, "Shortage of Research Abets Sexual Harassment Confusion," *Personnel Administrator,* November 1983, p. 62.
24. Diane Feldman, "Sexual Harassment: Policies and Prevention," *Personnel,* September 1987, p. 12.
25. Ibid., p. 13.

26. Faley, "Sexual Harassment: Critical Review," p. 597.
27. Petersen and Massengill, "Sexual Harassment—A Growing Problem," p. 86.
28. Kronenberger and Bourke, "Effective Training," p. 880.

SOME ADDITIONAL REFERENCES

Chusmir, Leonard H., and Douglas E. Durand. "What Managers Don't Understand about Sexual Harassment." *Management Solutions,* August 1987, pp. 27–33.

Clarke, Lillian Wilson. "Women Supervisors Experience Sexual Harassment, Too." *Supervisory Management,* April 1986, pp. 35–36.

Dwyer, Paula. "Sexual Harassment: Companies Could Be Liable." *Business Week,* March 31, 1986, p. 35.

Gutek, Barbara A. *Sex and the Workplace: The Impact of Sexual Behavior and Harassment on Women, Men, and Organizations.* San Francisco: Jossey-Bass Inc., 1985.

Seymour, Sally. "The Case of the Mismanaged Ms." *Harvard Business Review,* November–December 1987, pp. 77–87.

Improving the Functioning of Work Groups

The four techniques, methods, and programs of applied management described in the next four chapters focus primarily on the small work group. Distinctions among the individual, group, and organizational level are not absolute. Obviously, a small work group is composed of individuals, and the larger organization is composed of both individuals and small groups. Also, small group techniques, such as quality circles, are used to enhance organizational effectiveness.

As with any of the behavioral science–based techniques presented in this book, those described in this part stem from a core of theory and research. Chapter 9, Conducting an Effective Meeting, is derived from both group dynamics and organizational communication. Chapter 10, Building Teamwork, is based on a number of sources including group dynamics and organization development. Chapter 11, Production Work Teams, describes an approach to organization design based on socio-technical systems—an attempt to interrelate principles of organization structure with principles of motivation through job enrichment.

Chapter 12, Quality Circles, describes a program aimed at improving the quality of goods and services by soliciting employee suggestions. Quality circles are rooted in the canons of participative management. Although still in widespread use, many questions have been raised about their effectiveness.

Chapter Nine

Conducting an Effective Meeting

The executive staff of a building maintenance company held a meeting to deal with a major decision facing the company: whether to locate their expanded company headquarters downtown or in a suburban office park. The executives used a combination of intuition and common sense to guide the conduct of the meeting.

Building Maintenance, Inc., a firm of 325 full and part-time employees is engaged in the cleaning and general maintenance of offices and shopping plazas. Starting as an operation of "one man and one van" about 10 years ago, BMI has grown into the largest firm of its kind in its region. Bud, the founder and president of BMI, is the major shareholder of this privately held firm. The other four members of the executive team are also major shareholders. At present, the company is headquartered in an old office building scheduled for demolition.

The pending demolition has forced the firm to face a relocation decision. Bud has called a 10 A.M. meeting of the executive team to address this problem. Two days before the meeting he sent a memo announcing the meeting (see Exhibit 9–1).

The morning of the meeting, Bud rushed into his office at 10:10. Karen, Liz, Marty, and Nick were already seated.

Bud:

Sorry to be a few minutes late. I got tied up at the bank talking to a loan officer. You know how much detail those bankers can sometimes demand. The reason I called us together is to decide where to locate our new offices. I assume you've given some thought to this matter already.

Let me go over the alternatives I see. We can either relocate to some decent space in one of the newly refurbished downtown buildings, or we can get some slightly better space in a suburban park. Karen, as our financial officer, you must have some relevant facts and figures.

EXHIBIT 9–1 Memo Used by Business Owner to Announce Meeting

BUILDING MAINTENANCE INCORPORATED

"Your cleanliness is our business."

TO: The Executive Team (Karen, Marty, Liz, and Nick)
FROM: Bud
DATE: March 13th
SUBJECT: Office relocation

Demolition day is fast approaching. Let's meet in my office, March 15th at 10 A.M. to wrestle with this problem. We've got to relocate someplace. Put on your thinking caps and be prepared to reach a quick decision.

See you then.

Karen:

As you requested a few weeks ago, Bud, I have looked into a variety of possibilities. We can get the decent downtown space you describe at about $23 per square foot. And, we can get first-rate accommodations in a suburban office park for about $25 per square foot. Relocation costs would be about the same. So it's a wash with respect to rental fees.

Bud:

Now, we've heard it from the financial side. Marty, from your vantage point as sales director, where do you think we should relocate?

Marty:

That's what I like to see, a business owner who puts the customers up front at all times. I agree strongly that the demands of our customers should always carry the heaviest weight with respect to any internal decision we make. Too many large organizations fall victim to the trap of letting bureaucracy overshadow their concern for the external environment. At least, I read something to that effect in a business magazine.

Customers are influenced by image. So long as we have a good image, I think the customer will be satisfied. By the way, we are doing something that is negatively affecting our image to customers. Our customer-service representatives are just too rude over the phone. I think these gals should have proper training before we turn them loose on the customer phone. Remember, all we sell is service. Lots of other companies have good brooms, vacuum cleaners, and power-cleaning equipment. Our only edge is the good service we offer customers.

I'm glad I had the chance to make this point.

Bud:

Liz, what is your position on this relocation decision?

Liz:

As employment director, I have a lot to say about relocation. I agree with Marty that customer service should receive top weight in any decision we make about relocation. Customer service, of course, is a direct result of having an efficient crew of maintenance employees. A suburban office park may sound glamorous, but it could be a disaster in terms of getting help. Maintenance workers know how to get downtown and can afford to get downtown. The vast majority of them live in the city, and they are dependent on mass transit to get to work.

You typically need private transportation to get to an office park. The vast majority of our permanent and temporary employees do not own cars. And many of them that do own cars, usually can't afford to keep them in good repair. Many of the temporary help can only put gas in their cars on payday.

So if we relocate to a suburban park, we'll have to rent a small employment office downtown anyway.

Bud:

So you're telling us that maybe we should choose both alternatives. We should open an employment office downtown and move the executive office to a suburban office park.

Liz:

I agree with part of your reasoning, Bud. Yet, I think you're putting words in my mouth. I'm less concerned about where we put the executive office. My big worry is to have a location that makes it possible for us to hire the employees we need.

Karen:

Now, we're introducing a third alternative. We could have two offices downtown. One for the executive and clerical staff and one for recruiting and selecting help.

By the way, who was supposed to bring the coffee and pastry to this meeting? How can you make a big decision without refreshments?

Bud:

Nick, what do you think? Which location would be best for you as director of maintenance operations?

Nick:

I'm not in the office too much. I spend most of my time in the field overseeing our supervisors and their crews. Most of our help never see the office after they are hired unless they have a major problem. They report directly to the site. To them their place of work is the building or shopping plaza where they are assigned. Other things are more important than location.

One of the important things we should be considering is a big holiday party this year. Our biggest competitor holds a once-a-year party that every employee gets invited to. It's a real morale builder. I think it's cost effective in terms of how much turnover it reduces. Some of the cleaning help stay on for a couple of extra months just to attend the party.

So far nobody has mentioned the color and furnishings of the new offices. To me, office decor is as important as location.

Karen:

Nick, do you have any figures to prove the cost effectiveness of an annual company party? It can run about $25 for each person in attendance. We can expect that more than two thirds of the employees will bring a guest.

Nick:

So what? You can't put a dollar figure on morale.

Marty:

It looks like you folks have got the major issues out on the table. I really don't care where we locate so long as the needs of the customer come first. I'm eager to know what you folks decide. But right now I have to run. I have a luncheon appointment on the other side of town that could mean a big shopping-plaza contract for us. As I said before, I'm more concerned about customers than internal bureaucracy.

Bud:

Good luck with the sales call, Marty. However, I suspect you could have scheduled that luncheon for another day. This is a pretty important topic. I'd like you to stay five more minutes.

Nick:

Bud, you're the boss. What do you think should be our relocation choice? We'll go along with any sensible decision.

Bud:

It seems that it's premature for us to reach a decision on this important matter today. Maybe we should call in an office location consultant to help us decide what to do. In the meantime, let's talk some more about the office party. I kind of like that idea.

SUGGESTIONS FOR CONDUCTING A PRODUCTIVE MEETING

The BMI meeting illustrates an event that is repeated innumerable times every working day: Many meetings fail to accomplish their intended purpose because they are conducted poorly. In this chapter we describe a wide range of suggestions for conducting productive meetings, based on a mixture of experience, common sense, and research. A meeting in this sense is any gathering of people with a purpose in mind, including staff meetings, committee meetings, task force meetings, strategy sessions, and meetings called for the purpose of practicing participative management. The common thread to all these meetings is that the group is trying to solve some type of problem, and therefore either make a decision or lay the ground for making one.

As you review the suggestions for conducting meetings, relate them to the BMI meeting. The vignette was purposely chosen because it violates so many important principles and practices of conducting a productive (or effective) meeting. The suggestions are divided into two general categories: those dealing more with (*a*) the structure and process of meetings and (*b*) the people present at the meeting. Although most of the suggestions are aimed at the leader, many of them can be applied to other participants at the meeting. For example, the leader should strive to keep others from going off on tangents. At the same time, each person should share the responsibility of staying on track. Additionally, one participant can sometimes help another stay on track by making a polite request to that effect.

Dealing with Structure and Process

The *structure* of a meeting includes organization and agenda, timing, and physical arrangements. In this context, *process* refers to activities such as drawing up minutes, providing summaries, and directing effort toward surmountable problems. The 15 suggestions presented in this section reflect and summarize contemporary thinking about improving structure and process to make meetings more productive.

Have a Valid Reason for Calling a Meeting.   Many meetings are unproductive simply because there was no valid reason for calling them. A meeting is justified primarily when there is a need for coordinated effort or interaction on the part of participants. If straightforward, factual information needs to be collected or disseminated, memos can be substituted for meetings. Peter A. Turla and Kathleen L. Hawkins make this analysis:

> Before calling a meeting, assess whether the time invested in the meeting is going to equal or exceed the dollar yield. Do you need advice from all the people who will attend? Do you need group involvement to make a decision or solve a common problem? Do you need a group vote to approve new policies?[1]

Based on the above criteria, Bud was certainly justified in calling a meeting to decide about the new office location.

The underlying purpose of a meeting may be different from its stated purpose. For example, the leader may use it as a political forum to gain support for a project. Or certain group members may use the meeting to publicize their accomplishments or put down another group. Almost every meeting has some undercurrent of power play. By carefully observing what is happening, the meeting becomes more informative than one might have anticipated.[2]

Have a Specific Agenda and Stick to It.   Few people in a work setting would deny the importance of having an agenda, distributing it in advance of the meeting, and staying on track. Yet, this could be the most frequently violated principle of conducting a productive meeting. The agenda should be distributed about 24 hours prior to the meeting, even though the meeting and its general purpose should be announced much sooner. If the agenda is distributed too early, it may be lost or forgotten. Most people can prepare themselves for a meeting within 24 hours.

An agenda should, if possible, include at least one agenda item of high potential interest to each participant. An exciting agenda item adds a spark to the meeting that may spill over to other topics to be discussed. Examples of almost universally exciting agenda items include discussions of cash bonuses, salary increases, and layoffs.

Decide Carefully Who Should Attend.   Considerable time is wasted in meetings because planners do not carefully select participants. The skills, authority, and motivation of the participants should be appropriate for the task at hand. Barbara C. Palmer and Kenneth R. Palmer note that if you are orchestrating a group responsible for identifying and evaluating alternatives for toxic waste disposal, you would not want morticians, librarians, and driver education teachers involved, but chemists, botanists, biologists, physicians, and possibly urban planners.[3]

Another source of low productivity is the failure to invite people who are prepared or authorized to act, as opposed to those who cannot or choose not to make decisions. Inviting people to the meeting who regard attendance as a punishment rather than a reward can also contribute to an unproductive meeting.

It may also be important to invite to the meeting those people whom you are trying to convince, or whose cooperation you need. As one manufacturing manager commented, "I always invite representatives from finance and engineering to our key planning meetings. It helps explain to them some of the problems we face in making a product."

Schedule the Meeting at a Convenient Time and Location.   To minimize the risk of poor attendance, schedule a meeting at a time and location that will make it feasible for most people to attend.[4] Perhaps Bud should not have scheduled a meeting so close to lunchtime, knowing that the sales director would most likely have scheduled a business lunch. A preferred meeting time for most busy managers and professionals is at the start or toward the end of a working day. When the people required or invited to attend a meeting are from dispersed locations, it is helpful to choose a central site.

A related consideration is that some geographic locations are easier to reach than others, whether or not they are centralized. Time lost on ground transportation in major cities has become a concern for many business people. For this reason, many business conferences today are held at hotels located adjacent to airports. Teleconferencing is growing in popularity as a way of cutting down time spent traveling to meetings. However, the teleconference location must also be chosen with care.

Start and Stop the Meeting on Time.   Meetings that are held to their designated starting and stopping time contribute to an organizational culture of professionalism. When a meeting starts late, the prompt attendees are penalized and the latecomers are rewarded. A precedent may then be established for people to arrive habitually late for meetings. Short time limits should be set on meetings whenever possible (perhaps 45 minutes to one hour). The underlying reason is that meetings follow Parkinson's Law: They tend to expand (or contract) to fill the allotted time.

Some attention has been paid to *standup* meetings as a way of shortening their length.[5] If people are forced to stand, they are more likely to feel uncomfortable and will move quickly through the agenda to minimize discomfort. However, there are several real problems with standup meetings. Attendees cannot take notes comfortably; they may feel so awkward that their attention will be diverted; and, the meeting may not be taken seriously because it departs so far from standard business practice.

Direct Effort toward Surmountable Problems.   Many meetings are ineffective because participants spend time discussing "who is to blame for the problem," or "what should have been done to avoid the problem.[6] Rather than try to change the past, it is better to invest energy and time into dealing with how things can be improved in the future. To the credit of the BMI team, at least they did not spend time bemoaning the fact that they had rented space in a building so old that demolition in the near future was inevitable.

Keep Comments Brief and to the Point.   One of the major challenges facing the meeting leader is keeping conversation on track. Marty's well-intended comments about responding to customer needs is a good example of tangential discussion during a business meeting. One way for the leader to keep comments on target is to respond only to targeted comments. Another method is to ask the participant, "How does your comment relate to the agenda?" As a last resort, the leader might have to respond sternly, "You've made your point about that issue, but now we have to get back to the purpose of the meeting."

Participants, too, have an obligation to keep their comments focused on the problem at hand. Aside from lowering the productivity of meetings, irrelevant comments annoy other members. Participants can also play a leadership role by subtly asking other participants to avoid tangents.

Despite the importance of not making irrelevant comments, a meeting should allow some room for spontaneity and the introduction of important ideas that might be dealt with at a future meeting. A major underlying purpose of some meetings might be to foster informal discussion.

Provide Summaries for Each Major Point.   An effective way of keeping a meeting focused on important issues is for the leader to provide summaries of each major point after they are made. Doing so provides structure to the meeting and gives members the feeling that something specific is being accomplished. Instead of concluding that it was premature to reach a conclusion, Bud might have summarized the several different viewpoints offered about where the new office should be relocated. The group could then have possibly reexamined their thinking.

Repeat or Restate Unclear Comments.   Participants at a meeting often mumble or present their ideas in an unclear manner. The leader can play a valuable role in repeating or restating these comments so that they can be understood by other group members. If the leader does not understand either, the participant can be asked to "Please restate your point. Some of us did not follow you."

Set Up a Physical Structure That Encourages Communication.   A circular, semi-circular, or elliptical arrangement of members encourages verbal interaction. In contrast, a typical classroom arrangement discourages two-way communication among participants. A provocative analysis of ways that physical seating arrangements and layouts influence interaction at meetings is presented in Figure 9–1.

Another potentially important aspect of structure is the physical surroundings. It is better to meet in neutral territory such as a conference room or lounge rather than the meeting leader's office. A neutral location, similar to a circular seating arrangement, facilitates more open communication.[7]

Use Parliamentary Procedure Only for Legalistic Meetings.   Parliamentary law, as exemplified by *Robert's Rules of Order,* provides specific rules for conducting a meeting including such items as when motions can be introduced, who can second a motion, and what proportion of members have to vote affirmatively on a motion for it to be passed. These rules tend to discourage informal interaction, spontaneity, and creativity. Also, they tend to create a dreary, somber atmosphere that often detracts from group effectiveness.

FIGURE 9–1   Alternative Meeting Room Layouts

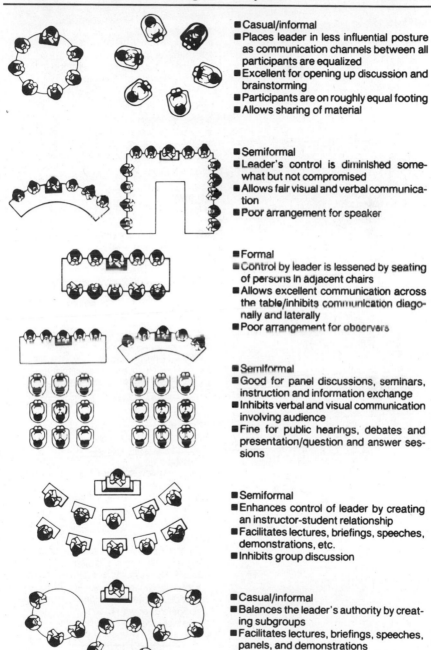

- Casual/informal
- Places leader in less influential posture as communication channels between all participants are equalized
- Excellent for opening up discussion and brainstorming
- Participants are on roughly equal footing
- Allows sharing of material

- Semiformal
- Leader's control is diminished somewhat but not compromised
- Allows fair visual and verbal communication
- Poor arrangement for speaker

- Formal
- Control by leader is lessened by seating of persons in adjacent chairs
- Allows excellent communication across the table/inhibits communication diagonally and laterally
- Poor arrangement for observers

- Semiformal
- Good for panel discussions, seminars, instruction and information exchange
- Inhibits verbal and visual communication involving audience
- Fine for public hearings, debates and presentation/question and answer sessions

- Semiformal
- Enhances control of leader by creating an instructor-student relationship
- Facilitates lectures, briefings, speeches, demonstrations, etc.
- Inhibits group discussion

- Casual/informal
- Balances the leader's authority by creating subgroups
- Facilitates lectures, briefings, speeches, panels, and demonstrations
- Allows group discussion and work

FIGURE 9–1   (Concluded)

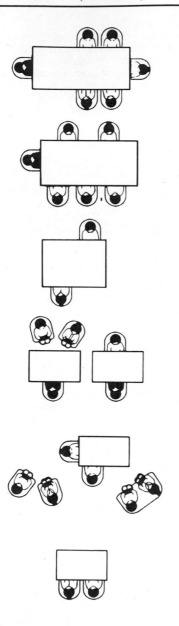

■ Casual/informal
■ Participants are on an equal footing
■ Facilitates cooperation
■ Inhibits visual and vocal communication
■ Allows sharing of materials

■ Casual/informal
■ Participants are on an equal footing
■ Allows visual and vocal communication
■ Allows sharing of material

■ Formal
■ Allows good visual and vocal communication
■ Establishes adversarial or superior/subordinate relationship (especially if a desk is involved)
■ Restricts ability to share materials
■ Creates psychological barrier between participants

■ Casual/informal
■ Permits independent activity/work and limited communication
■ Participants are on an equal footing
■ Makes sharing of materials difficult

■ Formal
■ Allows fair visual and verbal communication (head chair will receive most communication)
■ Leader/follower or boss/employee relationships established
■ Allows some sharing of materials

■ Formal
■ Establishes psychological distance between participants and leader
■ Nuclear group lessens authoritative posture of leader at opposite end of table
■ Established leader/follower, boss/subordinate or adversarial relationships
■ Restricts sharing of materials

SOURCE: From the book, *The Successful Meeting Master Guide,* by Barbara C. Palmer and Kenneth R. Palmer, pp. 92–93. © 1983. Used by permission of the publisher, Prentice-Hall, Inc., Englewood Cliffs, N.J.

Nevertheless, parliamentary procedure does have its place. Legislation (the making of rules and laws) usually requires the assistance of rules of order.[8] To illustrate, the boards that oversee the activities of licensed professionals in the United States and Canada conduct their meetings according to parliamentary procedure. At these meetings, rules sometimes are formulated that govern the behavior of self-employed professionals (such as specifying the amount of job experience an engineer must have before being qualified to obtain a license).

Use Handouts Sparingly.   Most people attending a meeting expect to receive at least one handout summarizing an important issue related to the central topic. With the almost universal availability of photocopying machines, the distribution of handouts at meetings has reached the point that many participants suffer from communication overload. Another problem with distributing handouts at a meeting is that it leads to participants' reading the handouts rather than listening to each other or making spoken contributions.

Take Minutes and Distribute Them Promptly (if Necessary).   A relatively small percentage of meetings require minutes. Yet minutes are necessary under conditions such as:

1. Policy affecting a large number of people or organizations is being formulated.
2. A high volume of business is being transacted.
3. A continuing need to consult the record of the group's activities is anticipated.
4. Follow-up implementation activities are assigned at the meeting.[9]

An effective practice is to prepare minutes that reflect an informal summary of the meeting, much like an extension of the agenda items. The minutes should be distributed within several days of the meeting to help dramatize their importance. Minutes of meetings held weeks ago tend to receive little attention from busy people.

Avoid Interruptions Except for Emergencies.   A real danger in holding a meeting near the work area of most of the attendees is that the meeting is likely to be interrupted for routine phone calls and requests for minor information. One meeting was interrupted because an administrative assistant wanted to know if her boss preferred mustard or mayonnaise on his roast beef sandwich. When minor interruptions are tolerated, it creates the impression that the subject matter of the meeting is not as important as routine events taking place outside the meeting.

Conclude on a Positive Note.   After the agenda is completed, or if the time deadline is near, the meeting should conclude on a positive note. The participants should leave with a feeling of having accomplished something worthwhile. If there has been much disagreement and not much visible progress, the leader should point out what went right in the meeting. For instance, Bud might have concluded, "Although we haven't agreed on anything specific yet, at least we have established what the major factors are in choosing a location for our new office."

Dealing with People

Our mention of people so far in this chapter has focused on the human aspects of improving the structure and processes of meetings, such as taking into account personal convenience in scheduling a time and place. Below we describe tactics that deal more directly with managing the people present at a meeting. The distinction we make between structure and process versus people is done more for convenience than in the interests of scientific rigor. An alternative would be to classify our discussion into formal versus informal aspects of conducting a meeting.

Serve as a Role Model.   The behavior of the leader sets the tone of the meeting. If the leader is insistent, domineering, and overly quick to criticize, group members are likely to behave in the same way or retreat into silence. In contrast, if the leader is calm, reasonable, and reflective, then others—within the limits of their personality—will tend to behave similarly.[10]

The Leader Should Be Both Task-Oriented and Relationship-Oriented.   Without effective leadership, most meetings are doomed to low productivity. For most situations, effective leadership style is characterized by a high concern for both the task and members. A high task orientation is necessary to keep the group moving toward accomplishing the goals of the meeting. A high relationship orientation is required to provide the kind of emotional support that encourages group interaction and creativity. A keen sensitivity to people is also necessary in running a meeting because of the many subtle interactions taking place (such as members dragging their heels when they disagree with a given proposal).

The Leader Should Share Power and Act as a Facilitator and Collaborator.   In order to encourage constructive ideas, the leader can share power and act as a facilitator and collaborator with members. In most meetings, the leader makes many statements that inhibit creative responses from participants. Accepting ideas from participants tends to spur creativity. Considerable skill is required to constructively modify or resist suggestions from the group without inhibiting imagination or further contributions. Extraneous concerns and flaws should be acknowledged as subproblems to be worked on, but the group's energy should be focused on building a solution.[11] Here is an example of what Bud could have done in this regard:

Liz:

So if we relocate to a suburban park, we'll have to rent a small employment office downtown anyway.

Bud:

Your point about the problems our labor pool would have in getting to a suburban location is a good one. I therefore understand what you mean about maintaining a downtown employment office. I agree that our labor force must be given top consideration. But I'm looking for a solution that will give us one cohesive, central office. We'll keep your point in mind.

Create a Supportive Atmosphere to Enhance Group Discussion. By being supportive of members, the leader plays a major role in creating an atmosphere that fosters discussion. Supportive behaviors include listening to ideas, giving verbal encouragement to the expression of worthwhile ideas, being tolerant of mistakes made by participants, and smiling frequently. Accepting criticism from group members also contributes to free discussion.

A poor atmosphere for group discussion is created by the opposite of behaviors just mentioned. The person who approaches the meeting with arrogance and self-righteousness, attempting to dominate others and impress them, will also inhibit group discussion.[12]

Listen Carefully to Members.   Listening to members serves important functions in addition to creating an atmosphere for group discussion. It enables the leader to gather information that could be vital in solving the problem facing the group. Active listening will also help the leader gauge how well his or her ideas are being accepted. If, for example, one or more participants change the subject after the leader contributes an idea, that idea requires further development and selling.

Strive for Balanced Contributions by Members.   To effectively lead a meeting, the leader must gently curtail the participation of domineering and garrulous members. Equally important, the leader has to coax more reticent members to contribute their ideas. A simple, but effective method of drawing people out is to ask their opinion about agenda items. Asking for factual answers is less helpful in encouraging a balanced contribution for this reason: The person may not know the answer and therefore become more inhibited out of embarrassment.

Give Participants the Opportunity to Assume a Leadership Role.
Yet another way of creating a give-and-take atmosphere and encouraging
a balanced contribution from members is for the leader to encourage
others to take over some leadership activity. One way of accomplishing
this end is to turn over a portion of the meeting to a member who is
responsible for a particular agenda item. When that agenda item is
processed, the leader can take the leadership role back gently. A less
formal way of encouraging leadership behavior among members is to
express appreciation for meritorious suggestions volunteered by them.

Encourage Candid Comments.   A dull, ceremonial meeting is characterized by participants offering only polite, psychologically safe comments. In contrast, an exciting, results-oriented meeting is characterized
by members contributing candid opinions about agenda items and related
topics. You will recall that Liz, the employment director, offered candid
comments about the importance of having a downtown office to accommodate maintenance workers. Without her contribution, the concept of a
suburban office location would have gone unchallenged. The leader can
encourage candid comments by not acting defensively or showing displeasure when an initial open comment is made.

Suppose a group member makes the comment, "It doesn't matter
what machine we purchase. The real problem behind our low productivity
is a group of top managers who are operating in the Dark Ages." To
encourage additional candid comments, yet still preserve a sense of
discipline, the leader might respond: "Okay, the way you see things, if we
want to improve productivity, we must examine corporate policy and top
management practices. Do you have any specific suggestions I can carry
forward?"

Nonverbal Communication Should Be Used Freely.   Another way of
keeping a meeting vital is for members to make ample use of nonverbal
communication to supplement their verbal communication. Without these
silent messages, the meeting can take on a stiffness much like a meeting
governed by parliamentary law. All the forms of nonverbal communication described in Chapter 6 would be relevant here, since meetings
are a natural setting for such communication. The leader can encourage
nonverbal behavior by serving as a model. Among the silent messages
widely used in meetings are table thumping, smiling, finger-pointing, and
leaning forward toward the person making a point.

Posture is another important aspect of nonverbal behavior during a
meeting. Dominance can be established by throwing one's head back and
speaking in a loud voice. At the other extreme, people who place their
hands behind their backs while being addressed may be perceived as
taking a subordinate role.[13]

Members Should Be Tolerant of Divergent Views.   The group leader plays a key role in creating an atmosphere that encourages diverse viewpoints. Participants can play an equally significant role by showing tolerance for extreme viewpoints and controversial opinions. Toleration can be communicated by subtle behaviors such as a nod of approval or a wink after another participant has expressed an extreme viewpoint. The nod, wink, or similar behavior does not necessarily imply agreement, but it does imply acceptance of divergent views.

Encourage Group Interaction.   We mentioned the importance of the leader's encouragement of group discussion. Similarly, the leader should encourage group *interaction*. A meeting loses the advantage of two-way communication when all communication pathways are between the leader and members. It is more effective for the participants to react to each other's comments. At times, tactful challenges are in order. When Nick, the director of maintenance operations, took off on a tangent about the importance of the company party, another member of the team might have said, "Nick, I can't disagree with the importance of the party, but let's deal with the problem of office location."

Although group interaction is welcome, whispers and other side comments should be discouraged. The most effective technique of quelling whispering is for the leader to stare in silence at the whisperers until they stop.

Translate Jargon for Outsiders.   Jargon generally receives negative commentary, yet it serves the useful purposes of shortening communication and fostering a feeling of group belonging. The jargon of one technical group may be unfamiliar to an outsider attending the meeting. Rather than trying to eliminate jargon, the terms should be defined for outsiders. This has the advantage of making the meeting more informative for the outsider. For instance, in one meeting a computer scientist referred to "32-bit architecture." With a smile, he turned to the noncomputer people in the meeting and commented, "That's hacker's jargon for how much data the computer can store. And by the way, a hacker is simply a computer freak."

Strive for Consensus, Not Total Acceptance.   Few groups composed of assertive individuals will arrive at total agreement on most agenda items. It is more realistic to strive for consensus—a state of harmony, general agreement, or majority opinion with a reasonable amount of disagreement still present. When consensus is achieved, each member should be willing to accept the plan because it is logical and feasible. The following suggestions are designed to help the leader achieve consensus:

1. Accept the idea that "there's more than one way to skin a cat."

2. Encourage the team members to clarify and build on one another's ideas. Encourage the entire team to be sure that everyone's ideas are heard.

3. Avoid vigorous or heated arguments in favor of one person's position, especially your own. Encourage the team not to let itself be railroaded by one or two people.

4. Avoid easy ways out—such as majority vote, averaging, and coin flipping—unless the issue is virtually meaningless. Such selection methods may leave team members with strong differences of opinion. Then you have no consensus at all.

5. Shoot for win-win solutions (or plans) if at all practicable. This means that everyone feels reasonably comfortable with what is going to happen. This is where you should be when you believe that you have a consensus.[14]

Participants Should Delay the Expression of Strong Emotion. Experiments suggest that the expression of emotion about decision problems should be delayed until after alternatives to the problems have been generated. Two dysfunctional consequences are associated with the early expression of strong emotion: a reduction in group energy and a narrowing of the range of accepted ideas. High levels of emotion will sometimes hinder the capacity of the group to think clearly about the task at hand and also foster misunderstanding and poor communication within the group.[15] An example of such early display of emotion would be cheering when the first acceptable tentative solution to the problem at hand arises. The leader should help restrain emotion from members until additional alternatives have been explored.

Avoid Disruptive Behavior. The leader also may have to act as suppressor when participants engage in behavior that has a debilitating effect on meetings. According to Palmer and Palmer, the most frequent behaviors of this kind are inept humor, personal anecdotes, domination of the discussion, switching topics in midstream, side conversations, unconstructive cynicism, repetition of arguments, and insistence on questioning decisions already made by the group.[16] In all these instances, the disruptive person may have to be dealt with assertively by the leader (or other members).

Manage Conflict as Needed. Healthy, open discussion inevitably brings about interpersonal conflict. Instead of trying to suppress or ignore this conflict, the leader should consider dealing with it openly. An interpretation of the difference of opinion between the two participants can be helpful in turning the conflict into a constructive force.

Too little conflict in a meeting could mean that members are lapsing into overconformity of thought. The participants may get so accustomed to avoiding friction that politeness and consideration take precedence over disagreement, even of a polite nature. In this type of situation it may prove beneficial for the leader to stimulate conflict by throwing out good-natured challenges such as "I can't believe that everybody agrees on this point. Somebody must have at least one reservation about this proposal."[17]

Provide Refreshments When Motivation Is a Problem.   A cultural fact of organizational life is that many people expect refreshments at meetings. When participants, or their organizations, pay to attend meetings (such as conventions, professional meetings, and trade shows) refreshments are mandatory. For briefer meetings, on the company premises, refreshments are optional. Yet, many people expect to be offered food and beverage during the meeting. Since eating and drinking take time away from the meeting, and do cost some money, refreshments should not be served indiscriminately. As a rule of thumb, since the lack of refreshments can dampen satisfaction and motivation, they should be served primarily when satisfaction and motivation are potential problems. Following this logic, refreshments are mandatory at Saturday morning meetings!

The Argument For and Against Following Suggestions for Conducting Effective Meetings

Although all of the suggestions presented in this chapter may not work all of the time, they have high potential for being cost effective for two reasons. First, managers spend a substantial amount of time in meetings, perhaps up to two thirds of their average workday. Second, it has been estimated that about half of time spent in meetings is wasted.[18] This waste can be translated into two types of costs. One is the cost attributed to the salaries and benefits paid to the participants while they are attending the meeting (computed as the hourly salary, plus benefits multiplied by the time spent attending and traveling to and from the meeting). The other are the opportunity costs—productive work the people might have done if they had not been at the meeting.

One argument for ignoring the suggestions in this chapter is that if rational people want to make meetings more effective, they will. Perhaps the time wasted in meetings is really functional. The gabbing and ceremonial activity that takes place in a meeting relieves tension and helps build a sense of camaraderie among workers. Another argument in opposition to these suggestions is that the time wasted in meetings is not a real cost, owing to Parkinson's Law. After people have wasted time in a meeting, they scurry to finish up their day's work. If they did not attend the meeting, they would work at a more leisurely pace the remainder of the day.

Guidelines for Action and Skill Development

To improve the productivity of the meetings you chair and/or attend, use the suggestions made in this chapter as a checklist of steps that can be taken or factors that can be considered. Not all of these suggestions will be applicable to every meeting. The major points in the chapter are summarized below to assist you in using them as a checklist.

Checklist for Improving the Productivity of Meetings

	Do It Now	Should Do It	Not Appl.
Dealing with Structure and Process			
1. Valid reason for meeting.	____	____	____
2. Stick to specific agenda.	____	____	____
3. Select attendees carefully.	____	____	____
4. Convenient time and place.	____	____	____
5. Stop and start on time.	____	____	____
6. Work on surmountable problems.	____	____	____
7. Brief and pointed comments.	____	____	____
8. Provide summaries for key points.	____	____	____
9. Repeat, restate unclear comments.	____	____	____
10. Physical structure for communication.	____	____	____
11. Limited use of parliamentary procedure.	____	____	____
12. Use handouts sparingly.	____	____	____
13. Send minutes soon after meeting.	____	____	____
14. Minimize interruptions.	____	____	____
15. Conclude on a positive note.	____	____	____
Dealing with People			
1. Serve as a model.	____	____	____
2. Task and relationship-orientation.	____	____	____
3. Power sharing by leader.	____	____	____
4. Supportive atmosphere.	____	____	____

5. Listen carefully to group members.   ____   ____   ____
6. Balanced contribution by members.   ____   ____   ____
7. Participants given a chance to lead.   ____   ____   ____
8. Encourage candid comments.   ____   ____   ____
9. Free use of nonverbal communication.   ____   ____   ____
10. Tolerance of divergent views   ____   ____   ____
11. Encourage group interaction.   ____   ____   ____
12. Translate jargon for outsiders.   ____   ____   ____
13. Strive for consensus.   ____   ____   ____
14. Delay expression of strong emotion.   ____   ____   ____
15. Avoid disruptive behavior.   ____   ____   ____
16. Manage conflict as needed.   ____   ____   ____
17. Serve refreshments if needed.   ____   ____   ____

The checklist just presented can be used for skill building. During meetings you attend or chair, make a serious attempt to practice the applicable behaviors outlined in the checklist. For instance, if you think group discussion is very important in your meeting you would take note of point 10, "Physical structure for communication." In referring back to Figure 9–1, you would then choose the "casual/informal" seating arrangement. Another example of how this checklist can be used for skill building, would be the application of point 8, "Provide summaries for key points." If you chair a meeting, remember to stop at certain checkpoints to provide oral summaries of key topics. If your summaries seem to add to the productivity of the meeting, you will most likely incorporate summaries of key points into your repertoire of skills.

An important general skill to develop in conducting a meeting is to find a way to keep people listening. Even at high levels in organizations, many people daydream, whisper, or work on other matters while attending a meeting. A powerful antidote to this problem is to frequently ask people their opinion about issues that surface. Rather than risk being embarrassed by not having heard the issue, most attendees will stay alert. Another antidote to the problem of nonlisteners is for the meeting leader to confront the daydreamer or whisperer with a comment such as, "Are you with us?"

DISCUSSION QUESTIONS AND ACTIVITIES

1. Why do so many people say they hate meetings?
2. Identify one or two political reasons for conducting meetings.
3. For which of the standard functions of management (planning, organizing, leading, controlling, and so forth) are meetings used?

4. How would you handle the situation if your boss went off on a tangent during a meeting and you believed that this behavior was lowering the productivity of the meeting?

5. Organizations sometimes send key personnel to a "retreat" for purposes of formulating strategy or dealing with other important matters. Why are such retreats likely to be more productive than meetings held on organizational premises?

6. For what purposes do you think standup meetings are best suited?

7. Use the Checklist for Improving the Production Meetings to analyze the next meeting you attend. If time permits, bring your findings back to class.

NOTES

1. Peter A. Turla and Kathleen L. Hawkins, "Meaningful Meetings," *Success!,* June 1983, p. 40.
2. "Meetings Don't Have to Be Boring," *Personal Report for the Executive,* December 1, 1986, p. 6.
3. Barbara C. Palmer and Kenneth R. Palmer, *The Successful Meeting Master Guide* (Englewood Cliffs, N. J.: Prentice-Hall, 1983), p. 31.
4. Ibid., p. 31.
5. Stan Kossen, *The Human Side of Organization,* 3rd ed. (New York: Harper & Row 1983), p. 110.
6. Gary Dessler, *Human Behavior: Improving Performance at Work* (Reston, Va.: Reston Publishing Company, 1980), p. 277.
7. "The Best Meetings Are Usually the Liveliest," *Personal Report for the Executive,* May 14, 1985, p. 5.
8. Palmer and Palmer, *The Successful Meeting,* p. 107.
9. Ibid., p. 164.
10. "The Best Meetings Are Usually the Liveliest," p. 5.
11. George M. Prince, "Creative Meetings through Power Sharing," *Harvard Business Review,* July–August 1972, p. 53.
12. Palmer and Palmer, *The Successful Meeting,* p. 33.
13. Joe Kelly, "Surviving and Thriving in Top Management Meetings," *Personnel,* June 1987, p. 34.
14. Francis X. Mahoney, "Team Development, Part 4: Work Meetings," *Personnel,* March–April 1982, pp. 52–53.
15. Richard A. Guzzo and James A. Waters, "The Expression of Affect and the Performance of Decision-Making Groups," *Journal of Applied Psychology,* February 1982, pp. 67–74.
16. Palmer and Palmer, *The Successful Meeting,* pp. 128–29.
17. "The Best Meetings are Usually the Liveliest," p. 6.
18. Joan Hamann, "Turning Meetings into All-Win Situations," *Personnel Administrator,* June 1986, p. 62.

SOME ADDITIONAL REFERENCES

Daniels, William R. *Group Power: A Manager's Guide to Using Meetings.* San Diego, Calif.: University Associates, 1986.

Fox, William M. *Effective Group Problem Solving: How to Broaden Participation, Improve Decision Making, and Increase Commitment to Action.* San Francisco: Jossey-Bass, 1987.

Kirkpatrick, Donald L. *How to Plan and Conduct Productive Meetings.* Rev. ed. New York: AMACOM, 1987.

Smeltzer, Larry R., and Jeanette A. Davy. "Teleconferencing: Reach Out to Train Someone." *Personnel Administrator,* June 1987, pp. 211–19.

The 3M Meeting Management Team. *How to Run Better Business Meetings: A Reference Guide for Managers.* 2nd ed. New York: McGraw-Hill. 1987.

Chapter Ten

Building Teamwork

The principal of a small CPA firm was concerned about the limited amount of teamwork and cooperation among the six accountants and two secretaries who comprised the rest of his firm. In an attempt to rectify the situation, the owner sought the advice of an industrial and organizational psychologist.

"The reason I sought your advice," said John Zeman, "is that my firm isn't really working like a firm. We're just a bunch of individuals serving separate clients. I'm the owner of the firm, but I feel like I'm just the landlord."

"What makes you feel that you are just the landlord?" asked Gil Peterson, the industrial and organizational psychologist.

"The point I'm getting at is that it seems as if I just rent space to the six accountants who work in my office. They are cordial to each other, but they don't work together as a team. Each accountant in the office does his or her own thing. We don't really benefit by being a firm. We're independents, not a true group."

"I like your analysis," said Peterson. "It's a common problem among professionals who serve clients. Often they do not give much thought to working as a team. Instead, they are content to work quite independently. Before recommending any tentative solutions to your problem, it would be best to meet with you and the rest of the firm for about a two-hour session."

"Okay, how about Friday afternoon, the 14th of next month at 2:30 for a session?" said Zeman. "This will give me time to go back to the people working for me and make sure they can arrange their work schedules to fit this meeting. As much as I want to improve teamwork at my firm, client service comes first."

Zeman, Peterson, and the six accountants met in the conference room at Zeman's office. Zeman opened the meeting by explaining its purpose: "As I mentioned to all of you individually, I invited Dr. Gil Peterson to meet with us to get our perceptions of whether we need better teamwork among ourselves. If it appears that we do need improved teamwork, we want to get your suggestions of what should be done. If it seems advisable, Gil will then make a few suggestions for me for improving teamwork."

Following is an abridgment of the major comments made by the professional members of Zeman's firm:

Ken:

I could see the need for more teamwork. Yet I'm concerned that we really don't have much time for teamwork. John keeps strict track of the amount of time we bill to clients. Most of our bonus is based on the level of our billings. If I spend time with talking to the other professionals or the secretaries in the office, my billings will go down. And so will my bonus.

Allison:

There goes Ken again, thinking like an accountant. (Laughter from the group.) Seriously, I can see why John is concerned. We don't do enough in the way of teamwork. We can't even get out for lunch as a group because we need heavy coverage in the office during those hours. And during the tax season, we barely have time to grunt at each other when we pass in the halls at 10 P.M. Let's do something together as a team. Maybe we should attend an occasional local NAA (National Association of Accountants) meeting together.

Brad:

I'm the senior accountant in the office except for John who hired me. My vantage point might therefore be useful. I can see the need for more coordinated effort among us if that is what you mean by teamwork. However, there are some built-in limits to teamwork in a small CPA firm. I know that several of us would like to become partners in this firm somewhere down the road. If we coordinate too much and exchange ideas, it will be difficult for John to figure out who is making the biggest contribution. We are cordial to each other, but there is always the hidden concern that we each want to gain an edge over our colleagues. I don't think it's anything out of the ordinary.

Jose:

I'm the newest member of the firm, so my vantage point should be of particular interest also. I don't buy the idea that we are worried about getting the edge over one another. We're not working as a team because John hasn't organized us to work in teams so far. Maybe if we had a few more large clients, we could work together on those clients. It's not John's fault. We get too many of the sole-proprietorship accounts and tax preparation for individuals. We're small potatoes, and teamwork is for big potatoes.

Matthew:

> This has been a very polite meeting so far. What I have to say isn't so polite. But I guess we wouldn't be paying a consultant if we didn't want some straight talk. I won't name names, but we do have some negative vibes among a few members of the firm. The people I'm talking about respect each other professionally, but they don't get along personally. John should see a few of the cold stares that go on in our little firm. If these people could iron out their personal differences, you would see a lot more teamwork.

Lorraine:

> Matt's comments are not untrue, but they obscure the fact that the members of our firm get along pretty well. Nobody has left in the two years that I've been here. Our turnover of secretaries is also quite low. We would work together more as a team if John had more time to work with us as a team. This is the first meeting we've had in five months. I know that John is busy. He has the biggest client load of us all. He barely has time to supervise what we are doing.

John:

> I guess I should make a few comments now. The reason I asked Gil to visit us is that I don't think we work enough as a team. The problem could be my fault. The few comments you have made today have been an eye-opener for me. I intend to study the problem further. I'll take your recommendations seriously. I'll also listen carefully to what Gil recommends.

Gil then met once more with John and the other members of his firm. Based on what he heard in both sessions, and general information about teamwork, Gil made these tentative recommendations to John:

Above all, John should promote the concept of teamwork among the staff of the firm. The fact that a meeting has already been held on the topic is a good starting point. The idea of teamwork has to be promoted at every opportunity.

A financial incentive system should be developed that rewards the staff for individual contributions as well as the total performance of the firm. Profit sharing helps reinforce the idea of teamwork.

Teamwork will not take place unless the staff works on some team projects. John should capitalize on any opportunity to attract clients large enough to justify the services of more than one CPA.

Communication sessions should be held among staff members approximately once a quarter to openly discuss any interpersonal problems existing within the group. It may be beneficial for the consultant to conduct these meetings to help protect against their getting out of control.

A group breakfast, lunch, or dinner should be scheduled approximately every other month to foster solidarity and camaraderie.

John should spend more time interacting with staff members to help them develop the feeling that they are working for a firm. An important part of this interaction should be a discussion of the goals and strategy of the firm.

Next, John Zeman discussed these recommendations with the members of the firm. Although Matthew and Lorraine made a few skeptical comments, the consensus was that the recommendations were worth a try. John agreed and announced the first "solidarity meeting." He brought to the meeting a box of T-shirts in various sizes, all carrying the logo, *The Zeman Demons*.

Six months later, John telephoned Gil Peterson to inform him that the teamwork experiment was successful. Both John and the group perceived themselves to be more of a true firm than in the past. One important sign of teamwork is that group members were now sharing information with each other about difficult client problems. Another was that the group had identified and approached three individuals who wanted to join the firm as soon as an opening developed.

STRATEGIES AND TACTICS FOR ENCOURAGING TEAMWORK

The situation of the accounting firm illustrates a simple but useful approach to enhancing teamwork that involved several tactics and strategies. Such approaches can be divided into three categories: (*a*) informal tactics and strategies, (*b*) formal tactics and strategies, and (*c*) team-building meetings that require the assistance of an internal or external consultant. The emphasis in this chapter, however, is on approaches to building teamwork aside from formal team building. Managerial judgment and intuition must be used to choose which of these many strategies or tactics will probably best fit a given circumstance.

Informal Tactics and Strategies

The tactics and strategies described in this section do not require changes in structure, policies, or procedures. Most of them concern the interpersonal aspects of managing people such as John Zeman speaking to group members about teamwork.

Serve as a Model of Teamwork.   According to Paul S. George, perhaps the most effective way to encourage the emergence of teamwork is by example. If the leader reveals important information about ideas and attitudes relevant to the work of the group, members may follow suit. Self-disclosure fosters teamwork because it leads to shared perceptions and concerns.[1] For example, John Zeman might share with the group his concerns about competition from a new CPA firm that opened offices across the street.

Develop a Norm of Teamwork.   An overall strategy the team leader should use to promote teamwork is to cultivate the attitude among group members that working together effectively is an expected standard of conduct. (A *group norm* is defined as an informal rule adopted by a group to regulate and regularize group members' behavior.)[2] A direct way of accomplishing this end is for the leader to make explicit statements about the desirability of teamwork. Normative statements about teamwork made by powerful group members can have a similar effect. The manager of an information systems department at a food manufacturing company used the following comments (with good results) to help foster a norm of teamwork:

> My boss is concerned that we are not pulling together as a cohesive team. And I can see some merit in his argument. We are performing splendidly as a group of individuals, but I see a need for an improved united effort in our group. We need to share ideas more, to touch base with each other, to pick each other's brains more. From now on when I evaluate performance, I'm going to give as much weight to group effort as I do to individual contribution.

Encourage Cooperative Behavior.   An obvious but often overlooked method of building teamwork is to encourage cooperation rather than intense competition within the group. One method of encouraging cooperation would be for the manager to praise employees for having collaborated on joint projects. Another would be to assign tasks that require input from several people in order to be completed. One manager of a chemical department encouraged cooperation by sending out two chemists on trouble-shooting assignments from time to time. They were asked to present a joint recommendation for overcoming the problem.

Minimize Personal Friction.   A common sense strategy of merit for promoting teamwork is to have friends work together and enemies work apart. Assigning people to tasks according to their social preferences is only feasible when group members are arranged into small subteams. A potential disadvantage is that overly friendly workers may socialize too much on the job. But as magazine publisher Peter Diamandis puts it, "I have a hiring policy that's revolutionary. It took me 48 years to figure this out. I only hire people I like. Up until recently I hired experts; I hired people with great reputations. I hired all sorts of people who were sent to me for different reasons, and a lot of them didn't work out. So I decided to go back to basics and hire only the people I like, figuring that at the very least we'd all have a lot of fun. And it's turned out very well. Everybody takes on a lot of responsibility and does very well."[3]

Encourage Competition with Another Group.   One of the best-known ways to encourage teamwork is to rally the support of the group against a real or imagined threat from the outside.[4] Beating the competition makes more sense when the competition is outside your own organization. When the enemy is within, the team spirit developed may become detrimental to the overall organization.

A plant manager told his supervisors: "Our sister plant in Montreal is way ahead of us in preventing lost-time accidents. We don't have to take this challenge lying down. Let's wish them the best of luck in reducing accidents, but let's create even better luck for our own plant." By the end of the year the Ontario plant *did* reduce accidents a trifle more than did the Montreal plant.

Keep Communication Channels Open.   Many minor problems between the manager and subordinates fester into major problems. The major problems, in turn, adversely affect team spirit and productivity. Early intervention in these problems could have prevented them from becoming a disruptive force. In order to work through little problems, the group leader should keep open channels of communication with the group.

> One supervisor made it a practice to have lunch once a month with seven subordinates. It was called the "anything goes" lunch. One problem the group brought up was that the supervisor was being negligent in ordering office supplies for them. This simple problem was resolved before it escalated into ill will between the supervisor and the group, thus hampering teamwork.

Encourage and Provide Emotional Support.   Good teamwork includes emotional support to members. Such support can take the form of verbal encouragement for ideas expressed, listening to a group member's problems, or even providing help with a knotty technical problem. The leader can provide such support and also encourage other members to help each other. A case in point is a pressroom supervisor who uses a straightforward method of encouraging emotional support within the workgroup. Should one of the press operators arrive at work looking forlorn, he would say to another press operator: "Buddy up to _____ today. I think he could sure use some encouragement. He seems to be under the weather."

Practice Equality.   A team leader does not have to like all team members equally well. But leaders should try to make assignments on the basis of merit, otherwise they run the risk of being accused of favoritism. Equality thus means that each department member has an equal chance of obtaining whatever rewards the leader or manager has to offer providing that person performs well. Playing favorites detracts from teamwork because most people do not wish to cooperate with a selected one or two employees who receive undeserved rewards.

Reach Out to Isolates.   In many groups, at least one member is friendless and often lonely. If the manager can involve such individuals in group social interaction, teamwork will increase because one more person will become part of the team. If the isolate is adamant about not getting involved with others, and the others do not want the isolate, intervention may backfire. One supervisor skillfully facilitated a loner becoming involved in the group. She asked that individual to be acting-department head on a day that supervisors were asked to hand out good news about a cost-of-living adjustment. Being a bearer of good news helped ease the isolated employee into a position of group acceptance.

Orient New Members.   New workers should be carefully introduced to the group to give them a chance to become psychologically part of the work unit. Many companies use a big-brother or big-sister program whereby experienced workers help assimilate new workers to the formal requirements of the job and the informal mores of the group. Improved teamwork is often the result.[5]

Encourage Shared Laughter.   George observes that laughter is a natural team builder that enhances understanding and empathy, essential ingredients to group cohesiveness. Simple techniques work well such as daily calendars with humorous stories, in-group jokes at staff meetings, and pictures or words hung on the walls of the entrance hall.[6] The Zeman Demons T-shirts were worth a good laugh and led to the group scheduling a bowling night together.

Formal Tactics and Strategies

The tactics and strategies for building teamwork described in this section require changes in structure, policies, or procedures. These types of changes might also be classified as administrative, because they require some administrative action to implement (such as providing group incentives).

Make the Task the Boss.   Teamwork is fostered when group members pull together toward a common goal. One way of accomplishing this is to make the "task the boss," a concept illustrated by the training film, "Task Oriented Team Development."[7] The underlying premise is that an agreed-on goal, rather than the leader per se, directs the team. This idea complies with the generally accepted principle of group dynamics that working toward a common goal enhances group effectiveness. An important contribution of the leader is to help the group realize the path toward goal attainment. A basic example of the latter would be for the leader to fight for appropriate support services for the group.

A practical way of helping the group realize a common goal is to conduct group meetings devoted to goal setting and strategy (long-range goals and plans). The hoped for outcome of such meetings would be an awareness by group members of common goals. Three useful discussion questions for goal-setting meetings are:

1. Where are we headed as a group?
2. Who are we?
3. What are we trying to accomplish?

Allow for Physical Proximity among Members. Group cohesiveness, and therefore teamwork, is enhanced when team members are located close together and can interact frequently and easily. The late William Glueck offers this explanation: "This may be due to the ability of the members to maintain eye contact if they are located close together. Eye movement, direction of gaze, and mutual eye contact are important nonverbal interactions that influence group effectiveness."[8] Whether or not this eye-contact explanation is valid, sharing a location seems important for group cohesiveness.

Use Group Incentives. A key strategy in encouraging teamwork is to reward the group as a whole when such rewards are deserved. Assume a manager receives a compliment from higher management that he or she has done an outstanding job. The manager in question would share this praise with the group since most accomplishments of a manager reflect group effort. A popular form of group incentive is to reward good group performance with an organization-paid banquet. One company threw a roast beef and beer party to celebrate making a record shipment of industrial pumps.

Rotate Leaders and Job Assignments. Two types of job rotation contribute to teamwork. One type is recommended by William G. Hahn. He observes that it is an effective practice to rotate the team leaders on some preset frequency. This gives each team member a chance to learn the required skills and eliminates some petty problems related to the leadership of the group by reinforcing the idea of team leadership being more of a coordination role, and less of an authoritarian role.[9] Rotation of leaders is more likely to be practiced at the first level of management among professional or technical groups than at the executive level.

Another type of rotation is to give group members a chance to cross-switch jobs. This type of rotation encourages identification with the team as a whole rather than with individual jobs. Rotation promotes cooperation and teamwork in another subtle way. Workers come to appreciate the problems faced by other workers within the department as they perform each others' jobs.

Get Team Members to Share Ideas. Idea sharing is a robust approach to developing teamwork because the exchange of information requires a high level of cooperation. David A. Stumm, the sales and training manager for Duracell Corporation, explains how a manager heightened teamwork through idea sharing:

> To get us working together, he'd say, as if in passing: "John has some ideas he wants to try; with your experience you ought to be able to help him. The two of you tell me what you want to do." Since I didn't want my boss to think only John had ideas, the situation was competitive. But the proof that I was good would be if John and I made good together—so we cooperated intensely. We became excited and committed ourselves to making things happen. We outsold all the other divisions in the company and our success ratio rose with every win.[10]

Use Team Symbols. Teamwork on the athletic field is enhanced by team symbols such as uniforms and nicknames (*Fighting Irish, Orangemen, Lady Longhorns,* and so forth). Symbols are also a potentially effective team builder in the office, factory, or store. Trademarks, logos, mottos, and other indicators of products both advertise the company and signify a joint effort. Company jackets, caps, T-shirts, mugs, luggage tags, and business cards can be modified to symbolize an organizational subunit.[11]

Social symbols, such as symbolic group activities, can also identify and build team unity. Many groups use ceremonies such as award banquets to recognize group effort, thus reinforcing collaborative effort. A recommended approach here is to organize a ceremony announcing the successful introduction of a new product or service that resulted from a team effort.[12]

Establish a Shared Physical Facility. The importance of physical proximity as a builder of teamwork was described previously. A related technique is to create the opportunity for team members to share a physical facility such as a conference room, research library, or beverage lounge. It is recommended that these areas be decorated differently from others in the building and a few amenities be added such as a coffee pot and refrigerator. Team members can then use these areas for refreshments and group interaction.[13]

Follow Through on Commitments. Managers who are negligent in following through on commitments to their subordinates may lose support of the group. In addition, the group may become demoralized and teamwork may consequently suffer. Commitments to employees include major and minor matters, such as conducting performance reviews on time, ordering supplies for the department, helping employees process benefit forms such as medical claims, and inquiring about job transfer or promotion possibilities. Following through on commitments also contributes to teamwork because it enhances a feeling of trust between the subordinates and the manager.

Have Team Members Critique Each Other.   Constructive critique among team members can lead to a feeling of closeness and mutual concern about doing things right. Because this type of critique is unlikely to occur spontaneously, the leader may need to establish a formal feedback mechanism for the critique. One such approach would be to have a critique session at the end of a staff meeting. Each member would critique the other members on how well they contributed to the meeting. For instance, one person might say to a co-worker: "I liked your idea about attracting big clients. But you just left us hanging. You posed the problem, but you provided no specific details about how to attract big clients."

If the critiques are too pointed and extensive, some group members will be inhibited from making statements that are likely to be criticized by others. Nevertheless, critique is an important part of the team building exercises training programs for leadership excellence such as the Managerial Grid.[14]

Provide for Shared Meals.   Sharing meals is a natural opportunity for developing teamwork because dining together is symbolic of camaraderie. Breakfast meetings have gained in popularity because they are less disruptive of regular work than luncheon meetings, and less disruptive of family life than dinner. Too many business breakfasts and dinners, however, detract from teamwork. Group members who regard these meetings as an intrusion on personal time will come to resent the shared meals. The consequent grumbling will detract from teamwork.

Strive for Long-Term Membership in the Group.   Team building and attrition work against each other. A spirit of cooperation is fostered when team members recognize that they will be working together relatively permanently. (This strategy has been one of the pillars of the Japanese strategy for achieving work group harmony.) Team members should be organized so they perceive themselves spending the foreseeable future together as a team; the result is likely to greater degrees of interpersonal commitment. The promise of permanence is important. As George notes, "No amount of money or time spent on formal team-building efforts make up for shredding interpersonal fibers by upsetting and separating the team too often. Organizing teams with an eye on a long-term membership goes the extra mile toward natural development."[15]

Team Building as a Method of Building Teamwork

A standard way of building teamwork is through team building, an organization development technique that seeks to improve the cooperation and effectiveness of work groups through self-analysis and change. The common format is for a consultant to work with a natural work group to clarify objectives and tasks, roles and relationships, and to provide training in interaction skills.[16]

A Specific Team-Building Program.   Team building takes many different forms, all centering on the idea of improving teamwork and solving work problems. A representative team-building program developed by Jeffrey P. Davidson is described here. Its purpose is to accomplish work goals and generate team spirit along the way. The team-building activity consists of seven weekly 2-hour sessions involving a work unit of between four and seven people. The sessions proceed as follows:[17]

Session 1:   The team assembles and begins to identify general areas in which the group's work problems lie. Group members discuss the importance of assuming responsibility and minimizing the blaming of others. A questionnaire asking for information about goals and methods of resolving conflict is administered.

Session 2:   The group brainstorms to develop a consensus on team problems and agree on group goals, such as "We will develop a new plan for fund raising from individuals by April 30 of this year."

Session 3:   The team considers potential obstacles it may create to prevent itself from accomplishing its mission. Members are instructed to ask themselves: "How can I communicate with others to obtain results that contribute to the team's mission?" Team members write problem statements in the form of how-can-I questions, such as "How can I get a valid list of potential contributors to our agency?"

Session 4:   After completing the problem statements, the group divides into three- or four-person subgroups to help one another solve problems. Action plans are drawn based both on brainstorming and fact finding. Each subgroup member has the opportunity to examine others' problem statements and actions plans. In this way, additional input into problem solving is obtained.

Session 5:   Participants negotiate with one another to overcome work problems. The problems may be technical, administrative, or interpersonal. For instance, one person might say to another: "I could accomplish my data analysis sooner if you would stop looking over my shoulder while I'm working."

Session 6:   Team members assemble in three-person subgroups, each consisting of two individuals who bargain and one third party who observes to help resolve conflicts. Members often report that as a result of this process, "They have subdued their egos for the good of the team; individual assignments have not changed, but are now pursued with a new perspective and vigor; for possibly the first time, the whole unit is seeking the same bottom line."[18]

The session ends after team members write out agreements they have made, such as "I will get the data analysis on time, if you give me the figures on time and in usable form."

Session 7:   Here the members develop subunit goals based on the individual performance goals they have developed in the previous sessions. Representative subunit goals include simplifying the financial reporting system or obtaining a valid list of potential donors. During this session, members also share thoughts about the team-building process.

An eighth session is sometimes held to evaluate progress since the first meeting. The questionnaire administered in the first session is repeated. Participants compare how much progress they have made in clarifying goals, resolving conflict, and improving teamwork.

Results Achieved with Team Building.   Davidson reports that results from the model of team building just described almost always reflect progress over the seven-week period. His results are substantiated by other researchers who report favorable results with team building. When specific rather than general interpersonal and task issues are worked on, the results are more likely to be positive.[19] Nevertheless, not all research about team building reports positive results. For instance, a team-building experiment with hard-rock miners in a metal mine found that team building did not improve productivity.[20]

THE CASE FOR AND AGAINST
BUILDING TEAMWORK

The most cogent argument for attempting to build teamwork is that a cohesive team can consistently outperform a collection of talented individuals, both in sports and in business. The reason is that on a cohesive team, the members work together in the pursuit of a common goal.[21] A related argument for the importance of making an effort to build teamwork is that the legendary successes of individuals such as Lee Iacocca are really the accomplishments of teams of workers.[22]

Empirical evidence about the importance of promoting teamwork rather than individual contribution is supplied by the U. S. Army. In 1986, the Army replaced a system that assigned soldiers to their units individually in favor of a system that keeps teams of soldiers together for their entire tours of duty. As explained by a U. S. Army spokesperson: "We discovered that individuals perform better when they are part of a stable group. They are more reliable. They also take responsibility for the success of the overall operation."[23]

On the other hand, maybe we are concerned too much about getting people to work together and to like each other. Too much cohesion has some undesirable consequences such as overconformity and group-think—the end point of consensus whereby group members begin to think alike. In order to be creative many organizations need more boat rocking, more mavericks, and less mutual admiration. Organizations move forward via the individual ingenuity of a relatively few pioneers. If we rely excessively on teamwork and cooperation, these people may hold back from making their contributions.

Another argument against teamwork is that people who rely too much on teamwork will not receive recognition for their individual ideas, thus retarding their careers. Also, exploring and pursuing your own ideas can hasten self-development.[24]

Guidelines for Action and Skill Development

In order for teamwork to live up to its potential, managers must surrender some of the power they have over team members and become part of the team. John Naisbitt makes the following recommendations for becoming a *high-touch, Information-Age manager* (his term for someone who practices team management):

1. Recognize that people are the organization's most valuable resource. It is therefore important to be a teacher and mentor, not an order-giver.

2. Treat employees with the same respect accorded to customers. Employer-employee relationships should be based on care, trust, and honesty.

3. To minimize conflict, the goals of individuals and the organization must be balanced.

4. Positive discipline should be substituted for negative discipline. When a problem arises, confront the worker and ask how the issue might be resolved.

5. Create a team in which all members participate in decision making, everybody's input is actively solicited and considered, and people are challenged to take risks and work at their highest level.[25]

DISCUSSION QUESTIONS AND ACTIVITIES

1. How does honesty on the part of the team leader contribute to a spirit of teamwork?
2. In what way might friction in the workgroup make a contribution to organizational goals?
3. Why does competition with another group facilitate teamwork?
4. How can car pooling contribute to teamwork?
5. What are some of the practical problems of rotating the group leader?
6. What is your opinion of the value of an employer sponsoring athletic teams for employees as a way of promoting teamwork on the job?
7. Ask two experienced managers what they think is a good way of promoting teamwork on the job. Be prepared to report your findings back to class.

NOTES

1. Paul S. George, "Teamwork without Tears," *Personnel Journal,* November 1987, p. 129.
2. Daniel C. Feldman, "The Development and Enforcement of Group Norms," *Academy of Management Review,* January 1984, p. 47.
3. "Magazine Publisher Diamandis," *MBA Executive,* April/May 1980, p. 9.
4. H. Joseph Reitz, *Behavior in Organizations* 3rd ed. (Homewood, Ill.: Richard D. Irwin, 1987), p. 290.
5. George Strauss and Leonard R. Sayles, *Personnel: The Human Problems of Management,* 2d ed. (Englewood Cliffs, N. J.: Prentice-Hall, 1967), p. 200.
6. George, "Teamwork without Tears," p. 124.
7. "Team Building," CRM/McGraw-Hill film, 1983.
8. William F. Glueck, *Management* (Hinsdale, Ill.: Dryden Press, 1977), p. 164.
9. William G. Hahn, personal communication, 1987.
10. David A. Stumm, "Teamwork and Tin Men," *Success!,* October 1987, p. 22.
11. George, "Teamwork without Tears," p. 126.
12. Ibid., p. 126.
13. Ibid., p. 128.
14. Robert R. Blake and Jane S. Mouton, *The Managerial Grid III,* Houston: Gulf Publishing, 1985, pp. 118–22.
15. George, "Teamwork without Tears," p. 129.
16. Reitz, *Behavior in Organizations,* p. 576.
17. Jeffrey P. Davidson, "A Task-Focused Approach to Team Building," *Personnel,* March 1985, pp. 16–18.
18. Ibid., p. 18.
19. R. W. Woodman and J. J. Sherwood, "The Role of Team Development in Organizational Effectiveness: A Critical Review," *Psychological Bulletin,* 88 (1980), pp. 166–86.

20. Paul F. Buller and Cecil H. Bell, Jr., "Effects of Team Building and Goal Setting on Productivity: A Field Experiment," *Academy of Management Journal,* June 1986, pp. 305–28.

21. *Effective Team Building,* AMA Extension Institute, audio-cassette/ workbook, 1987; Steven S. Ross, "Teamwork: Key to Business Success," *Business Week's Guide to Careers,* April 1986, p. 64.

22. Robert B. Reich, "Entrepreneurship Reconsidered: The Team as Hero," *Harvard Business Review,* May–June 1987, p. 82.

23. Ibid., p. 82.

24. Srully Blotnik, "The Truth about Teamwork," *Success!,* June 1987, p. 20. (Although Srully's statement of his sample size has been publicly discredited, his insights are still considered valid.)

25. John Naisbitt, "The New Teamwork," *Success!,* March 1986, p. 8.

SOME ADDITIONAL REFERENCES

Blake, Robert R., and Jane Srygley Mouton. *Spectacular Teamwork.* New York: John Wiley, 1987.

Dyer, William. *Team Building: Issues and Alternatives.* 2nd ed. Reading, Mass.: Addison-Wesley, 1987.

Goodman, Paul S., and Associates. *Designing Effective Work Groups.* San Francisco: Jossey-Bass Inc., 1986.

Hardaker, Maurice, and Bryan K. Ward. "How to Make a Team Work." *Harvard Business Review,* November–December 1987, pp. 112–20.

Lynch, Robert. "The Shoot Out among Nonteam Players." *Management Solutions,* May 1987, pp. 4–12.

Nanda, Ravinda. "Training in Team and Consensus Building." *Management Solutions,* September 1986, pp. 31–36.

Appendix to Chapter Ten

THE TEAMWORK CHECKLIST

Directions: The purpose of this checklist is to serve as an informal guide for diagnosing teamwork. Both the leader and group members should complete the checklist.

	Mostly Yes	Mostly No
1. Members of the group regard themselves as being part of a team.	____	____
2. Group discussion is frequent, and it is usually pertinent to the task at hand.	____	____

3. Group members understand what they are trying to accomplish. _____ _____

4. People listen to each others' suggestions and ideas. _____ _____

5. Disagreements are tolerated and an attempt is made to resolve them. _____ _____

6. The group members pull for each other. _____ _____

7. The group likes to compete against other groups. _____ _____

8. Should one member falter, the others would help that person. _____ _____

9. There is a well-established, relaxed working relationship among the members. _____ _____

10. There is a high degree of trust and confidence among the leader and subordinates. _____ _____

11. The group members strive hard to help the group achieve its goal. _____ _____

12. Suggestions and criticisms are offered and received with a helpful spirit. _____ _____

13. There is a cooperative rather than a competitive relationship among group members. _____ _____

14. We often meet together outside of regular hours, including having meals together. _____ _____

15. The leader and members hold a high opinion of the group's capabilities. _____ _____

16. We share ideas and opinions on many tasks. _____ _____

17. There is ample communication within the group on topics relevant to getting the work accomplished. _____ _____

18. Group members feel confident in each others' decisions and judgments. _____ _____

19. We enjoy many laughs together. _____ _____

20. The leader of the group coordinates our activities but does not dominate us. _____ _____

Total   _____ _____

Scoring and interpretation: The larger the number of statements answered *mostly yes,* the more likely good teamwork is present, thus contributing to productivity. The answers will serve as discussion points for improving teamwork and group effectiveness.

Chapter Eleven

Production Work Teams

> An electronics firm was experiencing quality problems with their line of TV receivers, and a related problem of low job satisfaction among its production workers and supervisors. To remedy these problems, the firm decided to reorganize its assembly-line operation into small work teams, called self-managing work teams or production work teams.

"Let's review quickly why we are getting together today," said Jack Ross, manufacturing vice president of Chartwell Electronics. With him were Dave Cooper, general manager of Chartwell's Yellow Junction plant, and Meryl Butwid, corporate industrial engineering consultant.

Jack:

We've hashed over this same problem many times during the last several years. I've listened to dozens of suggestions, I've read many industry studies, and I've made some of my own observations. Now we are ready to act before we lose an important segment of our business.

For the last few years we have been in trouble with our line of TV sets. Our price is still competitive, but just barely. We get a lot of squawks from retail outlets that our sets are coming back to the store for refund or replacement. I have to admit, some shoddy merchandise has been getting through. I'm not so sure I would give my own mother a Chartwell TV for a present if she didn't have ready access to a service center. During the last six months, our share of the market declined 25 percent. Our sales were down 15 percent, while industry sales as a whole were down only 7 percent.

Meryl, will you go ahead and tell Dave and me your latest analysis of the problem?

Meryl:

I want to point out that Dave and his staff members are in essential agreement with my diagnosis of the problem. They may not all agree on my solution, but at least we have a consistent viewpoint of the nature of the beast. We have a growing epidemic of the blue-collar blues, not just in the Yellow Junction plant, but all over. Many of our workers, perhaps one half to two thirds, are burned-out. They've lost whatever spark of enthusiasm they once had for their jobs. Our supervisors are becoming discouraged dealing with so many technical and morale problems.

It's rumored that many of our workers themselves believe we are producing inferior TV sets. A joke circulating around our plants these days is that if you want to enjoy Super Bowl Sunday, visit a friend who owns a competitor's TV. Because our production jobs are so boring, our problems with turnover, absenteeism, and tardiness have increased sharply.

We know there must be a better way. The better way we have formulated is the team approach to job enrichment. Some call it job redesign, but the latest buzz word is *production work teams*. The team approach to production work has been used in Europe since the mid-1960s. The sociology behind it is that many workers feel alienated because their work lacks challenge and meaning.

The concept is quite simple. Teams of from 8 to 12 workers will cover a full set of tasks, and team members will decide which people will perform which tasks. It will be as if we have 10 small TV making shops in the plant instead of one large assembly line. It's like setting scientific management back 100 years. We'll have small groups of generalists, rather than a large number of employees performing specialized, narrow tasks. I know that Dave would have some comments about the reorganization and retooling necessary to convert from a traditional assembly to autonomous work groups.

Dave:

I've studied the situation carefully including getting loads of input from our manufacturing engineering department. We're talking about a couple of hundred thousand dollars worth of revamping for just one assembly line. We would have to rearrange work stations. We'd have to tear down some partitions. We'd have to select and train the right people. We'd have one line out of operation for three months during the tooling-up process.

An analysis performed by Meryl and the plant staff suggests that we should start small. Our worst problems are with the portable black and white TV sets. Maybe that's because the production of those sets is so routinized. About one half the Yellow Junction capacity is devoted to the manufacture of our black and white portables.

Another solid reason for beginning this experiment at Yellow Junction is that the union there is so cooperative. Nick Langdon, the local president, is willing to let us try this for one year before we negotiate the new job structure into the next labor agreement. Nick says his senior people are frightened that the Yellow Junction plant might close. We've already had one small layoff due to a softened demand for our TVs.

Jack:

It sounds like we have our experiment with work teams pretty well planned. I'd say let's get moving with the project. We'll start committing resources to the project right away. I'd like to see the system online by January 1.

Nine months later, Jack and Dave made one of their regular visits to Yellow Junction to evaluate progress on the project and offer whatever advice and support they could offer. Meryl Butwid was on site, working with a consultant. She offered the visitors a brief explanation of the current status of the project:

Meryl:

We've been in full operation for about two months. The format seems to be working. In essence, each group of nine workers has total responsibility for the assembly task. The team also deals directly with staff groups such as purchasing and quality control. We use a team leader but not a supervisor. Some of our supervisors have been selected as team leaders. Others chose to take staff jobs or work as assemblers on the color TV line until a supervisory position opened over there.

It's too soon to tell for sure, but team spirit is high, attendance is up, and our quality department says manufacturing defects are way down. The number of units shipped in a week is slightly behind the assembly line format. Ken Phillips, the consultant who's been advising us on this project, has a few comments.

Ken:

I think we're going to get the increase in quality and morale that you are seeking. But it will take awhile. Not every employee who volunteered to work on a team has the immediate skills necessary to perform as a team member. Some people lack the confidence necessary to handle all the responsibility. We're asking people to become TV makers instead of specialists in putting together some miniscule part. It's much like asking somebody to change part of their self-image.

We're also asking people to become responsible members of a team. If they are out one day, they have to feel somewhat guilty about letting the team down. The assembly line is so much more depersonalized. Another big change is that young inexperienced employees are now working as co-equals with higher paid, more senior employees. Dealing with the status difference makes some people feel awkward. One gal told me that she had to bring a part back for rework to an older woman. That woman happened to be her occasional babysitter when she was six years old. That's heavy stuff for a 20-year-old raised in Yellow Junction.

On one of my trips here, I had my hair trimmed at the local barber shop. I heard a comment that makes me think production work teams will be around a long time. One older man said to another, "If you're looking for a spiffy wedding present for your daughter, why not get her a Chartwell portable TV made at Yellow Junction? These days they outperform the Japanese models."

Research Evidence about Production Work Teams

The team approach to production used at Chartwell is gaining acceptance throughout the world as a method of improving productivity and quality in both manufacturing and office settings. Fourteen years ago, fewer than two dozen manufacturing plants in the United States organized work into self-managing teams. Today team structures are used in several hundred offices and plants, especially new, highly automated plans with work forces of 25 to 500 employees.[1] One reason this approach is not well known is that the same approach to work design carries different labels. Production work teams are also referred to as *autonomous work groups, semiautonomous work groups, sociotechnical systems, production teams, self-managing work teams,* and *group job enrichment.*

The common element to all these work arrangements is that a small team of workers is assigned responsibility for performing a major function. The self-managing work team stands in contrast to a production operation in which individuals perform highly specialized tasks and have very limited decision-making authority.

Published research about the effectiveness of self-managing work teams has been consistently positive. Here we will present current evidence along with an updating of information on classical studies of autonomous work groups such as those conducted at the Gaines pet food plant in Topeka, Kansas.

Volvo Trucks.   The Volvo Tuve truck assembly plant was designed as a single product (trucks) workshop of 25 blue-collar and 25 white-collar employees. Although comparisons between the team-oriented production process at Tuve versus other Volvo plants are difficult, a comparison with an older truck facility seven kilometers away showed Tuve to be 16 percent more efficient. For example, absenteeism averaged 16.5 percent at Tuve, compared to 20 percent at the truck facility with a more traditional assembly-line maufacturing process.[2]

Volvo Automobiles.   The Volvo automotive plant opened at Kalmar, Sweden, in 1974. Kalmar's work force is divided into approximately 20 production teams of 15 to 25 persons each. The team assembles a major unit of a car such as door assembly, electric wiring, or fitting upholstery in an average of 20 to 40 minutes. Members of the team can exchange jobs or change teams if they so choose. Team members can also vary the work pace, keeping up with the general flow of production but speeding up or pausing as they wish. This is possible because car-carrying trolleys can be delayed for awhile both before entering and after leaving each work team's area.

Production costs at Kalmar are 25 percent lower than at Volvo's plants organized on an assembly-line basis. The continuing success of the Kalmar plant has prompted management to build a new plant at Uddevalla, Sweden, following the same principles of work design.[3]

New United Motor Mfg. Inc (NUMMI).   General Motors and Toyota entered into a joint venture, NUMMI, to manufacture Chevrolet Novas in Fremont, California. Workers at NUMMI are organized into teams with substantial control over their jobs. Although NUMMI uses less automation than the average U.S. automotive plant, the quality of the the cars produced generally outranks the best from GM's most highly automated plants.[4]

Lansing, Michigan Plant of General Motors.   The self-managing work team structure used so successfully at NUMMI was implemented at a GM plant in Lansing, Michigan. Workers define their own jobs and monitor the quality of their output. The work teams conduct their own daily audits and also have "stop-line" cords that enable them to close down the line if they encounter a problem. The work teams have enabled the plant to eliminate 37 percent of the audit jobs in its first year of operation and has reduced the cost of making a car by 21 percent.

The Lansing plant manager reports that the use of self-managing teams has boosted the quality of his plant's cars (such as the Pontiac Grand Am and Buick Somerset) nearly 46 percent. According to the manager, "When you let workers set up their own jobs, they are tougher on themselves than they would be if you set up the job for them."[5]

Rohm & Haas Co. Plexiglass Plant.   Rohm & Haas is an example of union-management cooperation in converting existing plants into the team arrangement. The Aluminum Workers Union collaborated with the Rohm & Haas management at a plexiglass manufacturing site in Knoxville, Tennessee. Within four years after the plant began to shift toward self-managing work teams, productivity, as measured by square feet of plexiglass produced per worker hour, had increased approximately 60 percent.[6]

Shenandoah Life Insurance Co.   In the early 1980s, Shenandoah Life installed a $2 million system to automate processing and claims operations at its Roanoke, Virginia, headquarters. The results from computerization were disappointing. It still required 27 working days and handling by 32 clerks in three departments to process a representative claim. The delays stemmed from the elaborate maze of regulations, not from defects in the technology. To speed up the claims processing and capitalize on automation, the company grouped clerks into semiautonomous teams of five to seven members. Each team now performs all the functions previously distributed over three departments. Team members learned new skills that brought increased job satisfaction and pay.

As a result of organizing by teams, the typical case-handling time decreased to two days, and customer complaints about service were virtually eliminated. Within six years of installing semiautonomous work teams, Shenandoah was processing 50 percent more applications and queries, with 10 percent fewer employees.[7]

Gaines Pet Food, Topeka, Kansas.   In the late 1960s, General Foods experienced negative employee attitudes and diminishing productivity at some of its manufacturing plants. To combat these problems, management began to design new plants to operate with a minimum of supervision. One well-publicized example took place at the Gaines Pet Food plant in Topeka, Kansas. The plant was designed to permit work teams to control production, packaging, and shipping technologies rather than to let technology control people.

Production was built around teams consisting of 7 to 14 members. Three teams were used per shift: processing, packaging, and shipping and office duties. Each team was responsible for dividing its own work among team members, interviewing and hiring job applicants, and establishing internal policies and decision making within their own area of responsibility. All teams were responsible for their own quality control and such diverse functions as industrial engineering, maintenance, and housekeeping. Workers were encouraged to learn and perform as many jobs on the team as they are capable of doing. When workers learn more skills, they are compensated accordingly.

The early results from this experiment in self-managing teams were encouraging but not all glowing. On the positive side, about 70 people were soon operating a plant originally estimated by industrial engineers to require 110 people to operate effectively. After the first 18 months of operation, overhead was 30 percent lower than in conventionally operated plants in the same division of the pet food operation. Turnover and absenteeism were much lower than industry norms. The plant operated for almost four years before its first lost-time accident. Altogether, an estimated annual cost savings of $1 million was achieved.[8]

Fifteen years after the experiment began, The Gaines Foods plant still uses teamwork, both in the office and factory. The current plant manager says that Topeka produces the same pet foods as a sister plant in Kankakee, Illinois, at 7 percent lower labor costs.[9]

Despite these positive results, the Gaines plant did experience difficulty being integrated into the larger organization. In addition to the formation of self-managing teams, other aspects of a traditional bureaucratic structure were modified. Phillip L. Hunsaker and Curtis W. Cook make this analysis:

> Because power was shifted downward within the Gaines plant, traditional functional management and professional job classifications were eliminated. Staff at the home office experienced difficulty in their attempts to commu-

nicate with unassigned counterparts in Topeka. Over time, the power shifted back to a structure that central management could control; in part this resulted from adding on traditional management positions such as plant controller and manufacturing services manager.[10]

Hunsaker and Cook note further that the organizational culture must support an innovation such as autonomous work group, or the innovation will not endure. At Gaines, the traditional structure of the rest of the organization may have prevented the spread of self-managing teams, but it did not negate completely its benefits.

Sherwin-Williams.   A familiar paint manufacturer is the setting for a dramatically effective application of the team approach to work restructuring. Top management at the Sherwin-Williams Company supported the concept of improved work design.[11] The chief executive officer was committed to making the venerable paint manufacturer an efficient, low-cost producer in today's highly competitive paint market. The company needed a new plant and new equipment plus a well-trained flexible and productive work force. He believed that these goals could be reached by arranging the work to be done in teams. Simultaneously the sociotechnical system would be designed to suit autonomous work groups.

The paint company's Richmond, Kentucky, plant was chosen as the site for the self-managing work teams. One important factor was that the residents of this community have a strong work ethic. Another was that Sherwin-Williams had no other facilities in the area, so it had no traditions in the community that it would have to follow or deviate from. Also, since the community is agricultural, prospective employees had little previous industrial experience that might have predisposed them against Richmond's new work structure and policies. Many members of the work force still work the family farms.

The plant technology is another background factor that helps provide insight into the potential application of autonomous work groups. The Richmond plant is designed to manufacture and package automobile paint. A different formula is required for each color. Since Sherwin-Williams supplies paint for a six-year stock of factory package colors for major U.S. automobile manufacturers, the plant produces many different products. Considerable operating flexibility is required to cope with frequent production changes. The technology also requires careful production and quality control. In addition to sophisticated manufacturing equipment and process, the attention and judgment of skilled operators are key factors in making quality paint.

Specifics of the New Design.   The design engineer's report for the project specified that the operation of the plant would be performed by work teams without supervision: "In order to make the work for the individual more varied and challenging, an attempt was made through the computer control system to reduce the routine inventory accounting, log entering, and other paperwork control to a minimum." The system is designed to permit a technician to have the total responsibility for the manufacture of a batch of paint from its inception to its final storage as a finished product ready for shipping. In order to achieve this end, it was necessary that the technician have adequate and reliable control of all variables in the batch.

Using the team approach as the guiding principle, industrial engineers, assisted by a sociotechnical systems consultant, followed two key guidelines in designing the plant: (1) they made the layout follow the actual flow of the product in its manufacture and (2) the work space was kept open to allow interaction and communication among team members. Figure 11–1 depicts the product flow.

FIGURE 11–1   Product Flow on the Packaging Line

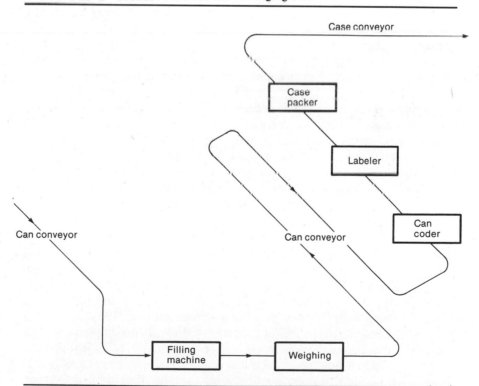

As an extension of the autonomous work group structure, the plant organization structure is relatively flat. Absent are production superintendents, assistant plant managers, and supervisors. Coordination across the functions (raw materials, manufacturing, and packaging) and across shifts of operations is accomplished by appropriate team leaders. The matrix form of organization replaces the traditional, functional arrangement. (A matrix organization is a project organization superimposed on a functional organization.) Following the matrix format, team leaders have both a functional (e.g., raw material) and a shift (e.g., second shift) reporting relationship.

Each autonomous work group is assigned a whole task to perform. Instead of building in people redundancy, the approach builds in skill redundancy within each team. All team members acquire the skills necessary to perform all aspects of the team's work. Because the teams are relatively self-managed, the team members themselves decide on job rotation within the group—provided they have received training in the skill area to which they are assigned.

The Compensation Package. A unique feature of compensation under team structuring is that people are paid for what they know, not what they do. The more skills you have, the more valuable you are to the team. An employee's skill level is subject to peer review. As with managerial personnel, all operating personnel at Richmond are salaried, yet they also receive shift premiums and overtime pay.

Management decided to pay Richmond employees at a level that would place them in the top 25 percent of companies in central Kentucky. The rationale was that the company did not want to attract employees who were primarily interested in high pay. Yet, it did want a compensation package that would attract and retain qualified employees for the new plant.

Implementation. Most of the design work for the autonomous work group arrangement took place before the Richmond plant's management team had been identified and released of other responsibilities to work on the start-up. All 10 start-up team leaders and 7 members of the plant manager's staff had previous experience in various Sherwin-Williams locations. Much of the experience was in places with an atmosphere quite different from the Richmond plant. Some of their plants were characterized by poor labor-management relations, old equipment, and supervisory practices emphasizing close checking up on employees.

Two questions were asked repeatedly through the implementation process: "Will this activity increase the commitment of team leaders and members? Does it help us accomplish our technical and business objectives?" Richmond's management believes that the three implementation steps—employee selection, employee training, and team building—were crucial factors to the plant's successful operation on a team basis. These three phases are described in the next three sections.

Recruitment and Selection.   The Richmond recruitment and selection strategy took into account the fact that not every person is suited to work in a team setting. Recruiters relied heavily on employee self-selection, after giving prospective employees a candid account of the new operation.

Three key steps were included in the selection procedure: (1) Each applicant received a personal interview with several staff members and team leaders along with a tour of the facility (with spouse, if applicable). (2) Applicants were urged to discuss the job opportunity at home before reaching a final decision. (3) Those who were still interested were given final consideration by the team leaders.

Orientation and Training.   New employees benefited from an extensive orientation program, which included the usual plant tours, a film about the team approach to work, and an employee handbook. Simultaneously, employees were given technical job training. A unique feature was a segment of the orientation and training designed to help employees become responsive to customer needs. Trainees were given tours of job shops in which Sherwin-Williams paints were actually used. In this way the consequences of substandard quality and late deliveries were dramatized. The employees saw and heard for themselves directly from the customers.

Team Building   Team-building activities were designed to give the employees the skills to support and confront each other constructively at work—both vital skills for the functioning of an autonomous work group. Team building began with a session attended by the plant manager, his staff members, and the team-building consultant. One activity at this level was to design team-building sessions for team leaders, the next level down in the organization.

During the two-and-one-half day team-building session designed by plant management, team leaders worked on problems they anticipated in implementing the management philosophy at Richmond. An underlying aim of the sessions was to help the supervisors shift to the role of team leaders—one that emphasized helping, coordinating, and consulting.

Results.   A number of worthwhile results for the Richmond plant, and therefore the company as a whole, stemmed from the self-managing work teams, as summarized next.

1. Autonomous work groups led to efficiencies in the utilization of human resources. The original estimate of the work force needed at the new plant was 200. At last report the facility was operating with 160 employees, a 25 percent reduction.

2. Absenteeism for work-team members was 2.5 percent in contrast to all-plant average of 6.7 percent. The 2.5 percent figure is also remarkably low for any type of production operation. Turnover was reported to be negligibly low.

3. Productivity is objectively measured to be 30 percent higher than in sister plants. Of striking significance, the cost per gallon of paint in this facility is 45 percent lower than in other plants manufacturing automotive paint. Plant management attributes 75 percent of the cost reduction to human factors, and not to the physical structure of the plant or new technology.

4. The Richmond facility now produces the highest quality paint manufactured by Sherwin-Williams. Ninety-four percent of its production is rated excellent by the technical department in contrast to a 75 percent all-plant average. The field sales organization is highly enthusiastic about the Richmond product quality. *Consumer Reports* has proclaimed Sherwin-Williams automotive paint (made at the Richmond plant) as the best produced in the United States.

5. Failure cost, defined as production that does not meet product specifications, is down 25 percent. Paint returned from customers is down 75 percent, and product availability (a measure of prompt service) is at a record high level.

6. The Richmond facility is the only Sherwin-Williams plant that had no lost-time accidents in its first 1,108 days of operation (the end of the study period).

7. Self-managing work teams at the Richmond plant have made a positive contribution to the quality of work life. The first annual attitude survey indicated such high job satisfaction with job design, team work, and organizational climate that it was attributed the "honeymoon effect." Yet, the second annual survey resulted in even higher ratings. It is not unusual for employees to tell visitors. "This is the best place I've ever worked. Management cares about you, and the work is fun."

The Argument for Production Work Teams

Several arguments can be advanced for production work teams. Of prime importance, companies using the team approach to work restructuring report substantial improvements in employee motivation, and these improvements can be linked directly to the achievement of financial goals. Work teams also improve productivity by giving production systems greater flexibility in meeting dynamic market demands.[12]

Increased job satisfaction is another important positive consequence of self-managing work teams. Many workers prefer teamwork because it offers a greater variety of job tasks compared with repetitive jobs in an assembly line. A team coordinator in a GM plant makes the following comment in support of the job satisfaction argument: "Once in a while I get bored and switch jobs with someone just to relieve the tedium. I couldn't do this before we switched to work teams."[13]

Self-managing work teams make another contribution to organizational effectiveness because they handle many discipline problems taken care of in the past by members of management. If the problem is not resolved by discussion with the team leader, the problem is discussed openly at a team meeting. Most employees choose to resolve the problem rather than experience the embarrassment of public discussion.[14]

The Argument against Production Work Teams

Despite the advantages just mentioned, self-managing work teams are not suited to improving productivity and satisfaction in every work situation for the following reasons.

1. Self-managing work teams may not fit into an organizational culture characterized by a strong belief in a bureaucratic authority structure. The traditional idea that a manager's primary function is replaced with the idea that a manager should encourage employees to use initiative.[15] Managers who think only in terms of a top-to-bottom flow of authority would probably not allow self-managing work teams to function properly.

2. You need a relatively high-quality work force for the team concept to be effective. To work effectively as team members, employees have to be mentally flexible, alert, and possess at least average interpersonal skills. In many plant and office locations, such employees are not available. Or if they are available, the employer may not be able to offer high enough wages to attract them.

3. The cost of introducing autonomous work groups can be prohibitive. A European specialist in industrial management notes that in plants where machines of the same type, such as lathes or drilling machines, are laid out together, they must be rearranged so different kinds of machines are grouped together. Furthermore, "If the work groups produce a large range of components or complete products, they may all need almost the same configuration of equipment. This means tooling and machinery surpluses. Buffer stocks are also needed so that each work group can work at a different pace. Placing buffer stocks between work groups may neutralize a classical advantage of the production line—the small quantities of material in work in progress."[16]

Thus, the cost of converting an existing facility to work teams might be so high that the only feasible approach is to select a new location for the conversion.

4. Autonomous work groups might be limited in their effectiveness to that portion of the work force who seek the type of stimulation found in team arrangements. A sizable portion of the

work force—perhaps as high as 70 percent—prefer to perform repetitive tasks independently.

5. When labor unions are present, designing jobs into teams could result in complicated, difficult-to-resolve labor-management issues. A major problem is that instead of multiple job classifications, a teamwork plant usually has only one or two. Production and maintenance work, usually separate job categories, tend to merge into one fluid work system.[17] Other issues include these: Which employees will be denied membership in the new work groups? How do you establish wage rates for employees who can perform in six different jobs? Is the employee who interacts directly with a supervisor from another department required to be a member of the bargaining unit?

6. Self-managing work groups are poorly suited to situations in which one department is dependent on another for getting work accomplished. Because each unit operates independently, they are not attuned to adhering to each other's production schedules.

Guidelines for Action and Skill Development

To properly house a team operation, an organization must be redesigned thoroughly and a systems point of view maintained. First, attention must be paid to the design and layout of the physical setting. Building space must allow for the product flow and for the interaction of people necessary to perform teamwork. Second, it is usually necessary to create a relatively flat organization structure whereby team members are in control of a significant amount of their work.

Autonomous work groups are the most effective when the status barriers between managers and operative employees are broken down. Doing so permits the establishment of an atmosphere of trust and open communication.[18]

Employees must be carefully chosen who show pride in their work and enjoy working cooperatively with others. Self-nomination or asking for volunteers for the autonomous work groups will decrease selection errors.

To avoid the ambiguity (and therefore the stress) often associated with the unpredictable income of pay systems based on group performance, pay plans for self-managing work team members should combine a fixed income with a group bonus. Experience suggests that the fixed portion of the wage should be based on job evaluation results and employee skills. Typically, between 70 and 90 percent of an employee's wages are fixed. The group bonus is then divided equally among the team members.[19]

The optimal number of employees for the team normally is between 10 and 15. When the work teams are larger, job satisfaction and productivity cease to improve, owing perhaps to a lack of cohesiveness and interaction among members.

It may be necessary to transfer employees who do not make it as team members or team leaders to more traditional jobs. Some people are not suited to self-managing work teams even though they might nominate themselves for such assignments.

Most employees require a job that grows in challenge or another job they can aspire toward within or outside the work team. Otherwise employee disgruntlement will mount, and organizational effectiveness might suffer.[20]

DISCUSSION QUESTIONS AND ACTIVITIES

1. What similarities do you see between self-managing work groups and the teams that compose a task force, committee, or project?
2. Identify an office operation you think could be adapted well to a self-managing work team. Explain why.
3. What is the underlying reason that self-managing work teams often lead to improvements in product quality?
4. How might the information presented in Chapter 10 about building teamwork be applied to increase the effectiveness of self-managing work teams?
5. Do you think work-team structuring would be as effective in Los Angeles and New York as it is in Kalmar, Sweden, and Richmond, Kentucky?
6. Interview a person who works in manufacturing and obtain his or her opinion on the probable value of self-managing work teams. Be prepared to discuss your findings in class.

NOTES

1. "Management Discovers the Human Side of Automation," *Business Week,* September 29, 1986, p. 71.
2. Paul Bernstein, "Efficiency Is Up and Absenteeism Down at New Volvo Plant," *World Wide Report,* December 1983, p. 94.
3. "Management Discovers the Human Side of Automation," p. 74.
4. "Why Image Counts: A Tale of Two Industries," *Business Week,* June 8, 1987, p. 139.
5. Ibid.
6. "Management Discovers the Human Side of Automation," p. 79.
7. Ibid., p. 70.
8. Richard W. Woodman and John J. Sherwood, "A Comprehensive Look at Job Design," *Personnel Journal,* August 1977, pp. 384–90, 418.

9. "Management Discovers the Human Side of Automation," p. 79.
10. Phillip L. Hunsaker and Curtis W. Cook, *Managing Organizational Behavior* (Reading, Mass.: Addison-Wesley, 1986), p. 573.
11. Ernesto J. Poza and M. Lynne Markus, "Success Story: The Team Approach to Work Restructuring," *Organizational Dynamics,* Winter 1980, pp. 3–25.
12. Panagiotis N. Fotilas, "Semi-Autonomous Work Groups: An Alternative in Organizing Production Work?" *Management Review,* July 1981, p. 52.
13. "Management Discovers the Human Side of Automation," p. 72.
14. Donald F. Barkman, "Team Discipline: Put Performance on the Line," *Personnel Journal,* March 1987, p. 60.
15. "Management Discovers the Human Side of Automation," p. 72.
16. Fotilas, "Semi-Autonomous Work Groups," p. 51.
17. "Management Discovers the Human Side of Automation," p. 79.
18. Poza and Markus, "Success Story," p. 24.
19. Fotilas, "Semi-Autonomous Work Groups," p. 53.
20. Edward M. Glaser, "Productivity Gains through Worklife Improvement," *Personnel,* January–February 1980, p. 73.

SOME ADDITIONAL REFERENCE

Bernstein, Aaron, and Wendy Zellner. "Detroit versus the UAW: At Odds over Teamwork." *Business Week,* August 24, 1987, pp. 54–55.

Gmelch, Walter H., and Val D. Miskin. *Productivity Teams: Beyond Quality Circles.* New York: John Wiley, 1984.

Melohn, Thomas H. "How to Build Employee Trust and Productivity." *Harvard Business Review,* January–February 1983, pp. 56–57, 60–61.

Plous, F. K., Jr. "Redesigning Work: A Chicago Bank Eliminates the 'Paperwork Assembly Line'." *Personnel Administrator,* March 1987, p. 99.

Sims, Henry P., Jr., and James W. Dean, Jr. "Beyond Quality Circles: Self-Managing Teams." *Personnel,* January 1985, pp. 25–32.

Appendix to Chapter Eleven

IS A PRODUCTION WORK TEAM WELL SUITED TO YOUR SITUATION?

Directions: Respond *Yes* or *No* to the following statements. The greater the number of Yes responses, the higher the probability that a production work team (or self-managing work team) will enhance productivity in your situation.

Organizational Characteristic	Yes	No
1. The cost for conversion from an assembly line to a team operation would not be prohibitive.		

	Yes	*No*
2. Teamwork is valued in our organization.	_____	_____
3. Our employees have a strong work ethic.	_____	_____
4. Our operative employees display initiative frequently.	_____	_____
5. Union-management (or employee-management) relations are generally good in our firm.	_____	_____
6. Top management in our firm practices decentralization of authority.	_____	_____
7. Upper management is accustomed to receiving suggestions from below.	_____	_____
8. Our work force is of generally high quality with respect to education, training, and skill level.	_____	_____
9. Many of our employees have good interpersonal skills.	_____	_____
10. Many of our employees appear to be seeking more responsibility.	_____	_____
11. Much of our work could be divided into independent units without creating a major disturbance.	_____	_____
12. We do not have huge status differences between managers and operative employees.	_____	_____
13. Many of our employees show pride in their work.	_____	_____
14. Most of our supervisors could learn to live with a decrease in their amount of formal authority.	_____	_____
15. Our basic operations could stand some productivity improvement.	_____	_____

Chapter Twelve

Quality Circles

A manufacturer of paper products observed that its main competitors were producing products of higher quality and, consequently, were increasing their market share. To help cope with this problem, the company decided to use quality circles (QCs) to help bring about needed improvements. QCs were initiated in both manufacturing and support areas.

Joe, the systems analyst, arrived at the conference room at 1 P.M. David, Roy, Steve, Mary, and Kristin, the five system designers, were already seated around the conference table. Joe's first comments were the following: "Hi, folks. It looks like all of us from our software group are here, so we can get started. To begin with, let me briefly review why we are here today. Our goal for the first meeting of our quality circle is to identify ways we can improve our design techniques and implement these improvements.

"Top management believes that if every key department in the company upgrades the quality of its output, these improvements will be reflected in the quality of our product. This is true even if we are a support group not directly involved in the manufacture of paper.

"Here is a handout that provides a basic definition of and framework for the quality circle format to be used throughout the company (see Figure 12–1). Keep it with you as a reminder of what we are doing. Because I've received some QC training, I'm both the circle leader and the facilitator.

"As you know, the quality circle concept was originally developed in the United States and was later successfully applied by Japanese industries. To get our circle started, we're going to brainstorm ways we can improve our design techniques. As the weeks go by, we'll be tackling many different problems and using many different problem-solving techniques."

FIGURE 12–1 Quality Circle Handout

A quality circle is a group of employees that meet regularly to solve problems affecting its work area. Generally, 6 to 12 volunteers from the same work area make up the circle. The members receive training in problem solving, statistical quality control, and group process. Quality circles generally recommend solutions for quality and productivity problems, which management then may implement.

A facilitator, usually a specially trained member of management, helps train circle members and ensures that things run smoothly. Typical objectives of QC programs include quality improvement, productivity enhancement, and employee involvement. Circles generally meet four hours a month on company time. Members may get recognition but rarely receive financial rewards.

SOURCE: Edward E. Lawler III and Susan A. Mohrman, "Quality Circles after the Fad," *Harvard Business Review,* January–February 1985, p. 66.

Steve:

> I see one problem in our design techniques. Our programs do not follow the program standards, especially the format. Frequently we have to refer to some of the programs written a few years ago to make changes and modifications as desired, but it is difficult for us to read other people's programs. If all the programs were written according to the standards, we could save a lot of time and be much more efficient.

Mary:

> I agree with Steve 100 percent. We should give top priority to developing a methodology to police standards for design and programming.

Roy:

> I have another suggestion. The problem I often encounter is that many programs have incomplete documentation, and some programs have no documentation. Without documentation, it is difficult to understand what the program intends to do and how the program structure does things.

Kristen:

> The insufficient documentation also makes it hard to trace other related programs. For example, if I make a change in one program due to lack of documentation, I sometimes don't know which subprocedures and calling procedures also need to be changed.

David:

> I found some unnecessary comments in the documentation. We should produce documents that describe techniques for enhancing program flexibility, and the documentation should be readable.

Mary:

> I think we should review the current programs and check the structures and documentation. If they don't meet the standards, or there are holes in the

documentation, we should take the time and effort to improve the quality of our design. We can do this project once and for all. It will benefit us in the long run.

Joe:

Mary, I hear what you're saying, but I do not quite agree. I believe that it will be too expensive to accomplish this task now. Many programs are running fine, and the chances are slim for us to refer back to them for changes or modification. Besides, concepts such as standard structures and good documentation are based on subjective opinions. Let's come up with some ideas that have feasible benefits.

Roy:

I am working at level 4, and every day I deal with massive amounts of raw data. The programs produce different status reports and statistical analysis on a long-term basis. Good documentation is therefore critical here. At present I spend too much time just writing documentation for programs. I think we should investigate an easier method for writing documentation. Suppose a new method can reduce 100 hours per year from my documentation time, and that the software department charges the production department $50 per hour for my time. The company can therefore save $5,000 per year.

Joe:

Good, and in the long run, the work force can be reduced.

Steve:

I suggest that we work on a project to identify current tools for measuring system or program performance. My concern is how can we better measure the efficiency of a system or program. Response time is one good measure because it depends on a program's efficiency. If a program is written efficiently, it should minimize the memory space and CPU (central processing unit) time. Response time should therefore be relatively shorter. We now waste too much time waiting for the computer to respond.

Mary:

Another way of measuring a program's efficiency is to have Joe, the most experienced person in our group, "walk through" our programs before we test or install them on the production floor. If Joe finds too many bugs, we can assume the program is not written efficiently.

David:

I don't like this idea. First of all, it is not fair to the new designers. Secondly, it will discourage people easily and therefore have a negative effect on morale.

Roy:

Going back to the problem of response time, we can also apply some human factors principles. People get tired and frustrated if they wait too long for the computers, so they just give up. Shortening response time will therefore cause people to make more extensive use of our computers.

Mary:

I would like to point out that by reducing the response time we can reduce the work force in the long run.

Roy:

Shorter response time will also use less system resources, which will speed the disk access time.

Steve:

The operators on the production floor will be more effective if computer response time is reduced.

Kristen:

Talking about operators on the production floor reminds me that we should consider the possibility of reducing the size of log files. Too many messages are printed on the paper when we log on and off every time. If we can modify our system programs and just display these messages on the screen, we can save a lot of paper; and paper costs money. If every 1,000 lines of paper cost the company $1.20, we can then save $10,000 in a year.

Mary:

I think saving $10,000 per year is too conservative an estimate. I would say $15,000 per year is more accurate.

Joe:

I am also thinking about standardizing Screen/1000 program documentation. There is no documentation feature on the Screen/1000 package; it is therefore difficult to learn. If we can reduce the time it takes to familiarize a new designer with the Screen/1000 package, we can save up to $4,000 per year.

Steve:

Improving the training on use of Screen/1000 is definitely a good idea. I remember that I had a difficult time learning that software package.

Joe:

We've achieved excellent results so far. We have brainstormed ideas that can improve our design techniques. However, we can choose only one or two projects because we have been allotted just 192 working hours to implement the improvement. Also, management wants our first QC output to work as smoothly as possible.

Roy:

I think we should work on the project of investigating an easy method of documentation.

Mary:

Because my job is mostly involved with coding, I vote for working on the project of reducing response time.

Joe:

By applying cost-benefit analysis, I would say that we should work on the project of reducing the size of the log files. Everybody has to log messages in log files so that it will benefit the entire company. Besides, it is fairly easy to accomplish the task.

The other members of the group nodded their heads in agreement. The single agenda for forthcoming QC meetings was to develop ways of reducing the size of log files.[1]

A LOOK AT SOME OF THE EVIDENCE

Quality circles, on balance, appear to be making a positive contribution to productivity (including quality), profits, and morale. A current review of 33 research studies of QC results indicates that 16 reported uniformly positive results, 9 studies demonstrated mixed or nonsignificant results, and 8 studies reported uniformly negative results.[2] Although QCs have received less attention in the last few years than in the previous decade, the quality circle method is still widely used. Because of their widespread use, QCs are subject to frequent evaluation by both businesspeople and researchers. Here we will report on several types of evaluation methods, sampling first the positive and then the negative evidence.

Favorable Outcomes with Quality Circles

Positive results with QCs have been reported in many types of organizations, using both organizational outcomes (such as productivity, quality, and cost savings) and individual outcomes (such as job satisfaction). Here we examine a synthesis of 16 studies, plus an experimental evaluation of 11 QCs in one organization.

Synthesis of Sixteen Studies.   In their review of 33 studies of QC effectiveness, Murray R. Barrick and Ralph A. Alexander identified 16 that showed uniformly positive results. The positive results were reported both in terms of individual and organizational outcomes. Fifteen of the studies were conducted in work settings that include the following: electronic equipment makers, hospital employees, factory and shop employees, nine manufacturing plants, Tektronix, Tenneco, the Department of Defense, and Martin Marietta. One of the studies was conducted in a laboratory with psychology students.

An impressive aspect of these findings was the lack of a positive-finding bias. Specifically, there was *not* a tendency for less rigorous studies to report positive results, and more rigorous studies to report negative results.[3] Evaluation studies of applied management techniques are often subject to a positive-finding bias.

Experimental Evaluation of Eleven QCs. In an attempt to evaluate the appropriateness of quality circles to American firms, a team of researchers set up a one-year field experiment at a metal fabricating facility of an electronics firm.[4] The subcomponents made by this facility are used by other divisions in the manufacture of electronic instrumentation products. Management of the facility was receptive to improving product quality and morale since both were seen as being below satisfactory levels.

Eleven quality circles, averaging nine production employees each, were established. A control group, consisting of employees doing comparable work, but not assigned to QCs, also was established. The research question was, "Do employees who have received circle training and started a viable circle process have higher performance and better attitudes on the job than employees in the control group?" The researchers also wanted to investigate whether the quality control program was cost effective.

Performance was measured by a computerized monitoring system created out of the company's existing employee performance reporting system. Both quantity and quality measurements were taken. Employee attitudes were assessed by the Hackman-Oldham Job Diagnostic Survey, which measures employee attitudes about the specific work task they perform. Five job characteristics were combined into a single index called the Motivating Potential Score (MPS). The time period for the measurement process was one year, including the baseline data period.

The major result of the circle program was its positive impact on reject rate, as shown in the top half of Figure 12–2. Per capita reject rates for quality circle participants dropped by one third to one half of the former rate by the time the program had run three months. The reject rates for the control group surprisingly increased during the same period.

An explanation offered by the researchers for these results is that circle members tackled the issues of internal communication as a top priority item. For example, one of the initial projects implemented by the QCs was improving training manuals and procedures, including translating materials into a worker's native language, if the workers desired. Careful attention to better training in fundamentals prevented many errors.

Circle members made fewer errors. In addition, those errors the circle members did make tended to be less expensive to scrap or rework into usable parts. The explanation given for these results is that circle training instructs employees how to prioritize problems on the basis of dollar impact on the company. The cost savings generated by the lower reject rate represented a 300 percent return on investment in the cost of the program. However, the QC program did not increase those produc-

FIGURE 12–2   Impact of Quality Circles on Employee
Performance and Attitudes

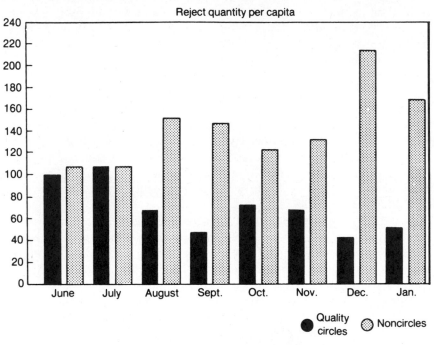

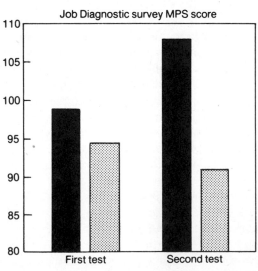

SOURCE: Justin Y. Shimada, Kenneth M. Jenkins, and Lewis N. Goslin, "Quality Circles Meet the Challenge," *Business Forum,* Spring 1983, p. 20. Reprinted with permission.

tion rates that were more dependent on orders and production technology than on quality. The researchers emphasized that the focus in this experiment was on quality, resulting in an increase in the net usable quantity produced.

To assess the impact of quality control circles on employee attitudes, two separate measures were taken of both the experimental and control groups. Prior to training about the QC method, both groups took the Job Diagnostic Survey (JDS). As anticipated, no significant difference was found between the two groups. Six months later, the JDS was read-ministered. By this time, the QC participants had been trained, were meeting regularly, and were solving operational problems with the circles.

The second testing indicated that the Motivating Potential Score for the circle participants increased, while the control group showed a decrease (see Figure 12–2 bottom). No other changes were present in the work environment that would affect the experimental group differently than the control group. The researchers therefore concluded that the improvement in employee job attitudes could be attributed to the circle training program and the problem-solving activity. The job characteristic most influenced by the quality activity was skill variety—the extent to which the job requires a variety of different skills. According to research-ers, the QC process affects attitudes primarily because it becomes a recurring part of the job itself.[5]

Negative Outcomes with Quality Circles

Despite the favorable outcomes described above, many negative outcomes with QCs have also been reported. Tai K. Oh reports that quality circle programs have failed in more than 60 percent of the American organizations implementing them.[6] A survey conducted by the consulting firm of A. T. Kearney reported that 80 percent of the Fortune 500 firms had started some type of quality circle program since 1980. Eighty-three percent of these firms dropped the program within 18 months.[7] A review of the results of the first surge of QC activity in the United States revealed that as many as 75 percent of initially successful programs were no longer in operation after a few years. Even Lockheed, one of the American pioneers in this method, has decreased its involve-ment with this method.[8]

Synthesis of Eight Studies. The review of 33 studies reported previously, identified eight studies in which quality circles had negative consequences for the individual and/or the organization. One of these negative results was found at a division of Honeywell; one at a computer firm; one among government employees; and five at the Department of Defense. Barrick and Alexander hypothesized that the organizational climate in the Department of Defense may not have been appropriate for the conduct of quality circles. Also, the quality circles may not have been conducted long enough to obtain good results. In the one Department of Defense study that did achieve positive results, data were taken after the QC was in operation 13 months.[9]

A Study of Quality Circles in Twenty-Nine Companies. Only eight quality circles were found to be cost-effective in one study of 29 companies. Woodruff Imberman investigated the 21 unsuccessful QC efforts and found 4 major causes of failure. First, in many firms the employees intensely disliked management. Their antagonism carried over to the quality control circles, which some employees perceived to be a management ploy to reduce overtime and trim down the work force by increasing productivity. Second, most organizations did a poor job of selling the QCs. Instead of conducting individual discussions with employees, they relied on flip charts, booklets, and formal management presentations. The workers were left wondering, "What's in it for me?"

Third, the supervisors chosen to lead the circles received some training in human relations and group dynamics, but they felt that little of this information satisfied the specific needs of their own departments. Fourth, most of 21 firms regarded the QC programs as merely a way of improving the efficiency of production techniques. They did not realize that QCs cannot succeed unless top management is willing to shift its philosophy toward emphasizing good human relations among employees themselves, and between management and employees.[10] This last point hints at the importance of establishing the conditions that allow a quality circle program to succeed.

KEY ELEMENTS OF A SUCCESSFUL PROGRAM

Quality control circle programs show some variation from company to company, whether these companies are engaged in manufacturing or service. Among the points of difference are how frequently they meet, how much authority is granted to the team leader or supervisor, whether they use a group facilitator in addition to a supervisor, and how much coordination there is with the already existing quality control department. Based on the judgments of several observers and some current research, the successful programs have certain elements in common. A successful or effective quality circle is one in which (a) a high number of improvements are suggested, (b) a high number of suggestions are adopted, and (c) a high level of member satisfaction with the circle exists.[11]

The key elements of a successful program are tied in with systematic application of principles of human behavior, the use of quantitative problem-solving techniques, and sound managerial judgment. A synthesis of these key elements is presented next.[12]

1. *Program goals are stated explicitly.*   Objectives should be made clear to avoid confusion or unreasonable expectations from the circle program. Among the goals of QC programs are improving product quality, increasing productivity, improving communications between workers and supervisors, decreasing product costs, improving the quality of work life, and preparing workers for future supervisory assignments.

2. *Good employee-management relations already exist.*   As noted by John D. Blair, Stanley L. Cohen, and Jerome V. Hurwitz, quality circles are not likely to succeed in organizations suffering from acrimonious union-management conflict or high levels of distrust between employees and management.[13]

3. *Top management is committed to the program and believes in decentralization of authority.*   Without commitment from top management, the initiation of a QC program is inadvisable. Commitment includes financial and emotional support from management. A philosophy of decentralization allows latitude to operating units to be given freedom to run their circles and attack the problems they deem advisable.

4. *Circle members establish high performance norms and form a cohesive group.*   Effective QCs establish realistically high goals and pursue those goals as a cohesive group. The group cohesiveness also contributes to a spirit of teamwork among members

5. *Circle members have relatively high self-esteem.*   Two researchers measured the self-esteem of circle members and circle effectiveness at a computer manufacturer. A quality circle was designated as relatively successful if it had generated at least two solutions to problems that upper management accepted and implemented. A positive association was found between group member's self-esteem (feelings of self-worth) and the group's success.[14]

6. *Circle leaders use a participative leadership style.*   Quality circles are a direct application of participative management. It therefore follows logically that participative leadership contributes to QC effectiveness. In contrast, when the circle leader acts in a highly authoritarian role, the members are usually unresponsive.[15]

7. *The right people in the right area are selected.*   For quality circles to be effective, the program manager has to be enthusiastic, persistent, and hard-working. The team leader and facilitator must be energetic and cooperative. Another important step in getting the program off the ground is to select an area of the company where one can expect cooperation and enthusiasm from participants.

8. *The program is well publicized throughout the firm.*   Once the program is started, information about it should be disseminated widely throughout the firm. Better communication results in less resistance and fewer negative rumors about the program. The content of the communication should be open and positive.

9. *Long-term results are emphasized.*   In successful QC programs, management views the QC as a long-term investment and does not push impatiently for short-term results. Because the quality circle method involves careful study and analysis of the problems tackled, quick fixes are not in order. Nor are QCs designed to operate in a crisis mode. In support of the importance of the long term, the analysis of 33 QC programs found that positive results took awhile to accomplish, as described previously.[16]

10. *The QC program is customized to meet the needs of the firm.*   A subtle source of failure for some QC programs is the use of a canned set of procedures that do not pay attention to local circumstances. A circle participant whose work is data processing may have difficulty with the translation of a case from automobile manufacturing. A workable compromise is to use standard training as a framework and build on it with the unique problems of the firm in question.

11. *Membership in the circle is voluntary.*   Volunteerism facilitates bringing people into the program who are eager to contribute. However, some volunteers prove to be employees simply looking for time off from their regular duties. Employees who desire to contribute their ideas will generally perform better than employees who are arbitrarily assigned to the QC.

12. *Ample training is provided.*   Quality circle members generally need some training in group problem solving and interpersonal skills. At a minimum, the circle leader will need skills in group participation methods. Otherwise, he or she will wind up conducting lectures about topics such as quality improvement and productivity improvement. Leaders and participants will also need training in the use of whatever statistical and problem-solving methods are to be used. Following are eight major problem-solving techniques and their purposes.[17]

a. Brainstorming is used to identify all problems, even those beyond the control of the circle members.

b. A check sheet is used to log problems within the circle's sphere of influence within a certain time frame.

c. A Pareto chart graphically demonstrates check sheet data to identify the most serious problem (i.e., those 20 percent of the problems that cause 80 percent of the major mistakes).

d. A cause-and-effect diagram graphically demonstrates the cause of a particular problem.

e. Histograms or bar charts are graphed showing the frequency and magnitude of specific problems.

f. Scatter diagrams of "measle charts" identify major defect locations by having dots on the pictures of products, thus identifying dense dot clusters.

g. Graph and control charts monitor a production process and are compared with production samples as illustrated in Figure 12–3.

h. Stratification, generally accomplished by inspecting the same products from differing production areas, randomizes the sampling process.

13. *Creativity is encouraged.* As illustrated in the opening case and mentioned above, brainstorming, or variations thereof, fit naturally into the quality circle method and philosophy. Maintaining an attitude of "anything goes" is particularly important, even if rough ideas are later refined. If half-processed ideas are shot down by the leader or other members, idea generation will extinguish quickly.

14. *Projects are related to members' actual job responsibilities.* Quality circles are not arenas for amateur speculation about other people's work. People make suggestions about improving the quality of

FIGURE 12–3 A Control Chart Used in Quality Circles

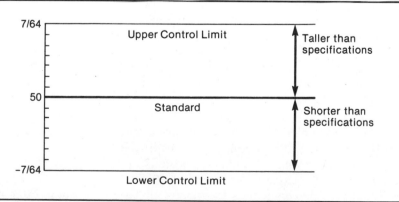

NOTE: The prescribed length of the product is 50 inches. The acceptable range of the length (tolerable limits) is plus or minus 7/64 inches, or from 49.891 inches to 50.109 inches.

work for which they are already responsible. Thus a lawn-mower manufacturer is not plagued with sorting out suggestions from the quality circles at divisions engaged in the manufacture of something entirely different such as lawn chairs. (We are not taking the dogmatic position, however, that productive innovations in one field cannot come from people outside that field.)

15. *Members receive a mixture of internal and external rewards.* QC members should receive both internal and external rewards based on the success of the program. Internal rewards include personal satisfaction, enjoyment of the challenging tasks, and a feeling of pride. External rewards include recognition and bonus money for useful suggestions. Paying for useful suggestions, however, is controversial because it may create resentment among employees who are not involved in a circle.

THE ARGUMENT FOR AND AGAINST QUALITY CIRCLES

It appears that the quality circle method has become a standard technique for improving quality and productivity in both manufacturing and service organizations. Nevertheless, QCs have been widely criticized. Both sides of the argument should therefore be examined.

Advantages of Quality Circles

A major argument for quality circles is that they represent a low cost, efficient vehicle for unleashing the creative potential of employees. In the process, highly desirable ends are achieved. In addition to quality improvements, QC programs have increased productivity, job satisfaction, morale, and motivation. It has also been reported that QCs have improved communication, changed the emphasis in problem solving from fire fighting to prevention, enhanced employee commitment, reduced the reliance on authority to accomplish a task, reduced delivery times, and enhanced the coordination of work.[18] Many of these positive outcomes lead to improved quality of work life.

Another favorable feature of these circles is that they are perceived positively by management, workers, the union, and stockholders. A firm contemplating implementing such a program thus does not run the risk of internal or external opposition. (It is conceivable, however, that opposition will be forthcoming if management fails to develop a formal reward system for quality circle contributions.)

Quality circles contribute to organizational effectiveness in another important way. They have emerged as a useful method of developing present and future managers. An example of this oft-repeated phenomenon is furnished by C. Philip Alexander. He reports that a major computer manufacturing firm established a quality circle separate from the training department. After the program had been operating two years, the director of training observed that the supervisors who were quality circle leaders were significantly more self-confident, knowledgeable, and poised than other supervisors who were attending the regular training program. The director believed that the supervisors' involvement in the QC training programs and activities were the major contributor to this difference.[19]

Disadvantages of Quality Circles

A major criticism of quality circles is that many of them are not cost-effective. If they were, fewer of them would be abandoned by management after an initial burst of enthusiasm. Even more pessimistic is the criticism that the purported successes of QCs may be attributable to factors other than the actual quality circle program. One explanation is that the attention paid to employees by management may be the force behind the gains in productivity and morale (the well-known Hawthorne effect). Another possible explanation of the successes of quality circle programs is that the gains are due to improved group dynamics and problem-solving techniques.[20] Therefore, an entire QC program need not be conducted just to achieve these gains.

A discouraging argument has been advanced that quality circles may not be suited to the North American workers. Matsushita Electric, a leading user of the quality circle method in Japan, does not use circles in its U.S. plant (located in Chicago) because it does not consider the American worker suited to circle activities.[21] Perhaps Matsushita management believes that Americans are too self-oriented to be group oriented.

Quality circles may prove to be breeding grounds for friction and role confusion between the quality control department and the groups themselves. Unless management carefully defines the relationship of quality circles vis-à-vis the quality control department, much duplication of effort (and therefore waste of resources) will be inevitable.

Exclusive reliance on volunteers for the circles may result in the loss of potentially valuable ideas. Many nonassertive people may shy away from participation in the circles, despite their having valid ideas for product improvement.

Some employees who volunteer to join quality control circles may be doing so for the wrong reasons. The circle may develop the reputation of being ''a good way to get away from the line for awhile and enjoy a coffee break and a good bull session.'' (To counter such an abuse of the quality circle program, QC group members might monitor the quality of input from their own group members.)

Guidelines for Action and Skill Development

Quality circles should be used as group suggestion programs. In this way management relies on the initial enthusiasm and knowledge of workers who get an opportunity to meet and make suggestions. Furthermore, the circle does not necessarily have to be a permanent structure.

Quality circles can also be used to deal with temporary or critical organizational issues. For example, in introducing new technologies, retooling for new product lines, or helping to solve problems about customer complaints, circles can be used to work out bugs as well as to help employees accept change.[22]

Avoid using the quality circle as a "garbage can" for unresolved controversies of the past. Fresh problems, whose solutions have a chance of being accepted, should be offered to the circle.[23]

Membership in the circle should be voluntary and on a rotating basis. In many instances a team member will soon run out of fresh ideas for quality improvement. Rotating membership will result in a wider sampling of ideas being generated.

Quality circles should be implemented on a pilot basis. As the circle produces results and wins the acceptance of managers and employees alike, it can be expanded as the demand for its output increases.

Management must make good use of many of the suggestions forthcoming from the quality circle, yet still define the limits of the power and authority of the circle. On the one hand, if none of the circle's suggestions are adopted, the circle will lose its effectiveness as an agent for change. Circle members will become discouraged because of their lack of clout. On the other hand, if the circle has too much power and authority, it will be seen as a governing body for technical change. Under the latter circumstances, it is also possible that people will use the circle for political purposes. A given individual who wants to get a technical modification authorized may try to influence a member of the quality circle to suggest that modification during a circle meeting.

Managers can use quality circles as a transitional vehicle in moving toward a more participative management system and culture. QCs can also be used in making a transition to self-managing work teams. Circles prepare employees for self-managing teams by developing the appropriate skills and knowledge.[24]

To develop skill in conducting a quality circle, the leader should follow closely the above suggestions in addition to those offered in the chapter section Key Elements of a Successful Program. Training in group dynamics and methods of participative management will be particularly helpful. If the right structure is established for the circle, it will facilitate skill development. Experience suggests that it is best to begin with about nine members and a leader. It may also prove helpful at the outset to appoint a group facilitator (an internal or external consultant) who can help the group run more smoothly.

DISCUSSION QUESTIONS AND ACTIVITIES

1. A worker told a researcher, "I don't trust the quality circle program. Management plants its spies in the circle, so they can be informed of any person who has complaints about the company." How can top management best deal with this concern?

2. In what way might quality circles dilute the power of supervisors and higher-level managers?

3. What application do you see for quality circles in service organizations, such as the public assistance (welfare) department, hospitals, and banks?

4. What similarity and differences do you see between a suggestion system and a QC?

5. Typically the team leader of a QC is not the regular boss of the circle members. Why do you think things are arranged this way?

6. To what extent do you think it is realistic to expect production workers to learn the statistical and problem-solving techniques typically used in a quality circle?

7. Try to locate a person who has participated in a quality circle. Record that individual's description of the method and results of his or her quality circle experience.

NOTES

1. Case researched by Sandra Koo, Rochester Institute of Technology, 1987.
2. Murray R. Barrick and Ralph A. Alexander, "A Review of Quality Circle Efficacy and the Existence of Positive-Finding Bias," *Personnel Psychology,* Autumn 1987, p. 583.
3. Ibid., p. 585.
4. Justin Y. Shimada, Kenneth M. Jenkins, and Lewis N. Goslin, "Quality Circles Can Meet the Challenge," *Business Forum,* Spring 1983, pp. 18–21.
5. Ibid., p. 21.
6. Mitchell Lee Marks, "The Question of Quality Circles," *Psychology Today,* March 1986, p. 38.
7. Thomas Peters, "Workers Can Make, Break Company," Syndicated column, August 2, 1987.
8. John D. Blair, Stanley L. Cohen, and Jerome V. Hurwitz, "Quality Circles: Practical Considerations for Public Managers," *Public Productivity Review,* March/June 1982, p. 14.
9. Barrick and Alexander, "A Review of Quality Circle Efficacy," p. 57.
10. Berkeley Rice, "Square Holes for Quality Circles," *Psychology Today,* February 1984, p. 17.
11. Sandy J. Wayne, Ricky W. Griffin, and Thomas S. Bateman, "Improving the Effectiveness of Quality Circles," *Personnel Administrator,* March 1986, p. 81.

12. Wayne, Griffin, and Bateman, "Improving the Effectiveness of Quality Circles,"; Sud Ingle, "How to Avoid Quality Circle Failure in Your Company," *Training and Development Journal,* June 1982, pp. 57–59.
13. Blair, Cohen, and Hurwitz, "Quality Circles," p. 16.
14. Joel Brockner and Ted Hess, "Self-Esteem and Task Performance in Quality Circles," *Academy of Management Journal,* September 1986, pp. 617–23.
15. Laurie Fitzgerald, "Quality Circles—Three More Obstacles," *Training and Development Journal,* May 1982, p. 7.
16. Barrick and Alexander, "A Review of Quality Circle Efficacy," p. 587.
17. George Munchus, III, "Employer-Employee Based Quality Circles in Japan: Human Resource Policy Implications for American Firms," *Academy of Management Review,* April 1983, p. 257.
18. S. G. Goldstein, "Organizational Dualism and Quality Circles," *Academy of Management Review,* July 1985, p. 514.
19. C. Phillip Alexander, "A Hidden Benefit of Quality Circles," *Personnel Journal,* February 1984, p. 54.
20. Blair, Cohen, and Hurwitz, "Quality Circles," p. 12.
21. Munchus, "Employer-Employee Based Quality Circles," p. 261.
22. The first two guidelines are from Edward E. Lawler III and Susan A. Mohrman, "Quality Circles after the Fad," *Harvard Business Review,* January–February 1985, p. 70.
23. Henry P. Sims, Jr., and James W. Dean, Jr., "Beyond Quality Circles," *Personnel,* January 1985, p. 29.
24. Lawler and Mohrman, "Quality Circles after the Fad," p. 71.

SOME ADDITIONAL REFERENCES

Hutchins, David. *Quality Circles Handbook.* New York: Nichols Publishing Company, 1985.

Landon, David N., and Steve Moulton. "Quality Circles: What's in Them for Employees?" *Personnel Journal,* June 1986, pp. 23–26.

Marks, Mitchell; Edward J. Hackett; Philip H. Mirvis; and James F. Grady, Jr. "Employee Participation in a Quality Circle Program: Impact on Quality of Work Life, Productivity, and Absenteeism." *Journal of Applied Psychology,* February 1986, pp. 61–69.

Pati, Gopal C.; Robert Salitore; and Sandra Brady. "What Went Wrong with Quality Circles?" *Personnel Journal,* December 1987, pp. 83–87.

Smeltzer, Larry R., and Ben L. Kedia. "Training Needs of Quality Circles." *Personnel,* August 1987, pp. 51–55.

Whatley, Arthur A., and Wilma Hoffman. "Quality Circles Earn Union Respect." *Personnel Journal,* December 1987, pp. 88–93.

Part IV

Improving Productivity and Quality at the Organizational Level

In this part of the book we examine four approaches designed to improve productivity and quality at the organizational level. All of these approaches involve substantial changes in the way an organization operates and in its culture. To be successful, approaches of this nature should not be considered isolated programs or "hot topics," but as part of a total commitment to high quality and productivity.

Chapter 13 describes approaches to building a commitment to quality from as many organizational members as possible. The changes are more pervasive than simply conducting a program of quality improvement. Chapter 14 describes how some firms are deliberately fostering product innovation within small organizational units in order to help the firm cope with a changing environment. Successful intrapreneuring is based on a knowledge of individual and group creativity. Chapter 15 describes how some firms attempt to hasten decision making and reduce costs by decreasing the number of layers of management. Modifying the structure in this manner is based on an understanding of the theory of bureaucracy.

Chapter 16 describes Japanese management practices and their application to the American firm. In addition, we look at some of the controversy surrounding the true merit of Japanese-style management. Japanese management is based on well-established concepts of participative management and group behavior.

Chapter Thirteen

Building Quality Awareness

> Top management at Xerox Corporation decided that in order to compete successfully in the present economy the company had to upgrade the quality of its products and services. The route they chose was to implement a program to heighten quality awareness among all employees.

At Xerox Corporation managers are outfitted with plaques for their desks inscribed with the company motto on quality: Leadership through Quality. Framed diagrams of problem-solving techniques adorn the walls of company conference rooms. A whole vocabulary has sprung up to express the company's emphasis on quality. Workers are part of *family groups*. Managers espouse a formula called *LUTI*, an acronym for *learn, use, teach, inspect*.

The lingo and the framed diagrams on quality are just the external signs of a massive training effort. Xerox had 103,000 employees worldwide trained about quality in one year in seminars that lasted from two days to a week.

Xerox's emphasis on quality has clearly brought about a turnaround for the company, analysts say. But it is only in the past two years that the company has begun to regain some of its overall market share in copiers. The lag may have had to do with the enormity of the undertaking. Xerox has had to refashion its corporate and employee outlook as well as its marketing and product development strategies.

Xerox's training seminars teach basic problem-solving techniques and ways to ensure quality products. The process focuses attention on the needs of the customer, a strategy Xerox sees as crucial for combating competition.

"Every single employee has a responsibility to ensure satisfaction," said Charles L. Sabino, who leads training sessions for the company. "In training people on concepts, we do not want people just to understand them but to buy into them."

The change in corporate culture amounts to a revolution. Every employee is expected to consider quality issues and bring them to the attention of others. Lines of communication between management and workers have become much more open, the company claims, and individual employees have more autonomy.

Convincing employees to adopt these principles in their daily work is no easy task. Especially among middle managers, the new process has met with resistance. "The company is excellent in developing processes; there are probably hundreds of processes," said Tom Boucher, a manager attending a training session on quality techniques. "But to get the worker to apply the principles is a little bit more involved. You can't just tell the worker to do it."

David T. Kearns, president and CEO of Xerox, has estimated that any company that does not pay more attention to quality, risks losing as much as a quarter of its annual revenues to inefficient operation.

Analysts find that the changes within Xerox have brought results. "One of the things that is quite clear is that over the last five years there has been a sharp improvement in Xerox quality," said Eugene Glazer of Dean Witter Reynolds. He noted, "I don't know if they reached the end of the line, but they've come a long way." Lynn Ritter, a senior industry analyst at Dataquest Inc. said the company has not grown by leaps and bounds since the training program started in 1983. However, if Xerox hadn't started to focus on its competitors and on quality, its market share would have declined further.

Even a competitor, Canon USA Copier Products, has noted that Xerox has become more competitive, especially with its "10" copier series.

To Xerox, the investment in training programs is well worth it. The company credits its quality process, as well as other programs introduced in the early 1980s, with helping the company regain market share in the copier industry.[1]

The company's training sessions teach every employee to be more aware of the importance of quality, in addition to providing training in specific techniques of statistical quality control. A marketing manager who attended the program made this comment about the benefits of the Leadership through Quality program:

> A lot of clear messages come through about the importance of quality. Above all, we learn that quality is the job of every employee. It's not just a responsibility assigned to quality specialists. Quality improvement is much more complicated than inspecting a product for defects and then making any appropriate adjustments. Quality begins with the design of a product or service and ends with a satisfied customer.

Quality can mean a technically sound product design, an on-time delivery, a smile when greeting a customer, or a courteous response by the telephone operator when a customer calls.

Some of us held after-hours rap sessions when we were in the training program. At one of these sessions the group concluded that quality boiled down to every worker in the company, including the president, putting forth his or her best effort every day. I heard somewhere that a parachute manufacturer developed the best quality program possible. The parachute makers were required to take a jump in a randomly selected parachute they had packed. You can imagine how hard these workers tried to build quality into the packing of parachutes. I think Xerox is striving for the same level of quality awareness in every employee.[2]

STRATEGIES AND TACTICS FOR QUALITY AWARENESS

Xerox Corporation, as well as many other firms, has learned that improving the quality of products and services involves both the learning of quality techniques and the development of quality awareness among employees. Our concerns here are with the "soft side" of quality improvement—strategies and tactics for quality awareness. Although abstract and less tangible than techniques such as the Taguchi method of measuring deviations from conformance, developing quality awareness can have a much bigger payoff. As Tom Peters says, an important aim of quality awareness strategies and techniques is to "Get quality into the air with high tingling intensity."[3]

Create a Corporate Culture of Quality.   It is generally acknowledged that improving quality requires an upheaval in corporate culture. According to Karen Pennar, engineers, designers, marketers, administrators, and production workers have to collaborate to ensure quality, and they all have to understand that they are critical to the process. Quality-improvement that does not include a corporate culture that embodies quality is likely to be shallow and short-lived. "If the process is half-hearted or poorly planned, quality will become simply another fashionable word in the executive's lexicon or yet another trendy promotion vehicle for new goods."[4]

Get Top Management Commitment to Quality.   Without a commitment by top management to quality improvement, quality awareness is unlikely to pervade the organization. One important way of demonstrating this commitment is for the director of the quality control department to report to a member of top management.[5] A study of room air-conditioning manufacturers in the United States and Japan supported this point. It was found that high levels of quality were associated with strong commitment to that goal, and that Japanese managers were more committed to quality than were American managers.[6] An example of how managerial actions can demonstrate commitment to quality took place at The Ducane Co., a manufacturer of top-quality barbecue grills.

> Once while walking the floor of the factory, John Ducate, Jr., president of Ducane Industries (the parent company), found flaws in tons of castings for the grill's chassis. "The castings weren't poured properly," he explains. "They looked pitted and rough." At a cost of several thousand dollars, Ducate sent the parts back to be remelted and his workers to take a refresher course on pouring aluminum.[7]

Include Quality in the Organizational Strategy.   Quality awareness heightens when quality becomes part of organizational strategy and not just protecting consumers from annoyances.[8] If a statement about quality is not contained in the organization's strategy, quality will be subordinated to other goals. Some companies use quality as their strategy in gaining their desired market share. Panasonic, the electronics firm, uses its ability to produce high-quality products as its key marketing strategy.[9]

Develop a Company Policy about Quality.   Once quality is built into strategy, the groundwork is laid for establishing a company policy about quality. Policy, in turn, further increases awareness of the importance of quality. Philip B. Crosby says that the main rule about establishing a policy about quality is that it should be clear enough to avoid misunderstanding. He recommends that a policy about quality should include this statement: "We will deliver defect-free products and services to our clients, on time." A representative quality policy has been developed by Milliken (textiles):

> Milliken and Company is dedicated to providing products and service designed to be at that level of quality which will best help its customers to grow and prosper. Its operational areas (Research and Development, Marketing, Manufacturing, Administrative, Service) will be expected to perform its functions exactly as written in carefully prepared specifications.[10]

After the strategy and policy about quality are formulated, they must be reinforced by other methods to bring about awareness of quality. The remaining tactics help reinforce strategy and policy.

Make Quality an Objective of Each Manager.   The desire for quality should be as important as meeting production schedules and producing a high volume of goods. Managers should be held as responsible for achieving quality objectives as they are for achieving quantity objectives. A convenient way of achieving this end is to include in the performance appraisal an evaluation of how well quality objectives were attained. In this way managers are rewarded for achieving quality.

Communicate Widely the Concept of Quality.   A basic strategy for bringing about quality awareness is for key people in the organization to communicate information about quality at every appropriate opportunity. The methods used to spread the word about quality vary in sophistication, but all make some contribution to quality awareness. Tom Peters urges managers to make regular calls to or visit work places to chat with employees from all levels and organizational functions. They should ask questions such as "What's our progress on the quality-improvement process here?" As a consequence of these chats, organizational members will be seizing the opportunity to tout their accomplishments in improving quality.[11]

Many companies distribute inserts about quality into pay envelopes (such as those distributed by Payroll Inserts) that contain catchy quotes about quality. An example: "Customers may not know or care how quickly you did the job, but they always care how well you did it. William H. Spoor, Chairman Pillsbury Company."[12]

Another way of communicating the importance of quality is to praise quality. Supervisors who praise good finishes, durability, and quick service are urging a course of action that produces quality.[13]

Crosby recommends a ground-level approach to communicating the importance of quality. He claims that one of the most effective methods of reminding people of the importance of quality turns out to be floor mats containing such slogans as "Do It Right the First Time." Studies show that floor mats are more effective reminders than posters.[14]

One more way of communicating the importance of quality is to express a visible interest in quality, as recommended by Tom Peters. Two such means suggested by Peters are to conspicuously display books about quality in one's office and to let it be known that one is away from the office attending a seminar on quality.[15]

Present Top Management Speeches about Quality.   An effective way of communicating the importance of quality is for the CEO to make frequent brief speeches about the importance of quality. The speech can be delivered at company meetings and to stockholders. Here is a script recommended by Crosby:[16]

> I recognize that quality is a very popular subject today. Our customers are concerned about it, the nation is concerned, we as a company and as individuals are concerned.
>
> We have done a great deal of investigation on the subject and have learned quite a bit. One thing that has come through very clearly is that there are no simple, painless cures for solving the problem of quality. It takes determination, education, and then a clear process of implementation.
>
> Our studies show that a company gains improvement quickly when it takes quality seriously. They also show that it takes several years before it all becomes part of the routine, if it ever does.

We have also learned that quality begins with senior management. So every member of management is attending special classes to help us develop a common language of quality and recognize what our individual role is. Everyone in the company will attend classes on this subject.

We are going to deliver defect-free products and services to our customers. After all, this is what we told we will do in our advertisements and discussions. There is no more important task for our team to accomplish.

The company that delivers what it says it will deliver is the company that will lead its industry.

We have the people, the equipment, and the knowledge to make it all happen. We are committed to quality forever.

Conduct Five-Minute Quality Updates. To keep quality awareness in the forefront of people's minds, begin meetings in all functional areas with a five-minute quality update. Additionally, recommends Peters, every agenda item, no matter how indirectly related to quality, could begin with a brief discussion of the quality implications of the item. For instance, a discussion of employee recruitment could be related to how the selection of high calibre personnel leads to the production of high-quality goods and services. As a follow-up, a full-dress quality review can be conducted each quarter.[17]

Emphasize Meeting the Customer's Requirements. Corning Glass Works has a quality-awareness program similar to the one at Xerox Corporation. The simple, yet powerful, principle, "meet the customer's requirements" is the driving force behind the Total Quality Management System. *Customer* is defined as any person with whom an employee has a job-related relationship. These people include someone who actually buys a Corning product or service, is a co-worker, supervisor, supervised employee, or supplier. Meeting the customer's requirements is considered to be the very foundation of every employee's job at Corning.

To be able to meet customer requirements, employees must first understand those requirements. Also, the requirements must be documented and reviewed regularly to plan for necessary changes and to avoid future misinterpretation. To determine how well an employee is doing, the customer is sometimes asked whether requirements are being met on time, the first time, 100 per cent of the time.[18]

Promote the Idea of Error-Free Work. The argument continues to rage over whether or not it is practical to strive for zero defects—the absence of defects in a product or service. A slightly less stringent approach is to promote the idea *strive to do error-free work*. The Corning program recognizes that errors cannot be eliminated. The purpose of the principle of striving for error-free work is to create an attitude that errors are not acceptable. Corning no longer operates on the basis of an "acceptable quality level" with an allowable percentage of defects. Instead, the new attitude prompts employees to ask why an error has occurred, track down the root cause, and take action to prevent a reoccurrence.[19]

Make Frequent Use of Sayings that Promote Quality.   Awareness of quality can sometimes be accomplished through sayings and slogans incorporated into speech and posters. Sayings and slogans developed by others that promote quality include: "I make the difference" (The Rockefeller Group); "We want to give the best customer service of any company in the world" (IBM); "Quality, service, cleanliness, and value" (McDonald's); and "Quality Is Job 1" (Ford). Another approach is for managers to develop their own slogans that promote quality.[20] The proprietor of a typewriter store uses this slogan, "My work is a reflection of me."

Sports talk can also be used to encourage quality performance.[21] Examples include, "You pulled a hat trick with your quality performance last month," "Every defect is a 20-yard penalty against us," or "An error-free worker is a 20-game winner."

Stress the Importance of *Kaizen*.   Quality awareness can be regarded as a gradual process rather than a crash program. It therefore fits well the spirit of *Kaizen*, a philosophy of continuing gradual improvement in one's personal and work life. *Kaizen* also means roughly, "Every day in every way, I'm getting better and better." Companies use *Kaizen* to program themselves with positive thinking so that some small improvement takes place everyday.

Kaizen is a long-term gradual improvement, involving a series of small, sometimes imperceptible changes. The spirit of *Kaizen* improves quality awareness because it prompts employees to be constantly on the lookout for small improvements. Workers are also encouraged to look for things that are not quite right, but are not yet full-blown problems.[22]

A restaurant owner promoted the spirit of Kaizen among her workers. Several of them decided to begin uncluttering the restaurant by removing some of the less attractive paintings from the wall and some of the bar decorations. Soon a few customers began to comment favorably on the cleaner decor. Given this encouragement, the owner and the workers decided to shift to an art-deco motif (characterized by a stark, clean, and modern look). Business increased substantially. The owner attributed much of this increase to the high quality appearance of the restaurant.

Think Anthropomorphically.   To anthropomorphize is to attribute human qualities to animals or things, such as saying "The Dow Jones was feeling gloomy this morning before making a comeback late in the day."

William J. Gorden recommends that supervisors should think of how violinists hug and stroke their instruments, the bond that develops between sailors and their ship, and the insignia that pilots and crew paint on their aircraft.

After making these visualizations, the supervisor can then serve as a role model to others about having a fond affection for equipment and machines.[23] Employees, in turn will show the same care for their equipment and machines, which will ultimately lead to quality awareness and improvement. The logic is that workers who have a genuine concern for their equipment and tools will want to achieve output of high quality.

Conduct Supplier Meetings about Quality. A company needs high-quality components and materials to produce high-quality products and services. Quality awareness is therefore also important for a company's suppliers. Sharp, the electronics firm, exemplifies this approach. The company teaches many of its suppliers how to produce high-quality components. In this regard, part of Crosby's program on quality improvement includes recommending the following policy statement: "Suppliers are educated and supported in order to ensure that they will deliver services and products that are dependable and on time."[24]

An adjunct to informing suppliers about quality specifications is to attempt to raise their general level of quality awareness. A frank discussion with suppliers about the company's quality strategy will be helpful in communicating this message. Ford and Motorola are two of many companies that award certificates to suppliers who meet all of their quality specifications. Awards of this type are helpful in promoting quality awareness among the company's actual and potential suppliers.

Develop Excellence in Human Relations. A strategic, yet indirect, method of developing quality awareness throughout the firm is the excellence in human relations program developed by Ford Motor Co. *Excellence in human relations* is a major tenet of the company's mission statement and guiding principles. The reasoning is that if employees are treated in an excellent manner from a human relations perspective, they will be motivated to produce high quality goods and services. Employees who are treated fairly and with dignity, and therefore in a high-quality manner, will reason that they should turn out work of high quality.

However pontifical the principle of excellence in human relations sounds, it has contributed to a superior quality image of Ford Motor Co. products. The Taurus and Sable autos, for example, are known to compete favorably on quality with autos from any country.[25] Both cars were developed since the principle of excellence in human relations was developed. However, many other factors—such as intensive study of the quality features of Japanese autos—also are responsible for the high quality of the Taurus and Sable (despite a few electronic problems).

The Argument for Building Quality Awareness

A major argument in favor of building quality awareness is that many executives and consultants believe that the true path to quality improvement is through a change in corporate culture. Xerox president David Kearns, for example, believes that achieving "100 percent fault-free quality" requires a profound cultural change.[26] The heralded quality-improvement program developed by Crosby includes many of the ideas for promoting quality-awareness described in this chapter.[27] Many of the exhortations of Tom Peters also center on the theme that "thinking quality" is the most valid approach to quality improvement.

Building quality awareness is also important because it is a logical approach to competing favorably in international competition and forging ahead in domestic markets. As observed by David A. Garvin, "The quality of products presents both a problem and an opportunity for U.S. manufacturers—a problem, because foreign competitors are often far ahead in offering products of superior quality; an opportunity, because American consumers are increasingly concerned about the quality of goods and services they buy."[28]

The Argument against Building Quality Awareness

The argument against building quality awareness is not that quality awareness is unimportant, but that there are better documented methods of improving quality. One such method is statistical process control. Developed by W. Edwards Deming, it is a technique for spotting defects at the point they are made rather than in after-the-fact inspection of a finished part or product. Another modern approach to quality improvement is "robust-design," developed by Genichi Taguchi. The basic premise is simple: Instead of constantly tinkering with production equipment to assure consistent quality, the product should be designed to be robust enough to achieve superior quality despite fluctuations on the production line.[29]

Recent research also suggests a more tangible approach to quality improvement than the intangible approach of developing quality awareness. Quasar, a Matsuhita subsidiary, purchased a television plant from an American company several years ago. Many of the managerial staff were replaced with its own managers, yet the operative work force was left almost intact. Quasar installed its own quality assurance systems and began to incorporate quality into the design and manufacturing processes. The essential steps taken by Quasar to assure high-quality products were straight-forward approaches that any company can take, including the following:

1. Thorough life-cycle testing of product components.
2. Use of a pilot line to plan production and work out some of the bugs.

3. Development of a detailed description of the process and instructions for operators of what to do and how to do it.

4. Predesign of work stations to minimize chances of operator error.

5. Separation of adjacent assembly lines containing similar parts to reduce chances of mixes.

Extraordinary improvements in quality took place. Quasar achieved a defect rate of 15 per 100 sets built, 10 times better than the American average.[30] Instead of a working on profound changes in the corporate culture, Quasar used some common-sense, low-technology methods of improving quality. Conceivably, however, these quality-improvement techniques could have heightened quality awareness.

Guidelines for Action and Skill Development

Suggestions for developing quality awareness have been the central topic of this chapter. A few additional suggestions, however, are in order that will facilitate converting awareness into actual quality improvement.

The manufacturing or operations process must be in control. Running a tight "operations ship" is necessary to achieve quality products and services. An in-control operations process includes such things as well-maintained machinery and office equipment, good housekeeping, well-trained employees, and an efficient quality control operation.

Managers and employees at all levels who achieve high quality should be rewarded. Rewards can include public recognition, cash bonuses, company-paid vacations, high performance appraisal ratings, promotions, or compliments. Some companies recognize high-quality performers by such designations as "Quality Person of the Month."

Deal openly with the problem of quantity versus quality. Many workers believe that lip service is paid to quality while high quantity (such as sales volume and meeting demanding production schedules) is what really counts. It is important to allow employees to vent their feelings about this topic; then explain how both quantity and quality are important (if true).

DISCUSSION QUESTIONS AND ACTIVITIES

1. Why do you think American companies have become so concerned about product quality in recent years?

2. Give an example of how quality awareness could be applied to customer service.

3. What is your reaction to the argument of a clothing manufacturer who

said, "Quality is for the big companies. Our clothing is designed for the discounters whose customers are looking for $10 shirts and blouses."

4. Identify an organization you would classify as having high quality awareness. What is the basis for your conclusion?

5. Philip B. Crosby argues that "quality is free." What does he probably mean?

6. Interview three consumers and ask them what the term *quality* means to them. Be prepared to compare your answers with those of classmates.

NOTES

1. Excerpted and adapted from Michelle Lavender, "Xerox 'Family' Pushes Quality," Rochester *Democrat and Chronicle*, December 6, 1987, pp. 1F, 4F.
2. Interview conducted by Vashuda Badri, November 1987.
3. Thomas Peters, "Quality Starts with Zealous Supervisor," syndicated column, November 8, 1987.
4. Karen Pennar, "America's Quest Can't Be Half-Hearted," *Business Week*, June 8, 1987, p. 136.
5. Philip B. Crosby, *Quality without Tears: The Art of Hassle-Free Management* (New York: McGraw-Hill, 1984), p. 101.
6. David A. Garvin, "Quality Problems: Policies, and Attitudes in the United States and Japan: An Exploratory Study," *Academy of Management Journal*, December 1986, p. 666.
7. Nancy K. Austin, "Quest for Quality," *Success!*, January/February 1987, p. 14.
8. David A. Garvin, "Competing on the Eight Dimensions of Quality," *Harvard Business Review*, November–December 1987, p. 102.
9. Jack Reddy and Aber Berger, "Three Essentials of Product Quality," *Harvard Business Review*, July–August 1983, p. 159.
10. Crosby, *Quality without Tears*, pp. 101–102.
11. Peters, "Quality Starts with Zealous Supervisor."
12. "Quality First!" *Payroll Inserts*, not dated, p. 5.
13. William I. Gorden, "Gaining Employee Commitment to Quality," *Supervisory Management*, November 1985, p. 31.
14. Crosby, *Quality without Tears*, p. 111.
15. Peters, "Quality Starts with Zealous Supervisor."
16. Crosby, *Quality without Tears*, pp. 103–4.
17. Peters, "Quality Starts with Zealous Supervisor."
18. William H. Wagel, "Corning Zeroes in on Total Quality," *Personnel*, July 1987, pp. 4–5.
19. Ibid., p. 5.
20. Gorden, "Gaining Employee Commitment," pp. 30–31.
21. Ibid., p. 31.
22. Scott DeGarmo, "Managing with Kaizen," *Success!*, April 1987, p. 1;

Massaki Imai, *Kaizen: The Key to Japan's Competitive Success* (New York: Random House, 1987).

23. Gorden, "Gaining Employee Commitment," p. 32.
24. Crosby, *Quality without Tears,* p. 167.
25. William J. Hampton, "Why Image Counts: A Tale of Two Industries," *Business Week,* June 8, 1987, p. 139.
26. John A. Byrne, "Culture Shock at Xerox," *Business Week,* June 22, 1987, p. 106.
27. Crosby, *Quality without Tears,* throughout book.
28. Garvin, "Quality Problems," p. 653.
29. Hamptom, "Why Image Counts," p. 142.
30. Martin, R. Smith, "Improving Product Quality in American Industry," *The Academy of Management Executive,* August 1987, p. 243.

SOME ADDITIONAL REFERENCES

Hesterman, Ellen W. "Model for Implementing a Participatory Program in Statistical Process Control Areas." *Personnel,* November 1986, pp. 53–58.

"I Know It When I See It." Video with discussion guide. New York American Management Association, 1987.

Rubenstein, Sidney P. *Participative Systems at Work: Creating Quality and Employment Security.* New York: Human Sciences Press, 1987.

Shetty, Y. K., and Vernon M. Buehler. *Quality Productivity and Innovation.* New York: Elsevier Science Publishing Co., 1987.

Towsend, Patrick L. *Commit to Quality.* New York: Wiley, 1986.

Wholey, Joseph S. *Organizational Excellence: Stimulating Quality and Communicating Value.* Lexington, Mass.: Lexington Books, 1987.

Chapter Fourteen

Intrapreneuring

The five large companies described here each faced the challenge of fostering the innovative spirit characteristic of many small entrepreneurships. Each firm chose a slightly different method of achieving product breakthroughs by way of intrapreneuring—the existence of entrepreneurial behavior and thinking within a large organization.

3M. Arthur Fry, a Minnesota Mining and Manufacturing chemical engineer, was bothered when pieces of paper that marked his church hymnal fell out when he stood up to sing. Fry was aware that Spencer Silver, a scientist working at 3M, had accidentally discovered an adhesive with weak sticking power. Under most circumstances, low adhesion would be bad, but for Fry it was good. He reasoned that markers made with the weak adhesive might stick lightly to something and then would readily detach. Because 3M allows employees to spend 15 percent of their company time on independent projects, Fry began working on the idea.

Fry made samples of the light-sticking paper and then distributed the small yellow pads to secretaries within the corporation. The enthusiastic reaction by the secretaries gave 3M an impetus to begin marketing the product under the name *Post-it*. The product has become a legendary success with annual sales of over $100 million.

General Electric. Jacques Robinson was given the opportunity about seven years ago to manage GE's video products division in Portsmouth, Virginia. One of his responsibilities was to expand its product base to include a long list of products for home information and entertainment. Robinson maintained an open-door policy for anyone with fruitful ideas. One person who took advantage of this policy was Howard R. Stevenson, Jr., a technical whiz since his high school days. He had spent his entire professional life with GE, most of the time working on radar.

Although not discontent enough to leave the firm, Stevenson felt stifled. He therefore welcomed the opportunity when GE offered him a transfer to Portsmouth. Shortly thereafter, Stevenson found a creative challenge. Ordinary TV sets are much less effective than monitors in displaying numbers, letters, graphics, and images from home computers, video games, and video cameras. Working at night in his cluttered home workshop, Stevenson designed circuitry that elevated standard television sets to monitor quality. The monitor became an immediate marketing success, and Stevenson's career has become rejuvenated. He says, "I like the atmosphere of taking risks, trying things."

IBM.   Ten years ago, International Business Machines Corporation adopted the concept of independent business units (IBUs) that operated as separate organizations. Growing in number, the IBUs each have their own miniboard of directors. An independent business unit has the authority to decide on its own manufacturing and marketing strategy, usually without asking for approval from corporate headquarters. One unit is developing automatic teller machines; another is building industrial robots.

IBM's most heralded IBU produced the company's personal computer. A dozen executives led by Philip D. Estridge established headquarters in Boca Raton, Florida, in 1980. They were given as much money as they needed and a mandate to get IBM into the personal computer business as soon as possible. Given this amount of latitude, the group broke some of IBM's most hallowed traditions such as supplementing the IBM sales organization with retail outlets. To control costs and hasten development, the IBU bought most of its parts from outside suppliers (among them a South Korean company), rather than from inside IBM. The PC family, including the Personal Systems/2 computer, has become a notable success. Its only setback was the ill-selling PC Junior, which was discontinued. The dozen people in the original PC group grew into the entry systems division, which now has over 10,000 employees.

Hewlett-Packard.   Over seven years ago, this well-known electronics firm awarded engineer Charles House a medal for "extraordinary contempt and defiance beyond the normal call of engineering duty." House achieved this distinction by ignoring an order from the founder of the firm, David Packard, to stop working on a type of high-quality video monitor with a giant screen. Despite the admonition, House persevered and succeeded in developing the monitor. The monitor is of such high quality that it has been used to track NASA's manned landings and also in heart transplants. Early estimates were that the market for such large-screen displays would only be 30 units. Within three years, 17,000 of them had been sold for gross revenues of $35 million.[1]

Xerox Corporation. Faced with the challenge of speeding up the development of new products, Xerox decided to sequester relatively small groups of employees in five research and development groups throughout the United States and Canada. In the Rochester, New York, "skunk works," a group of people work on special, secret products with code names like *Chainsaw, Bulldog,* and *Yardbird.* It is called a *skunk works,* similar to other companies, because it's off in a corner, where smelly (or devious) things are often hidden. The Rochester skunk works employs fewer than 100 people from backgrounds in engineering, research, marketing, and administrative services. From the outside, the skunk works resembles a dilapidated factory or an abandoned building. Much of the building is also in a state of disrepair. The facility has been the birthplace of four major photocopiers. Two of these copiers have generated close to $3 billion in sales since 1978.

A new company was spawned from the skunk works that in 30 months designed, produced, and sold the first desktop copier made in the United States in eight years. It is used mostly for engineering applications. Because it is one yard wide, the copier has been given the code name Yardbird.

Nearly 20 patents were achieved in developing the Yardbird. It uses no more electricity than a toaster, can be installed in a trailer at a construction site, can make copies on any kind of paper or vellum, will take copies from a variety of sources, and makes copies of copies. It can make copies a yard wide and indefinitely long—the longest one so far being 500 feet. Xerox plans to sell the copier throughout the world including Europe, South America, and China. By one estimate there's a market for as many as 100,000 machines. If this estimate were accurate, Yardbird would generate $360 million in revenue.

An industry analyst, Brian Fernandez, said, "The engineering copiers in the past have been so big and so expensive and so fixed-place. The Yardbird is smaller than anything I've heard of. I think Xerox did a fairly good job on the machine. It's different. It's unique. It demonstrates once again why the company needs a skunk works."[2]

ORGANIZATIONAL ACTIONS TO FOSTER INTRAPRENEURSHIP

The different aspects of intrapreneuring practiced by the five companies just described are but a sampling of steps taken by companies to encourage entrepreneurial behavior for the good of the firm. Here we describe 10 principles of intrapreneurship or steps organizations are taking to encourage entrepreneurial behavior. Although Gifford Pinchot III coined the term, *intrapreneurship,* the same type of activity has been referred to in the past as, *divisional incorporation, subsidized start ups,* and *venture task teams.* And intrapreneurs were labeled *corporateurs.*[3]

Develop a New Culture or Modify the Present One.   The corporate culture must be compatible with intrapreneuring. Above all, authoritarian beliefs have to give way to permissiveness that grants intrapreneurs the freedom to do things their way. The Foresight Group (founders of the training program called *Sweden's School for Intrapreneurs*) contends that most companies have to develop a new culture. This does not mean that the existing values and myths or the traditional heros of the old culture must be abandoned. "Rather, new values, models, and myths must be given priority. Bureaucrat and controller must coexist with, or give way to, designer, and entrepreneur."[4]

When Pacific Telesis needed to develop new information services, it drew up six corporate commitments dedicated to implementing their plans at all levels. One reads like an intrapreneurial manifesto and specifies cultural values:

> We are creative, can-do people. We have the freedom to act and innovate to meet our customers' needs as though each of us owned the business. Strategy guides our direction; sound judgment guides our execution. We take prudent risks and are accountable for our actions.[5]

In most situations, revamping the organizational culture will be difficult. A realistic approach is to therefore modify those aspects of the culture that might be inhibiting intrapreneurship.

Identify Intrapreneurs Early in Their Careers.   Intrapreneurs are considered to be self-selecting; the organization cannot appoint people to this role. Intrapreneurs are typically people who are in the creative throes of a new idea and also have the energy and determination to pursue their own vision. They will follow this pursuit with or without the company's permission. Because intrapreneurs may arise from any part of the organization, a mechanism such as a multidisciplinary review board should exist to identify them as soon as possible.

Once the intrapreneurs have been identified, a formal system of assigning each one to a senior executive "champion" may prove valuable. The champion or sponsor helps facilitate the path for the intrapreneur administratively as an aide in obtaining budget approvals and other resources.[6]

Conduct Innovative Work in Small Organizational Units.   The skunk works at which new photocopiers were developed illustrate the important intrapreneurial principle of conducting innovative work in small organizational units. Geographic isolation is also helpful because it contributes to group cohesiveness and team spirit. The benefits of conducting innovative work in small organizational units is so well accepted that it would be unusual to find a large organization that ignores this approach. Tom Peters makes this comment about the prevalence of skunk works:

> It would not be difficult to argue that 3M, Hewlett-Packard, Digital Equipment, and Johnson and Johnson today are nothing more than collections of skunk works. I think all the evidence says that if you want to get down to the optimal size, you'll get down to the 100 person unit. The companies that push the farthest in that direction are going to be the next wave of successful companies."[7]

The decentralized units for innovation are essentially multidisciplinary project teams that report to an intrapreneur. It is not necessary for all the team members to be intrapreneurs, but they must be able to function in an ambiguous and dynamic environment. Team members are relieved of their regular responsibilities for the life of the project. If the project becomes successful enough to form a separate division of the company, project members usually have the option of being permanently assigned to the new division.

Reduce Physical Barriers to Interaction.   To foster intrapreneurial behavior it is helpful to reduce physical barriers that could inhibit the human interaction that leads to cross-fertilization of ideas. One of Hewlett-Packard's tactics is to implement its "next bench" philosophy. "People are not isolated behind office walls," says Kitty Woodall, a communications manager in corporate personnel. "People work in common areas by design. We go out of way to encourage a rubbing of elbows and an exchange of ideas."[8]

Lounges for technical personnel are another way of facilitating verbal interaction that could lead to the development of innovative ideas. Elimination of office walls has two potential disadvantages: (1) Many professionals will not work for an organization in which they have no hope of having a private office, and (2) innovation often requires an intensity of concentration not possible while working in a bull-pen–style office.

Grant Freedom to the Intrapreneur.   The most consistently espoused principle of intrapreneurship is that the intrapreneur needs freedom to operate effectively. *Freedom* in this context refers to such things as freedom to fail, freedom from budget restraints, freedom to make decisions without the usual multilevel approvals, freedom to pursue one's own interests, and freedom from deadlines. David Taylor, who headed the development and production of one of the copiers developed at the Rochester skunk works, says, "Freedom is very important in this kind of environment. The freedom of the environment allows people to do things much more openly." Another employee at the same skunk works commented, "We try to create and nurture an environment where people don't feel intimidated by failure."[9]

Multilevel approvals restrict the freedom of the intrapreneur, and they also result in a distorted perception of the concept for which approval is sought. The top decision maker hears only translations of the intrapreneur's original concept and will not have the opportunity to hear the intrapreneur's enthusiastic pitch. To circumvent this problem, Pinchot recommends that a direct relationship be established between the doer and the approver; intrapreneurs must be able to get face to face with decision makers.[10]

Allow for Some Corporate Slack.   Closely related to the principle of allowing intrapreneurs freedom is allowing slack or breathing room in resource allocation. As Pinchot observes, "When all corporate resources are committed to what is planned, nothing is left for trying the unplannable."[11] In practice this could mean incorporating into budgets a fund for emergency allocations. It could also mean a flexible budget that overcomes the need for intrapreneurial begging or "theft" of corporate resources in order to pursue a new undertaking.[12]

Corporate slack can also mean the freedom to use a portion of one's time in exploring new ideas with an unknown payoff. Many organizations, including 3M, IBM, Textron, and Du Pont allow some technical personnel to spend 5 to 15 percent of their time exploring ideas of interest to them.[13]

Avoid Traditional Controls.   Tight control systems may be characteristic of a professionally managed organization, but they can also act as a constraint on innovation. It may be difficult to justify an intrapreneurial operation from the standpoint of a projected return on investment. However, without the products stemming from an intrapreneurial unit the organization may go out of business in the future. It would therefore make sense not to deny funding to an intrapreneurial operation because it could not provide a convincing forecast of short-range return on investment.

Another type of control that should be avoided is transferring the old management structure onto a new operation as soon as it seems successful. A lesson in this regard comes from Exxon Corporation. After starting several new businesses in the 1960s and 1970s, the company proceeded to smother them with rules and regulations until they expired one by one. Tom Peters says the key is to protect the intrapreneurs from the planners.[14]

Create Changes in the Reward System. Organizational rewards should fit the preferences of intrapreneurs in order to keep these people with the firm. Insufficient or the wrong type of rewards are unlikely to decrease the effort of intrapreneurs. Rather than withdraw from work, the poorly rewarded intrapreneur will often become an entrepreneur—or an intrapreneur for another firm.

An effective reward for most intrapreneurs is the opportunity to engage in further intrapreneurial work; the more successful the intrapreneur is in developing new products, the more new products he or she is given a chance to develop. Profit sharing or "intrapreneurial pay" is another important reward for intrapreneurs. Although intrapreneurs may not be motivated primarily by money, they may look on profit sharing as a form of recognition and feedback.

Rosabeth Moss Kanter recommends that corporate employees who are responsible for new ventures should participate in its future profits. Most such pay plans pay the venture participant a base salary, generally equivalent to their former job level. In addition, they are asked to put part of their compensation "at risk"; the percentage of their "ownership" is determined by the part they put at risk. Intrapreneurs under this type of pay plan would no longer receive the other type of bonuses and profit sharing they would have received in their regular job.[15]

Dual career paths are another recommended change in the reward system for intrapreneurs. Intrapreneurs may come from many different places in the organization and thus be promoted into the position of team leader or project head. After the intrapreneur starts producing, it may be advisable not to promote that person into a higher-level administrative position. It is unwise, for example, to promote an intrapreneur to a vice presidency that demands heavy adminstrative responsibilities, including extensive meetings. Doing so may limit the intrapreneur's opportunity to do innovative work.[16] A valued promotion for the successful intrapreneur might be to handle a bigger intrapreneurial budget or to become the organization's chief intrapreneur.

End the Home-Run Philosophy. Pinchot observes that many large organizations approach innovation with gigantic success as their single goal. The senior-level executives reason that if an innovation cannot be projected to reach from $50 to $500 million in sales within a decade, it cannot have a significant impact on growth or earnings per share. The flaw in their logic is that several medium-size successes might equal one large success. These businesses pursue innovation with criteria such as these: (1) The business must not be risky; it must be based on proved technology and well-defined markets; (2) there must be no significant potential competition in the market.

This quest for a home run, rather than merely getting on base, is a mistake that establishes unrealistic criteria for innovations. An important reality to recognize is that multimillion dollar industries often began by serving very small markets. For example, mechanical refrigeration was first used on ships for exporting meat and later in food-processing plants. The jet engine and many other innovations (such as instant fruit drink) were first used for military or aerospace purposes. Even more convincing, the nonwoven business that dominates the textile market today began modestly as a $15,000 per year operation within Du Pont that sold lens wipers.[17]

Allow for Continuity of Responsibility.   Intrapreneurs should be allowed to continue with the innovations they have brought to fruition. This is true because intrapreneurs are not merely content to think of a brilliant idea and then turn it over to others for manufacturing and marketing. Invention alone is a meritorious creative activity, but the intrapreneur typically has a strong desire to build an "intraprise" (an enterprise within an existing organization).

INDIVIDUAL ACTIONS FOR BECOMING MORE INTRAPRENEURIAL

The presentation so far has focused on what the organization can do to foster intrapreneurship. For those interested in becoming an intrapreneur, it is also worthwhile to examine some of the skills and behaviors required of intrapreneurs.

Be Willing to Take Risks.   Risk taking is characteristic of both entrepreneurs and intrapreneurs. Intrapreneuring is an insecure path that carries with it constant transition and possible failure. One risk is that the innovation championed by the intrapreneur may fail, losing money for the firm and credibility for the innovator. Another risk exists even when the intraprise succeeds. Once implemented, innovations eventually become standard company practice. Then the intrapreneur may feel compelled to develop another self-created innovative activity. A career path of this type does not lend itself well to promotion to a senior-level executive position.[18] (If the intrapreneur is not interested in becoming a top executive, as stated previously, the risk here is small.)

The risk-averse individual is therefore not suited for intrapreneurship. A plausible suggestion for becoming more of a risk taker is to begin taking small risks and see what happens. If you savor the rewards of success and can absorb pain from losses, your risk-taking propensity may increase.

Redefine Your Relationship with the Company. Barbara A. Potter suggests that the way to become intrapreneurial is to redefine your relationship with your company. "Ask not what the company can do for you, but what you and the company can do together." However little freedom you are granted, you can perform a small intrapreneurial act. Maintain a notebook of possible areas for innovation. Formulate solutions to problems and steps to implement them. These problems could be related to product development, cost savings, or administrative efficiencies. When you identify a challenge that fits organizational goals, you might be able to incorporate it into your job function. Take the initiative to solve the problem rather than being told to proceed. The following scenario illustrates this approach:

> Bronwin McGarva, a manager in corporate financial communications, listened when Pacific Telesis publicized its commitment to attracting the best people and identified a need she could help fill. As a self-appointed talent scout and recruiter, she attends lectures, seminars, and conventions, making contact with speakers and trainers. Then, using her inside knowledge of project needs and the on-line communication system she oversees, she "markets" the speakers and trainers internally.[19]

Become More Valuable to the Company. The more valuable the individual is to the organization, the more leeway he or she will receive. Pinchot recommends building trust and value credits by extending oneself when given an assignment. Take your job specifications and devise a way to be innovative so the results are even better than those requested. The result could attract a sponsor who is impressed by your initiative. Sponsors are important for the intrapreneur because they can be a shield from faultfinders and can help him or her gain access to organizational resources.[20]

Become a "Cluster Specialist." To enhance your credentials for becoming an intrapreneur, William Houze recommends that you become a cluster specialist, a person who has technical depth in related technologies, crafts, markets, or skills. Elvin Montgomery, a clinical psychologist and consultant with Arthur Young, is an example of such a person: "I didn't want to be limited by traditional psychology. But I didn't want to abandon all that I had learned." Following an interest in what makes an effective clinic, he conducted his dissertation on the clinic rather than the patient. "Eventually I saw myself as a therapist of organizations rather than individuals."

By both generalizing and integrating his skills, knowledge, and interests, he created a cluster specialty: social systems, organizational behavior, and new organizations. This was exactly the constellation of skills and interests Arthur Young needed to adopt the Swedish Foresight intrapreneurial programs to American business. The same cluster of skills were also needed to manage the new Arthur Young intrapreneurial program.[21]

Maintain a Professional Management Style. Entrepreneurs are known for their resistance to professional management techniques such as maintaining careful controls and delegating responsibility. In recognition of this fact, many entrepreneurs hire professional managers to run their operation once it achieves substantial growth. Many entrepreneurs follow the same pattern of deemphasizing professional management.

Because large, complex organizations prefer all units to be professionally managed, it would be to the intrapreneur's advantage to practice professional management. In general this refers to following the fundamentals of planning, organizing, directing, controlling, and rational decision making. Being both a professional manager and an intrapreneur gives the organization the best of both worlds.[22] The suggestion was made earlier in the chapter that the organization should relax controls in order to accommodate the intrapreneur. The implication was that the organization should be willing to bend on some aspects of professional management. It is a safer strategy for the potential intrapreneur to assume that the organization will welcome traditional management practices.

Learn to Function with a Minimum of Structure. A successful intrapreneur has to learn to operate with less structure than a corporate employee in a more traditional role. Because intrapreneurships are not part of the mainstream of the organization, they will have fewer policies, rules, and regulations guiding them. Even the dress code may be relaxed for employees working at a geographically detached intrapreneurial unit. In some organizations, the budget for the intrapreneurship may not allow for the usual amount of staff support. To cope effectively with such an environment, the intrapreneur will have to handle ambiguity and a lack of structure.

Learn to Use Informal Influence Processes. Intrapreneurs face the same key challenge as other types of project leaders. Instead of using formal authority to get the resources and cooperation they need, they often have to rely on informal influence processes. As one skunk works leader said, "I have to charm people outside our group to get what I need to accomplish our work." In many innovative start ups, the intrapreneur must cross departmental boundaries and rely on a network of allies. When the intrapreneurship is endowed with substantial support, such as the IBM group that launched the PC, informal influence processes are less necessary.

Another reason for learning to use informal influence processes well is that employees who are attracted to an intrapreneurial venture may not respond well to formal authority; they are less authority conscious than most employees. In short, the intrapreneurial leader must rely more on personal than formal power.

The Case for Intrapreneuring

One argument in favor of intrapreneuring is that it has resulted in many products that have proved valuable to society, profitable to the corporation, while at the same time it has created excellent career opportunities for intrapreneurs and their staffs. Similarly, intrapreneuring gives large organizations the chance to be as innovative as small organizations. Another argument in favor of intrapreneuring is that in a number of appropriate situations, being an intrapreneur is preferable to being an entrepreneur, as described by Pinchot:

> You have a burning vision that is inherently more intrapreneurial than entrepreneurial (for example, an idea that offers a way to improve the company business).
>
> You want to conduct new activities, but your desire to stay with the friendships and the security of the corporation is stronger than your desire for a chance at great wealth.
>
> Funding for your idea is easier to come by inside the corporation than outside.
>
> You want to try an innovation on the inside before risking your own funds.
>
> You are dependent on the company name or on its marketing channels to successfully launch your intraprise.
>
> You need constant access to the company's proprietary technology to stay competitive and to remain enthused.[23]

Intrapreneuring represents the best of all possible worlds for some individuals. As Albert Shapero of Ohio State University has written: "Corporate managers who are sent off to head subsidiaries often react similarly to entrepreneurs to the exhilaration of being on their own. Our research suggests not only that many managers can be transformed into intra-corporate entrepreneurs but also that once a manager has had a taste of the entrepreneurial experience it is very difficult to lure the manager back to the corporate world."[24]

In sum, intrapreneuring can be exciting, combining the capacity and security of a large corporation with the freedom and innovativeness of the entrepreneur.

The Case against Intrapreneuring

One argument against intrapreneuring is that if too many corporate employees compete to become intrapreneurs, the result would be detrimental to the organization, if not chaotic. So many people would be spending so much time looking for interesting things to do outside of their job descriptions that the organization's regular work would not get accomplished. To counteract this problem, the organization could enforce a policy that a specific percent of one's time can be invested in pursuit of personal projects—such as done at 3M.

Another problem with too much emphasis on intrapreneuring is that it glorifies the attention seeker, deemphasizes teamwork, and denigrates traditional management practices. This type of thinking is an offshoot of the current trend toward glorifying entrepreneur and castigating professional management. In proper perspective, both intrapreneurism and entrepreneurism are one aspect of a professional manager's job.[25] Organizations cannot grow and prosper on intrapreneurism alone; professional management is still vital to the long-term success of an enterprise.

Guidelines for Action and Skill Development

According to Oliver L. Niehouse, intrapreneuring is likely to work best under three conditions. First, the environment must be flexible. For instance, an intrapreneurial effort may have to be freed temporarily from bottom-line performance. Second, the decision-making process may need to be altered so that intrapreneurs can present, get approval for, and implement sound ideas rapidly. For example, the creation of automatic teller machine banking took only about a year, which is a relatively short time for a major financial development. Third, intrapreneurs must be able to take risks without fearing the consequences of possible failure. Intrapreneurs should be reassured that their jobs are not on the line should they try and fail.[26]

The Foresight Group recommends seven initial steps to the organization that intends to embark on intrapreneurship.

1. Determine and carefully describe the kinds of entrepreneurial ideas and opportunities that top managers are interested in and willing to support.
2. Define the groundrules for the future relationship between the corporation and the intrapreneur.
3. Identify the amount of first-risk money top management is willing to invest and also possible future investments.
4. Specify the expected results from the venture such as profitability and volume of employment.
5. Make management aware of the cultural values and changes in rules that are needed to bring about innovation.
6. Inform employees about the upcoming new venture and its most important consequences.
7. Identify the potential intrapreneurs.[27]

DISCUSSION QUESTIONS AND ACTIVITIES

1. In what way does the research and development function in an organization differ from intrapreneurism?
2. Is the term intrapreneur simply a modern synonym for inventor?
3. Why wouldn't large organizations be better off simply buying small companies with promising products than bothering to create intrapreneurships?
4. Give two examples of an intrapreneurial idea (real or not yet tried to your knowledge) not related to a new product or service. Enlist the help of a corporate employee if necessary.
5. What is the difference between intrapreneuring and a quality circle program?
6. Should business schools begin offering courses or majors in intrapreneurship? Explain your reasoning.

NOTES

1. The first four cases are as reported in John S. DeMott, "Here Come the Intrapreneurs," *Time,* February 4, 1987; "The Knockoffs Head for a Knockdown Fight with IBM," *Business Week,* December 21, 1987, p. 112.
2. David Dorsey, "Skunk-Working," *Rochester, Democrat and Chronicle,* May 11, 1986, pp. 1F, 6F, 8F.
3. Mack Hanan, "Make Way for the New Organization Man," *Harvard Business Review,* July–August 1971, p. 132.
4. Keith Atkinson, "Intrapreneurs: Fostering Innovation inside the Corporation," *Personnel Administrator,* January 1986, p. 44.
5. Beverly A. Potter, "Intrapreneurs: New Corporate Breed," *Business Week's Guide to Careers,* December 1985, p. 66.
6. Franck A. de Chambeau and Fredericka Mackenzie, "Intrapreneurship," *Personnel Journal,* July 1986, pp. 42–43.
7. Quoted in Atkinson, "Intrapreneurs," p. 46.
8. Potter, "Intrapreneurs," p. 66.
9. Dorsey, "Skunk-Working," p. 1F.
10. Gifford Pinchot, "Promoting Free Intraprise!" *Across the Board,* March 1985, p. 34.
11. Ibid.
12. de Chambeau and Mackenzie, "Intrapreneurship," p. 43.
13. Pinchot, "Promoting Free Intraprise," p. 34.
14. Atkinson, "Intrapreneurs," p. 44.
15. Rosabeth Moss Kanter, "From Status to Contribution: some Organizational Implications of Changing Basis for Pay," *Personnel,* January 1987, p. 22.
16. Atkinson, "Intrapreneurs," p. 45.
17. Pinchot, "Promoting Free Intraprise," pp. 36–40.
18. Potter, "Intrapreneurs," p. 71.

19. Ibid., p. 66.
20. Ibid.
21. Ibid., p. 71.
22. Joel E. Ross and Darab Unwalla, "Who Is an Intrapreneur?" *Personnel,* December 1986, p. 46.
23. Gifford Pinchot III, "The Age of the Intrapreneur," *Success!,* January 1985, p. 60.
24. Ibid., p. 61.
25. Roger Kaplan, "Entrepreneurship Reconsidered: The Antimanagement Bias," *Harvard Business Review,* May–June 1987, pp. 84–89; Peter Drucker, *Innovation and Entrepreneurship: Practice and Principles* (New York: Harper & Row, 1985), p. 17.
26. Oliver L. Niehouse, "How-To Guide on Successful Care and Feeding of Intrapreneurs," *American Banker,* March 21, 1986.
27. Atkinson, "Intrapreneurs," p. 45.

SOME ADDITIONAL REFERENCES

Goleman, Daniel. "The Psyche of the Entrepreneur." *The New York Times Magazine,* February 2, 1986, pp. 30–32, 59, 60, 68.

Hutton, Thomas J. "Recruiting the Entrepreneurial Executive." *Personnel Administrator,* January 1985, pp. 35–42.

Kidder, Tracy. *The Soul of a New Machine.* New York: Avon, 1982.

Pinchot, Gifford III. *Intrapreneuring.* New York: Harper & Row, 1985.

Polsky, Walter L., and Loretta D. Foxman. "Intrapreneurship: Charting New Courses." *Personnel Journal,* August 1987, pp. 116–18.

Appendix to Chapter Fourteen

DISCOVERING YOUR INTRAPRENEURIAL PERFORMANCE QUOTIENT*

Intrapreneurial Style

Each of the following items describes some aspect of intrapreneurial managerial behavior on the job. Circle the response that most nearly reflects your degree of agreement or disagreement with this type of behavior (0 = Strongly Disagree; 1 = Disagree; 2 = Undecided; 3 = Agree; 4 = Strongly Agree). Respond according to the way in which you would actually behave on the job. Add the numerical values for your responses and enter score on the intrapreneurial style (IS) profile.

In their behavior on the job, supervisors and managers should:

1. Try to avoid letting the systems and procedures of the organization get in the way of innovation   0   1   2   3   4

2. Pursue innovation through administrative (managerial) as well as technical (scientific/mechanical) means   0   1   2   3   4

3. Improve productivity and encourage innovation by delegation   0   1   2   3   4

4. Encourage "idea champions" who are willing to risk failure to bring their idea to fruition   0   1   2   3   4

5. Recognize that mistakes and false starts, kept within bounds, are the necessary byproducts of risk taking   0   1   2   3   4

6. Orchestrate spirit and discipline within the organization's structure and among organization members   0   1   2   3   4

7. Stay close to the customer, providing service and quality as the most important ingredients of company success   0   1   2   3   4

8. Encourage creativity (thinking up new ideas) and innovation (making things happen) as well as independent thinking, if necessary   0   1   2   3   4

9. Constantly seek new markets, new
products, and new uses for old products   0   1   2   3   4

10. Assist in institutionalizing and articulating a
strategy of intrapreneurship, innovation,
and productivity   0   1   2   3   4

Intrapreneurial Personality

Each of the following items describes some aspect of beliefs and/or behavior on the job that suggests an intrapreneurial personality. Circle the response that most nearly reflects your degree of agreement or disagreement with this type of behavior (0 = Strongly Disagree; 1 = Disagree; 2 = Undecided; 3 = Agree; 4 = Strongly Agree). Respond according to the way in which you would actually behave on the job. Add the numerical values for your responses and enter score on the intrapreneurial personality (IP) profile.

In my behavior on the job, I should:

1. Focus on results (effectiveness), not on
activity   0   1   2   3   4

2. Question the status quo and have a desire
to change things when the need is clear   0   1   2   3   4

3. Be a Pygmalion—perceive employees as
responsible people who want to get results   0   1   2   3   4

4. Be motivated by problem solving and
rational decision making   0   1   2   3   4

5. Be ambitious and competitive   0   1   2   3   4

6. Believe that the reward is in the work as
much as in the pay   0   1   2   3   4

7. Be frustrated by restrictive bureaucratic
systems and develop a knack for operating
within these constraints   0   1   2   3   4

8. Develop an ability to resolve conflict and
friction   0   1   2   3   4

9. Understand that the organization is a
system of interrelated technical subsystems
and that my "niche" is a part of the whole   0   1   2   3   4

10. Be motivated by effecting change and
innovation, not only for myself but for
employees as well.   0   1   2   3   4

Intrapreneurial Performance Quotient (IPQ) Profile

Your Perception of a Proper Intrapreneurial Style (IS)		*Your Perception of Intrapreneurial Personality (IP)*
Readiness Range	40 38 36 34 32	40 38 36 34 32
Transi- tional Range	30 28 26 24 22	30 28 26 24 22
Nonreadiness Range	Below 22	

Your intrapreneurial performance quotient (IPQ) equals the combined score on the IS and IP scales. To see how you rate as an intrapreneur, see below.

Score	Interpretation
60–80	You are definitely an intrapreneur.
40–59	You are well suited to being an intrapreneur but are not quite there yet.
Below 40	You had better remain in a bureaucratic organization

Chapter Fifteen

Creating Flat Organization Structures

A specialty chemical plant wanted its work force to be committed to the company and to perform up to its potential. The method plant management chose was to run the plant with an unusually flat organization structure, almost eliminating supervision and creating a high degree of participative management.

After working three years in two low-level manufacturing jobs, Carla LeBlanc had grown skeptical about her talents. Displays of initiative provoked sneers from her supervisors. But those painful, frustrating days are behind her. LeBlanc still works in manufacturing, but her newest job has boosted her self-esteem and erased many of her insecurities.

For the past five years, the native Texan has worked as a process technician at Rohm & Haas Bayport Inc., a six-year-old specialty chemical plant in LaPorte, Texas, near Houston. There the participative management concept has been taken to the limit: All 67 employees play an active role in managing the plant; technicians like LeBlanc routinely perform a variety of tasks without supervision; workers even evaluate one another and interview job applicants.

"The idea is to push responsibility and know-how farther and farther down into the organization, so that every person is a manager. We're trying to transfer ownership for decision making to the people who are going to get the work done," says plant manager Bob Gilbert. "I can make the best decision in the world, but if it's not accepted by the people who are going to promulgate that decision, it isn't worth anything."

At Bayport, the management team numbers a meager four execu-

Introductory text in this chapter excerpted, by permission of the publisher, from Don Nichols, "Taking Participative Management to the Limit," *Management Review*, August 1987, pp. 28–32. © 1987 American Management Association, New York. All rights reserved.

tives. A finance director shares the front office with Gilbert. Out in the plant, two manufacturing managers head the two operating units: Bayport Diphenyl (BDP), which produces Blazer, a herbicide used on soybeans; and Bayport Specialty Monomer (BSM), which manufactures a monomer used in making automobile paint and film for photographic plates. Only those two managers separate the plant manager from the 46 process technicians and 15 technical people (engineers and chemists) who keep the operation running. Unlike plants operated more traditionally, Bayport has no shift supervisors.

Approximately one half of the technicians work exclusively for the BDP chief; the other half answers to the BSM manager. Neither unit leader gives his staff much direction. Instead, the technicians make operating decisions among themselves, working in teams varying in size from four to seven people.

The technicians staff the plant around the clock, seven days a week, splitting their workday into 7 to 7 shifts. Four teams work each day, two per shift—one in the Blazer division, the other in the monomer operation. Teams work four consecutive days, then are relieved by four others following the same schedule. When teams return to work after resting four days, they pull the opposite shift: Those that worked night duty switch to days and vice versa.

The technicians work in the control room, the lab, the rack area, and materials handling (inbound and outbound shipments). They rotate jobs with other team members every 4 to 12 weeks, a practice that keeps boredom low and motivation high. The multiskilled workers train one another, read manuals, and view videotapes.

Bob Gilbert said, "Some people can't work in a system like this. It's too threatening to them. But there is a whole bunch of human resources out there that American industry isn't tapping—resources that we are trying to tap here. Lots of people could do this if they tried. People just don't reach out and try doing things like they ought to."

A task force—a specially appointed team of technicians, technical people, and management—tackles major problems, sometimes spending weeks or months trying to resolve them. The evaluation system used by technicians has been studied repeatedly and modified.

Originally, technicians in each unit completed written evaluations on one another every six months and gave them to their manufacturing manager. After studying the data, the manager met privately with each technician to give an evaluation. This "middle man" approach created fiction, so the technicians began face-to-face meetings. Rating peers who worked different days was difficult, so employees' evaluations were narrowed to members of their own teams and those who relieved them.

The plant's participative management system attracts a lot of attention. Gilbert frequently finds himself explaining it to other curious executives. Occasionally, skeptics even force him to defend it.

"Everybody wants to know how much better we are doing than other Rohm & Haas plants. That is a hard question for me to answer because we don't make the same products anyone else does," he says. Still, the plant manager readily offers a few facts and figures that seem to speak well of the Bayport facility and its innovative operating policies. Not too long ago, a customer's inspectors visited the plant to make a quality audit. They never had given a supplier's plant a higher grade than 83 percent, but Bayport scored 96. Another time, when representatives of a potential customer made a visit, they decided to buy all of their company's needed supply of a particular product from the plant. The Bayport staff would have been satisfied with an order half that size.

"In the past three quarters, we have not shipped any out-of-specification (unacceptable quality) product from our monomer division, and our volume has gone up. That compares to 30 to 40 percent in-spec when we first started operating," Gilbert brags. "In the specialty chemical industry, if someone is shipping 90 to 95 percent in-spec, they are doing very well."

Other Rohm & Haas operations are taking cues from Bayport. Plants in Bristol, Pennsylvania; Houston, Texas; Knoxville, Tennessee; and Louisville, Kentucky, have introduced less sophisticated, but similar management systems.

The idea of team participation and team management is diffusing into the company. "But we're still way out ahead of the others," Gilbert says. "I like to think that we've created a good system of working that benefits both our people and Rohm & Haas."

Why Organizations Are Using Flat Structures

Rohm & Haas used a flat organization structure—one with relatively few layers of management—in order to practice participative management. Flat organization structures are used currently to achieve several other purposes. A primary reason for eliminating one or more layers of management is to reduce personnel costs. Payroll costs are important because they often represent approximately 75 percent of the cost of operating an organization. Cost reduction is seen as particulary important today in order to become more competitive with foreign rivals. In the public sector, cost reduction is seen as necessary to cope with dwindling budgets. Achieving cost reduction by decreasing the number of managerial layers is now considered to be a formal turnaround strategy.[1]

As described in Chapter 3 about crisis management, reducing the number of managerial layers also serves the purpose of speeding up decision making. With more layers of management, more approvals are required, thus increasing the amount of time required to make a decision. Also, lower levels of management can communicate directly to top management instead of going through a ponderous chain of command. A related reason for creating flat structures is to reduce staffing because of other negative consequences of overstaffing. Charles Ames, chairman and CEO of Acme-Cleveland Corporation says, "Many companies still have fat staffs, lots of layers, and overcentralized control. People don't even know all the products their company makes anymore."[2]

Flat structures are also helpful in fostering decentralization as illustrated by the French company Carrefour S.A., whose annual sales are $6 billion. Carrefour is the pioneer of the hypermarket concept (a giant store selling food and other goods). The company stays lean by decentralizing as many functions as possible to their retail outlets. A headquarters staff of less than 20 employees, including secretaries, guides the business. Only one layer of management is between the central office and stores—a group of regional managers.[3]

Finally, flat structure is used by some organizations simply because a streamlined organization fits the spirit of the times. As Ames expounds, "We are in turbulent times, and we must begin managing for survival in turbulent times. We must be geared to a more competitive environment, breaking apart overloaded organizational structures and streamlining, emphasizing producer people over support staff, getting our cost/profit ratio more in line, taking the bull by the horns, and doing what we have to do to survive."[4]

Suggestions and Procedures for Creating Flat Structures

Creating flat structures would seem self-explanatory, yet some information has emerged that can make the process more effective in achieving its intended results and less disruptive to the people displaced.

Identify the Need for Trimming Down the Management Work Force.   As part of the control function of management, senior executives should stay alert to the possible need for reducing managerial layers. Michael L. Tennican, an organization planning consultant, believes that many organizations are overstaffed with managers. He points out that the impressive productivity gains in factories have yet to be matched in the offices. His firm's survey of 200 representative companies indicated that from World War II to the mid-1960s, they resembled pyramids, with four out of five employees working in direct production jobs. Tennican says that the pyramid has been turned upside down. There are now four managers for every production worker.

According to Tennican, poor managerial practices are responsible for much of this top-heavy structure. Diversification, for example, breeds hierarchy as headquarters adds more staff to keep senior executives supplied with information and to provide the expertise that the present managerial staff lacks. Another sign that managerial overstaffing may be taking place is when people are assigned the job title *manager* to evade pay limitations to individual-contributor positions. In one case, such policies resulted in a factory where each supervisor was responsible for only 4 employees, compared with a span of control of 40 at a rival's factory.[5]

Tom Peters also recommends that senior executives examine the prevailing span of control to find out if managers are supervising too few employees. (The larger the average span of control throughout the organization, the fewer the layers of management.) He reports that many firms today have moved toward an organization structure in which the ratio of managers to nonmanagers is 1 to 100 at the bottom of the firm and 1 to 20 at the top. Peters, however, disagrees with Tennican about the typical spans of control. Peters says that the traditional number of employees supervised by one manager is about 1 to 15 at the bottom and 1 to 5 at the top of the organization.[6]

Change the Organization Structure to a Simpler Design.   After the need for reducing the number of managerial layers has been identified, the next step is to simplify the organization structure. Figure 15–1 illustrates this process. Assume that manager A has three direct subordinates,

FIGURE 15–1   The Contrast between a Tall and a Flat Organization Structure

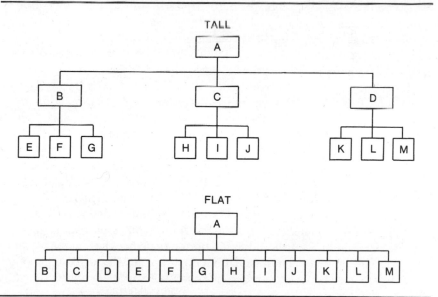

NOTE: This figure represents the contrast between two organizational subunits. A comparison between two total organizations would depict several more layers of management.

managers B, C, and D, and that each of these managers has three direct subordinates. Managers B, C, and D are then all assigned to their work groups as individual contributors. Although all workers are retained, their organizational units are no longer separate entities. Manager A has now increased his or her span of control from 3 to 12. If managers B, C, and D are transferred or terminated to reduce costs, manager A now has a span of control of nine.

Make the Changes Quickly Rather Than Gradually.   The argument rages whether, in times of layoff, to attempt to make all the cuts at once or over a protracted period of time. If alternative placement is not available for the managers affected, reductions in staff are much less disruptive if done all at once rather than gradually. A key argument in favor of making the changes quickly is that the survivors deal better with the downsizing if they are reasonably assured that no further cuts will be forthcoming. However, if managers are not sure if they will be eliminated next, the ambiguity creates considerable stress. As many managers have said after an initial period of restructuring, "We are all waiting for the other shoe to fall."

Another human resource problem stemming from gradual cuts is that the organization may lose many competent managers who are worried about job security. Rather than wait to be terminated, some of the more qualified managers may look for better opportunities in another firm. Less competent managers may also spend a good deal of work time conducting a job search and worrying about losing their jobs.

The argument for the incremental approach is that laying off managers one at a time over a period of time is less likely to be interpreted as a sign of organizational malaise than a blitz. Shock waves throughout the organization are thus avoided. Also, it is easier for the organization to find new jobs for displaced managers one at a time than to place a large number all at once. One company that decided to eliminate two layers of management, carried out the downsizing over a two-year period. Whenever a suitable position in sales or customer service became vacant, a middle manager was invited to switch jobs. A layer of management was thus eliminated through attrition rather than through layoffs.

The incremental approach is therefore recommended when it appears feasible to offer managers suitable individual-contributor jobs. In many situations, middle managers would prefer to leave the company rather than be reassigned to a nonmanagerial position. IBM is an example of one firm that successfully used the incremental approach in reducing its managerial positions. A few years ago 5,000 middle managers and staff people were reassigned to customer-contact positions over a one-year period.[7]

Use Multiple Approaches to Staff Reductions.   When the displaced managers are not absorbed into other positions, flattening the structure results in staff reductions. Multiple approaches to accomplishing this reduction can help reduce human trauma and inconvenience. Exxon implemented a downsizing program that illustrates multiple approaches to staff reduction. Nearly all of its 42,000 salaried employees were offered the chance to leave through several different options. Over 6,000 employees accepted the invitation. The cutbacks were part of a restructuring program that included the consolidation of several division headquarters and the elimination of many managerial positions.

Exxon offered employees too young to retire a voluntary severance plan. A manager with 20 years seniority, for example, received about a year's salary in severance, plus benefits earned from an employee savings plan. A 55-year-old employee with a salary of $50,000 and 30 years at Exxon would be offered an early retirement plan that added three years of age and three years of service to the employee's record. These figures would then be used in calculating pension rights. The employee would receive a company pension of about $24,000 annually for life, adjusted periodically for changes in the cost of living.

When reducing the management work force, companies can sometimes use their unique abilities to help these managers regain employment. After Eastern Airlines was acquired by Texas Air, the decision was made to lay off 442 managers in order to stay competitive. Management employees cut from Eastern receive two weeks of salary, payment for unused vacation, and severance pay equal to one week for every year of employment with the firm, up to a maximum of 26 weeks. Eastern also offered laid-off employees who were looking for jobs in other cities "space available" passes on its flights.[8] Because managers often must relocate to find new employment, the Eastern flight passes were seen as especially helpful and valuable.

Du Pont is another example of a company that uses a flexible approach to attrition. During a four-year downsizing effort, employees were offered two different voluntary attrition programs. For example, a manager might be able to retire immediately with a lump-sum cash benefit and a smaller retirement. Or the same manager might be able to postpone retirement for five years and receive no cash settlement but a higher pension. Du Pont's attrition policy proved to be effective from both a financial and a public relations standpoint.[9] Nevertheless, Du Pont did lose a number of people they wish had stayed.

Provide Adequate Support Mechanisms for the Displaced Managers and Professionals.   The managers and professionals (for example, planners and coordinators) who lose their jobs under restructuring may need various forms of support. Middle managers often require more help than other categories of employees in coping with layoff. "We're not altogether sure that it isn't the white-collar people who suffer more," says Jeanne Gordus, who has designed programs to help thousands of unemployed auto, glass, and steel workers. "Middle-management employees are so attached to their jobs that they have greater stress and emotional problems," Gordus said.[10]

Developing these support mechanisms begins with a preplanning for layoffs in order to treat employees with dignity and respect instead of rushing them out the door.[11] Developing some of the options just described is one example of planning.

The next step in providing adequate support to the laid-off manager is to offer the person a candid, but sympathetic statement of why the person was chosen to be laid off. Because *every* manager is not eliminated in an organizational flattening, the person may wonder why he or she was targeted for removal. An appropriate statement from the bearer of the bad news might be, "We decided to lay off 90 percent of the managers at your level. Your performance has been above average, but we are retaining only those 10 percent of managers with outstanding performance appraisals and who have critical skills that no other managers in the firm possess. You will receive high marks on any employment reference."

The generally most useful support mechanism for the dismissed manager is outplacement services, a systematic approach to helping the individual find new employment outside the firm. Outplacement includes career counseling, instruction in conducting a job campaign, administrative support such as clerical help and telephone privileges, and support groups (see Chapter 20).

Provide Job Security to Survivors. Robert M. Tomasko writes that the demographics of the 1980s have been a challenge for many organizations and their managers. The postwar baby boomers reached middle-management age at a time when downsizing of organizations eliminated many of the positions they hoped to occupy. "Companies that have responded to this by pruning back their organizations *and* working hard to provide job security for those selected to remain will be one step head of the others in having loyal and committed people to deal with the demographics of the 1990s."[12]

One way of shoring up the prospects of job security is to explain to the remaining managers that they are a select cadre of managers on whom the organization hopes to build its future. John F. Welch, Jr., the CEO of General Electric Co., follows this approach. Welch contributed heavily to the decision to eliminate one quarter of GE jobs. For the remaining 350,000 employees he has redefined what it means to work at GE:

The job of the enterprise is to provide an exciting atmosphere that's open and fair, where people have the resources to go out and win. The job of the people is to take advantage of this playing field and put out 110 percent. . . . The people who get in trouble in our company are those who carry around the anchor of the past.[13]

Words alone are not sufficient to convince the survivors that their job security is not threatened. It is equally important to manage the company in such a way that job security appears high. At postdownsized Apple Computer, temporary help is used to staff up to 10 percent of jobs. The heavy reliance on temporary help suggests to people hired for permanent jobs that the company considers them to be part of an elite work force.[14] The reliance on temporary help for some positions increases job security in another way. Current employees, middle managers included, believe that if further downsizing is necessary, temporary workers can be readily trimmed, thus saving the jobs of permanent workers.

Integrate Management Development with Flattened Structures. Within most newly trimmed operations, middle managers, well aware of the thinning ranks around them, become worried about their own future and job security. They are also concerned about strong competition for fewer management positions from maturing baby boomers. Loyalty to a particular company thus declines. Oliver L. Niehouse advises top management to select their most promising managers carefully. These managers can then be assured that they will be receiving management development along with a possible series of lateral moves. The combination of training plus broadening of experience should make the individual an attractive candidate for promotion.[15] With prospects of promotion being reasonably good in an era of retrenchment, the promising managers might then show more loyalty to the firm.

Use Task Forces to Solve Special Managerial Problems. After restructuring, downsizing, or delayering has taken place, fewer managers exist to solve problems. An antidote to this problem is for taskforces, composed of top-level and first-level managers, to solve special problems. After the problem is solved, the managers return to their regular assignment full time. The task-force can function part-time, or full-time according to the magnitude of the problem being addressed. The taskforce approach makes it possible for an organization to operate efficiently with a fewer number of managers occupying full-time, permanent positions. Special problems suitable for the taskforce analysis include the following: whether or not to acquire or be acquired by a particular firm; how to reduce operating costs; how to create better career opportunities for the physically challenged; and how to respond to an organizational crisis.

Advantages of Flat Organization Structures

Flat organization structures are gaining in acceptance because they offer several key advantages to the organizations, as already described in the discussion about why firms are using these trimmed-down structures. Here we reexamine the same issue with some additional information.

A key advantage of flat structures is that they are a contributor to organizational effectiveness, including productivity. Ken Iverson, chairman of the profitable steelmaker Nucor Corp., makes this point about excessive layers of management, "The most important thing American industry needs to do is to reduce the number of management layers." At the bottom of the Nucor structure is the supervisor; the supervisor reports to a department head who reports to the general manager who reports to the president and chairman's office.[16]

Flat structures, to repeat, hasten decision making because fewer managers provide input to the same decision. As John Welch of GE sees it, an overstaffed bureaucracy can muck up the works. He recalls that while climbing the organizational ladder, corporate staff "bothered my people, by meddling and nit-picking, demanding reports, presentations, facts, and figures that contributed nothing to making and selling better products."[17] Flat structures also speed up decision making because executives can communicate directly with their sources of information without going through intermediaries.

A subtle advantage of flat structures is that they help prevent second guessing by layers of managers. The second guessing is designed to serve as a system of checks and balances, yet it may serve to prevent innovation. At one point in the history of Xerox, the presence of second-guessing staffers hampered the company's ability to adapt existing products to local markets and make the technological advances necessary to develop new ones. One consultant told of a frustrated Xerox manager who had been trying for nine months to obtain approvals to add more intense light bulbs to copiers so the company could compete in Egypt, where penciled information is copied frequently.[18]

Flat structures will also help organizations cope with the upcoming shortage of people available for managerial positions. The labor shortage currently exists among people in the work force age 21 and under.[19] By about 1995, a shortage should exist of people for entry into middle-management jobs. With fewer of these jobs to fill, there will be less of a labor shortage.

In some instances, the creation of flat structures performs a social good. Some of the more talented middle managers and professionals who are forced to leave the organization wind up working for smaller firms who need big-company expertise to grow. Also, the more entrepreneurial of the laid-off middle managers begin new companies of their own, thus creating jobs.

Disadvantages of Flat Organization Structures

Most of the great organizations have been built with pyramid-shaped rather than flat structures, so the traditional hierarchy must offer some advantages. One notable advantage is the presence of a large pool of well-educated, intelligent, and resourceful people at middle levels in the organization. These individuals serve important functions such as providing useful input to decision making, searching for new opportunities, and freeing up the time of top management so the organization can do more than respond to emergencies.

The multilayered structure offers the important advantage of providing for the development of future executives. Working as a middle manager or staff person gives the aspiring executive an opportunity to manage other managers and professional workers. Without this type of experience, it would be difficult to function effectively as an executive.

An entirely flat organization structure is also unrealistic. As John Hartley, a retired management professor puts it, "The fad of flat structures will disappear in time. I would like to see a large organization in which the members of the executive suite would spend much time communicating directly with first-level supervisors."[20]

A disadvantage of creating a flat structure suddenly is that many good people will be forced to leave the organization. They may face the trauma of long-term unemployment because other organizations are also trimming down. A related problem of downsizing is that it may not achieve its intended result—getting rid of the fat and keeping the muscle. During a downsizing at Exxon, the company lost some of the people it wanted to keep and kept some of the people it wanted to lose. Many talented managers slipped out the door with a financially attractive severance program because they were able to find new jobs fairly easily.[21]

Guidelines for Action and Skill Development

After an organization has been flattened, certain actions must be taken to keep it trimmed down and therefore efficient (lean and mean). First, keep the pay system from building excess management back into the company. Employees should be able to advance in pay without having to become managers. A recommended approach is to develop a two-track pay scale that enables people to advance substantially in income either as a manager or a staff professional.

Second, slow down the upward-only fast track. Career paths should be designed that cover lateral as well as vertical moves. People should be excluded from mid-level and senior staff jobs until they have had some experience in the line organization.

Third, make it difficult for managers and professionals to get hired. Only those individuals of exceptional promise should be hired into management training programs, and temporary help should be used wherever feasible.[22]

As a manager working in a flattened structure, learn to develop habits of self-sufficiency because there will be less help available to perform a variety of administrative tasks and supply you information. In many instances, the personal computer in your office becomes your information-gathering middle manager of the past.

A danger in most downsizings is that many talented people will exercise their option to collect a sizable chunk of cash and then find new employment. It is therefore advisable to communicate quickly to these talented people that they are vitally needed in the organization.

DISCUSSION QUESTIONS AND ACTIVITIES

1. In what specific ways does the trend toward flat organization structures affect your future?

2. One reason flat organization structures have become popular is that the contribution of some managerial and professional activities has been questioned. What are some managerial and professional activities that you think might be wasteful?

3. How would quality circles and self-managing teams fit into a philosophy of flat organization structures?

4. What is your opinion on the controversy of whether layoffs should be made suddenly versus gradually?

5. What is your position on Niehouse's contention that offering management development programs to managers will induce them to remain with the organization?

6. Speak with someone who has been a member of an organization going through downsizing. Gather that person's perception of some of the problems created by downsizing and be prepared to discuss your findings in class.

NOTES

1. Charles R. Gowen III and Joseph W. Leonard, "Turnaround Strategies to Reverse Declining Corporate Performance: Analyzing a Survey of Turnaround Symptoms, Actions, and Results," (Submitted for publication, 1988).
2. Kirkland Ropp, "Restructuring: Survival of the Fittest," *Personnel Administrator,* February 1987, p. 46.
3. Robert M. Tomasko, "Running Lean, Staying Lean," *Management Review,* November 1987, p. 46.

4. Ropp, "Restructuring," p. 46.
5. "America's Leanest and Meanest," *Business Week,* October 5, 1987, p. 81.
6. The Tom Peters Group, *A World Turned Upside Down* (Palo Alto, Calif.: Excel, 1986), p. 16.
7. "How IBM Is Fighting Back," *Business Week,* November 17, 1986, pp. 152–157.
8. Kirkland Ropp, "Downsizing Strategies: Reducing the Trauma of Reducing Employees," *Personnel Administrator,* February 1987, p. 63.
9. Ibid.
10. Sharon Warren Walsh, "White-Collar Layoffs Snatch Away More Than Just a Job," *Washington Post,* syndicated story, March 16, 1987.
11. Tomasko, "Running Lean, Staying Lean," p. 38.
12. Ibid., p. 37.
13. Ibid.
14. Ibid.
15. "Lean Companies Keep Talented Managers," *Business to Business,* October 17–November 9, 1986, p. 1.
16. Thomas Peters, "Revolution Needed in the Organization," syndicated column, April 5, 1987.
17. Russell Mitchell, "Jack Welch: How Good A Manager?" *Business Week,* December 14, 1987, p. 94.
18. "A New Era for Management," *Business Week,* April 25, 1983, p. 55.
19. "Help Wanted," *Business Week,* August 10, 1987, pp. 48–53.
20. Personal communication, January 1988.
21. Ropp, "Downsizing Strategies," p. 64.
22. Tomasko, "Running Lean," pp. 36, 37.

SOME ADDITIONAL REFERENCES

Bohl, Don Lee. *Responsible Reductions in Force,* Amacom Briefings & Surveys. New York: AMACOM, 1987.

Ginzberg, Eli. *Resizing for Organizational Effectiveness: A Report of a Workshop.* New York: Center for Career Research and Human Resource Management, Graduate School of Business, Columbia University, 1985.

Harrison, Robert W., and William G. Layton. "How Troxel Manufacturing Restructured Itself." *Management Review,* March 1988, pp. 43–46.

Milne, Michael J. "Scott Paper Is on A Roll." *Management Review,* March 1988, pp. 37–42.

Nienstedt, Phil, and Richard Wintermantel. "Restructuring Organizations for Improved Productivity: A Case in Point." *Personnel,* August 1985, pp. 34–40.

Smallwood, W. Norman, and Eliot Jacobsen. "Is There Life after Downsizing?" *Personnel,* December 1987, pp. 42–46.

Chapter Sixteen

Japanese-Style Management

About 15 years ago, Honda of Japan decided to begin manufacturing in the United States. Top management chose to adapt *Nenko*—a system of cohesiveness and coordination developed by Japanese companies—to its new subsidiary, Honda of America.

Thirty years ago, when the American market for motorcycles was stagnating, Honda decided the time was ripe to enter the United States through the establishment of a sales office, American Honda. Only 160 motorcycles were sold during their first year in business, but Honda was determined to succeed.

By 1960, Japanese motorcycle manufacturers had a decade of developing high production volumes of small motorcycles in their domestic market behind them. Only 4 percent of motorcycle production was exported at the time, but large economies in the production of small motorcycles had already been achieved. As a result, cost reductions due to large-scale operations placed Japanese motorcycle manufacturers in a highly competitive position. Honda used this position to its advantage and started to market its small motorcycles in the United States.

However, for Americans living in the early 1960s, the motorcycle brought to mind images of the rough and rowdy Hell's Angels. Honda decided to change this negative image. Advertisements stating, "You meet the nicest people on a Honda" and a retail price of under $250 (compared to $1,000 to $1,500 for the larger American and British motorcycles) soon convinced many Americans to purchase a Honda. By 1964, nearly half the motorcycles sold in the United States were Hondas. American Honda sales soared from $500,000 in 1960 to $77 million in 1965, and Honda was producing thousands of units a year in a once-dormant market.

Nine years later Honda commenced plans to build manufacturing facilities in the United States, in keeping with its policy of setting up plants in countries where its products are marketed. On September 10, 1979, the first Honda motorcycle built in America rolled off the production line in Marysville, Ohio. Today, approximately 60,000 motorcycles are produced every year in the Marysville plant.

Honda's success in the American motorcycle market has led to automobile production in the United States. The company's automotive manufacturing plant in Marysville now produces about 150,000 Accords a year. Workers are cross-trained to rotate jobs and can quickly shift production from one model to another whenever necessary. Retooling for new models can also be performed rapidly—within just a few minutes. Honda workers can change the shapes of doors or fenders.

In addition to parts shipped from Japan, Honda purchases parts from local suppliers, with whom it establishes long-term relationships in order to maintain "just-in-time" purchasing. Shipments from key suppliers are delivered by a dedicated carrier contracted to meet Honda's schedule. Honda shies away from using common carriers who deliver at their own convenience, because the company's just-in-time production is planned around on-time deliveries. Most of the plant's inventory consists of only several hours' worth of supplies.

When Shoichiro Irimajiri, president of Honda America, moved from the Suzuka factory in Japan in mid-1984 to assume responsibility for operations in Ohio, he left behind a factory where the average employee had seven years of experience in manufacturing automobiles. Arriving at the Ohio plant, he found that the average American auto worker had less than one year's experience. Whether Honda would be successful in applying its approach to manufacturing automobiles in the United States was an uncertainty. Honda soon discovered that it was no problem at all.

In January 1985, *Car and Driver* magazine stated: "There is nothing wrong with a Honda Accord. Nothing. How many other cars can one say that about?" And, in December of 1985, *Consumer Reports* rated the quality of the Honda built in Ohio as high as those imported from Japan. According to company executives, the Accords produced at the Marysville plant are manufactured at roughly the same cost as those built by the parent company in Japan.

A company observer says:

> Honda's success in America can be attributed to an emphasis on cooperative labor relations. Rejecting traditional American management practices by which workers have been treated like machines, Honda has transplanted the Japanese philosophy of treating employees as the company's most valuable asset. Competing through quality, the Honda way begins with the recognition that human potential is limitless and [with] the creation of a safe working environment that fosters creativity, involvement, and pride.

Senior management at Honda of America lists five principles that guide its policies:

1. Proceed always with ambition and youthfulness.
2. Respect sound theory, develop fresh ideas, and make the most effective use of time.
3. Enjoy your work and always brighten your work atmosphere.
4. Strive constantly for a harmonious flow of work.
5. Be ever-mindful of the value of research and endeavor.

Everyone who works at Honda's Ohio plant is known as an associate. Distinctions between management and labor are so blurred that visitors often remark, "I can't figure out who is in charge." Everyone wears the same white uniform. Everyone parks in the same parking lot where there are no reserved spaces. Everyone eats in the same cafeterias. And everyone shares the same desks. The desk of President Shoichiro Irimajiri is in the same room as a hundred other workers, with no walls around him.

At Honda, everyone is encouraged to improve on existing practices. The entire approach to quality is based on respect for the individual's intelligence. Quality is not mandated by placing quality inspectors at each step of the manufacturing process. Instead, each associate is trained to take pride in and be responsible for the quality of Honda's products.

Should a problem arise, management goes to the shop floor and asks the associates for their solutions. Honda has a saying that there is more knowledge on the factory floor than in the office. They have found from experience that the associate most directly involved is often the one best qualified to solve problems and improve the quality and process of production. Irimajiri elaborates:

> In order to make this reliance on our Associates succeed, our Associates have to understand our commitment to continuous improvement. We have to eliminate the fear of making and reporting mistakes. False pride that seeks to hide problems is one of the greatest barriers to quality. We encourage our Associates to tell of problems in their areas and then to apply their creativity to solving them.

The Ohio plant has remained nonunionized. Honda associates earn an average of $11 per hour, slightly less than the $13 or $14 hourly wages made at GM or Ford. Even so, Honda's company benefits, training, and working conditions seem to compensate for this; and attempts to unionize the plant have yet to be successful. As one Honda worker noted, "Receiving $2,000 bonus checks and responses to aired grievances within two days probably makes most of us wonder what a good union could possibly do."[1]

STRATEGIES AND TECHNIQUES OF JAPANESE-STYLE HUMAN RESOURCE MANAGEMENT

The Honda experience provides a sample portrait of the nature of the adaptation of Japanese management to North America. Japanese companies operating in Japan, as well as in other countries, tend to follow the same model of *Nenko*. Nevertheless, in order to understand how Japanese-style management works, it is important to summarize its most frequently observed elements. The term *Japanese-style* refers to an adaptation of pure Japanese management to another culture—typically the United States. Nevertheless, there is substantial overlap between the human resources practices of Japanese firms in Japan, those operating in the United States, and Theory Z firms. *Theory Z firms* are a group of large American business organizations such as IBM, Eastman Kodak, and Hewlett-Packard who have always operated in a manner similar to large Japanese firms.[2] To complicate matters a little further, the Japanese-style firm in the United States is also referred to as *The American Transitional Model*, a transition from a pure Japanese model to an American adaptation of the model.[3]

The philosophies, strategies, and techniques of Japanese-style management described in this chapter focus on human resource management. Very worthwhile Japanese production techniques such as *kan ban* (just-in-time inventory control), quality circles, and statistical process control are outside the scope of this discussion.

Emphasis on the Humanistic Aspects of Work.   The philosophical bedrock of Japanese human resource management is an emphasis on the importance of people. A survey of personnel executives working at Japanese-owned companies in the United States found that 58 percent of these managers believe that "the core of Japanese management is the deliberate attention to humanistic aspects of work."[4] Thus Japanese management emphasizes the importance of solid relations between manager and subordinates and among subordinates. Because employees are perceived to be key resources, the growth of the whole person rather than exclusively his or her job skills, is emphasized. One way in which the firm displays this holistic concern is through substantial benefit packages and employee programs.

Unique Company Philosophy.   Japanese CEOs typically articulate a company philosophy designed to give their firm uniqueness (a practice, of course, similar to most large firms everywhere). Often these philosophies describe the firm as a family, distinct from any other firm. All employees are supposed to develop a system of mutual obligations, extending beyond what they are paid to do. Workers are supposed to be as loyal to the firm as they are to their families and villages. One consequence of this loyalty is that workers do whatever is needed for the corporation's benefit, including working overtime or taking evening courses in order to become more valuable employees.[5]

Wa, or harmony and teamwork, is also incorporated into most company philosophies. Employees who "buy into" the firm's unique philosophy will presumably not be motivated to join another firm and thereby be forced to work under another philosophy.

Long-Term Employment for Some Employees.   Large Japanese firms have traditionally relied on an internal rather than an external labor market in matching the number of employees on board to the number of jobs that need to be filled. The strategy begins with hiring male employees on graduation from high school or university with the expectation of keeping them permanently. The female work force, however, is temporary, and many of the less desirable jobs are given to temporary workers or subcontracted outside the firm. These practices give employers flexibility in adjusting the size of their work force to present economic conditions while maintaining employment for full-time male workers.[6]

Intensive Socialization of Employees.   A major objective of Japanese human resource policies is to develop cohesiveness throughout the firm. To accomplish this end, as many workers as possible must fit naturally into the culture of the firm. A young person, for example, who balked at such ideas as singing company songs or socializing with co-workers after hours would not be invited to join the firm. The basic criteria for hiring new employees are moderate views and a personality capable of entering into harmonious relationships with other employees.

Lengthy Orientation and Training.   Japanese companies invest more time in orienting and training employees than do their American counterparts. In Japan, formal orientation to the company can take as long as two weeks, frequently conducted at an off-company site such as a resort. In a survey of 100 American employees in Japanese-owned companies, Richard G. Novotny found that these companies are not particularly strong on orientation and training. He offers this explanation for the difference:

> This lower level of orientation and training for U.S. employees is probably a result of the high turnover rates in this country (U.S.) compared with the Japanese practice of lifetime employment. The Japanese apparently feel that it does not pay for them to extensively orient and train Americans as they would Japanese, since the former may not stay with the company long enough for the orientation and training to be cost-effective.[7]

Emphasis on the Team Concept.   In the Japanese model of management, the group is more important than the individual. Correspondingly, the success of the work group is more important than the success of one individual. Group members share values and goals and are accustomed to working together to achieve them. At Toyota, for example, employees work in teams of 5 to 10 members. Each team is autonomous and takes full responsibility for production checking and improving quality standards, cost, maintaining safety standards, training new team members, housekeeping, and *Kaizen* (making gradual improvements). Team members share responsibility for team performance and are encouraged to support each other. The team participates in goal setting, and the group is evaluated regularly. Consequently, employees work together as a unit. The pressure to perform a job correctly comes not only from management but from peers.[8]

The emphasis on the team concept does not exclude the possibility of Japanese workers being imbued with a strong sense of individual achievement. However, in a Japanese-style work culture, individual achievement is rewarded with acceptance from the group. The ambitious manager or individual contributor strives hard to excel in order to be seen worthy by the group.

Consensus Decision Making.   It is widely acknowledged that Japanese managers involve subordinates in the decision-making process; there is some disagreement, however, as to the form and extent of this participation. According to Kae Chung and Margaret Ann Gray, the type of decision making characteristic of Japanese business is best described by the word *nemawaski,* meaning rootbinding. Each person has a sense of running the firm because almost nothing gets done until all the people involved agree. The Japanese believe that differences can best be resolved by gathering as much information as possible from as many sources as possible. Consequently all parties are well informed, everyone has time to adjust to the upcoming decision, and all committed to the implementation of the decision once consensus is reached.

Although this form of participative decision making can be agonizingly slow, the implementation phase proceeds swiftly because of the high level of commitment.[9]

Individual Commitment to the Organization.   Despite the emphasis on group responsibility, the individual also has obligations to the firm. As explained by Chung and Gray, "The chief responsibility is that of loyalty to the group due to long-term commitment between the firm and the individual. Duties include continual development of skills, improvement of quality control, maintenance of social harmony, service to the firm, and interaction with its members outside of the normal working day. The Japanese systems will not function without such individual commitment to their organizations.[10]

Information Sharing among All Employees.   A pervasive theme of Japanese-managed firms is information sharing among all employees. It manifests itself, for example, in supervisors giving production workers almost any information they desire, such as the cost of materials and profit margins on the product being manufactured. Information sharing is seen as a vehicle for involving employees in the work process and obtaining their commitment.

Information sharing is fostered by the open communication system characteristic of Japanese offices and factories. Work spaces are open and crowded, allowing supervisors to be aware of what employees are doing and vice versa. It is rare even for high-ranking executives to have private offices. In factory environments, the supervisor and senior plant manager are constantly on the floor talking about problems, helping with units of work, conversing with outsiders, and instructing new employees.[11]

Presence of Management among the Work Force.   Japanese firms have brought attention to the importance of "management by wandering around." Managers intermingle freely among workers on the shop floor, in the office, in meetings and discussions, and at informal social events. The managers who do the wandering around may be the employees' immediate supervisor, or a higher ranking manager.[12] Lower-ranking Japanese managers apparently are not concerned that their subordinates have the opportunity to communicate directly with higher levels of management. An example of the physical presence of management in Japanese-style management is the fact that the president of Honda of America's desk is situated in the general work area.

Belief in Kaizen.   *Kaizen* was described in Chapter 13 as an important contributor to quality awareness. It is also a reflection of the Japanese philosophy of wanting to make work easier for employees and not to overburden them. One interpretation of *Kaizen* is that it is a process of finding waste in machinery, materials, labor, or methods of production. It is also a procedure by which team members collaborate to plan their own jobs to simplify them, thus assisting the team to work more efficiently.

Each production task is constantly subject to the process of *Kaizen;* the workers take the initiative to meet and discuss ways to make the job easier and to perform it more efficiently. Each job is *"Kaizened"* to eliminate as much waste (*muda*) as possible. In production jobs, waste can result from such activities as waiting for another task to be completed, rearranging materials, handling parts that will be needed later, unpacking parts, and going to another department to retrieve parts.

Through *Kaizen* production, efficiency improves, and workers can design many aspects of their own job. The more creative workers can think about how their jobs can best be performed. By designing their own jobs, workers generally experience improved job satisfaction and an improved feeling of self-worth.[13]

Flexible Job Classifications.   A cornerstone for achieving high productivity in Japanese firms is flexible job classifications for production workers, managers, and professionals. One executive argues that, "the most effective Japanese management technique is the opportunity for employees to work outside their job classification in order to better understand the company."[14] A survey of Japanese-owned firms in the United States showed that less than one third of the companies use clearly defined job descriptions. Instead, over 43 percent have classifications that are not as broad as those in Japan, but not as specific as those in other companies in the United States.[15]

Japanese employers believe that satisfactory productivity cannot be achieved unless they can quickly shift the most capable employee into a job when needed, for either a temporary or permanent assignment. This flexible approach makes it relatively easy to find substitutes for absent employees. Because workers have many skills, it is easier to keep them employed when work declines by reassigning them to different jobs. The existence of work teams is also dependent on the presence of multiskilled employees.

At the managerial and professional levels, flexible job classification takes the form of job rotation early in a person's career. This extensive and prolonged training enables workers to learn different facets of the business and form a network of friendships. Once assigned to a more permanent position, individuals become generalists with an awareness of how the work of one department affects another, and how it affects the superordinate goals of the total organization.[16]

Emphasis on Seniority for Pay and Promotion.   In Japanese human resource management heavy emphasis is placed on seniority rather than merit for achieving organizational rewards. Employees of a given age group, particularly during the first several years of employment, receive comparable pay. Owing to the concept of long-term employment, Japanese workers learn to wait a long time for individual recognition in the form of promotion and salary increases. Bonuses are typically tied to the performance of the total firm. In some of the more prosperous firms, these bonuses may amount to as much as five months' pay.

Evaluation of the Person, Not Only Results.   Most modern performance-appraisal systems in Western countries attempt to measure employees by the results thay achieve instead of personal attributes and behavior. Japanese management, in contrast, believes strongly in measuring personal attributes (such as loyalty and enthusiasm) and behavior (such as creativity), as well as direct performance. In most Japanese firms, personality and behavior, rather than output are the key evaluation criteria. In this way, hard-working employees do not experience a sense of failure and frustration when productivity is low due to factors beyond their control.

Group performance is another factor frequently used in individual evaluation. Peer pressure is therefore placed on individuals to perform well, and this pressure functions as an organizational control. The use of group performance measures in evaluating individual contribution encourages the norm of cooperation so important to the Japanese management model.[17]

The emphasis on evaluating personal attributes begins in recruitment. When being hired into Japanese firms, candidates are sought who possess a general attitude and approach to problems that are likely to be receptive to Japanese ideas about how organizations should be run. Among these desired characteristics are problem-solving ability, recognition of the importance of the group, and a capacity for obedience and company loyalty.[18]

Implicit, Informal Control.   Japanese managers rely heavily on unstated controls that are not part of a formal control system. These implicit controls focus on the long-term development of employees rather than on short-term performance. In this manner, a manager would be tolerant of a subordinate's mistakes if the manager thought they constituted a good learning experience. A short-term, performance-oriented viewpoint would be less tolerant of beginner's mistakes.

Group norms, developed slowly over a long period of time, are an important source of implicit control. Another informal control is exercised by differences in the way managers treat subordinates. The reason this type of control is so effective is because there is little room for manipulation of organizational rewards such as promotion and pay.[19]

Recognition of Employees as Experts.   A key assumption of Japanese management is that workers, if motivated and sufficiently loyal, are intelligent enough to perform their duties without the need for extensive supervision and rules. The intelligent, well-motivated employee quickly becomes an expert in performing his or her specialized task. Therefore, the first step taken to improve productivity is to get the worker's opinion on how this might be achieved. This has sometimes taken the form of asking a production worker to help redesign the machine he or she operates regularly. Quality circles and *Kaizen* are both based on the principle of the "in-house expert."

The Evidence and Opinion in Favor of Japanese Management

Glowing pictures have been painted of Japanese management. A strong argument in favor of Japanese management is that Japanese companies have been very successful in competing with American and European companies. Japan has made notable inroads into many markets, with an array of products including: Automobiles, radios, binoculars, watches, textiles, trucks, steel, motorcycles, televisions, cameras, clocks, shoes, ships, castings, bicycles, tape recorders, telescopes, timers, hats, machine tools, printing presses, and the list appears to be growing.[20]

The logic of this argument is that if Japanese companies are doing so well competitively, the management systems guiding this growth must be meritorious.

Another compelling argument in favor of the Japanese model of management is that Japan is a country about the size of California, with few natural resources, yet it has become the third most powerful industrial nation. It has been outpaced industrially only by the United States and the Soviet Union. Japanese industry was more heavily hit by the oil crisis of the 1970s than were other countries, yet its productivity grew rapidly during this period. From early 1970s to the early 1980s, Japanese productivity grew at an annual rate of 8 percent while the productivity of American industries grew less than 2 percent. However, by the mid- and later-1980s Japanese productivity increases had slowed down, and the rate of American productivity increases was 3.6 percent in 1988. Many of the American gains were attributed to a penchant for organizational leanness so prevalent in the late 1980s.

Another indication of the potential value of Japanese-style management is that Japanese-controlled firms operating in the United States and Canada have generally prospered. By the late 1980s there were over 550 Japanese manufacturing and/or parts-assembly companies located in these two countries, and the number is rapidly increasing.[21] Among these prospering firms are Toyota in partnership with GM in Fremont, California, Anne Klein (high-fashion women's clothing), and Japan Photo Center (retailing) in Canada.

The Evidence and Opinion against Japanese Management

Despite the initial enthusiasm about Japanese management, a more balanced perspective emerged. We summarize the reservations and concerns about both Japanese management itself and the indiscriminate application of Japanese management practices of Western firms. We devote more attention to the negative than to the positive because the arguments for Japanese management are already well publicized and, therefore, well known.

American Productivity and Quality Can Match That of the Japanese. Although the Japanese approach to human resource management has contributed to high productivity and quality, the American approach can also yield excellent results. A case in point is the Ford Motor Co. plant in Batavia, Ohio. Recently, Ford announced it would stop purchasing automatic transaxles from Mazda in Japan and consolidate all manufacturing of the sophisticated transmissions in Batavia. The reason given was the better quality and higher productivity of the Batavia plant. Three years previously the plant manager said, "We were going to close our doors because we could not make a quality product competitively."

The plan for rejuvenating the Batavia plant was straightforward. It borrowed from the techniques that Americans had helped the Japanese develop: a teamwork approach to labor-management issues, a system of statistical process controls, and a customer-oriented attitude throughout the plant.[22] (The counterargument here is that Americans can perform as well as the Japanese if they use Japanese-style management.)

A related issue is whether or not all Japanese products are truly of higher quality than those made in America. One important example is the comparison between automobiles made in the United States with those made in Japan. In terms of low maintenance and reliability, Japanese cars probably have the edge. However, when safety is considered the Japanese advantage diminishes. The Highway Loss Data Institute studies the relative claim frequency of automobiles and pickup trucks. An average claim frequency is 100, with the figure being adjusted for the fact that young drivers prefer certain vehicles. The higher the claim frequency the poorer the safety factor.

In general, heavier vehicles are the safest with the GMC Suburban receiving a claim frequency of 35; and the Mitsubishi Tredia with a frequency of 162. Comparing 28 small, two-door models, the Japanese cars have no better safety record than cars made in the United States (including those made by Canadian subsidiaries) or Europe. Specifically, 7 of the 14 cars with the highest safety rating are Japanese, and 7 of the 14 cars with the lowest rating are Japanese.[23]

Japanese Management Is Best Suited to Imitation Rather Than Innovation. Japan remains a net importer of foreign technology because its technical work force does better at imitation than innovation. The emphasis on work group harmony, obedience, and consensus curtails innovative thinking and behavior. Japanese industries thus concentrate on "core technologies" such as the 64K RAM (random-access memory) chips and robots. But they are forced to purchase most of the "peripheral technologies" needed for manufacturing and testing along with the product. According to Nicholas Valery, this means that "Never learning to make the really difficult part of their big systems, Japanese firms stay technologically 10 years behind their American rivals."[24]

Japanese Management Is Not Suited to Pursuing Aggressive and Risky Ventures. Japanese-style managerial practices that emphasize consensual decision making and group harmony are not suited to firms pursuing aggressive and risky ventures. Chung and Gray make this analysis:

> The Japanese systems are good at managing the nuts and bolts of manufacturing activities, but the emphasis on group harmony and consensus can easily smother creative thinking and innovative behavior. When technological innovation is the key to organizational survival, the American way of managing people, stressing creative ideas and individualistic performance, can be more advantageous than the Japanese approach.[25]

Human Resource Management Practices Are a Small Factor in Japan's Industrial Success. The success of Japanese industry can be attributed to factors other than a superior style of human resource management. Among these key nonmanagerial factors are a supportive government policy, low-cost financing that facilitates capital expansion, friendly labor unions, and a work force culturally conditioned to be obedient and cooperative. (Some American firms locate their manufacturing facilities in the rural south to achieve some of these advantages. The presence of a strong work ethic among rural people contributes to high productivity.) Some of the success of Japanese industries in worldwide markets can also be attributed to the heavy competition Japanese firms face domestically, particularly in electrical goods. To survive and prosper at home, Japanese firms must turn out electronic equipment so low priced that it competes favorably overseas. The argument has been advanced that much of the success of Japanese industry is attributed to the type of hard decision making involved in such competition, rather than only from skills in managing people.[26]

The research of Andrew Weiss contributes further to the argument that not all of Japan's success can be attributed to superior human resource management. He compared the practices of five Japanese electronic companies with those of Western Electric Company. Weiss concluded that superior productivity in Japan is not attributable to an "Oriental" style of management or to Japanese corporate culture. Instead, it hinges on straightforward decisions made by Japanese manufacturers that can be summarized as follows:

1. *More engineering support for production workers.* In the Japanese companies, one engineer was present for about every four workers. In Western Electric, the ratio is one to eight. The high level of engineering support usually increases productivity.

2. *Selective hiring.* The Japanese firms studied hire selectively and recruit the elite of the Japanese labor force. Job applicants are thoroughly tested for intelligence, skill, and motivation. References are also carefully checked. Not all American companies place such an emphasis on careful screening of job applicants.

3. *Considerably higher pay to experienced workers.* Experienced Japanese workers stay with the firm because they are paid so highly. And because newer workers are paid much less, they make a substantial contribution to profitability. The wage differentials are less in American companies.

4. *Substantially higher pay for top employees over the lifetime of their employment.* Despite the emphasis on seniority, high-performing employees are amply rewarded. For example, a 50-year-old employee in the top 10th of the pay scale would earn twice as much as a 50-year-old in the bottom 10th.

5. *Healthy investment practices.* One of many examples is that Japanese companies invest more extensively in equipment than do American companies. Although the Japanese equipment may not be more advanced, the fact that more of it exists boosts productivity.[27]

The Most Effective Elements of Japanese Management Are American in Origin. The more publicized Japanese techniques of human resource management and manufacturing are based on ideas borrowed from the United States. American organizational psychologists pioneered in the development of participative leadership techniques as early as the 1950s. Quality control methods, including quality circles, were developed by Deming about the same year and later introduced to Japan. Furthermore, as Linda S. Dillon has observed,

> The real success of the Japanese approach lies in what they were able to learn from the United States in the early postwar years: the value of controlling costs, working hard, saving money, and giving customers value for their dollars. It was their ability to adapt those concepts to a Japanese culture that led to their productivity gains and subsequent worldwide envy.[28]

Cultural Differences Create Problems in Adopting Japanese Management. A number of managers and scholars have expressed concern about the transferability of Japanese human resource management to North American industry. One frequently expressed opinion is that Japanese management practices are best suited to a culturally homogeneous work force. Since members of the homogeneous work force share similar values, they are more likely to cooperate well with each other and be committed to the company. Workers do what is expected of them and do not block productivity improvements. The culturally diverse work force in North America cooperates less well with each other and with the firm.

Another reservation about the transferability of Japanese techniques is that collective decision making is less important in a culture with good written communication. Dillon believes that Japan's penchant for consensus decision making and quality circles are in part responses to the difficulties of the Japanese language. It is so complicated to prepare written documents that the Japanese rely on methods in the work place that favor oral communication. The typical office arrangement features employees in one work unit sharing a common office. Desks are arranged so that everyone is readily aware of what everybody else is doing.[29] Management by "wandering around" is another practice that decreases the necessity of preparing written communication.

Japanese Management Is Unsuited for Firms in Weak and Unstable Positions. Firms in relatively stable and dominant positions are better able to adopt the Japanese model than those in weak and unstable positions. The main reason is that they can provide their employees with long-term, and sometimes lifetime, employment and make substantial investments in employee training. Because they do not have to worry about short-term survival, they can take a long-range perspective.[30]

Many Japanese Managers Suffer from Poor Working and Living Conditions. A final argument against Japanese-style human resource management is that it has led to poor living and working conditions for many Japanese managers and other workers. One problem is the stress created by a work schedule that requires 12-hour days, entertaining customers late at night, six-day work weeks, and little or no vacation time. As a result the suicide rate of Japanese managers has doubled during a period in which the population increased by only 8 percent.[31]

Severe job stress for Japanese managers also results from very few of them being promoted into key positions. Those left behind have few authentic responsibilities and sit at their desks looking out the window or reading newspapers, waiting until they reach age 55 so they can officially retire. It is extremely difficult for a Japanese manager to find work in another large company. Despite their grief over being "shelved," Japanese managers are expected to remain enthusiastic and conceal their complaints.[32]

Another concern about Japanese management is that it has failed to produce a comfortable life-style for most Japanese managers. Urban dwellers spend 26 percent of their disposable incomes on food compared with 15 percent for Americans. The price of real estate has made owning a single-family house almost unattainable for most Japanese. The average price of a small, three-room condominium two hours from downtown Tokyo was $228,000 in 1987. A comparable apartment in town cost several million dollars.[33]

Guidelines for Action and Skill Development

A common misinterpretation of Japanese-style management is that it is a straightforward system or technique to be installed, much like PERT (program review and evaluation technique). To work effectively, Japanese management must be incorporated into a philosophy of management that places primary value on human resources and internalizes the values behind participative management (such as every worker has the potential to contribute good ideas).

Non-Japanese companies should take the following steps to determine which Japanese practices are appropriate for their firms:

1. Review company procedures that have proved to be problem areas.

2. Identify features of Japanese management that may be substituted for unsuccessful techniques.

3. Jointly establish a strategy with employees for implementing an on-going monitoring and evaluation system.

If this process shows beneficial results, other aspects of Japanese management may be attempted. This approach can be implemented without massive personnel changes or significant capital investment. Additional costs are minimal and are related to training and reorganization expense.[34]

The adoption of a Japanese management system requires the careful selection of employees who can function effectively under the new system, a major investment in continuing employee training and development, decentralization of decision making, and sharing with employees of the benefits stemming from productivity improvement. Also necessary is the development of a close partnership between management and any labor unions representing the company employees.[35]

DISCUSSION QUESTIONS AND ACTIVITIES

1. Which techniques described in other chapters of this text do you think fit the Japanese approach to human resource management?

2. Are the values of today's stereotype of an MBA graduate compatible with the Japanese philosophy of human resource management?

3. Japanese executives freely admit that many of their techniques are borrowed from behavioralists such as McGregor and Herzberg. Why did it take American industry so long to pay careful attention to these ideas?

4. How do flexible job classifications fit with the philosophy of job enrichment (making a job more satisfying by giving the worker more responsibility)?

5. How well do you think Japanese employees would respond to American managers running their companies in Japan?

6. Describe a control system that would be the opposite of a system based on implicit, informal controls.

7. Among the many American firms described as using a Japanese-style of management are IBM, GM, Hewlett-Packard, and Rockwell International. Find somebody who works for, or has worked for, one of these firms. Interview the person to see if his or her description of the firm's management practices fits the description of Japanese management presented in this chapter.

NOTES

1. Adapted and excerpted from Harris Jack Shapiro and Teresa Cosenza, *Reviving Industry in America: Japanese Influences on Manufacturing and the Service Sector,* pp. 163–65, Copyright 1987 by Ballinger Publishing Company.

2. William G. Ouchi, *Theory Z: How American Business Can Meet the Japanese Challenge* (Reading, Mass.: Addison-Wesley, 1981).

3. Shapiro and Cosenza, *Reviving Industry in America,* p. 13.

4. James S. Bowman, "The Rising Sun in America (Part Two)," *Personnel Administrator,* October 1986, p. 83.

5. Nina Hatvany and Vladimir Pucik, "An Integrated Management System: Lessons from the Japanese Experience," *Academy of Management Review,* July 1981, p. 471. Many aspects of our description of Japanese management are based on the Hatvany and Pucik article; Jon P. Alston, "Three Principles of Japanese Management," *Personnel Journal,* September 1983, p. 761.

6. Hatvany and Pucik, "An Integrated Management System" p. 471.

7. Quoted in Mary Zippo, "Working for the Japanese: Views of American Employees," *Personnel,* March–April 1982, p. 56.

8. Stanley J. Brown, "The Japanese Approach to Labor Relations: Can It Work in America?" *Personnel,* April 1987, p. 26.

9. Kae H. Chung and Margaret Ann Gray, "Can We Adopt the Japanese Methods of Human Resources Management?" *Personnel Administrator,* May 1982, p. 43.

10. Ibid. p. 43.

11. Hatvany and Pucik, "An Integrated Management System," p. 473.

12. Audrey Freedman, "Learning from New U.S.-Based Neighbors," *Conference Board Record,* July 1983, p. 32.
13. Brown, "The Japanese Approach to Labor Relations," p. 26.
14. James S. Bowman, "The Rising Sun in America (Part One)," *Personnel Administrator,* September 1986, p. 114.
15. Ibid.
16. Chung and Gray, "Can We Adopt?" p. 42.
17. Hatvany and Pucik, "An Integrated Management System," p. 472.
18. Bowman, "The Rising Sun in America (Part One)," p. 67.
19. Chung and Gray, "Can We Adopt?" p. 43.
20. "Lessons in Success," brochure from George Plossi Educational Services, Inc., Atlanta, Georgia, 1984.
21. Shapiro and Cosenza, *Reviving Industry in America,* p. 24; "Can Japan Keep Its Economy from Hollowing Out?" *Business Week,* July 13, 1987, pp. 52–55.
22. Frank Swoboda, "Ohio Plant Beats Japanese in Quality, Productivity," *The Washington Post* syndicated story, December 27, 1987.
23. *USAA Car Guide: Safety and Insurance Ratings,* San Antonio, Texas, 1988; "How Safe Is Your Car?" *Aide,* Fall 1986, pp. 26–28.
24. Nicholas Valery, "The Fabled Giant's Might Is Dwindling," *The Economist,* July 9, 1983.
25. Chung and Gray, "Can We Adopt the Japanese Methods?" p. 46.
26. Ikujiro Nonaka and Johny K. Johannson, "Japanese Management: What about the 'Hard' Skills," *Academy of Management Review,* April 1985, p. 189.
27. Andrew Weiss, "Simple Truths of Japanese Manufacturing," *Harvard Business Review,* July–August 1984, pp. 119–25.
28. Linda S. Dillon, "Adopting Japanese Management: Some Cultural Stumbling Blocks," *Personnel,* July–August 1983, p. 77.
29. Dillon, "Adopting Japanese Management," p. 75.
30. Chung and Gray, "Can We Adopt?" p. 46.
31. Leslie Helm and Charles Gaffney, "The High Price Japanese Pay for Success," *Business Week,* April 7, 1986, pp. 52–54.
32. Bowman, "The Rising Sun in America (Part Two)," p. 87.
33. Larry Armstrong, "The Party Gets Stronger While the Government Gets Weaker," *Business Week,* July 13, 1987, p. 58.
34. Chung and Gray, "Can We Adopt?" p. 46.
35. Ibid., p. 46.

SOME ADDITIONAL REFERENCES

"A Hot American Car May Hit Japan: The Honda." *Business Week,* January 26, 1987, p. 50.

McCraw, Thomas K., ed. *America Versus Japan.* Boston: Harvard Business School Press, 1986.

Reich, Robert B., and Eric Mankin, "Joint Ventures with Japan Give Away Our Future." *Harvard Business Review,* March–April 1986, pp. 78–86.

Sethi, S. Prakash; Nobuaki Namiki; and Carl L. Swanson. *The False Promise of the Japanese Miracle: Illusions and Realities of the Japanese Management System.* Marshfield, Mass.: Pitman Publishing, 1984.

"Sony's Challenge: The Mighty Yen and Fierce Competition Are Forcing It into New Markets." *Business Week,* June 1, 1987, pp. 64–69.

Appendix to Chapter Sixteen

IS YOUR COMPANY JAPANESE MANAGEMENT ORIENTED?

Directions: Respond True or False to the following statements, as they apply to your organization. The greater the number of True responses, the higher the probability that a Japanese-style of management is suited to your organization.

Organizational Characteristic	*True*	*False*
1. Our concern for human resources goes far beyond paying lip service to the importance of people.	____	____
2. Relationships between managers and group members are generally quite good.	____	____
3. Good teamwork is found throughout our firm.	____	____
4. Most of our employees buy into the beliefs and ideas of the firm.	____	____
5. Our firm invests heavily in employee training and development.	____	____
6. The welfare of the work group is more important than the welfare of individual members.	____	____
7. Practically all important decisions in our organization reflect the consensus of group opinion.	____	____
8. Managers and group members engage in a free exchange of information.	____	____
9. Our managers wander freely around the work areas and talk to employees.	____	____
10. Our employees voluntarily point out areas of needed improvement and inefficiency.	____	____

11. Our managers and group members alike
welcome the opportunity to work outside of
their job classifications.   _____   _____

12. Our organization values seniority as reflected
in very high pay for more long-term
employees.   _____   _____

13. An employee's inner qualities are more
important than short-term results he or she
might achieve.   _____   _____

14. Our employees voluntarily control the
quality and quantity of their own work.   _____   _____

15. Experienced job holders are the people best
qualified to make suggestions for
improvement of their job operations.   _____   _____

Part V

Human Resource Management Programs

This part of the book describes human resource (or personnel) management programs designed to enhance human potential, improve productivity, or help displaced employees regain career thrust. Chapter 17 presents an in-depth look at a successful career development program and it also describes key components of other similar programs. Such programs are frequently based on theories of career development and occupational psychology. Chapter 18 describes outplacement programs, a method of helping surplus employees who are being dismissed find new employment outside the firm. Outplacement programs are part of career development and are based on counseling theory and well-established techniques of conducting a job search.

Chapter 19 describes gainsharing, a method of enabling workers to share in the monetary rewards associated with the productivity gains they have helped achieve. Gainsharing programs are based on reinforcement theory, especially positive reinforcement. Chapter 20 describes telecommuting, a program for allowing selected employees to work at home yet stay in touch with the office via telephones and computers. Telecommuting is gaining acceptance as many workers attempt to grapple with the problem of balancing work and family demands and lowering the cost of working.

Chapter Seventeen

Career Development Programs

> One of the world's largest hotel chains wanted to deal effectively with three challenges: creating lateral mobility for reservation agents, to provide managers the skills needed to coach employees on a variety of career moves, and assure retention of valuable employees. A career development program was selected to deal with these challenges.

Holiday Inns., Inc., faced the loss of several hundred reservation agents who felt that they had no place to move within the organization. The company was committed to retaining these agents and keeping their level of motivation high.

An analysis was completed of most Holiday Inns jobs to create data to form the basis for many of Holiday Inns's human resource programs including compensation, training, performance appraisal, and employee development. The analysis produced descriptions of skills for most jobs in the system. Because these descriptions were also viewed as invaluable career development tools, they were included in a set of career direction booklets that described families or clusters of jobs in Holiday Inns, Inc. It also specified the skills required in each and tied development activities to these skills. A career development model (or system) was developed to fit this information, as shown in Figure 17–1. Each of the components is described next.

Advisory Group. The reservations system director put together an advisory group made up of managers, the division director, and several hundred human resource consultants from the hotel division. The advisory group's role was to consult and react to the components of the program, monitor the program for six months, and help redesign and add other components as necessary after the program was implemented.

FIGURE 17–1   Holiday Inns, Inc., Career Directions System

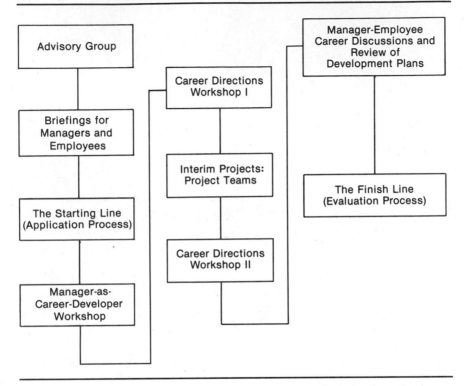

SOURCE: Zandy B. Leibowitz, Caela Farren, and Beverly L. Kaye, *Designing Career Development Systems* (San Francisco: Jossey-Bass Publishers, 1986), p. 165. Reprinted with permission.

Briefing.   The division director briefed the 30 line managers who supervised the 400 reservation agents. The briefing included an overview of the entire program, selection criteria, the application process, the career development model, and an outline of the manager-as-career-developer workshop. Each manager would be invited to the workshop. Managers were urged to give a similar briefing to all of their reservation agents and invite them to participate in the Career Directions program. Application forms were made available to all managers to distribute to their employees. This briefing not only demonstrated the commitment of the division director to the program but also gave him or her information about the managers' apprehensions at the outset of the program.

The Starting Line.   The four-page application form, called the *Starting Line,* assured that the reservation agents would begin to answer some of the questions needed for managing their own careers. One of the key elements of this process was for each applicant to perform two informational interviews with people outside his or her immediate area. One problem of the reservation agent's job was being confined to the telephone with limited chance to converse with anyone but customers. The application process was meant to ensure that they started talking to other reservation agents, from whom they were geographically separated, as well as other Holiday Inns staff members.

Other questions asked them to examine, for example, what factors were critical to them on a job, what their jobs lacked, what were the special contributions they made to the service industry, and to Holiday Inns Inc. A unique aspect of the application was that the criteria for selection were stated publicly on the form: All applicants were assured admission into the program if they (1) got the application in on time, (2) completed each question, and (3) had held the position for a minimum of one year. Over 100 agents applied for the workshop. The first 30 who met the criteria were assigned to the first program, the second 30 to the second, and so on. Employees said that filling out the form was a highlight of the program and really started them thinking.

Manager-As-Career-Developer Workshop. This three-day program, which preceded all employee workshops, was offered for all managers of reservation agents and touched on the basic skills needed in coaching and counseling employees. The program also helped managers examine their own careers. Managers left the workshop eager to enter into discussion with their employees, with a clearer perception of some of their own career goals.

Career Directions Workshop I. This two-day workshop focused on building a strong network of reservation agents and enabled them to take a hard look at themselves. Self-study instruments and exercises help them understand their specific skills, strengths, interests, values, and career anchors (primary interests or orientations). During the workshop, five-person teams were formed to work together on the interim research projects.

Interim Projects. The employee teams chose projects from a list developed by the advisory group. This component was designed to give the reservation agents an opportunity to work with each other for eight weeks and develop their leadership abilities, problem-solving abilities, presentations skills, and networking skills. The research projects included revising the Holiday Inns, Inc., orientation handbook, cataloging the factors that lead to success as a manager, and developing a dress-for-success sourcebook. These projects were completed and presented at the next gathering of the group (during the second workshop). They were also put in print for continual use by other employees in the newly set up career resource center. The division director felt that it was important to have employees make such contributions to the organization.

Career Directions Workshop II.   The second workshop, eight weeks after the first, entailed presentation of the research projects to the managers, goal setting, and developing planning. The reservation agents were encouraged to discuss their career goals and development plans with their managers, if discussions had not already begun in the interim between the two workshops.

Career Discussions.   Employees discussed their goals with their managers several times and got help and support for their development plans. Both employees and managers felt confident after these discussion of goals.

The Finish Line.   Six months after the second workshop, the entire group was brought together to evaluate the program. A form called *The Finish Line* let the employees note the progress they had made over the six months. A series of exercises allowed the reservation agents to talk about their accomplishments and new goals and acknowledge the support they received from their managers, the organization, and each other.

Program Evaluation.   Overall, the program has been highly successful. Of the first 100 applicants, nearly a dozen received new jobs as a result of the interviews they conducted for the *Starting Line* application. Other agents moved into management; many of them moved into other parts of the organization. Managers felt supportive toward the agents and no longer felt threatened by employee requests for new job opportunities. The organization became even more productive, and the program is used as a model in many other divisions of the organization.[1]

IMPORTANT COMPONENTS TO CAREER DEVELOPMENT PROGRAMS

The career development program at Holiday Inns, Inc., is only one example of a successful program. Career development programs vary considerably with respect to their degree of structure and components. Despite this variation, a set of components can be delineated that are associated with effective career development programs. Among them are (1) assessment of individual and organizational needs, (2) a human resource information system containing valid information, (3) development of realistic career paths, (4) dual career ladders, (5) integration of career development with management development and training, (6) managerial involvement in the career development of subordinates, (7) formal mentoring programs, (8) human resource specialists serving as advisors, (9) advisory groups, (10) networking, and (11) adaptation of the career development program to the organizational culture.

Assessment of Individual and Organizational Needs

A sensible early step in a career development program (CDP) is to diagnose what type of development is needed. Assessment from the individual's standpoint might answer questions such as:

What education and training do I need to achieve my goals?

What types of positions and career experiences do I need to achieve my goals?

What personal traits, characteristics, and behaviors require change in order for me to improve my professional effectiveness?

The appendix to this chapter presents a standard approach to career self-analysis. In addition to self-analysis, however, the assessment of individual needs for development should include input from present and previous managers, and perhaps professional assessors such as organizational psychologists.

Needs assessment from the organization's standpoint can be considered "human resources forecasting." It attempts to answer such questions as:

What types of skills and talents will be needed by this organization in the future?

Are we entering an era of retrenchment, stability, or expansion?

How well have we met our goal of providing equal employment opportunity?

Organizational needs assessment is accomplished by gathering information from managers, staff specialists, operative employees, and existing records. Figure 17–2 summarizes the primary methods of conducting an organizational needs assessment.

Human Resource Information System Containing Valid Information

A sophisticated method is needed of keeping track of both employees in the career development program and those who might be eligible for inclusion in the future. For most organizations, the method chosen is a human resources information systems (HRIS) or career development information systems (CDIS). An important component of the HRIS is the skills bank inventory. Its database includes an updated listing of the unique skills and job experiences of all employees in the organization, both those selected for the CDP and all other employees. When an attractive job opening develops that could be used for career develop-

FIGURE 17–2   Methods of Conducting an Organizational Needs Assessment for
Career Development Program

Questionnaires
    Can be open ended or forced choice.

One-to-One Interviews
    Can be formal or informal, structured or unstructured.
    Can be used to sample a large group.
    Can be conducted on the phone or in person.

Group Interviews
    Can be formal or informal.
    Can sample from a representative group of employees.
    Can use group problem-solving techniques such as brainstorming.

Records/Reports/Related Surveys
    Can include organization charts and data, such as attrition figures, length of
    service, and age profiles of employees. Can include existing data collection
    techniques, such as climate/attitude surveys or communication audits.

SOURCE: Zandy B. Leibowitz, Caela Farren, and Beverly L. Kaye, *Designing Career Development Systems* (San Francisco: Jossey-Bass Publishers, 1986), p. 23.

ment, a computer search is run to discover a fit between that opening and present employees.

A challenge facing the organization is to have valid information in the HRIS. The output in most human resource information systems is impressive on the surface—the reports appear to be scientific and valid because they are generated by a computer. However, the skills inventory and human resource forecasts contained in the system may contain many errors. Two career development specialists note that the majority of skills inventories actually contain information about education and experience—not skills.[2] It is also possible for the human resource forecasts to contain highly subjective estimates of future career opportunities in the firm. The basic input for these projections may be a hurried "guestimate" by a harried executive!

Alfred J. Walker, division manager (personnel data) at American Telephone & Telegraph Co., points out that users of the HRIS should be informed about the currency of the information within the system.[3] In this way some misperceptions they may have about the validity of the database can be minimized.

Development of Realistic Career Paths

The development of a career path—the sequence of jobs necessary to achieve personal and career goals—is an important component of many career development programs. The path can be displayed in a stepwise diagram or expressed verbally. A career path for a person in a food packaging company might choose the career path shown in Figure 17–3.[4] Observe that the individual has specified both professional and personal goals in the career path, thus striving for an integrated life.

An effective career path must match individual aspirations with organizational opportunities.[5] Much of career pathing is pure whimsy because it involves making plans for nonexistent opportunities. For example, in one CDP it was discovered that dozens of middle managers wanted to become international business liaison specialists—a person who served as a high-level intermediary between the home office and foreign affiliates. At the same time the company was planning to abolish

FIGURE 17–3 Career Path for Distribution and Marketing Professional in a Food Packing Company

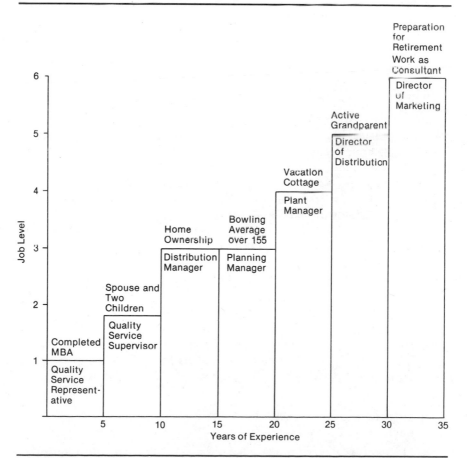

this position because its contribution to productivity was questionable. To minimize such problems, a realistic picture of company opportunities should be presented to employees. Answers to questions such as these might be provided:

- What are the prospects for promotion or transfer from the present job?
- What percentage of employees reach a certain target level in this organization?
- What are the pay ranges at various job levels?
- Where is the fastest growth (and, therefore, the best promotion opportunity) in the company?
- If I have reached a dead end, what are paths for moving down so I can move up faster somewhere else?
- How do I go about requesting a transfer without alienating my boss?[6]
- How do I learn about opportunities in other divisions of the organization?

Dual Career Ladders

Many salaried professionals, including scientists, engineers, information system specialists, computer scientists, and accountants are more interested in developing their professional expertise than in pursuing a career in management. A carefully designed CDP allows for such dual career progression; vertical growth is still possible for employees who want to remain as professional specialists. A prime example is Aetna Life and Casualty where the law department of nearly 100 attorneys has an approximately equal number of employees in both professional and managerial paths. Crossovers between the professional and managerial ladders are possible. An ideal dual career ladder is shown in Figure 17–4. An information systems specialist who became a principal information associate would be a person of national prominence and would earn the same compensation and benefits as the chief information officer.[7]

The dual career ladder has been around for many years, but is infrequently implemented effectively. Except for a handful of inventors and scientists, very few salaried professionals achieve the same prestige and income as executives.

Integrate Career Development with Management Development and Training

Career development is but one major aspect of management development. People should be assigned to management development programs

FIGURE 17-4   A Dual Career Ladder

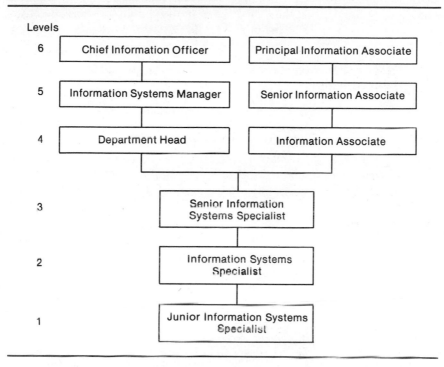

Levels

6	Chief Information Officer	Principal Information Associate
5	Information Systems Manager	Senior Information Associate
4	Department Head	Information Associate
3		Senior Information Systems Specialist
2		Information Systems Specialist
1		Junior Information Systems Specialist

on the basis of both individual and organizational needs. It would be folly, for example, to send a manager to a three-month advanced management training program at a university if that manager was seeking to get out of management or the organization had a surplus of managers.

The career development program at Dow Jones & Company, Inc. is one example of how career development and management development and training might be integrated. Labeled the *Druthers Program* ("If I had my druthers, I would . . . ."), it is supported by company-sponsored training and development programs. Seminars are provided on career planning and self-assessment. Career information briefings are provided by representatives from selected departments. The representatives explain job requirements and career alternatives within their departments. A special seminar coaches participants in how to present their qualifications in person and in writing.[8]

The assessment aspect of career development is well suited in helping achieve integration between career and management development. Formal assessment might reveal, for example, that manager A is deficient in oral communication skill. Manager A would then be assigned to an oral communication skill training program. During the assessment center, manager B might have proved to be an impulsive, haphazard decision maker. Manager B might be assigned to a decision-making training program. (If that didn't work, he or she should be reassigned to a position with very little decision making.)

Managerial Involvement in Career Development of Subordinates

An effective career development program requires that managers throughout the organization be skilled in helping subordinates build their careers. These skills include such things as coaching, conducting performance appraisals that help develop the person being evaluated, assisting in goal setting, and providing frequent feedback. Most skills of this nature can be acquired through training and practice. To reinforce training in career-development skills, managers should be rewarded for their contribution to career development.

Exxon is one of many firms that reward these skills. A company human resources professional observes: "A critical part of our management evaluation is how they do in helping to nurture and develop employees under them."[9] A Canadian computer company uses a slightly different approach to rewarding career-building skills. Each manager is required to pick and develop a successor before the manager will be considered for promotion. In this way, the career development of subordinates is linked to the career progress of the managers.[10]

A study was conducted of how employees perceived managers to have helped them with their careers. Four key roles for managers in career development were identified: coach, appraiser, advisor, and referral agent. A manager who is an effective career developer will use all four roles as appropriate.

In the role of *coach,* managers assist employees in identifying strengths, weaknesses, skills, interests, and values. In this way the employee moves toward answering the question, "Who am I?" As a coach, the manager maintains open communication, listens actively, and provides frequent encouragement.

In the role of *appraiser,* managers evaluate performance and relate it to advancement opportunities within the organization. The appraiser gives employees specific, timely, and frequent feedback to help them understand how they are perceived by the organization. An appraiser will also communicate to employees how the organization assesses their potential for handling administrative responsibility.

In the role of *advisor,* managers provide subordinates with information that will help them set realistic career goals and establish a career path. Managers who pass along both formal and informal knowledge, including political realities, are particularly helpful in this role. Another contribution as an advisor is helping employees set alternative goals thereby increasing their chances for achieving success.

In the role of *referral agent,* managers help subordinates develop action plans to support their goals. Action plans help employees answer the question, "How can I achieve my goals?" The employee might be referred to certain training programs or experiences (such as membership on a taskforce) that might help them realize their goals.[11]

Formal Mentoring Programs

The four roles just described that enable a manager to help others develop their careers are often incorporated into mentoring. The informal role of the mentor as a teacher, coach, and advisor is well known. Several organizations have also incorporated a formal approach to mentoring into career development programs. Among these firms are AT&T, Johnson & Johnson, Merrill Lynch, Federal Express, the Internal Revenue Service, and the U.S. Army. According to Michael G. Zey, the greatest contribution the mentoring process can make is developing the protégé into a full-fledged manager or professional. Training of the protégé often occurs in subtle ways: the mentor teaches the junior person both technical and interpersonal skills, familiarizes him or her with the corporate culture, and acclimates the protégé to the values and expectations of the organization. An exemplary formal program of mentoring contains seven distinct stages:

1. *Development.* During the program development stage, the goals, criteria of participation, and mechanisms of interaction are put into writing.

2. *Notification.* The implementing department should notify by memo the target audience of the existence of the formal mentoring program, the anticipated benefits to the company, and the length of the program. The notification can be considered an invitation to eligible groups such as all successful middle and senior managers and all incoming junior employees.

3. *Selection.* All interested candidates are interviewed individually, informed of the specifics of the program, and evaluated according to established criteria. Typically, those individuals of apparent management potential are selected into the program.

4. *Orientation.* All the senior and junior participants chosen should then attend an orientation meeting. This meeting usually serves as an ice-breaker between the mentors and juniors.

5. *Pairing.* A mechanism must be established for matching the protégé with the right sponsor. Many programs allow for independent selection of a partner such as an experienced executive identifying junior people in the organization for whom he or she would like to serve as a mentor. If the overseeing department (typically the human resources depart-

ment) assumes responsibility for partner pairing, it will be able to make those decisions based on information gathered in the selection phase.

6. *Implementation.* At this stage, the participants begin the actual mentoring, meeting at specific times and places. Some senior managers initiate the implementation phase by taking the protégé to lunch or breakfast.

7. *Evaluation.*   The primary criterion of a successful mentoring program is how well it has contributed to management development and training. Evaluation can take place in several ways. One way is for the mentor group and protégé group to meet collectively with the program formulators to give postprogram feedback and offer suggestions for improving the program for the next group. Suggestions from the mentors are particularly important because these people remain in the program as a mentor pool.[12]

The evaluation stage can also be used to debrief participants and to encourage senior executives to remain in the program as mentors. Evaluation can also take place during other stages of the program.

Human Resource Specialists Serving As Advisors

The major unit for career development is the employee and immediate manager. The human resource specialist should generally serve in the role of expert advisor who helps establish the program and serves as a consultant. If the human resource specialist becomes too heavily involved in the process, managers may be "taken off the hook." Another problem is that few organizations have the resources to provide individual counseling to all employees.

Despite the general wisdom of this strategy, there are times when professional career counseling for individuals is the intervention of choice. Among the situations that call for professional counseling are career dilemmas caused by the mid-life crisis, cases of severe career dissatisfaction, and modifying career plans to overcome stress disorders. As a result of professional career counseling, one manager came to realize that his stress symptoms were precipitated by the demands of his present job. He could no longer tolerate the daily confrontations with people. His stress symptoms subsided when he transferred to a position as a management information specialist.

Advisory Groups

A team of career development specialists observe that career development programs should be presented to the organization only after garnering wide, active support. One of the best ways to ensure the needed support and participation is to form advisory groups. The most important role played by these groups is to help develop an action plan, decide on first practical steps, and launch a career development program (CDP).

Advisory groups are composed of people with a variety of perspectives who can address career development problems in thoughtful, creative ways. These groups are usually made up of 6 to 12 members, representing different units and levels within the organization. Knowledge about the organizational culture, and personal influence, are more important than technical knowledge about career development as a qualification for being an advisory group member. Leibowitz, Farren, and Kaye describe the primary role of the advisory group in these terms: Advisory groups respond, critique, and comment; they have consultative power rather than line authority; and they need not become involved in the labor-intensive, time-consuming tasks usually associated with task-forces at the beginning of projects.[13]

Networking

Networking, the systematic use of contacts to gain advantage, is an informal part of most career development programs. It is widely recognized that networking facilitates career advancement. A long-term study of 457 managers from diverse organizations conducted by Fred Luthans, Richard M. Hodgetts, and Stuart A. Rosenkrantz provides empirical evidence about the contribution of networking to career development.

The researchers drew an important distinction between *successful* and *effective* real managers. (A *real manager* is the everyday manager who populates organizations rather than the superstars who receive so much publicity.) A *successful manager* is one who is promoted rapidly, while an *effective manager* is one whose subordinates are committed and whose unit achieves good performance. Successful managers are thus intent on achieving vertical mobility, while effective managers focus on achieving organizational goals.

One aspect of networking observed was interacting with others. Specific activities include seeking involvement in public relations activities by attending community events, handling customer/client relations, and meeting with country club members important to the organization. Another aspect of networking uncovered by the study was socializing/politicking. Specific activities include entertaining top-level managers in the organization, such as playing tennis with them; keeping an active social calendar; and socializing with employees in a lounge.

An important finding of the study was that successful managers engage in about 70 percent more networking than less successful managers. In contrast, networking was not particularly related to managerial *effectiveness*. Of the two types of networking activities, interacting with outsiders was more important than socializing and politicking. Networking thus did help managers advance their careers but was only marginally related to actual effectiveness.[14]

Adaptation of the Career Development Program to the Organizational Culture

Organizational culture, the system of shared values and beliefs characteristic of an organization, is an intangible but important influence on the potential effectiveness of a CDP. If the program does not fit the culture, its chances for success are diminished. A key cultural characteristic of one firm was distrust and secretiveness. Many people believed that being candid about any business mistakes or personal weaknesses would backfire—the information would ultimately be used against them. A career development program was initiated that required participants to discuss their strengths, weaknesses, and goals with immediate superiors. The level of compliance was so low that the program was discontinued after six months.

Based on practice in a number of organizations, here are six characteristics of an organization culture that favor the success of a career development program:

1. Business plans and forecasts are publicized (thus giving people an idea of future opportunities).
2. People have easy access to job information.
3. Networks foster innovation, high performance, and exploration of career options.
4. Enrichment, development, and mobility are valued.
5. Employees and managers are mutually supportive.
6. People fit the organization culture (for example, adventuresome people work for a risk-taking organization).[15]

If these characteristics did not prevail, the career development workers would presumably have to bring about the right changes. The first two characteristics would be the easiest to change while the last four would require considerable long-term effort.

THE CASE FOR AND AGAINST CAREER DEVELOPMENT PROGRAMS

Career development programs are now a stable aspect of human resource management. Almost all large firms, and many smaller firms, offer some type of CDP, even if it involves only reimbursing employees for job-related courses. Despite their widespread use, CDPs have both strengths and limitations.

The Case for Career Development Programs

A convincing case can be made for the formal use of career development programs. Ideally, a properly planned and executed program serves the good of individuals, the organization, and society. Following are several of the potential benefits of a soundly conducted CDP.

Integration of Individual and Organizational Goals. Career development helps identify the link between attaining individual and organizational goals. As one certified public accountant commented after a career-planning session with her boss, "I'm working for the right firm. If all goes according to plan, the firm will benefit from having its first woman partner, and I'll make enough money to buy what I want in life."

Saving Money. Career development programs can be cost-effective, as exemplified by a program at First Chicago. During its first two years of implementation, 130 officers were matched with open positions. Twenty-five of the matches resulted in placements. Program expenses during this period were calculated at $175,000. Savings (based on the 30 percent executive-search-firm fee that would have been charged to fill the vacancies from the outside) were calculated at $215,000—a net gain of $40,000 during the period studied.[16]

Communication of Concern for the Welfare of Individuals. An organization that helps employees plan their careers is demonstrating by its actions that it cares about the employees' welfare. The payoff to the organization is often a high degree of employee loyalty and commitment.

The Demonstration of Social Responsibility. Properly executed, career development programs are one way of contributing to the good of society. People with satisfying careers enjoy better mental health than their dissatisfied counterparts.

Implementation of Affirmative Action Programs. A career development program is a logical response to the charges that an organization is not fulfilling its responsibilities toward women, selected minorities, or ethnic groups. Without a solid program of career development, it is difficult for previously discriminated against groups to advance into higher-level positions.

Reduction of Turnover and Other Personnel Costs.   Several studies demonstrated that when the enterprise makes a determined effort to help its employees plan their career, the result is lower turnover and personnel costs.[17]

Reduction of Mid-Career Problems.   When employees properly plan their careers, they are less likely to fall victim to obsolescence and mid-career crisis. Burnout, too, can sometimes be minimized (see Chapter 4).

Enhancing the Contribution of Performance Appraisal Systems. The presence of a CDP can lead to better use of performance appraisal systems because the results of the appraisals can form the basis for career counseling by managers.[18]

Encouragement of a Strategic Point of View.   Career development involves strategic thinking because it projects careers into the future. Allowing for certain career-development activities thus contributes to the future effectiveness of the organization. Today's management trainee who rotates through different organizational functions is preparing for senior responsibility 15 to 20 years from now.[19]

The Case against Career Development Programs

As with any other program or set of strategies described in this book, career development programs sometimes have negative side effects.

Most Career Planning Exercises Contain a Good Deal of Fantasy and Wishful Thinking.   In the process of self-analysis, many individuals present a biased, unrealistic description of their personal strengths and goals. Almost everybody filling out a career development inventory lists "dealing with people" as a personal strength. Many people engage in goal setting so fanciful that their chances of success are less than 1 in 500. Despite the current trend toward pursuing a well-balanced, high quality life, an amusingly large number of people list as a career objective, "Chief executive officer of a major business corporation."

Some Career Development Activities Are an Invasion of the Individual's Privacy.   Career planning usually includes the individual divulging personal goals to a manager or staff specialist. The goals stated by many individuals are not particularly well integrated with or in the best interests of the organization. Many people plan to start a business of their own somewhat in competition with at least one product or service of their current employer. In the interests of candor, the person might reveal such a goal. To the disadvantage of the individual, he or she might now be perceived as disloyal and, therefore, out of consideration for major assignments in the future.

Career Development Programs Create an Elite Group of Crown Princes and Princesses.   When a handful of people are designated as fast trackers, they become part of a self-fulfilling prophecy. Since they are known to be an elite group, their managers may tend to give them undeservingly high performance evaluations. Management's judgment in making them an elite group is, therefore, vindicated. Another problem with the crown prince and princesses effect is that other equally deserving employees may emerge who are not given equal consideration.

Resource limitations frequently preclude organization-wide implementation of a career development program. In these instances, efforts are targeted at those areas and people having the greatest potential payoff to the organization.[20] The people selected for the limited program are thus perceived as being crown princes and princesses.

Career Development Programs Often Give Rise to Disappointed Expectations.   After participating in a CDP, many individuals believe that they should be receiving promotion shortly. When the promotion does not materialize, they experience disappointment. Sometimes this disappointment translates into joining another organization that offers the person more responsibility. The underlying problem is that the CDP resulted in higher expectations for the employee.

Another way in which career development programs sometimes disappoint expectations is that they may train employees for opportunities that may never be available. At the other extreme, some employees desire a secure, unchanging environment. Their expectations of being able to remain in such an environment are disrupted by a development program that emphasizes lateral moves and promotion.

Guidelines for Action and Skill Development

If you are employed by an organization sponsoring a CDP, you should obviously follow the program and work within the system. However, you can help subordinates develop their careers without the benefit of a formal program. Among the informal actions you can take are encouraging subordinates to establish career goals, providing them feedback on where you think they need development, and sharing with them information about organizational opportunities.

Dealing with the career development of subordinates is a responsibility of major consequence. It is better to err on the side of being noncommittal than giving people negative information which could alter their lives. One example: "You are unsuited for a career in business." Similarly, when you do not feel you are qualified to handle a given employee concern (such as, "Would I be more successful if I went back to college?"), seek professional assistance.

A formal career development program requires top management support in order to reach a high degree of effectiveness. If you are part of top management, give the CDP such support. If you are a lower-ranking manager or staff specialist, lobby for such support.

The presence of a career development program in your organization should not be interpreted as shifting responsibility for career planning and development from the individual to the organization (specifically the human resource department). As an individual, you still have the primary responsibility for managing your own career. And as a manager, you still have a heavy responsibility for helping subordinates develop their careers.

When implementing a career development program, it is important to emphasize growth within a job and horizontal growth, as well as vertical growth. The reason is that CDPs are generally interpreted as vehicles for moving upward in the organization. Counseling people about the reality that all growth cannot be vertical, can help minimize *some* discontent. One aspect of growth within a job appealing to many managers and professionals is the development of new skills.

DISCUSSION QUESTIONS AND ACTIVITIES

1. In recent years, career development programs have multiplied in number and received much publicity. What forces do you think have made CDPs so popular in recent years?

2. Where do people seeking help with career problems usually go for assistance?

3. What would be the advantages and disadvantages to an individual of going outside the organization for help with career planning (such as paying for the services of a career counselor)?

4. What do you think is the underlying reason that CDPs tend to reduce turnover?

5. It is not unknown for a person to quit a firm after completing the early phases of a CDP. Why do you think this happens?

6. What facts about an individual do you think should be included in the company HRIS? Why?

7. What facts about an individual do you think should not be included in the company HRIS? Why?

8. Identify two other techniques described in another chapter in this book that you think are well suited to career development. Explain your choices.

NOTES

1. Excerpted and adapted from Zandy B. Leibowitz, Caela Farren, and Beverly L. Kaye, *Designing Career Development Systems* (San Francisco: Jossey-Bass Publishers, 1986), p. 165.
2. Elmer H. Burack and Robert D. Smith, *Personnel Management: A Human Resource System Approach* (New York: John Wiley, 1982), p. 455.
3. Alfred J. Walker, "The Analytical Element Is Important to an HRIS," *Personnel Administrator,* September 1983, p. 34.
4. The jobs in the path, but not the figure, are from Kenneth B. McRae, "Career Management Planning: A Boon to Managers and Employees," *Personnel,* May 1985, p. 57.
5. Cherlyn Skromme Granrose and James D. Portwood, "Matching Individual Career Plans and Organizational Career Management," *Academy of Management Journal,* December 1987, p. 717.
6. The first five questions are from Marilyn A. Morgan, Douglas T. Hall, and Alison Martier, "Career Development Strategies in Industry—Where Are We and Where Should We Be?" *Personnel,* March–April 1979, p. 25.
7. Joseph A. Raelin, "Two-Track Plans for One-Track Careers," *Personnel Journal,* January 1987, p. 96. Figure 17–4 is based on concepts from Raelin, p. 99.
8. Richard K. Broszeit, " 'If I Had my Druthers. . . .' (A Career Development Program)," *Personnel Journal,* October 1986, p. 87.
9. Abby Brown, "Career Development 1986," *Personnel Administrator,* March 1986, p. 48.
10. Douglas T. Hall and Francine S. Hall, "What's New in Career Management?" *Organizational Dynamics,* Summer 1976, p. 29.
11. Zandy B. Leibowitz and N. Schlossberg, "Training Managers for Their Role in a Career Development System," *Training and Development Journal,* July 1981, pp. 72–79.
12. Michael G. Zey, "Mentor Programs: Making the Right Moves," *Personnel Journal,* February 1985, p. 56.
13. Leibowitz, Farren, and Kaye, *Designing Career Development Systems,* p. 194.
14. Fred Luthans, Richard M. Hodgetts, and Stuart A. Rosenkrantz. *Real Managers* (Cambridge, Mass.: Ballinger Book Company, 1988), pp. 3, 16–17, 21–22, 43–44, 72.
15. Ibid., pp. 49–50.
16. Ibid., p. 174.
17. William F. Glueck, *Personnel: A Diagnostic Approach,* 3rd ed. (Plano, Texas: Business Publications, Inc., 1983).
18. Betsy Jacobson and Beverly L. Kaye, "Career Development and Performance Appraisal: It Takes Two to Tango," *Personnel,* January 1986, pp. 26–32.

19. Andrew J. DuBrin and R. Duane Ireland, *Management and Organization,* 6th ed. (Cincinnati, Ohio: South-Western, 1989), p. 601.
20. Comment made by W. J. Heisler in a book review appearing in *Personnel Psychology,* Spring 1983, p. 166.

SOME ADDITIONAL REFERENCES

Betz, Nancy, and Louise E. Fitzgerald. *The Career Psychology of Women,* San Diego, Calif.: Academic Press, 1987.

Hall, Douglas T., and Associates. *Career Development in Organizations.* San Francisco, Calif.: Jossey-Bass, 1986.

London, Manuel, and Edward M. Mone. *Career Management and Survival in the Workplace.* San Francisco, Calif.: Jossey-Bass, 1987.

Nusbaum, H. J. "The Career Development Program at Du Pont's Pioneering Research Laboratory," September 1986, pp. 68–75.

Raelin, Joseph A. *The Clash of Cultures: Managers and Professionals.* Cambridge, Mass.: Harvard Business School Press, 1986.

Vondracek, Fred W.; Richard M. Lerner; and John E. Schulenberg. *Career Development: A Life-Span Developmental Approach.* Hillsdale, N.J.: Erlbaum, 1986.

Appendix to Chapter Seventeen

THE CAREER DEVELOPMENT INVENTORY

Directions: Complete the following questionnaire for your personal use. You might wish to make up a worksheet before putting your answers in final form.

1. How would you describe yourself as a person?
2. What are you best at doing?
3. What are you worst at doing?
4. What are your two biggest accomplishments?
5. Write your own obituary as you would like it to appear at the termination of your life.
6. What would be the ideal job for you?
7. Why aren't you more rich and famous?
8. What career advice can you give yourself?
9. Describe the two peak experiences in your life.
10. What are your five most important values? (The things most important to you.)
11. What are my long-range work (professional) goals?

12. What are my intermediate-range work (professional) goals?
13. What are my short-range (professional) goals?
14. How realistic are those goals in terms of opportunities in my place of employment or in my field?
15. How well suited are my qualifications and skills for achieving those goals?
16. What personal improvements must I make to achieve my goals?
17. What do I want to achieve in my personal life?

Chapter Eighteen

Outplacement Programs

A company that owns and operates several groups of department stores, acquired another group of stores. After sorting out their need for executives, top management decided to terminate several senior managers. To assist these managers make the transition to other employment, the company contracted the services of an outplacement firm. One of the senior managers who was terminated describes her experiences with the outplacement program.

"Life looked pretty grim for me that unforgettable day in November, just last year. I was one of the taskforce members to help our company to decide whether or not to purchase the midwestern group of stores. My argument against the acquisition was that we would be diluting our strengths by purchasing stores that would serve the same markets we were already serving. I thought we would be better off rejuvenating some of our existing outlets. Maybe my negative vote put me on the hit list. Whatever the true reason, the president told me over lunch that my position would be terminated December 31. He told me not to take it personally—I wasn't being terminated, just my position. Because they had no other position to fit an executive of my stature, the only sensible alternative was to dismiss me.

"Unfortunately, at age 51 I still needed every penny of my salary and bonus. With a condo, two children, and a BMW, I could not live on unemployment insurance or a minimum-wage job. I had to find another top-level merchandising position. The next few days were definitely the most difficult. I knew that this was the worst possible time of the year to find a retailing job. Hiring for top jobs in the industry would be postponed until the results from the Christmas season were known. Besides that, it was general knowledge that once you hit age 50, jobs become much scarcer in retailing management.

"The president told me that in addition to four months' severance pay, I was entitled to receive outplacement counseling at the company's expense. According to Gary (the president, Gary Moran) the outplacement firm had an excellent reputation. They would help me overcome the natural trauma of being without a job, and they would help me quickly regain employment. I assumed wrong that the outplacement firm would match me up with one of many executive openings in their files. Later, I learned that finding you a job directly is not part of an outplacement firm's act.

"I showed up at Knoll and Houseman the following Monday morning because I didn't want to waste any time becoming re-employed. I gave the receptionist my name, assuming that she was expecting me. After a few minutes of checking, she told me to wait and that my counselor would be with me shortly.

"When the counselor met with me, he mentioned that I looked nervous and preoccupied. Of course, I was nervous and preoccupied. I felt frightened and humiliated, thus making me appear nervous. Somewhat to my disappointment, the counselor spoke with me for about 15 minutes. I was then ushered into a small conference room and told to take a group of tests and questionnaires. It was annoying to spend four hours taking tests because I wanted to jump right into looking for a job.

"After taking the tests and answering the many questions about myself, I began to see some purpose in what I was doing. The questions about my experiences and accomplishments were particularly helpful. They made me think about who I was professionally and where I had been. Up to that time, I hadn't given enough serious thought to the specific nature of the contribution I was making to my company.

"The counselor told me that my tests results showed that I was an intelligent, resourceful person, with no outstanding hangups that would prevent me from becoming re-employed at the appropriate level. He also told me that the questions I was forced to answer about myself provided the raw data I needed to prepare a good job résumé. Again, I was eager to start my job search, but I was sensible enough to realize that you needed a good résumé to get started.

"I was referred to a slick looseleaf binder containing models of good résumés. I found one that seemed well suited to my career, so I modeled mine after that. A résumé specialist on the staff then worked with me to perfect what I had developed. Three days later, she had 100 copies of my résumé ready, reproduced on high-quality paper.

"Next, I requested another meeting with my counselor. His schedule was full, so I had to wait two more days. I was getting a little anxious about the days rushing by. I also knew that it would be difficult to get many job interviews with the holidays coming up soon. But I was reassured by other clients sitting around the office that a job search takes longer than most people expect. A rule of thumb I heard was that to find a job it takes about one month for each $15,000 of annual income. If that were true, I could face an eight-month search. I decided to ignore that rule of thumb.

"My counselor told me that he was pleased with my progress, and that I was now ready to hone my self-marketing skills. This translated into my practicing how to speak to people over the phone about job openings and how to conduct myself in job interviews and informational interviews. The purpose of the informational interview was to speak to people about my interests but not to actually look for a job. I was pleasantly surprised to hear how well I sounded on tape and how professional I looked on videotape.

"With my pile of résumés at hand and the practice interviews under my belt, I felt ready to begin my formal job search. I asked my counselor where I should start sending my résumés. He told me that sending unsolicited résumés to prospective employers is too amateurish. Instead, he told me that I should use a cover letter to accompany each résumé and to send both to qualified leads.

"When I asked where I would find the list of qualified leads, my counselor told me that the leads would come through my contacts. My next assignment was to draw up a list of every possible person I knew who could conceivably help me find a suitable position or could refer me to someone who might help me. When I asked my counselor why I needed outplacement counseling if I generated my own leads, he replied: 'Our job is to help you find a job, not find a job for you. If you're looking for leads, write to executive search firms and employment agencies.'

"My counselor's comments sparked an important insight. The outplacement firm was a resource for helping find a new job, but it was only one resource. Fired up with that insight, I then pored over classified ads in national and local newspapers. I used the many directories in the Knoll and Houseman library to come up with a list of executive search firms who might help me. I ordered another 100 copies of my résumé.

"My job hunting had now become a 45-hour-per-week job. After having sent out about 50 résumés, I checked back in with my counselor to discuss my progress. He confronted me with the fact that I was taking the easiest and least efficient approach to finding a job. He told me to concentrate more on telephoning my contact list and setting up in-person appointments.

"I did line up about six people who said they would speak to me. It felt awkward asking professional acquaintances to help me find a job. I was supposed to appear cool and polished, but I felt like I was asking for handouts. A few people were cordial, but others treated me like I was wasting their time. The most painful part was watching my contacts squirm in their chairs and look at their watches.

"The holiday week was most depressing. I felt so desperate calling on people to help me find a job when most people were contemplating their year-end bonus.

"Each day I checked in at the outplacement office to see if there were any mail or phone messages for me. The first six responses to my letters of inquiry were basically form letters of rejection. The best response I received was a hand-written note from an old acquaintance wishing me good luck in getting back on track. Gradually I began to speak to other job seekers and Knoll and Houseman about my experiences. They were helpful in cheering me up and telling me not to be discouraged, that a good job was as close as my next interview.

"My first warm lead came the day after Martin Luther King, Jr.'s, Day. A department store in Chicago was looking for a general manager, and they thought I might qualify. They mentioned that the job would pay about $25,000 less than my last salary. Because it required a relocation and a substantial pay cut, I declined to fly out for an interview.

"Thirty more days went by with no apparent progress in getting myself re-employed. I received about 25 more rejection letters from retail organizations I had written to, either by an unsolicited letter or in response to a classified ad. No executive search firm I contacted showed any interest in me. Several of them told me that they would never touch an unemployed executive; their clients wanted them to find people working and at the peak of their careers.

"A promising lead finally turned up from an unexpected source. When my counselor practically forced me to contact everybody I knew, I scheduled a luncheon date with the former personnel director of our company who had since taken a job at a dress manufacturer. She told me that she had no leads for me at the time, but she would keep me in mind should any lead turn up. As it worked out, the secretary of the president of her company called me to say that the president wanted to talk to me in a hurry about a key job opening.

"I went for the interview the next day. The three top marketing people in the company had quit *en masse* to form their own competitive company. The president said he might be suing the three managers for breach of contract, but in the meantime he needed a marketing director in a hurry. I spent three hours at the company, visiting with the other managers at headquarters. I was told that if negotiations proceeded further, I would have to visit the company factories in Tennessee and Puerto Rico.

"With great enthusiasm, I requested another meeting with my counselor. He congratulated me on my progress and told me that since I would now probably begin to receive job offers, I should attend the negotiation workshop. It sounded like a good idea, so I did attend the next session. We were taught how to negotiate such things as equitable compensation, perks, an employment contract, and relocation allowance if needed.

"Two days later, the president did call me. He wanted to have lunch with me as soon as possible to carry our discussion one step further. During the main part of the meal, he went into great detail about the company's strengths and weaknesses. He told me the company needed an executive with a retailing background because large retailers were their primary market.

"As soon as the coffee was served, the president offered me the job at $5,000 more per year than I was making at my old job. Before he could practically finish his sentence, I said that I would take the job and that I would be thrilled to give the position my full professional effort. I wanted to communicate my true level of enthusiasm for the job before he changed his mind. Besides that, I didn't want to appear small-minded by asking about employee benefits. I figured I could learn about those later.

"The job has proved to be a challenge, and the firm had more problems than even the president knew about. The pressure is tremendous, but I feel I have grown professionally by getting executive experience in directing the marketing effort of a retailer. With this kind of experience, I might qualify for the presidency of a manufacturer or retailer in the future.

"I did get somewhat frustrated with the outplacement firm and with my counselor because it didn't seem like they were doing that much for me. Yet they did force me to make use of my contacts, and they helped me develop insight into conducting a job search. If I was forced to lay off a manager in my firm, I think I would refer that person to Knoll and Houseman."[1]

Outplacement Goals and Components

The outcome of the outplacement program described above was successful—the terminated executive was returned to appropriate employment.[2] She did not simply find a job, but she obtained a challenging position that fit her professional background. The major goal of an outplacement program, according to the president of a Cincinnati-based outplacement firm, "should be to provide a compassionate transition for employees who no longer fit into the corporate picture—for whatever reason."[3]

In the current era of downsizing, large numbers of managers and other employees are terminated by their employers. As a consequence, outplacement programs conducted by either the companies themselves or consulting firms have proliferated. It would be unusual to find a large organization that did not use outplacement services on laying off a large number of employees. The specific goals of these programs include the following:

Minimize the trauma of termination for employees and their families.

Help terminated individuals quickly develop a positive outlook, thus channeling energy and activity into constructive pursuits.

Provide a structure, sense of purpose, and direction for those who otherwise might be floundering.

Encourage participants to fully explore their skills, interests, and alternative career paths before embarking on a job search.

Enhance the probability of finding a rewarding and challenging position more easily, faster, and more economically.

Improve employee morale in relation to a layoff.

Promote a positive public image surrounding the outplacement.

Reduce costs associated with termination.[4] (Severance pay and insurance costs are lower when terminated employees become re-employed quickly.)

To achieve these goals, most outplacement programs have four components as would be implied from the Knoll and Houseman program. First is personal evaluation, whereby outplaced employees obtain a clear evaluation of themselves. Using tests, interviews, and other diagnostic procedures, outplacement counselors identify the counselee's strengths and weaknesses. Many outplacement firms hire licensed psychologists to conduct or supervise the personal evaluations. Former employees are also taught to identify their transferable skills and professional goals, so they can seek positions that will further their careers.

Second is counseling and coaching about such topics as résumé writing, job search techniques, using contacts to advantage, and interview techniques. When the job search lingers on, the candidates are provided with additional help, including gentle prodding to persist in the job search. (Discouragement, despair, and self-pity are common problems among laid-off managers.)

Third is institutional support in the form of a base of operations for conducting the job search. Included here are office space, telephones, clerical support, and photocopying privileges. Fourth is emotional support in the form of job seekers working together to help one another find a job. These people form their own support groups, discuss the job market, share tips, and bolster each others' egos.[5]

Some Research about Outplacement Programs

Relatively little formal research has been conducted about outplacement programs or services. Two exceptions are a pair of studies that included an assessment of participant reaction to outplacement. Information about both studies is presented in the following paragraphs.

Fortune 500 Firms.   William E. Fulmer examined management outplacement services from the point of view of practicing executives. Specifically, the objective was to learn how extensive the practice is and to learn what managers think of the service.

Methodology.   A two-page questionnaire was designed to learn first hand of the experiences executives had with management dismissals and with outplacement services in particular. The questionnaire was mailed to the chief operating officer of Fortune 500 firms. These firms were chosen because they represented a sample that was easily identified and because their size and financial strength gave them the resources necessary to set up outplacement services. The chief operating officer of each organization was chosen because the executive was not only currently in a position to discharge other managers but would probably have had to do so on a number of occasions. Fulmer expected the response rate from this sample to be small but that the experiences of those who responded would more than offset this advantage.

The usable response rate to the survey was 12.8 percent or 64 chief operating officers. The results of the questionnaire were tabulated, and a series of cross tabulations and chi-square tests were conducted to determine if there were any significant differences in various categories of chief operating officers. In particular, the differences between the experiences and opinions of long-term and short-term chief operating officers were examined.

Findings.   Exhibit 18–1 shows that most of these chief operating officers had fired several managers in recent years. In fact, one experienced executive had fired 100 managers in the last five years. Exhibit 18–2 shows that 62.5 percent (40/64) of all executives responding to the questionnaire reported that their corporation provided some form of

EXHIBIT 18–1   Number of Managers Fired in the Last Five Years *(by 63 Short-Term and Long-Term Chief Operating Officers (COOs))*

Number of Managers Fired	By Short-Term COOs		By Long-Term COOs		Total
	Observed	*Expected*	*Observed*	*Expected*	
0–5	32	29	13	16	45
6–100	8	11	10	7	18
Total	40		23		63

$x^2 = 2.88$, d.f. $= 1$, p $= .047$

EXHIBIT 18–2   Companies with Outplacement Services *(64 responses)*

Out-placement Services	Short-Term COOs		Long-Term COOs		Total
	Observed	*Expected*	*Observed*	*Expected*	*Total*
Yes	29	26	11	14	40
No	12	15	12	9	24
Total	41		23		64

$x^2 = 2.39$, d.f. $= 1$, $p = .12$

outplacement services to those managers who were fired. Although the difference in the prevalence of such services was not significant at the 10 percent level, this exhibit does show that companies headed by a relatively new chief operating officer seemed much more likely to make outplacement services available to the discharged managers. (In this study, COOs with six years or less in the job were considered short-term, while those with more than six years were considered long-term.)

The most common types of outplacement services provided by respondents were severance pay (35 percent), new employment assistance (35 percent), job contacts (15 percent), and personal counseling (14 percent). Most of these services, other than severance pay, were provided by outside consultants (79 percent) rather than in-house personnel (21 percent).

Although 75.8 percent of all executives responding to the questionnaire reported that their last discharge was either "difficult" or "very difficult," Exhibit 18–3 shows that the level of difficulty was greater for relatively new executives. While 28.2 percent (11/39) of all relatively new

EXHIBIT 18–3   Level of Difficulty of Last Firing of Subordinate *(62 responses)*

Level of Difficulty	Short-Term COOs		Long-Term COOs		Total
	Observed	*Expected*	*Observed*	*Expected*	*Total*
Not Difficult	6	10	9	6	15
Difficult	22	20	13	13	35
Very Difficult	11	8	1	5	12
Total	39		23		62

$x^2 = 7.63$, d.f. $= 2$, $p = .022$

executives described their last discharge experience as being "very difficult," only one experienced executive described this last experience in such a way. The difference in the perception of the two groups was significant at the 5 percent level.

Given the results shown in Exhibit 18–3, it is not too surprising that relatively new executives placed a significantly higher value on outplacement services than did experienced executives. As Exhibit 18–4 indicates, 33.3 percent (13/39) of all relatively new executives found outplacement services to be "very helpful" whereas only one of the more experienced executives found the service "very helpful." The difference in their perception was statistically significant at the 5 percent level.

Conclusions. Some form of management outplacement service is quite widespread among Fortune 500 firms, although in many cases such services involve little more than severance pay. Furthermore, most executives who responded to the questionnaire felt that the services were somewhat helpful. The most significant conclusion that can be drawn from the data is that relatively new executives were much more likely to value the help of outplacement services when faced with a management discharge than long-term executives.[6]

The present author's explanation of these findings is that the long-term executives may have developed more effective networks than the short-term executives by virtue of their longer experience. The long-term executives could more readily rely on their own resources in helping a dismissed manager find new employment and were therefore in less need of outplacement services.

Large, Medium, and Small Organizations. A more recent survey of outplacement services was conducted for the American Management Association by The Redford Group, Inc. One hundred companies of different sizes from a sample of 210 firms answered a variety of questions

EXHIBIT 18–4 Opinion of Outplacement Services *(61 responses)*

Opinion of Outplacement Services	Short-Term COOs		Long-Term COOs		Total
	Observed	*Expected*	*Observed*	*Expected*	
Very Helpful	13	9	1	5	14
Somewhat Helpful	20	22	14	12	34
Not Helpful	6	8	7	5	13
Total	39		22		61

$x2 = 7.25$, d.f. = 2, p = .026

about the outplacement services offered and the effectiveness of these services as perceived by the participants.

Scope of Services. Fifteen specific outplacement services were offered by the firms in the study. In order of frequency of use, they are as follows:

1. Résumé development.
2. Interview training.
3. Benefits counseling.
4. Skill/interest assessment.
5. Job market information.
6. Out-of-area job searches.
7. Mailings to other employers about available employees.
8. Follow-up services (offering long-term help to those in need).
9. Career resource center (including employment information, office supplies, and office equipment).
10. Counseling on personal finance.
11. Counseling on family matters.
12. Peer support groups.
13. On-site unemployment setup.
14. Remediation and basic education (including high-school equivalency exam preparation).

A general tendency was found for large firms to offer more services than small firms, yet small companies were the most likely to provide job market information. Large firms were more than twice as likely to provide financial or family counseling, and they were also more likely to provide a career resource center.

Effectiveness of the Services. Company officials were also asked which of the different outplacement services were the most effective. The response categories reported in the study are related to, but not identical, with the 15 benefits described above. As shown in Figure 18–1, management networking with area employers to develop employment opportunities was perceived to be the most helpful aspect of outplacement. Networking often consisted of managers in the outplacing company calling other managers in the area to explain that the employees being outplaced were of high quality.[7]

The Case for Outplacement Services

To the extent that outplacement programs achieve the goals described previously, they made a substantial contribution to individual and organizational welfare. Some of the more specific benefits of out-

FIGURE 18–1 Most Effective Outplacement Procedures as Perceived by Company Officials

	All	Size				Category			
		No Answer	Large	Mid	Small	Mfg.	Service	Other	No Answer
Management networking	43 46.2%	4 50.0%	9 42.9%	12 46.2%	18 47.4%	16 40.2%	21 50.0%	6 54.5%	0 0.0%
Paid time off for job search	29 33.3	3 37.5	5 26.3	8 36.4	13 34.2	11 39.3	13 27.7	5 41.7	0 0.0
Relocation opportunities at other company units	20 27.4	2 25.0	10 35.7	5 26.3	3 16.7	7 31.8	9 22.5	10 100.0	0 0.0
Liaison with private agency	15 28.8	2 50.0	5 45.5	3 16.7	5 38.5	5 29.4	8 36.4	2 33.3	0 0.0
Liaison with public agency	7 20.0	0 0.0	2 20.0	2 20.0	3 25.0	3 17.6	3 23.1	1 20.0	0 0.0
Job fairs	6 33.3	0 0.0	4 36.4	1 25.0	1 33.3	2 33.3	3 33.3	1 33.3	0 0.0
Job market data	2 18.2	1 100.0	0 0.0	1 100.0	0 0.0	1 33.3	1 16.7	0 0.0	0 0.0

SOURCE: Reprinted, by permission of the publisher, from Don Lee Bohl, *Responsible Reductions in Force, p. 77.* An American Management Association Research Report on Downsizing and Outplacement. © 1987 American Management Association, New York. All rights reserved.

placement programs are also worth noting. A major advantage of out-placement services is that, on average, 85 percent of the job seekers find a new position that is more satisfying and pays better than the one they lost.[8] The potential savings in human suffering, misery, and lives are therefore substantial. For example, suicide rates increase dramatically for dismissed workers.[9]

Outplacement programs are often cost-effective because they usually reduce the time required for a successful job search in half. As a result, less money is required for unemployment compensation and severance pay. If the length of unemployment is reduced, the employer's unem-ployment tax rate is reduced.[10] However, if the dismissed manager is given a lump sum severance payment independent of how long it takes to find a new position, no severance money is saved.

Outplacement services make a contribution in preventing public relations problems and morale problems. A resentful firee can do a lot of damage, making public complaints about the organization or passing trade secrets to competitors. Also, employee morale will be adversely affected if a former employee complains of unfair treatment or is known not to be able to find another job.

Successful outplacement can spare an organization from a serious public relations gaffe in the event of large-scale dismissals or the firing of a prominent company executive. Suits for wrongful discharge are less likely to occur when the fired manager receives the benefit of carefully conducted outplacement services. Because of these public relations and legal issues, major outplacement firms consult with public relations and legal professionals.[11]

A subtle advantage of outplacement services is that they contribute to a lean staffing philosophy. When effective outplacement services are available, there is a tendency to be less concerned that surplus employees will be unable to regain employment if they are dismissed.

Another advantage of outplacement is that it provides dismissed workers with the emotional support they vitally need when conducting a job search. The support comes from both counselors and other job seekers assigned to the same outplacement service.

Lastly, outplacement services are beneficial because they provide many dismissed workers with insights they can use in gaining new momentum to their careers. One outplaced executive said, "The out-placement counselor helped me realize that I had lost two key jobs because I was so rigid in my thinking. Once my mind was made up, I blocked out any new evidence that might make me rethink my position." A classic example of new career insights is provided by the president of the world's largest outplacement firm:

> Though not a gifted athlete, an executive from a financial institution loved sports fiercely, watching or playing just about every game he could. At

mid-life, he somehow lost interest in his work and eventually lost his job. The natural inclination, given his extensive business connections, was to land another similar position at a bank, insurance company, or Wall Street firm. However, outplacement analysis unearthed the financier's personal feelings. As a result, he took a gamble and accepted a financial manager's job with a small sporting goods manufacturer. He went on to buy the company and build it into a casebook success story, relishing every minute of the work as pure fun.[12]

The Case against Outplacement Services

Outplacement programs also have their disadvantages. A primary consideration is that their contribution may be overstated. Although they typically claim an 85 percent success rate, this figure might be inflated for two reasons. First, they often avoid taking on the most-difficult-to-place managers, thus decreasing their chances of lack of placement.[13] Second, is the issue of how much an outplacement service contributes beyond which job seekers could accomplish without the service. Specifically, the success rate of dismissed managers in finding new employment on their own might be close to the 85 percent success rate claimed by outplacement services.

A similar argument is that outplacement services do relatively little for individuals that they could not accomplish for themselves. Job seekers usually have to scour up their own job leads, including getting in touch with executive search firms. The outplacement firms are purposely not affiliated with employment agencies or executive search firms in order to avoid a conflict of interest. The conflict is that the outplacement firm might feel obliged to place a client with an affiliated employment agency even though he or she may not be qualified for a position.

Outplacement firms can also be criticized for placing people into humiliating situations just so it appears the client is making progress in finding employment. One such humiliating experience is being encouraged to obtain interviews with contacts who have no interest in trying to help the job seeker find new employment.[14]

Another concern about some outplacement firms is the qualifications of the counselors. Few of them are licensed mental-health practitioners and thus perhaps should not be dealing with such important issues as helping a person plan a comeback. Some of the people referred to outplacement services are really in need of psychological counseling in order to overcome the self-defeating behavior patterns that led to their dismissal. (In their defense, however, many outplacement firms refer emotionally distraught clients to other agencies for mental health assistance.)

A notable criticism of outplacement services is that they place too much emphasis on the marketing of employees. Using highly polished techniques, substandard employees are marketed into positions they are not qualified to fill. (Remember, however, that not all outplaced employees are poor performers. They may be declared surplus because of a merger or for political reasons.) Also, employers may be deceived into believing that certain applicants are more qualified than they are. Often this process leads to putting the same employees in a situation where they will once again be forced to look for new employment.[15]

Guidelines for Action and Skill Development

Full-service outplacement service is costly and usually reserved for middle- and upper-level management. Corporations generally feel more obliged to help higher-level managers with outplacement because these workers are more likely to have made a greater contribution to the organization's success during their employment. Lower-level management and nonexempt employees are more likely to be provided with partial or group outplacement services.[16] For example, Drake Beam Morin, Inc., the largest outplacement firm, offers a group outplacement counseling workshop that is recommended for employees whose salary is less than $35,000 per year

The individual who is outplaced should not expect the outplacement firm to take over his or her job campaign. Outplacement firms serve as coaches who guide the individual through the process, but they do not assume responsibility for finding people a job. As explained by Richard E. Miller, "In its finest form, outplacement counseling is simply a counseling relationship with the counselor as a tool, a resource, a helping hand."[17]

The counselor is the heart of the outplacement service. The two essential components of an effective and successful counseling relationship are the following: (1) sympathetic counseling to facilitate the separation (effective counseling includes knowing when to be supportive and when to push the client toward certain ends) and (2) strategic advice and counsel on conducting a successful job search. Understanding what qualifications employers are seeking is critical.[18]

Should your organization refer you for outplacement services, do not regard it as a personal tragedy. Being dismissed at least once during a managerial career has become commonplace.

DISCUSSION QUESTIONS AND ACTIVITIES

1. How could a human resources department demonstrate the cost-effectiveness of an outplacement program?

2. If you were a hiring manager, would you look to job seekers from an outplacement firm as a source of management talent? Why or why not?

3. How might a company offering outplacement services boost the morale of employees who have still not found employment?

4. Should an employee who has been discharged for poor performance be offered outplacement counseling? Why or why not?

5. Assume that you were making an annual salary of $50,000 and that your employer dismissed you. You were then told that you could receive company-paid outplacement counseling or receive $7,500 in cash (the outplacement fee). Which alternative would you choose and why?

6. Is outplacement simply a euphemism for "firing somebody in a nice way"?

7. Several outplacement firms allow the job seeker several months to use a private cubicle while job hunting. After that the person is moved to a bull pen arrangement with about 10 desks. What do you think of the fairness of this practice?

NOTES

1. Case researched by Vashuda Badri.
2. Richard E. Miller, "Outplacement Myths Unlock the Mystery of Its Ineffectiveness," *Personal Journal,* January 1987, p. 26.
3. "Outplacement Counseling Services," *Research Institute Personal Report for the Executive,* January 21, 1986, p. 5.
4. Brochure from Drake Beam Morin, Inc., 1988.
5. "Outplacement Counseling Services," p. 5.
6. Research adapted and reprinted from William E. Fulmer, "Management Outplacement Services: A View from the Top," *Personnel,* September 1985, pp. 18–19.
7. Don Lee Bohl, ed., *Responsible Reductions in Force,* An American Management Association Research Report on Downsizing and Outplacement (New York: AMACOM, 1987), pp. 60–83.
8. John Stodden, "Outplacement: Starting Over after You're Fired," *Business Week's Guide to Careers,* September 1985, p. 31.
9. Angelo Kinicki and associates, "Socially Responsible Plant Closings," *Personnel Administrator,* June 1987, p. 116.
10. Richard Hoban, "The Outplacement Option: Everybody Wins!" *Personnel Administrator,* June 1987, p. 187.
11. Stodden, "Outplacement," p. 32.
12. Ibid., p. 33.
13. Ibid.
14. Gerald C. Parkhouse, "Inside Outplacement—My Search for a Job," *Harvard Business Review,* January–February 1988, p. 70.
15. Joel A. Bearak, "Termination Made Easier: Is Outplacement Really the Answer?" *Personnel Administrator,* April 1982, p. 71.
16. Hoban, "The Outplacement Option," p. 191.

17. Miller, "Outplacement Myths," p. 30.
18. Loretta D. Foxman and Walter L. Polsky, "Career Counselor," *Personnel Journal,* November 1985, p. 35.

SOME ADDITIONAL REFERENCES

"Career Counselor: How to Select a Good Outplacement Firm." *Personnel Journal,* September 1984, pp. 94–97.

Duffy, Elaine M., and associates. "Behavioral Outplacement: A Shorter, Sweeter Approach." *Personnel,* March 1988, pp. 28–33.

Feldman, Diane. "Helping Displaced Workers: The UAW–GM Human Resource Center." *Personnel,* March 1988, pp. 34–36.

Kracki, Thomas J. "Outplacement en Masse: A Marketing Approach." *Personnel Administrator,* May 1987, pp. 90–94.

Piccolino, Edmund B. "Outplacement: The View from HR." *Personnel,* March 1988, pp. 24–27.

Chapter Nineteen

Gainsharing

> Long before the company opened an axle-manufacturing division, management decided to make maximum use of its human resources. The method management chose to accomplish this goal was gainsharing—a group incentive program that enables employees to share in the financial benefits of any improvements in productivity.

There are no supervisors at the Dana Spicer Heavy Axle Division facility in Hilliard, Ohio. In a recent year, the plant had $150 million in sales of their heavy truck axles, but not one of its operative workers punched a time clock or reported to a supervisor. To accomplish the goal of self-management, the company implemented a group bonus system referred to as a *performance gainsharing plan*. The plan makes provision for teams that allow nonmanagement personnel to be directly involved in decisions about how their work methods can be improved.

The Performance Gainsharing Plan. The self-management concept at Dana Spicer is based on the belief that all employees in the facility share common goals. Under the gainsharing plan, the current performance of the division is compared to a targeted level of performance. During a period in which actual performance exceeds the target, employees earn a bonus paid as a percent of their wages. The size of the bonus varies according to the amount of improvement. *Performance* at Dana Hilliard is defined as a ratio of labor costs to output.

Each work area has a team consisting of one to three nonmanagement employees, as well as a staff representative. Their job is to solicit ideas from the people in their area, investigate the feasibility of the ideas, and implement acceptable ones. Although most ideas are implemented at this level, those costing more than a certain dollar limit affecting more than one work unit are reviewed by a larger, plantwide team.

The larger screening committee consists of management, staff, and a nonmanagement representative from each team. It reviews the more ambitious ideas (such as redesigning the layout for assembling an axle) and facilitates cooperation between shifts and work units in setting goals, identifying problems, and improving the quality and quantity of suggestions.

The Making of Self-Managers.   When the plant opened a few years ago, the bulk of the work force had previously worked as supervised hourly production workers from largely unionized firms in the area. At Dana Hilliard they were put on salary and told that no supervisor would be looking over their shoulders. How hard they would work and what work methods they would use would be up to them. The object was to create a work force in which all employees cooperated in establishing and working toward common objectives.

From the outset, management established unusually high standards in selecting employees for the new operation. Applicants went through a series of multiple interviews with the personnel manager and plant manager. Employees were screened for blueprint reading ability and previous experience with assembly-type factory work. The successful candidate at Dana Hilliard had to demonstrate qualities such as initiative and a team-oriented attitude. The company was advised by a consultant that the gainsharing plan would work only to the extent that employees had the desire to generate good ideas, communicate them freely, make decisions on their own, and cooperate with other employees.

Once each month, most of the production workers are rotated to different jobs. The purpose is to teach each worker how to do every other job in the shop. "Here we want our people to know more than how to tighten up a few nuts on a few bolts," said Steve Cobb, plant manager. "We want them to understand how to assemble a total axle so that regardless of what job they are performing, they know that's contributing to the job coming ahead and the one that came from behind.

"I think that, as a result, we are building a better quality product. They can see the total picture—they're better informed about the product. Almost every single person out in this plant could take an axle and from scratch put the whole thing together."

Upward communication at Dana Hilliard is facilitated by the gainsharing plan's suggestion system that allows any person in the firm to have his or her idea formally investigated for effectiveness. In this way, bugs in the operation that may have been missed by engineering or management are caught and corrected. Everyone has a tool to make things happen.

Lateral communication is also enhanced because interteam meetings are a formal part of the system. When one area's team is working on a production problem that involves another area, they are encouraged to contact that team to work things out. Additional problems are brought up at the company-wide screening committee meeting each month, where all departments may work on problems together.

The company has a mechanism to see that employees get the feedback they need about their productivity and quality in a gainsharing program. Management holds a monthly meeting with employees to review the performance of both the Hilliard facility and the division as a whole. Each of the factors determining the earning of a gainsharing bonus is discussed, and those forces hurting the bonus (and productivity) are singled out. One month it may be unusually high material costs; in another, labor costs. This gives the workers an area to target for improvement in the coming month.

The only quality inspectors at Dana Hilliard are those who inspect materials coming into the plant. None is on the lines, because every employee serves as his or her own inspector. When a finished product comes off of the end of the line, it goes straight onto the truck. For practical purposes, the shipping department has been eliminated.

The employee's dual role as production worker and inspector is taken seriously. Anyone in the shop has the authority to shut down operations if he or she feels something is wrong with the quality of the product. They know that if it is unsatisfactory and comes back from the customer, the cost of the returned product is doubled and subtracted from any earned bonus.

Challenges in Implementing the Plan.   Substantial planning went into each step of the gainsharing plan, beginning with calculating the bonus. Dana Hilliard employees earn a financial bonus when productivity improves. Productivity is calculated as a ratio of labor costs to sales. Labor costs include direct and indirect labor salaries, overtime premium, absenteeism, rework, and related items. In a month in which the actual ratio of labor costs to sales is less than a specific targeted ratio, a bonus is awarded. Because the facility had only been in operation one year, it made sense to adjust the bonus calculation with a moving base periodically to "tighten it up," reflecting technological and other changes. Employees at Hilliard accepted the adjustments.

Management at Dana took deliberate steps to establish a participative culture. From the beginning, employees knew that participation was part of their job description. During a three-day orientation program prior to beginning work on the shop floor, all new hires went through the gainsharing plan guidelines and learned what would be expected of them. On a continuing basis after that, they received training in problem solving, team concept, motivation, and other participation-related skills that they need to make a real contribution.

Another approach to strengthening the participative culture is management's sharing of information with employees. Cobb explains, "How can you expect people to work with half a set of facts or with no facts? How can you ask them to work toward a common goal when they don't know where the product fits or how much it's going to sell for or how much it's going to cost to make it? How can people be expected to improve simply by someone just telling them that they've got to improve? People don't accept that. They've got to understand where their effort fits in with the total scheme of business activity."

Dana Hilliard has taken steps to ensure that a steady stream of suggestions stems from the gainsharing plan. During the company's first year under the plan, 115 suggestions were contributed. The number rose to 285 during the second year and stood at 400 by the middle of their third year.

Results of the Program.   The company and its employees are very pleased with the program. Direct labor efficiency during the third year of the plan was 45 percent higher than that experienced the year prior to implementation. Assembly scrap level and rework were cut in half over a two-year period. The gains in quality allowed the company to issue a 500,000 mile warranty on axles, unusual in the industry. The sales per employee were considerably higher than the industry average.

Job security has also been improved as a result of the gainsharing plan. Dave Bockman, personnel manager, notes, "Being more efficient has brought in more job security. With one suggestion, we were able to eliminate inventory. By eliminating inventory and going onto the just-in-time concept, we have cleared up floor space and made it available for more production. I've just finished hiring 21 people. We have never had a layoff in this plant, even during the downturn, even when everyone else was laying off."

Along with the job security, Dana Hilliard employees have also enjoyed substantial productivity bonuses. The gainsharing plan provided average monthly bonuses of approximately 12 percent and 16 percent for two consecutive years. Year-end bonuses of 11 percent and 16 percent were earned during the same years. And during the first five months of the latest year under the plan, monthly bonuses were averaging more than 20 percent.[1]

Goals and Typical Results of Gainsharing Plans

Gainsharing plans take on several different forms. The gainsharing plan at Dana Hilliard is carefully developed and provides insight into the nature of these plans. Additional insight about these plans can be obtained through a description of their typical goals and results.

Purposes of Gainsharing Plans.   The ultimate goal of any gainsharing plan is to improve productivity, whether the plan is implemented in a private or public organization. Goals of gainsharing plans include the following:

1. To increase employee involvement in the improvement of company performance.
2. To increase employee motivation and job satisfaction.
3. To improve the quality of work life within an organization.
4. To improve communications and cooperation between departments.
5. To give recognition for good work at the individual, departmental, and company level.
6. To provide employees' understanding of the problems and opportunities of the company, industry, and country.
7. To encourage employees at all levels to identify and help solve problems.

The gainsharing plan at Dana Hilliard achieved some of these goals including improved productivity and communications and cooperation. For example, as a result of the program scrap level and rework were reduced, and management shared much more information with operative employees.

Typical Results.   Based on their personal involvement with gainsharing plans, Larry L. Hatcher and Timothy L. Ross have reported on some of the potential results of gainsharing.

Identity.   When gainsharing is successful, an organization has "identity"—most of its members are familiar with its history and plans, and they share the same image of the organization. Employees at middle and lower levels perceive a meshing of organizational and individual goals. They believe that they will enjoy job security, increased job satisfaction, and cash bonuses as long as the company prospers, and they feel important because they understand their contribution to the company's success. At the same time, executives develop a recognition of and sensitivity to the goals of employees.

Employee Involvement.   Employee involvement is the underlying mechanism of most gainsharing plans. All of these plans capitalize on the knowledge of nonmanagement personnel, including operative employees. Employee involvement is so important for the success of gainsharing that most plans provide a formal system for obtaining the input of employees. Typically a two-tier system of committees reviews improvement ideas and facilitates communication across departments and between management and employees. A system used in a specific company works like this:

> Each department elects a team of one supervisor and one or more employee representatives. (Some companies pattern their involvement systems after quality circles by asking for volunteers to join teams.) Every team meets at least monthly to review employee ideas for productivity improvement in the department; it may implement those ideas that seem workable and will cost less than $200.
>
> More expensive suggestions, along with the teams' cost-benefits assessments, are referred to the plantwide review team of department, management, and union representatives. This larger group also meets monthly to monitor the departmental teams' activities, perform special duties, review the more ambitious suggestions, discuss the financial performance of the gainsharing plan, review overall company performance, and give employee representatives the chance to discuss their concerns with management and get new information that used to be unavailable to them.[3]

An involvement system helps build identity and commitment, yet a few gainsharing plans are basically group incentive systems that do not solicit employee input.

Cooperation. In companies with gainsharing plans, employees learn quickly that the company's success, and their own opportunity to earn bonuses, depends heavily on their ability to work cooperatively in the pursuit of shared goals. Because employees comprehend that *company results are what count*, they realize that they must learn about other departments and look at the bigger picture.

Sharing the Gains. The bonus allows employees to share the gains obtained through hard work. Calculating the bonus can be relatively uncomplicated such as the bonus ratio used at Dana Hilliard, or as complicated as calculating a profit-sharing bonus. Productivity can be interpreted to include quality levels, costs, and the quality of customer service. (At Dana Hilliard, a stiff penalty was imposed for any merchandise rejected by customers.) Plans can be designed around the goal of beating a target performance level, earning a specified return on investment, or bettering past performance (the most frequently used alternative).

The best-known plans, IMPROSHARE ©, the Rucker ©, and the Scanlon plan, each use different formulas. Many companies devise a formula best suited to their particular circumstances.

Research Evidence about Gainsharing Plans

The gainsharing plan at Dana Hilliard has been quite successful. Its philosophy of self-management, however, is best suited to smaller facilities where there are a small number of employees, a flat organization structure, fewer lines of communication, and single product that is not particularly complex.[4] Other gainsharing plans in a variety of settings have yielded good results. Published reports of unsuccessful plans are difficult to find.

The GAO Study. A U.S. General Accounting Office (GAO) investigated 36 manufacturing facilities that had implemented some form of gainsharing. The results showed the following results:

Companies with average sales of less than $100 million averaged annual work force savings (fewer employees required to accomplish the same amount of work) of 17.3 percent.

Companies with average sales of equal to or more than $100 million averaged annual work force savings of 16.4 percent.

- 80.6 percent reported improved labor-management relations.
- 47.2 percent had fewer grievances.
- 36.1 percent had less absenteeism.
- 36.1 percent had reduced turnover.[5]

The GAO is updating this study, and reports suggest that the findings are comparable—gainsharing plans are still achieving their goals.

Volvo. The Volvo plant at Kalmar, Sweden, has been engaged in gainsharing for several years in addition to their self-managing work teams. Kalmar workers receive their bonus twice per year, even though the results portion is calculated every 14 days. Seven bonus factors are (1) capital costs for total inventories; (2) man-hours per car, direct and indirect production workers; (3) consumption of added materials; (4) consumption of materials and supplies; (5) spoilage and adjustments; (6) quality index (based on a point-scoring system; and (7) hours worked by office workers.

The gainsharing program was favorably received by most of the employees, and a few quantitative results were obtained that relate directly to productivity and quality. Since the inception of gainsharing, capital costs for total inventories have declined substantially. The index of man-hours per car has reflected a steady decline of about five points per year. Some of this decline can be attributed to an improved operating system developed by industrial engineers. A survey of employee opinion indicated that 82 percent of employees believed that gainsharing stimulated their interest in achieving high quality.[6]

Duncan Manufacturing. Gainsharing produced good results at Duncan Manufacturing (a fictitious name for a real firm). A variety of analyses compared results of the 12-month period before implementation with those of the 18-month period following implementation. Financial improvements included a 49 percent reduction in scrap costs, a 17.3 percent increase in direct-labor efficiency, a 14.5 percent reduction in warranty costs, and a 6.6 percent reduction in indirect labor costs. Grievances dropped from 120 to 10, and all 10 were settled without arbitration.

Employee surveys revealed an increase in overall worker attitudes. Eighteen percent more employees thought interdepartmental cooperation was average or above average. Attitudes about a variety of other facets of morale increased, and 95 percent of employees voted to continue with the plan.

The researchers of this study note that the findings are impressive because economic conditions prohibited large bonuses. During the 18-month period, only eight bonuses were awarded, none of which exceeded more than 6 percent of employees' pay.[7]

Scanlon Plans and Lincoln Electric. Earlier research on gainsharing programs investigated the effectiveness of Scanlon plans and the profit-sharing program at Lincoln Electric Company. A study was conducted of 23 companies using the Scanlon plan, some of which had used the plan for many years. Eleven of the companies had achieved good results with the plan; 12 companies abandoned the plan because it either never led to productivity improvements or had lost its effectiveness.[8]

Lincoln Electric, a manufacturer of arc-welding equipment, has been the site of perhaps the most publicized example of gainsharing. Generous profit-sharing bonuses to employees have helped the company remain a leader in its field for over 50 years. It is not unusual for the average Lincoln Electric employee to receive a year-end bonus equivalent to his or her regular salary. Since the plan's inception in 1934, the company has paid more in annual bonuses than in base pay.[9] The assumption made by many managers and researchers is that the high level of employee motivation induced by gainsharing is largely responsible for the outstanding productivity.

Advantages of Gainsharing

As the research evidence suggests, gainsharing can contribute to improvements in productivity, quality, and job satisfaction and therefore should be given serious consideration by human resource managers and other executives. Testimonials for gainsharing claim that the method has improved product quality, improved the use of capital, reduced scheduling and delivery delays, reduced scrap, improved the quality of supervision, reduced unemployment, improved wage and benefit systems, and significantly raised employee satisfaction.[10]

An impressive advantage of gainsharing is that it may achieve important results other than those attributed to people striving to earn financial bonuses. A former director of human resources at the Marine Systems Division of Honeywell said that the gainsharing program should continue even if no money was distributed (i.e., gains were never shared). This is true because the large number of employees involved believe that gainsharing is a better way to manage, and they feel more effective by being part of the process. According to Rosabeth Moss Kanter, the most obvious benefit has come from the mechanism's fostering employees' opportunities to participate in new ways, and not from the prospect of financial remuneration.[11]

Another potential advantage of gainsharing is that it ends the squabbling over merit pay and the size of individual salary increases and bonuses. The people involved in most gainsharing plans receive group rather than individual bonuses on top of regular salaries and cost-of-living adjustments. (As described below, this could also be a disadvantage.)

Disadvantages of Gainsharing

Despite its glowing advantages, gainsharing can be criticized on several grounds. A leading concern is the "free rider" issue, in which a few low-performing members benefit from the hard work of the high-performing members. Resentment builds up when the poor performers receive the same bonus as everybody else.

Gainsharing plans also exert considerable pressure on people to perform well and reduce costs. A compensation expert reports that in the Dutch company, Philips, the twice-yearly bonuses can run up to 40 percent of base pay. "Managers say that a paper clip never hits the floor—a hand will be there to catch it. If a husband dies, the wake is at night so that no one misses work. If someone goes on vacation, somebody else is shown how to do the job. There is practically no turnover."

Similarly, at Lincoln Electric, peer pressure can be so great that the first two years of employment are called purgatory.[12] Another manifestation of the urge to cut costs in order to increase profits is that some managers will deliberately understaff in order to save money. A disadvantage is that some important tasks will go unattended that could strengthen the organization.

Gainsharing plans run into potential trouble when losses, rather than gains, are to be shared. Employees anticipate sharing in profits and may become disgruntled when they receive no bonus or are asked to receive a pay cut. The problem is particularly acute when employees receive over 25 percent of their compensation in bonuses.

Finally, some gainsharing programs have failed. Michael Schuster notes, "Most managers and companies have been led to believe that there is no downside risk. This is not the case." Some of the failures center on a concern of employees that they have not received a fair bonus. When bonuses are less than expected, serious morale problems may result.[13] A problem of this nature took place in a company operating under a Scanlon plan. Several workers complained that the company kept two sets of books and manipulated the bonus to exploit the workers. Also, some workers wanted to replace the incumbent union officials for cooperating in a speedup.[14]

Guidelines for Action and Skill Development

Similar to many methods of employee involvement, gainsharing plans often experience a quick plateauing of interest and results. Worthwhile suggestions about pressing problems are quickly used up. The antidote is to "feed the plan." Managers at all levels should be encouraged to submit the major operational problems facing them to the attention of the employee-involvement committees.[15]

The employee-involvement aspects of gainsharing might be initiated on an experimental basis. Supervisors who have high credibility among operative employees, peers, and supervisors should be encouraged to assume leadership roles at the outset. As more employees welcome the idea of making suggestions for improvement, the involvement program can be expanded.[16]

Executives responsible for a gainsharing plan must be prepared to engage in open communication with organizational members about organizational goals and organizational performance. If employees' bonuses are based in part on profits, they need to know how the company is performing and how the employee percentage is calculated.[17]

Some allowance may have to be made for rewarding exceptional individual performance within a gainsharing plan to satisfy the aspirations of some high achievers. A small individual incentive can be introduced into the total bonus program. Perhaps 5 to 10 percent of the bonus can be based on individual performance.

DISCUSSION QUESTIONS AND ACTIVITIES

1. What do you see as the difference between gainsharing and a typical profit-sharing program?

2. What similarity, if any, do you see between gainsharing and quality circles?

3. Assume that you are the manufacturing vice president of a large firm that recently implemented a gainsharing program. Explain whether or not you would be willing to abolish the quality department?

4. How well might gainsharing work in a bank?

5. How well might gainsharing work in a low-technology operation such as a pet kennel?

6. How well might gainsharing work at individual McDonald's restaurants?

7. What is your reaction to the following statement made by consultant, Karl F. Simpson, Jr.? "Management would be well advised to avoid gainsharing and the silly charade of giving away money in the vague hope that the bonus being paid represents a reward for increased labor and productivity. More time and money should be spent teaching managers the economic purpose of management and training them in the use of good, not necessarily popular, management practices."

NOTES

1. Excerpted and adapted with permission from Larry Hatcher, Timothy L. Ross, and Ruth Ann Ross, "Gainsharing: Living Up to Its Name," *Personnel Administrator,* June 1987, pp. 153–62.

2. Goals 1 and 3 through 7 are from Larry L. Hatcher and Timothy L. Ross, "Organization Development through Productivity Gainsharing," *Personnel,* October 1985, p. 44.

3. Ibid., pp. 42–45; the quote is from pp. 44–45.

4. Hatcher, Ross, and Ross, "Gainsharing," p. 162.

5. Reported in Hatcher and Ross, "Organization Development through Productivity Gainsharing," p. 49.

6. William C. Hauck and Timothy L. Ross, "Sweden's Experiments in Productivity Gainsharing," *Personnel,* January 1987, pp. 61–67.

7. Hatcher and Ross, "Organization Development through Productivity Gainsharing," p. 50.

8. J. Kenneth White, "The Scanlon Plan: Causes and Correlates of Success," *Academy of Management Review,* June 1979, pp. 292–312.

9. Charles Hillinger, "Big Bonuses at Lincoln Electric Get Big Results," *Professional Trainer,* Winter 1983, p. 1.

10. Robert J. Doyle. *Gainsharing and Productivity: A Guide to Planning, Implementation and Development* (New York: AMACOM, 1983).

11. Rosabeth Moss Kanter, "From Status to Contribution: Some Organizational Implications of the Changing Basis for Pay," *Personnel,* January 1987, p. 31.

12. Rosabeth Moss Kanter, "The Attack on Pay," *Harvard Business Review,* March–April 1987, p. 65.

13. Kanter, "From Status to Contribution," p. 33.

14. James W. Driscoll, "Working Creatively with a Union: Lessons from the Scanlon Plan," *Organizational Dynamics,* Summer 1979, p. 67.

15. Ibid., p. 73.
16. Michael H. Schuster and Christopher S. Miller, "Employee Involvement: Making Supervisors Believers," *Personnel,* February 1985, p. 28.
17. Driscoll, "Working Creatively with a Union," p. 73.

SOME ADDITIONAL REFERENCES

Denton, D. Keith. "An Employee Ownership Program that Rebuilt Success." *Personnel Journal,* March 1987, pp. 114–20.

Graham-Moore, Brian E., and Timothy L. Ross. *Productivity Gainsharing.* Englewood Cliffs, N.J.: Prentice-Hall, 1983.

Muczyk, Jan P., and Bernard C. Reimann. "Has Participative Management Been Oversold?" *Personnel,* May 1987, pp. 52–57.

Rosen, Corey M.; Katherine J. Klein; and Karen M. Young. *Employee Ownership in America: The Equity Solution.* Lexington, Mass.: Lexington Books, 1986.

Tharp, Charles G. "Linking Annual Incentives and Individual Performance." *Personnel Administrator,* January 1986, pp. 85–90.

Chapter Twenty

Telecommuting

A profitable travel agency faced two challenges simultaneously: more office space was needed, and the turnover of the technical support staff had become unacceptably high. The agency attempted to solve these problems by implementing a program of telecommuting—allowing some employees to conduct their work from home and communicate with the office by computer, telephone, and mail.

Susan Lepsch and Russel Stratton, co-owners of Lepsch and Stratton Travel Agency, met for breakfast at 7:30 on the first Monday in July. "Sue, this is it," said Russ. "Today is the first working day of the second half of the year. Either we take decisive action, or we stop complaining about too little office space and too much turnover. My latest figures show that we should expand from 4,000 to 5,000 square feet. We are currently paying $13 per square foot; new space in an office the size we want would cost approximately $16 per square foot. That's too much money. Our other overhead costs are also rising. Our volume of business isn't large enough to gamble on being able to cover that much increase in expenses."

Sue nodded in agreement before saying, "I get your point, Russ. If we expand to the amount of space we require, we'll be paying a premium rate on the entire floor space, not just the additional 1,000 square feet. As strange as it may sound, my digging into this matter may have uncovered a program that will take care of the space and turnover problem at the same time.

"My contacts in the human resources field tell me that one of the best ways to keep good office help is to give them a work schedule that makes life easy. We've been using flexible working hours for some time. It did reduce turnover at first, but once most small offices in the area offered flexible working hours, we lost our competitive advantage. What's hot now is letting some of your office help work out of their homes. It's called *telecommuting* or *teleworking*. If we had enough of our support staff working out of their homes, we could get by without the additional space."

"I'm willing to give the program a shot on the voluntary basis," said Russ. "With whom do you think we should start?"

"The likely candidates in our office are the five support specialists and one direct mail specialist. Those people could do a substantial portion of their work at home if they had the right equipment. Gaining access to our files from home would be the biggest hurdle. We could meet with them about once every 10 days in the office just to cordinate matters and let them know that we still care about them." Sue and Russ identified four volunteers for the telecommuting program.

September 1 was the launching date for telecommuting at the agency. The biggest equipment problem was to supply each telecommuter with a personal computer and modem for interfacing with computers at the office. Two of the telecommuters volunteered to use their own personal computers; two computers were transferred from the agency to the homes of the employees. The direct mail specialist took home an electronic typewriter to supplement the personal computer assigned to her. In addition, she was assigned combination fax machine and telephone.

During mid-November, Sue and Russ decided to evaluate how well the telecommuting program was working. To that date, neither partner had heard of any substantial complaint about the program either from the employees or from clients because of poor service. Sue and Russ agreed that it was important to evaluate the program because the current lease would expire at the end of March. If the program were working well, the present space could be retained, thus avoiding the expense and effort of relocation.

Sue began her evaluation of telecommuting by describing her experiences in supervising the work of Kim and Betty. "I was worried about the possibility of Kim not doing her job because she wasted time on the telephone. That proved not to be a problem. If Kim was gabbing on the phone excessively, it didn't drag down her productivity. She did all the work that was required.

"A problem did arise, however, that I didn't anticipate. After the first two weeks of the plan, both Kim and Betty seemed to get their week's quota done by Thursday morning. They would then have a day and a half to do whatever they wanted. I couldn't complain because they met their quota. Yet, if they were in the office, somebody could have found something constructive for them to do."

Russ spoke to Carol, the direct mail specialist, about her experiences with working out of her home. Carol replied, "My reaction has been mixed. Some parts of being a telecommuter are good, some parts are not so good. I enjoy being treated like a true professional. Nobody has to watch over me to see that I get my work done. I like saving commuting time so I have a little more time for reading the newspaper and taking care of errands.

"What I don't like is being so alienated from the office. I want to move up to supervisor if our agency expands substantially. If you two hardly ever see me, I could easily be passed over for promotion."

Sue asked Diane, one of the support specialists, for her reaction to working out of her home. With a gleam in her eye and a smile, Diane replied, "Telecommuting has helped make my life work. My biggest problem before working at home was that I had a latch-key child. Trevor, my son, is too old for child care, yet too young to be home unsupervised. He gets home around 3:15 in the afternoon. When he gets home, he knows I'm working, but it's better than my not being on the premises. By not worrying so much about Trevor on my working days, I feel much less stressed and much better able to concentrate on my work.

"Another great thing about having my office in my home is that the cost of working is gradually going down. Gas, lunches out with the gang from the office, and buying all those extra panty hose can add up. I can imagine that over a period of one year, being a telecommuter could save me about $1,200."

Russ interviewed Tony, one of the support specialists, about his experiences as a teleworker. "On a scale of 1 to 10," said Tony, "I would rate teleworking a 5. Sure, I like being able to avoid commuting on a day with inclement weather. And I like getting home from work at 4:31 after having stopped work at 4:30. The pay is the same so I have no complaints there."

"What reservations do you have?" asked Russ.

"To be frank," said Tony, "I miss the interaction with my office buddies. I never wanted to be a loner. If I did, I would have become a forest ranger. When I was at school, I studied in the library rather than at home for the same reason. I like people. I like taking coffee breaks with co-workers. At home, I drink my coffee at my desk. For a break, I take out the garbage. If I'm lucky I say hello to the garbage collector or to the mail carrier.

"To make matters worse, one of my neighbors brought me over some food and clothing. She thinks I've been laid off. I guess that being a telecommuter doesn't give others the impression that you're a big success."

After this round of interviews, Sue and Russ expressed optimism that telecommuting could make a contribution to the Lepsch and Stratton Agency. Sue mentioned, however, "I don't know how far we will go with telecommuting. But I do know that we will always need somebody around the office to talk to our clients both in person and on the phone."[1]

Telecommuting Principles and Procedures

The travel agency that decided to implement a program of telecommuting is not acting alone. Approximately 2.3 million people in the United States do some or all of their office work at home. Among these are 30,000 full-time telecommuters. A consistent prediction is that by 1990, the United States work force will include 20 million full-time telecommuters.[2] These estimates include both corporate employees (the "true" telecommuters), free-lance creative workers, and contract workers who are essentially temporary workers.

Enough momentum has been gathered with teleworking to specify some principles and procedures worth considering when conducting a formal telecommuting program within an organization.

Select the Right Jobs for Telework. As the two travel agency partners observed, not all jobs are suitable for teleworking. Marcia M. Kelly, a specialist in providing telecommuting equipment, notes that there are certain criteria to be met if a job is to be well suited for telework. The following checklist covers the questions that must be answered affirmatively when analyzing the potential of a job for telecommuting:

1. Does the job involve routine information handling?
2. Is there a high daily or weekly use of the telephone?
3. Is there relatively little face-to-face contact?
4. If the face-to-face contact is high, can the contact be scheduled so that the other independent tasks can be handled from a remote location?
5. Are terminals necessary for the job or can they be employed to accomplish a large part of the work?
6. Are job activities project-oriented so that tasks have an organized flow of information in a defined span of time?
7. Are there defined milestones or checkpoints in doing the work or components that can be delivered at certain times?
8. Is the job sufficiently self-contained so that it can be performed independently of others? If necessary, can it be integrated into the whole at a later time?
9. Is there minimal need for complex support, in terms of people and several types of equipment?
10. Is there minimal need for working space to accompany the job?

Kelly believes a wide variety of managerial, professional, and clerical jobs exists that can be performed independently on a location-independent basis. Among them are sales representatives, word processors, computer programmers, architects, catalog order takers, insurance agents, securities traders, and marketing managers. Kelly concludes that there are over seven million corporate and professional jobs capable of being converted to telework on either a full- or part-time basis.[3] Much of teleworking takes place from the office at home, but it can also be performed at small satellite locations, yachts, campsites, and recreational vehicles!

Select the Right People for Telework.   After the right jobs have been selected for telework, the right teleworkers must be selected. A starting point is to appoint only volunteers. Some potentially good teleworkers may not have a home situation suited to office work. Among the unsuitable factors are many other people present at home, no suitable place for a quiet office, and heavy interpersonal conflict at home. Volunteers for telework still need to be screened; they may not be suitable for telecommuting because they may lack other important traits and behaviors.

Above all, a teleworker must be an individual who has already demonstrated the self-discipline to work independently without much direct supervision. Workers who require frequent social interaction are unsuited for telework. Emotionally immature people, in general, are unsuited for telework because they may not be able to handle the responsibility of being on their own. One teleworker had to be reassigned to a traditional office because he spent at least half his work time at home in such activities as maintaining his car, watching soap operas, and taking his dog for long walks.

Geraldine DeSanctis adds that a telecommuter should have good planning ability, be well organized, and efficient in managing time. Good communication skills—telephone and electronic mail—are important.[4] The organizing skills tie in with self-discipline. Unless the teleworker can concentrate on the task at hand, he or she will lose productivity due to such distractions as the unavailability of recreation and food at home, television, the VCR, and conversations with co-dwellers.

Select Equipment and Assess Start-Up Costs.   Telecommuting requires installing equipment in the office at home. In many forms of telecommuting the individual is responsible for obtaining the equipment, while in a formal program of telecommuting the organization often makes some of the investment. Equipment frequently purchased by the individual includes a typewriter, telephone, personal computer with appropriate software, high-quality printer, modem for interfacing with the home-office computer, telephone answering machine, file cabinet, desk, and bookshelves. Personal photocopying machines are gaining in popularity for teleworkers. Owning a postage scale is another small but important investment for the complete office at home. A rough estimate of the costs involved in starting an office at home range from $2,000 to $6,000, depending heavily on the type of computer, printer, and furniture selected.

More advanced offices at home include speakerphones, which leave the person's hand free to check figures or papers while speaking to an office-bound co-worker. Integrated telephones are useful in conserving space and reducing desktop clutter because they combine a telephone, answering machine, speed dialer, and sometimes a speakerphone. A facsimile machine enables the teleworker to send a document or drawing over an ordinary phone line in as little as 17 seconds. Desktop publishing is possible at home with the appropriate microcomputer, software, and laser printer.[5]

Organizations typically pay for such equipment as terminals that link to the mainframe computer at the home office (not office at home), typesetting equipment, and specialized equipment such as used in creating engineering drawings. Such equipment, of course, remains the property of the organization. Purchasing terminals usually represents the largest cost of equipping offices at home, costing about $2,000 each.

As telecommuting gains acceptance, it is probable that organizations will develop policies about their financial contribution to the office at home. Until such policies are formulated, teleworkers are forced to quibble over such matters as whether or not they can take a box of computer paper back to their office at home.

Establish Appropriate Salaries. Salary administration is another important consideration in planning and implementing a telecommuting program. The organization must decide whether work will be paid according to a normal work week, with an annual compensation equivalent to the current income for on-site employees. An issue raised by Carol Ann Hamilton is whether a telecommuter who finishes an assignment in half a week should be expected to produce twice as much as office workers in order to be paid a regular work week.[6] One problem is that an office-bound worker can more readily do fill-in assignments when he or she has completed a major assignment.

It is easier to establish wages for employees exempt from overtime than for nonexempt employees. Whether or not overtime is justified is more apparent for office workers than for those employees working out of their homes. Because telecommuters do not have to spend time commuting to the office, it is easier for them to work long hours. An interesting benefits issue is therefore whether home-based employees should receive longer vacations if they routinely work 12- and 14-hour days.

The general principle here is to resolve thorny policy issues before employees begin working at home. Administratively, the easiest alternative is to continue paying teleworkers the same salary and benefits they received as office workers.[7]

Introduce Telecommuting on a Trial Basis.   A sensible principle that applies to telecommuting as well as to most human resources programs is to begin on a trial basis. Computer programmers and word processing technicians are two occupational groups well suited to launching a telecommuting program. This is true because both jobs required relatively little face-to-face contact with other people, and their work can be divided into deliverable milestones such as a completed program. A study by the Diebold Group, New York, corroborates the fact that programmers and word processors are well suited to telecommuting. It was found that workers for both jobs are project-oriented, can work without close supervision, and can communicate with the office electronically.[8]

Several companies' experiences with teleworking have validated the wisdom of starting with as few as three or four employees. A trial sample of this size usually provides sufficient data to evaluate the effectiveness of telecommuting, yet it is manageable enough to be monitored regularly.[9]

Develop Effective Communication Links.   An essential requirement of a successful telecommuting program is to establish effective communication links between teleworkers and the traditional office. Telephone, electronic mail, couriers (for the transfer of the machine-readable documents) are the most frequently used methods of communication among companies involved in telecommuting. Facsimile machines are also gaining in use as their unit cost has decreased.

Create Opportunities for Interaction with Co-workers.   Successful telecommuting requires that telecommuters spend some time at the regular office. A rule of thumb used by most companies with successful telecommuting programs is to require teleworkers to return to the office at least one day per week. William Atkinson notes: "They need to plug back into co-worker relationships, catch up on gossip, be apprised of company policy changes, discuss work progress and problems with their managers, and even be involved in birthday parties, company outings, and the like."[10]

Telecommuters need some office or desk space for their use when they return to the office. Such work space gives teleworkers a sense of belonging and also allows them to be productive on days they are not working at home. However, if teleworkers have as much office space as office workers, there will be no cost savings attributed to leasing or owning smaller quarters.

Among the frequently used methods of getting together with teleworkers are regularly scheduled department meetings, business-social functions, and special meetings to discuss the concerns of teleworkers. Feelings of isolation and alienation may arise when teleworkers are rarely seen in person. Another method of avoiding isolation is for telecommuters to join professional organizations. Such activity minimizes the loss of professional networks.[11]

Establish Quality Control Standards. F International is a computer consulting company with a work force of over 1,000 telecommuters in three countries. Steve Shirley, the founder, says that she (not an error) emphasizes quality control in order to organize and oversee so many employees working from home. Management inspects samples of the work produced by all employees. Samples are taken in several ways, as Shirley explains:

> Through the machine, through the kind of product, through the documentation, through the client's payment. That's the final quality control—the amount of repeat business. If something happens to that ratio, no matter how many controls we've got into, I know that something's gone wrong with our service. A service company grows by opening new accounts each month, and when clients come back to the organization, it means you're offering a high-quality product at the right price.[12]

Quality control of the free-lancers' work is done through frequent audits. Auditing takes place on a rotating basis so that the person who audits a teleworker one week might be audited by that person another week.

Establish Clear Criteria for Measuring Performance. A key requirement of a successful telecommuting program is to establish standards for measuring the output of the home-worker. The more tangible the output, the more readily it can be measured. Supervisors of teleworking activities have had to abandon measures of performance such as attendance, punctuality, and attitude.[13] The more tangible the output, the more readily it can be measured.

A recommended approach is to establish specific goals and completion times for each work-at-home project. A federal reserve bank executive says, "We have a major management by objectives (MBO) program for our employees. People are responsible for reaching certain objectives during the course of the year that they initiate and that are subsequently approved, perhaps with some modifications, by their managers. Our work-at-home option allows them to pursue these objectives at home when they think they can make more rapid progress there."[14]

Kline contends that the MBO program is probably the bank's chief insurance against potential abuse of the work-at-home option. Employees who shirk responsibility at home would experience difficulty in meeting their annual objectives.

F International measures telecommuter output by breaking jobs down into small parts. Management attempts to estimate the content of various tasks, whether managerial consulting, or technical. This is accomplished by breaking a job down into smaller tasks. One job, for example, might be broken down into 387 parts, each of which is estimated to be about a week's work. Output broken down into chunks can be more readily measured than more global accomplishments.[15]

Provide Promotional Opportunities for Telecommuters.   Employees who do most of their work at home may fall into the trap of being "out of sight, out of mind." Not being seen around the office frequently may lead to the overlooking of telecommuters as candidates for promotion. A telecommuting systems designer from Imperial Software Systems in Long Island put it in these terms, "Working out of your home has many advantages. The big problem I see however is that I run the risk of being treated like a subcontractor. I'm out of the mainstream, so I'm not thought of as somebody who wants to climb the ladder. To rectify this problem, I'm returning to the office full-time next month."

To prevent telecommuters from feeling neglected, management should be explicit about the impact of working at home on one's advancement opportunities. An official from Control Data says, "Telecommuters must be able to trust that their managers won't forget them because they're not in the office every day."[16]

To overcome the problem of teleworkers being "gone and forgotten," the DMR Group, Inc. suggests an upper limit of two years on telecommuting stints.[17] If the person works from home for more than this period of time, he or she will probably no longer be perceived as part of the organizational mainstream.

Be Aware of Legal Ramifications.   The legal ramifications of telecommuting are far reaching; a few of them are described here. A leading vexing question is, what if a telecommuter experiences an accident at home during normal working hours? Is it the company or the teleworker who is liable? Many Worker's Compensation Acts lack a clear definition of home-work situations. Each situation is evaluated on its own merits because the normal company safeguards are not present.[18]

If the employee lives in a zoned residential area, the office at home could violate local zoning laws. Generally, if the office at home is considered to be a secondary work area (similar to a study), no legal problems will ensue. The employee must abide by local building codes in modifying the home to accommodate the office at home.[19]

If the number of teleworkers continues to grow, it is conceivable that offices at home will have to pass governmental safety regulations pertaining to such matters as air purity, accident hazards, and fireproofing.

Inform Employees of the Tax-Deductible Aspects of the Office at Home.   A separate legal concern is income tax rulings surrounding the office at home. Because many people anticipate generous tax deductions for their office at home, it is important to communicate accurate written information about this topic. Above all, the firm's tax accountant should provide an interpretation of current tax legislation regarding working at home.

The government does provide some tax relief for working at home with write-offs for offices at home. Telecommuters must obtain a written statement that they are working at home for the convenience of their employer. If this is the case, telecommuters can deduct a portion of the mortgage payments (interest only) or rent, utilities, real estate taxes, repairs and painting, and depreciation. Usually, the office has to be a separate structure such as a detached garage or a room devoted exclusively to business.[20] The percent of the deduction is calculated by dividing the amount of square feet used exclusively for office purposes by the total square feet of the house or apartment. (For example, a teleworker who uses for business 275 square feet of a 2,750 square foot house would be able to deduct 10 percent of certain housing costs as a business expense.)

The above comments, of course, must be verified by the teleworker's tax preparer. Professional advice is particularly important because there are so many debatable deductions in relation to working at home. One teleworker, for example, wanted to deduct a mileage allowance for trips to the company office, claiming that these trips were a travel expense. The teleworker's tax advisor ruled against him, emphasizing that trips to the company office are a normal part of the job.

Make Provisions for Security of Information.   As noted by a survey of companies with telecommuting programs, computer terminals off the company premises do represent a potential security risk. The organization must therefore develop a strategy to ensure that telecommuters can access only the system or files they are authorized to work with.[21] So far, no widespread security problems have been observed.

Terminal usage from remote locations can trigger another nonauthorized use of computers—playing computer games. Because the at-home worker is not directly supervised, he or she has a greater temptation to use company computers for entertainment purposes. As with security problems, this type of abuse of privileges has not become widespread.

Advantages of Telecommuting

Telecommuting offers many potential advantages to both the organization and the individual. Of primary importance to the organization, telecommuting programs often increase productivity. Mountain Bell contends that its telecommuters are 35 percent to 40 percent more productive than their counterparts working on company premises. The company attributes much of this productivity to the independent work habits and goal setting used by teleworkers.[22] In general, where direct measurement is possible, productivity increases average about 20 percent. The productivity increase often takes place after an initial decrease while the employee adjusts to working at home.[23]

Another productivity advantage is that office-space rental usually decreases under a telecommuting program. Another cost savings occurs when employees are taken off the regular payroll and hired as independent contractors, because they do not receive many benefits. Blue Cross/Blue Shield adds to the financial gains from telecommuting by charging home workers a $2,400 annual rental fee for the use of a computer terminal provided by the company.[24]

The company also gains under telecommuting when new labor pools are opened. Among the people who might not be able to attend a full-time office job are people with very young children and some disabled people with impaired mobility. Telecommuting has also been tried successfully with prisoners. One example is Bayview, a state prison for women in Manhattan, where a group of 33 women sit at telephone banks answering calls forwarded to them from various Department of Motor Vehicle locations.[25]

A telecommuting program can also be a potent recruiting incentive to those candidates who would prefer to work out of their homes rather than in a company office. Similarly, telework can help retain valuable employees who prefer not to relocate or who will stay with a company to avoid shifting to an employer who would require that the person be physically present.[26]

A subtle advantage of telework is that it improves the performance appraisal process. Employees must be evaluated almost exclusively on the results they achieve because it is difficult to make judgments about attitudes and personality factors.

A widely reported advantage of telecommuting to the individual is that some aspects of child care are made easier. However, if the teleworker devotes too much time during the working day to child care, productivity will suffer. Telecommuting also helps the individual avoid some of the stress associated with commuting by auto or public transportation, which can be considerable in large metropolitan areas.[27] The stress associated with defending against office politics and attending frequent meetings is also lessened.

Telework also offers the opportunity to give back employees the power stemming from ownership of the tools of production they possessed prior to the industrial revolution. One major effect of the industrial revolution was to shift the locale of work from the home to the factory, thus separating the worker from the ownership of his or her work tools. It has been claimed that the reverse shift back to working at home will enable many workers to become once again owners of their workplace and work tools. The result will be to decrease their feelings of powerlessness and alienation.[28]

Disadvantages of Telecommuting

Many of the potential advantages of telecommuting can be turned around as potential disadvantages for organizations and individuals. A potential disadvantage for the organization is that it is difficult to build loyalty and teamwork when a large number of workers rarely come to the office and do not interact much with co-workers. Teleworkers are also difficult to supervise and therefore may have much more latitude to attend to personal matters when they should be thinking about company problems. Also, the organization may miss out on some of the creativity that stems from the exchange of ideas in the traditional office.

A substantial number of potential disadvantages to the individual stem from telecommuting. A major concern is that teleworkers have no protection from unscrupulous employers. Teleworkers often lose all of their benefits and work excessively longer hours to earn good pay. A claims processor from Sacramento contends, "I thought I would work when I wanted to . . . work around the needs of my family. It ended up that I was working continuously. I'd work late into the night, 11, 12, 1 in the morning to get things ready for the next day." She and seven other teleworkers have sued their employer for fraud. "Calling these people independent contractors was nothing but a subterfuge to save costs in labor," said their attorney.[29]

Many teleworkers miss the intellectual stimulation and socialization that occur in many offices away from home. Many of them also find it difficult to concentrate on work because of the many potential distractions. They often cheat by napping, watching TV, or running household errands.[30] If they are paid on a piecework basis, their productivity and earnings diminish.

Teleworking can result in an impoverished rather than an enriched job. One problem is that feedback on performance is limited. Much of the feedback that is received takes place over telephone wires and computers, thus missing out on the subtle nonverbal aspects of messages. Reduced contact and greater distance from other workers also adversely influences task significance (the impact of the job on the lives of others). As Boas Shamir and Ilan Salomon explain:

> It may be more difficult to perceive the significance of an individual's task when he or she is remote from the work organization, has less chances to observe other people at work, and has reduced opportunities for informal communication with members of the same organization.[31]

Above it was mentioned that avoiding commuting decreases stress. For some poeple, it is possible that avoiding commuting *increases* stress because they lose the buffer period between having to deal with work problems, then family problems.

Labor union leaders fear that physically separated workers will be difficult to unionize and mobilize for collection action. Employers may exploit this situation and employ individuals in conditions that would not have been acceptable if the workers were organized.[32] A spokesperson for the Communication Workers of America expresses the concern just mentioned: "Too many times, employers use this to isolate people, to prevent people from acting collectively, and to avoid paying people a decent wage."[33] Similarly, telecommuting programs have been accused of creating "electronic sweatshops," that rival the poor conditions of many pieceworkers in the garment industry.

Teleworking can also result in career retardation, as described previously. The teleworker who does not cultivate a network in the office winds up being overlooked for promotion and transfer to favorable assignments.

A final disadvantage of teleworking is that it fosters workaholism. Many teleworkers claim that having an office at home allows them to take a dinner break with the family; if they worked many miles from home, it would not be practical to come home to dinner before returning to work at night. The same situation leads to a work addiction because it is so easy to return to the project sitting there in an office at home. Many people with offices at home work regularly until 11 P.M. and many hours on the weekend.

Guidelines for Action and Skill Development

To tie together the principles and procedures for teleworking already presented, we present some summary guidelines to the individual and the organization. Here are six steps to follow, based on company experiences in many organizations, in establishing a telecommuting program:

Step 1. Select the jobs.

Step 2. Select the people.

Step 3. Train the managers and emphasize the difference between effective supervision and close supervision.

Step 4. Train the employees who will actually be doing the teleworking.

Step 5. Link the teleworkers to the office in addition to telephone lines and computer hookups. These links include office visits, staff support, and maintenance of their equipment.

Step 6. Take care of the technical aspects of telecommuting. Set up the equipment and services, such as telephone lines, in advance of the start-up date.[34]

The beginning telecommuter should take the following steps: First, create a separate work environment, preferably not in the bedroom. An office in the bedroom makes it difficult to separate oneself mentally from work. Second, set up a daily work schedule and stick to it the same as you would if working in an office on company premises. Third, equip the office with items such as a desk, filing cabinet, telephone answering machine, personal computer and letter-quality printer, and a copying machine.[35] A facsimile machine is also becoming important (see the chapter appendix).

DISCUSSION QUESTIONS AND ACTIVITIES

1. Identify five jobs you think would be well suited to telecommuting.
2. Identify five jobs you think would be poorly suited to telecommuting.
3. Are your work habits and personality well suited for telework? Explain the basis for your reasoning.
4. How far should an organization go in equipping the telecommuter's office at home? For example, what about carpeting, wall covering, bookshelves, and wall decorations?
5. Would you predict that teleworking would decrease or increase during a period of heavy cost cutting?
6. What is the difference between a telecommuter and anybody who works out of his or her house, such as a free-lance architect?
7. Talk to a full-time telecommuter and find out what that person perceives to be the advantages and disadvantages of telecommuting.

NOTES

1. Case researched by Jennifer Parkman.
2. " 'Two-Computer Yuppies' Fuel a New Boom," *Business Week,* November 9, 1987, p. 130; Connie Koenenn, "Telecommuting: A New Idea That Looks Better than It Is?" *Los Angeles Times,* August 10, 1988, p. 4V.
3. Marcia M. Kelly, "The Next Workplace Revolution: Telecommuting," *Supervisory Management,* October 1985, pp. 5–6.
4. Geraldine DeSanctis, "A Telecommuting Primer," *Datamation,* October 1983.
5. Kathleen Lander, "New Electronic Lifestyles," *Business Week's Guide to Careers,* October 1986, pp. 51–58.
6. Carol Ann Hamilton, "Telecommuting," *Personnel Journal,* April 1987, p. 97.
7. Ibid., p. 98.
8. Ibid., p. 99.

9. DeSanctis, "Telecommuting."
10. William Atkinson, "Home/Work," *Personnel Journal,* November 1985, p. 108.
11. Hamilton, "Telecommuting," p. 100.
12. Steve Shirley, "A Company without Offices," *Harvard Business Review,* January–February 1986, p. 127.
13. Naisbitt, "The Computer Commuter," p. 10.
14. Atkinson, "Home/Work," p. 107.
15. Shirley, "A Company without Offices," p. 131.
16. Atkinson, "Home/Work," p. 109.
17. Hamilton, "Telecommuting," p. 94.
18. Ibid., p. 98.
19. Ibid., p. 98.
20. "The New Keys to Home-Office Deductions," *Business Week,* July 6, 1987, p. 100; Jill MacNiece, "Technology Opens the Door for More to Work at Home," *USA Weekend,* January 16–18, 1987, p. 6.
21. Hamilton, "Telecommuting," p. 99.
22. Castro, "Staying Home Is Paying Off," p. 113.
23. Hamilton, "Telecommuting," p. 100.
24. Naisbitt, "The Computer Commuter," p. 10.
25. Michelle Levander, "Telecommuting," Rochester *Democrat and Chronicle,* September 21, 1987, p. 10D.
26. Kelly, "The Next Workplace Revolution," p. 3.
27. Boas Shamir and Ilan Salomon, "Work-at-Home and Quality of Working Life," *Academy of Management Review,* July 1985, p. 461.
28. Ibid., p. 462.
29. Levander, "Telecommuting," pp. 10D and 11D.
30. Shamir and Salomon, "Work-at-Home," p. 457.
31. Ibid., p. 458.
32. Levander, "Telecommuting," p. 10D.
33. Levander, "Telecommuting," p. 10D.
34. Kelly, "The Next Workplace Revolution," p. 7.
35. Paul and Sarah Edwards, *Working from Home* (New York: Tarcher, 1985).

SOME ADDITIONAL REFERENCES

Atkinson, William. *Working from Home: Is It for You?* Homewood, Ill.: Dow Jones-Irwin, 1985.

Friedman, Dana E. "Work vs. Family: War of the Worlds." *Personnel Administrator,* August 1987, pp. 36–39.

Ropp, Kirkland. "Mission Possible: Cases in Point." *Personnel Administrator,* August 1987, pp. 72–79.

"Telecommuting: Is Your Operation Ready?" *Research Institute Personal Report for the Executive,* July 15, 1986, pp. 4–5.

Townson, Monica. "The Electronic Cottage: Working for Peanuts in a 20th-Century Sweatshop." *The Financial Post Special Report,* Winter 1984.

Appendix to Chapter Twenty

FACSIMILE MACHINES

Personal facsimile (fax) machines are making it possible for more managers and professionals to work out of their homes. Telecommuters can now own a "personal fax" that plugs into any electrical outlet and contains a built-in telephone and photocopier. Copies of documents can be sent and received over telephone wires to another facsimile machine owner anywhere in the world. Worldwide communication is possible providing the machine is "G3 compatible"—able to communicate with most classes of facsimile machines.

Personal fax machines have some limitations. Incoming documents have to be torn off a roll of paper, and most models transmit only five pages at a time automatically. Personal faxes transmit a page in approximately 20 to 40 seconds, about the same time as a full-sized office machine. The price of most personal facsimile machines is somewhere between $1,000 and $1,500 (1988 figures).

A facsimile machine functions essentially as a scanner. As a sheet of paper is drawn across the machine, a stationary light bar shines on the document and translates light and dark into digital form (zeroes and ones). The modem translates the digital information into a wave, or analog form, necessary to transmit information over telephone lines. To hasten transmission, the data are compressed, using a software and hardware program through a series of integrated chips. The receiving unit translates the signals from analog form to digital, decompresses the data, and converts it to printed form.

Direct thermal fax machines, the most widely used, employ heat-sensitive paper. A print head, containing many heat elements, warms the paper, forming the letters. The heat is applied in very thin lines. Plain paper fax machines follow the same process. However, instead of thermal paper they use an imaging cartridge made of linked mylar that is similar to a large typewriter ribbon. The paper is pushed against the inked ribbon, and the image is reproduced. The most sophisticated technology, a fax/laser printer, relies on a series of light beams and a mirror within the machine.

SOURCE: As reported in "Fax Machines: The Personal Touch," *Business Week,* January 25, 1988, p. 118; Michelle Levander, "A Matter of Fax," Rochester *Democrat and Chronicle,* March 27, 1988, p. 1F.

Organization Index

Name Index

Acuff, Frank L., 93
Alberti, Robert E., 124
Alexander, C. Philip, 209, 212
Alexander, Ralph A., 200, 211
Alston, Jon P., 273
Altmaier, Elizabeth, 68
Ames, Charles, 248
Armstrong, Larry, 274
Aronson, Elliot, 69
Ashkenas, Ronald N., 6, 20
Atkinson, Keith, 239
Atkinson, William, 342
Austin, Nancy K., 19, 225

Badri, Vashuda, 225, 314
Baird, John E., Jr., 110
Baker, H. Kent, 124
Barkman, Donald F., 194
Baron, Robert A., 68
Barrick, Murray A., 200, 211
Bartlett, Kay, 139
Bass, Bernard M., 49, 53, 93
Bateman, Thomas S., 211, 212
Batten, Julie, 69
Bazerman, Max H., 89, 92
Bearak, Joel A., 314
Bell, Cecil H., Jr., 178
Benedict, Barbara, 53
Bennett, Stephen J., 35, 36
Berger, Aber, 225
Bernardo, Stephanie, 21
Bernstein, Aaron, 194
Bernstein, Paul, 193
Betz, Nancy, 298
Bishop, Jerry E., 69
Blair, John D., 205, 211, 212
Blake, Robert R., 177, 178
Blakey, James, 93
Blanchard, Kenneth, 100, 103, 110
Bliss, Edwin C., 8, 21
Blotnik, Srully, 178
Bohl, Don Lee, 287, 310, 314
Bourke, David L., 134, 139, 140
Bowman, James S., 273, 274
Bradshaw, David S., 133, 139
Brady, Sandra, 212
Brandt, Rhonda, 100
Bregman, Norman J., 93
Brockner, Joel, 212

Brohaugh, William, 21
Brooks, Earl, 93
Broszeit, Richard K., 297
Brown, Abby, 297
Brown, Stanley J., 273, 274
Buehler, Vernon M., 226
Buller, Paul F., 178
Bunker, Barbara Benedict, 53
Burack, Elmer H., 297
Byczkowski, John J., 35
Byrne, John A., 226
Byrnes, Joseph F., 92

Cameron, Kim S., 53
Casto, Maryles, 64
Chung, Kae, 263, 273, 274
Chusmir, Leonard H., 140
Clarke, Lillian Wilson, 140
Cohen, Stanley, L., 205, 211, 212
Conger, Jay A., 54
Cook, Curtis W., 185, 186, 194
Cosenza, Teresa, 273, 274
Crosby, Philip B., 219, 225, 226

Daniels, William R., 163
Davidson, Jeffrey P., 174, 175, 177
Davis, Flora, 110
Davis, Sandra L., 21, 124
Davy, Jeanette A., 163
Dean, James W., Jr., 194, 212
de Chambeau, Franck A., 239
DeGarmo, Scott, 20, 225
Deming, W., Edwards, 223
DeMott, John S., 239
Denton, D. Keith, 327
DeSanctis, Geraldine, 332, 341, 342
Dessler, Gary, 162
Diamandis, Peter, 168
Didato, Salvatore, 110
Dillon, Linda S., 270, 274
Dingham, Michael D., 46, 53
Dorsey, David, 239
Dovidio, John F., 110
Doyle, Robert J., 326
Driscoll, James W., 326
Driscoll, Jeanne Bosson, 139
Drucker, Peter, 240
Drury, Susanne S., 124

345

Subject Index